PAGES FROM A

Palo Alto

EDITOR'S

SCRAPBOOK

by Ward Winslow

How to Order:

Send a check or money order for $12 per copy, sales tax included, to:

Ward Winslow Writing
193 Hemlock Court
Palo Alto, CA 94306-4623
(415) 424-1128

Quantity discounts are available from the business address above.

On your letterhead include information concerning the intended use of the book and the number of books you wish to purchase.

Ward Winslow *1995*

PAGES FROM A

Palo Alto

EDITOR'S
SCRAPBOOK

by Ward Winslow

Published By
WARD WINSLOW WRITING
1 9 9 4

Cover design: Cheryl Kiehlbauch
David Lippenberger
Composite Arts, Sunnyvale, California

Graphic design: Joanna McClean
Stanford News and Publication Services
Stanford, California

Typography: Hundreds of newspaper compositors and, more recently, newspaper composition systems

Printing: Mike Rossi and associates
Shoreline Printing & Graphics, Inc.
Mountain View, California

Binding: Ed Tuite and associates
Pacific Finishing
Palo Alto, California

Publisher: Ward Winslow Writing
193 Hemlock Court
Palo Alto, CA 94306-4623

First Edition
Library of Congress Catalog Card Number: 94-90135

Winslow, Ward (Wardell V.), 1927 —
Pages from a Palo Alto Editor's Scrapbook/
by Ward Winslow
214 pages
8 ½ by 11 inch format
Includes index
ISBN 0-9641432-5-9

Published in Palo Alto, California
Manufactured in the United States of America

DEDICATION

To the *Palo Alto Times*, 1893-1979, and the *Peninsula Times Tribune*, 1979-1993, and the thousands of colleagues who over many years shared with me the task of putting out the Palo Alto area's daily newspaper.

CONTENTS

Pregnant on TV? ♦ Holiday Traditions ♦ Freed from Geography ♦ Peace Advocate ♦ Accessible Baylands ♦ Playing Fields ♦ USGS Day Care ♦ Photography and Funds ♦ Traffic Survival ♦ School in Mayfield ♦ Artists' Retreat ♦ Experience Lost ♦ Enduring Book Club ♦ Unfair Taxation ♦ Our Federal Labs ♦ Selling a House ♦ Phone-Line Politics ♦ Hothouse Wizardry ♦ Grandfather and Garbage ♦ Viva Italia ♦ The Irreplaceables

False Spring ♦ Sally's Eyes ♦ Installing Cable TV ♦ Fog Factor ♦ Staying Put's Payoffs ♦ Raychem ♦ Greenmeadow ♦ Filoli in Drought ♦ Elections Past ♦ Closet Celebrities ♦ Al Werry at 100 ♦ Golden Age of Gunn ♦ The Emperor and Palo Alto ♦ Rubber Pedestals ♦ Sorry, Sousa Fans ♦ Dinah's Shack Relics ♦ Little "Eeerma"

PREFACE

The target audience for this book is people who live now in the Greater Palo Alto area, or who once did. Most of the pages are, in fact, from my "scrapbook" of collected newspaper writings from 1943 to 1994. I've included a few new articles and some comments so no one who ventures 12 bucks will feel defrauded for having read it all before. (It would take a devoted and venerable fan to have seen every clip.)

"Greater Palo Alto" is the title of a recent telephone directory covering Atherton, East Palo Alto, Los Altos, Los Altos Hills, Menlo Park, Mountain View, Palo Alto, Portola Valley, Stanford and Woodside. That cluster of communities, perhaps with Sunnyvale and Cupertino added, is the area the Palo Alto Times served in its 1960s and '70s heyday. We called it the Midpeninsula. The Peninsula Times Tribune tried to bite off a larger chunk, but these places were its core.

Some people in some towns don't like being lumped with "Greater Palo Alto." I respect their wish for local distinctiveness. But Palo Alto has impacted them more than vice versa, I contend, and this geographical and social cluster still forms a community of interests, even without the glue of a local daily newspaper. What's more, in toiling as principal author of the Palo Alto Historical Association's book, *Palo Alto: A Centennial History*, I grew frustrated at having to focus strictly on Palo Alto without including many of its natural interties with neighboring cities and towns.

I have tried to select material that still, years or decades later, may be informative or interesting. The reprints are arranged in the order of phases of my journalistic career. If the reader notes time gaps, or heavy emphases on a particular area, my assignments as a Times newsman may explain them. Palo Alto recreation activities were an early beat. Then came south San Mateo County — mostly Menlo Park,

Atherton and East Palo Alto. Meanwhile, I covered prep sports with Paly High as my home base. After returning from Naval Reserve duty in the Korean War, I covered the Palo Alto Board of Education and general assignments for a time, then shifted to Santa Clara County government and local, state and national politics. After spending nearly a year in Washington, D.C., on a fellowship, I returned as an editorial writer, still doubling in politics for a while. As editorial page editor, the paper's whole ambit — and the rest of the world, too — became my beat. As managing editor for 2 1/2 years I did relatively little writing. After retiring, I freelanced local columns and "Special to ..." pieces.

There's another reason for some gaps. My scrapbook isn't complete. After Tribune Company of Chicago killed the Times Tribune on March 12, 1993, Tribune gave its clip files to the City of Palo Alto. They've been locked away for more than a year now. These files ought to be open to qualified researchers. Some of them, compiled before the Redwood City Tribune merged with the Times in 1979, should be repatriated to San Mateo County, where history groups await them.

I beg the reader's pardon if this book comes across as an ego trip. Hoping to get it to market before Palo Alto's Centennial is forgotten, I haven't lopped the bylines off most clips and sometimes have left in "thumbnail" mugs, creating a "Portrait of Dorian Gray" effect.

About bylines: I first used Wardell — my given name, school name and even name within the family while my grandfather was Ward. My nickname, Dode, stuck to the prep sports stuff, except once when a linotypist dubbed me Dope Wilson. Since the mid-'50s, I've trimmed the longer handle to Ward.

The reader is likely to notice that many of these pages betray personal experiences and relationships as a source. This is especially true for columns, where the writer traditionally has liberty to draw on his or her spouse, children, parents, neighbors and friends for material. Things close to the heart tend to make lively copy.

Printing marks and reduced photocopy sizes affect some of the print quality herein. I hope they remain readable anyway, and that the photos are recognizable if not elegant. Copy styles prevailing at the time of writing are retained.

Maybe there should have been more notes. For instance, on page 23 the Don Edwards elected president of the state Young Republicans is the same Don Edwards who became a liberal Democrat and is retiring soon after representing the San Jose area in Congress for 32 years. On page 26, Janice Kreutzmann's movement classes for boys presaged ballet training for defensive backs in college football. Her son Bill must have gotten rhythm — he's the Grateful Dead's No. 1 drummer.

Besides the notes, the new material is:
(1) a high school scrapbook leftover on page 3,
(2) an article on David Packard that stemmed from the long interview, but which I was too busy to market successfully in 1991-92, and
(3) errata relating to the Centennial history.

I am indebted to Steve Staiger, research librarian and historical association archivist, and Ken White, Paly High sports archivist and retired teacher, for help finding certain clippings. My appreciation goes also to the multitude of sourcepeople for this material, and to the colleagues, editors and printers who had a hand in the initial publishing, especially Carolyn Snyder and Bill Shilstone, both now at the San Jose Mercury News. Working with the book publishing artisans whose names are on the copyright page has been a joy.

Lastly, advance thanks to my beloved wife, Holly, who doubles as business manager of our little firm. Distribution of the book threatens to cut into her gardening hours.

Ward Winslow
April 25, 1994

——EDITORIAL——

Seven Gold Stars

Some time when you're walking down the hall, stop and look up at the red and white banner with seven gold stars on it. Seven gold stars, each one standing for a former Paly student who gave his life for his country.

Each star stands for a life, a life undoubtedly much the same as yours and mine, for those boys had experienced the fun of dancing at jolly-ups, the disappointment of flunking a test, the thrill of an exciting game and all the other little things which make up life at Paly, or life anywhere. Those boys loved their lives, and all the little things in them, but they gave them up, willingly, for something greater than themselves.

Are you doing right by those seven, by the millions of other men, some perhaps your own friends and relatives, who are willing to sacrifice their very lives for something greater than themselves? Have you done anything to make them happier, safer, or better fed and armed? How? Well, for instance, you can give athletic equipment to servicemen through the current school drive. Or you can say, "Sure, I'll take some" to the war stamp salesman Wednesday morning. Then too, the Victory Garden and the Red Cross work-room need workers on occasional noons. Why not write that serviceman brother, uncle, or father tonight? If you haven't already plans for some essential activity this summer you can sign up to harvest or process fruit. Have you ever said a prayer to hurry the end of this terrible war?

Sometime when you're walking down the hall, stop and look up at the flag with the seven stars. Those boys gave their lives. What have you given?   —WINSLOW.

The seven gold stars on the banner multiplied in the months after this editorial was published. By the time America's World War II dead were accounted, 74 Palo Alto High School graduates and former students — two of them women — had given their lives. The Korean conflict added three gold stars, Vietnam six.

The high school has a Gold Star Memorial Scholarship Fund, now dedicated to the 83 who gave what Lincoln termed that "last full measure of devotion." War-years classes having their 50th reunions are adding to the fund, which presently yields about $10,000 each year for scholarship awards to outstanding senior students.

▼

Boys risk lives in initiation prank

Five Palo Alto High School boys, allegedly pulling a prank as part of a club initiation, took a desperate chance on getting shot last night when they staged a fake "shooting" on University avenue, it was reported today by police.

L. O. Tanner of Motley's phoned police at 9 o'clock saying that four men in a black sedan had shot a man in front of the cafe. One of the men got out of the car, Tanner related, and threw the "dead man" into the sedan before it sped away toward Stanford.

Police overtook the fleeing car at South Palo Alto and found five high school boys in it. Had not the officers suspected a hoax the consequences might have been serious for the "killers."

There was also a falsified report to police of a burglary at a University avenue book store. Making such a report is a crime under the penal code. Police are investigating.

There was more to the fake murder story than the *Times* printed. The following handwritten account, a copy of which was sent to the paper but not published, has languished in a scrapbook until now.

The Times' editorialized reportage was correct in asserting danger. Such a stunt would be far riskier today with a crack police force on patrol than during World War II when police manpower was at low ebb. Also, involvement could have derailed some careers.

Foolhardy or not, the episode has become part of Paly High legend. At one Class of '44 reunion, eyewitnesses say, a master of ceremonies asked everyone who had taken part in the prank to stand, and nearly 100 did. Such is the stuff of legends, for, as recited below, only 17 took part. They will not be named here.

Whodunit

THE FAMOUS HOAX CRIME
September 17, 1943

THE OPERATIONS WERE CARRIED OUT ON A LARGE SCOPE, FOR INSTANCE INSTEAD OF ONE CAR AS REPORTED IN THE PALO ALTO TIMES, FOUR CARS WERE INVOLVED. SEVENTEEN BOYS PARTICIPATED RATHER THAN THE FIVE WHO WERE APPREHENDED. THE ENTIRE MANEUVER WAS REHEARSED TWICE, AND EACH PARTICIPANT KNEW HIS SPECIFIC DUTIES. HERE IS AN OUTLINE OF THE "SHOOTING" AS PLANNED AND CARRIED OUT —

Cars one and two were parked in front of the Stanford Theatre at 8:45 awaiting the signal from the finger man. In the foyer of Wideman's Clothing Store the "victim" also awaited the signal, which consisted of the lighting of a cigarette (which of course was not smoked) by the scout as he crossed University Avenue.

The signal was given when the coast was clear and car one, the murder car containing four persons armed with one blank-cartridged .32, one rubber dart pistol, and a child's movie gun, roared to a start. One blank was fired at the victim as he strolled out onto the corner, and he crumpled to the sidewalk in a remarkable display of acting.

Immediately car two drove up and three persons leaped out, two of whom seized the body and hurled it into the back seat, while the other guarded the proceedings. Then these behatted, overcoated figures jumped into the large, black sedan and it gunned down the subway, following the "murder car." At the sound of the shot, cars three and four staged a fake accident which blocked effectually the path of pursuit.

The incident completed sans flaw, all four cars met immediately at a rendezvous in the darkness of Stanford University. Having laughed a hearty laugh, the murder clothes were removed and all cars separated and headed for the home of one of the assassins, cars three and four coming through the town to observe the large assemblage of police and excitded citizens.

Car two, readily recognizable for its size, took to the backroads. However, as it crossed Alma Street at California Avenue it was apprehended by a squad car, whose officers advanced with drawn guns and questioned the murderers. Taken to the station, the five captured "criminals" were reprimanded for causing the sending out of a statewide alarm (the police had evidently thought it was a fairly convincing hoax).

That's the complete story. No Palo Alto High School initiation was connected with it. The purpose was solely to have fun, and put a little life in the "dead" town. However, we concede that if we were to do it again, we would tell the police beforehand, for we relish in no manner the thought of a policeman's bullet in our ... er ... backs!

— *One of the "killers"*

Swan Song

Class of '44 Approaches End
Of Palo Alto High School Career

Tomorrow night the class of nineteen hundred and forty-four will reach the end of the trail. Our twelve years of public schooling have been a long and hard, but enjoyable, struggle, and commencement will undoubtedly mark the end of the formal education of many of us, at least for some time. The outside world is ready and waiting for us.

As a class we don't claim to be the greatest that ever went to Paly High. Forty-four is just a good, strong, normal class, and its members have tried their hands at a lot of things. We've had writers, poets, athletes, artists, politicians, musicians, brains, lovers, B.T.O.'s, and even R.O.D. boys. Our efforts for student government produced a pretty good showing, and some activities have flourished under our reign. Though no oomph class, we've thrown some good parties and enjoyed ourselves for three years. We helped corral a few championships, and our gang has hung up some records for successors to shoot at. As students our showing has been acceptable. We've done a lot of things, and we surely realize that we've left a lot of things undone.

Some of us will be very happy to graduate, some very sad, and some apathetic about it all, but we, editorially, suspect that the great majority of the class is glad in anticipation of new experiences ahead, and at the same time filled with regret for leaving the place where we've spent so many unforgettable hours. A tinge of sorrow is not out of place, because, all kidding aside, the world we're going out into isn't very much like the one we've been in, and the high school period which tomorrow night's ceremonies will end will no doubt stand as one of the happiest periods in many of our lives, if not the happiest. High school at Paly has been great, and we're thankful for having had the privilege of attending.

There seems to be little more to say in this swan song, but since we, personally, are loath to lay down our editorial pen for the last time, we shall next say our thank-yous, and set down our last will and testament.

To Mrs. Naomi Gill, our hard-working adviser, goes our utmost appreciation for making such an effort to make the paper a success. Her counseling and alert eye have been invaluable.

The staff, especially managing editor Sally Mayock, come in for a big thank-you for their prolonged efforts through the last year. The printer, Miss Stella Ely, is last but not least on this credits list; we want her to know that we appreciate every little change she ever made for us.

To Marge Baker and Carolyn Crary, next year's editors, we reluctantly hand over the dear old Camp. We hereby bestow upon them the confusion and bother of deadlines, make-up, copyreading, and writing heads, of an ever-empty copy-paper drawer, of headline styles that won't count, and most important of all, we leave them a good healthy interest in everything that goes on around school—an interest you can't have too much of, an interest sometimes called school spirit. There is a fly-swatter in the editor's drawer in case someone persists in bothering you, an address book full of fictitious bylines to use on editorialized stories, and a half galley of useless overset down at the print shop with which to start next year; these items are now yours, together with our very best wishes for success.

And, for our career at Palo Alto High, that's 30.

—WINSLOW

Marge Barker's name is misspelled — a misprint, I hope.

Offset is marvelous for today's student newspapers. Still, I wouldn't trade my hours in Stella Ely's print shop on College Avenue for anything.

Otherwise, no comment, except that editors have been known to stretch their prerogatives.

Paly Players catch suspense and comedy in production of 'Arsenic and Old Lace'

By WARDELL WINSLOW

An excellent performance of "Arsenic and Old Lace," not only as a high school play but as real entertainment, was given by the Paly Players at Palo Alto High School last night.

The production, entirely planned, directed, and executed by students for the first time in the history of the school, caught both the suspense and comedy of Joseph Kesselring's play. The players were well-coached and moved through the action of the play at a good clip. Their timing was remarkable.

Costuming was very good and the set, though not elaborate, was well designed. Another good feature was the brevity of the intermissions, which helped preserve the suspense.

A great deal of credit should go to Hal Burdick, Jr., a high school junior, for his first big undertaking as a director. It was obvious that he and the entire cast and crew had put in plenty of work on the performance and thought in planning it, and they had a right to be pleased with the results.

All the major parts were very well handled. Special mention should be made of Flora Kirschner and Jo Bartky as Abby and Martha Brewster, the old maids who persuaded lonely men to sample their lace (with arsenic) elderberry wine. Miss Kirschner has outstanding stage presence.

Roger Morris was convincing in his performance of Teddy (Roosevelt) Brewster. Jack White handled well the difficult part of Mortimer Brewster, the drama critic who is finally relieved to find he isn't a Brewster after all.

Allyn Kreps was a sinister Jonathan Brewster, the nephew who returns to find his aunts have tied his record for murders. He made effective use of his hands and voice. Bruce Robinson delighted the audience in the dialogue part of Jonathan's sidekick, the face-lifting Dr. Einstein. As Officer O'Hara, the cop who wanted to write a play, Richard Bare was very good.

The Paly Players, separate from the regular high school Thespian Club, formed their group after some of the members got the idea of giving "Arsenic and Old Lace." After demonstrating in rehearsals that they could handle the play, they got a faculty "go-ahead." Though advised by Miss Jane Goodspeed and several other faculty sponsors, they handled the entire production themselves. Miss Goodspeed said the group had aided greatly in building interest in dramatics, especially among the boys.

Grant Spaeth acted as business manager and Jan Thompson was rehearsal secretary. Last night's performance was the only one scheduled, and proceeds will go to defray production costs and to the Gold Star Memorial Fund.

Though the Players have no plans for future productions at present, playgoers should be looking forward to another piece by the group. If it can match the standard set in the first performance, the Paly players will really have arrived.

This play review earned me my first *Palo Alto Times* byline. Although a college girl friend had been a leading lady in a rather good drama department, I'd never written a play review before. My mother had trod the boards in college, and came from a journalistic family. She helped me get in the essentials.

Spring Festival plans to be drawn at meeting tonight

Final plans for Palo Alto's 25th Annual May Fete will be drawn tonight at a meeting of the spring festival general committee in the Children's Theater of the Community Center at 8 p.m

The committee is headed by Mrs. Frances Merner, general chairman. Other members are Michael Ryan, Frank Lee Crist, L. Harold Anderson, Linn Winterbotham, Louis Olsen, Fred Glanville, Mrs. Hazel Robertson, William P. Johnson, J. E. Shuchat, Mrs. Edward E. Hardy, Mrs. Miner B. Adams, Grady (Tex) Fritz, John Leecing, Miss Marian Theobald, Paul Meyer, Mrs. Stanley Croonquist, and Mrs. Josephine O'Hara.

After trying me out on a few stringer assignments, Managing Editor J.R. Paulsen encouraged me to await an upcoming staff vacancy. Meanwhile, he had me cover the May Festival, which I did in more depth than ever before — or since. Here's the parade story, written on deadline (luckily, the deadline then was quite late).

I include the committee item to underscore how involved the city's leaders were in this annual event in those days. Oldtimers will recognize Councilwoman Frances Merner at the helm, plus leading lights of the municipal staff and the late '40s citizenry.

Thousands see Festival parade

Sun beams down on gaily costumed youngsters; pageant is postponed until next Saturday

By WARDELL WINSLOW

Thousands jammed University Ave. this morning as the sun beamed down on Palo Alto's 25th annual May Day parade. Business and traffic came to a virtual standstill at 10:30 as the giant procession began its trek down the Avenue.

People climbed to rooftops and hung from upper story windows as the colorful paraders, large and small, stopped and started frequently. Photographers, professionals and amateurs, were out in force.

At 10 o'clock people began to congregate on the Avenue to secure choice seats, some armed with camp stools and ladders, others carying toy balloons. Paraders moved back to Lytton Ave. where Frank Crist, master of ceremonies, blared lining-up instructions over a loudspeaker. Marshals grouped youngsters into starting positions. In the dog section leashes strained as skittish canines sniffed for fights and revolted against neck bows and hats. Small owners soothed them, but the barking went on.

At 10:30 two Cub Scouts moved out, carrying the May Day banner. Mayor J. Byron Blois, natty in a straw hat, and L. Harold Anderson, grand marshal, began their march, followed by the veterans' color guard.

With the flourishes of four wooden trumpets, the ladies of her court pulled the May Queen's chariot into line. Pretty, dark-eyed Queen Louise Starkie wrinkled her nose and smiled for cameramen.

The high school band struck up a tune, and majorettes stepped high.

Tiny girls pushed their doll buggies, helped along by Girl Scouts. One buggy was swathed in pansies; another carried a doll hospital and nurse. Disguised as a lamb in doll's clothing, George the lamb was pushed in a buggy. "One World" dolls filled one wagon.

The Palo Alto Military Academy band snapped into the line of march with precision. Hundreds of children in costume followed, led by a tiny accordian player who struck up "Come Join the Band." There were clowns and hula girls, pirates and 49ers, a giraffe and an ostrich, Dutch girls and Chinese rickshas, three boxes of soap, a pint-sized cowboy who got tangled in another's lariat, and many more. Dick Tracy and Tess Trueheart showed up along with Donald Duck, and there was a profusion of senoritas, fairies, and nymphs.

One woman with a rolling pin threatened a boy with pie in his hand and all over his face. A two-man elephant cavorted.

"The Bare State" stood out in the inanimate section as scantily-clad young ladies shared a wagon with teddy bears. Four girls in pajamas were "The Gay Nighties."

Cages and cages of cats moved ahead of the feathered and miscellaneous pet section. A monstrous turkey, an inert turtle, and a quiet parrot were thoroughly bored with it all.

The McKinley Elementary School band and drum corps from Redwood city piped the dogs along. A huge Great Dane marched ahead of a a little Chihuahua. . . . . a collie pulled his master along at a run. . . . One loose dog sniffed at his parading colleagues with the happy air of freedom. . . . . five caged pups set up an unhappy wailing.

Brownies, Girl Scouts, and Cubs marched in uniform, their hair slicked neatly in place. The NAACP junior drum corps drew a hand as they beat out a snappy cadence. The Palo Alto School Traffic Squads marched neatly.

Decked in miles of crepe paper, the tricycles moved into the line of march, their riders happily crashing into each other now and again. Tears flowed as one little girl's trike broke down and had to be sidelined for repairs. Bicycles followed, with their riders constantly hopping on and off in the stop-and-go traffic.

The Jordan Junior High band, a late entry, swung into action.

Whistles shrilled as the 1947 Redwood City Rodeo queen led the horse sections perched in a convertible, of all things. Ten groups of riders paraded and some had their hands full calming spooky mounts. Many of the riders dressed in costumes reminiscent of California a hundred years ago.

Full-sized floats from a number of organizations brought up the rear.

Following the parade a large part of the crowd flowed to the Lytton School grounds to inspect the paraders at close range until noon. Award ribbons were handed out there.

Mrs. Miner B. Adams, chairman of awards, and Mrs. Edward E. Hardy, chairman of judges, agreed that "every entry was good enough to win an award."

At 12 the horse show began at Rinconada Park, lasting for several hours. YMCA groups sold snack lunches. Swimming began at the Rinconada pool at noon, free to all youngsters. The pool will close at 5 p.m.

The annual Science Fair began at the Junior Museum at 1 and will be open until 6 p.m. At the Junior Bazaar there, small live pets, cookies, and other items are on sale.

The Children's Library opened at 1 and will stay open until 5 p.m. for inspection by all.

Tonight from 8 to 12 there will be dancing at the Community Center. Families will folk dance in the social hall; social dancing for adults will be in the reception hall; and teen-agers may dance in the Boy Scout Hall.

The annual pageant, scheduled for the Community Center lawn, was postponed because the lawn was too wet for the dancers. About 300 youngsters will go through their paces there at 1:30 on May 8, and the May Queen will be crowned then.

Tilton tells planning goals; nine others present views

Analyzing the land problem will be the first move in formulating a master plan for Palo Alto, L. Deming Tilton, the city's new planning consultant, said last night.

Land acquisition will follow this analysis and estimation of probable ultimate land demands as the number one program under the new plan, Tilton told a small audience attending a forum on city planning at the Community Center.

Tilton described the planning commission's job as selecting and putting together ideas, making them intelligible, and presenting them to residents.

"Standards already set in Palo Alto have established standards for planners," Tilton stated. "It will be substantially the same kind of community it is now, with improvements in certain places."

Another early move of the planning commission will be to protect against mistakes in the building of new sections in perimeter areas, Tilton promised. "We know what ought to be done. We will try to get these ideas across and set the highest possible standards to guide the developments emerging."

Tilton mentioned offstreet parking as an extremely important problem. He also referred to zoning as frequently becoming "a case of the tail wagging the dog." He hopes squabbles over minor zoning problems can be cut down or by-passed in drawing up the master plan.

Forum talks are preferred by Tilton as a method of determining community feeling on zoning problems. He called on groups to work for the good of the community as a whole in forming the master plan.

Tilton was introduced by City Councilman A. B. Morten. Morten also read a list of objectives drawn by Dr. Russel V. A. Lee chairman of the city planning commission.

These objectives were: final definition of the University Ave. area business district, and plans for neighborhood business areas; increase of quarters for city government; es-

tablishment of traffic routes; a civic center; development of parks and recreational areas in cooperation with the schools; and the tie-in of Palo Alto with neighboring communities.

Nine speakers, representing various city groups, precede Tilton in the forum, arranged by the civic league. Hugh Moran served as chairman.

Allan Reid of the chamber of commerce described a delinquency-free community as the goal of planning. The chamber, he said, is particularly interested in greater school facilities; better utilities, particularly water storage; disaster and smog control set-ups; offstreet parking; and arterial streets.

Mrs. Harold Severance, representing Palo Alto Branch, League of Women Voters, urged that the facts be slowly and carfully considered and the people be kept completely informed on planning work and the reasons for the various plans. She warned against injecting issues which could endanger passage of the main plan, and asked for simple, efficient, and businesslike plans for the future.

In calling for more adequate recreational facilities, Paul Meyer of the Youth Council said recreation is a public responsibility on a par with schools and health. He suggested the master plan should extend recreation to all groups without large centralized investments. Family recreation is better served by smaller plants, Meyer said. He pointed out a need for an indoor swimming pool.

Dr. M. K. Bennett of the library board repeated the board's request for a bond issue to establish a $92,000 branch library in South Palo Alto, and to make $37,000 worth of improvements in the main library. Though the city council has tabled the board's move to put the bond issue on the June 22 ballot, Bennett hopes action can be taken at an early date. The board feels, he said, that a new half million dollar building is necessary for a progressive main library, but that it is out of the question at present.

Mrs. Herbert F. Ormsby of the Garden Club called for good landscaping around future buildings and for lengthwise planting of new streets with the same kind of trees. She said the Garden Club plans to give both financial help and suggestions in the landscaping of the Crescent Park School and the Red Cross Building.

David Packard, representing the board of education and the PTA's, said Palo Alto will have to more than duplicate its present school set-up by 1960 because of a tremendous upswing in birth rate. He told of the long range plans now being considered by a committee sponsored by the board. Packard hopes for cooperation of other planners and the community, and that these plans can be fitted in with others.

W. W. Mackall said the South Palo Alto Civic Club will back things good for all of Palo Alto as a residential city.

Mrs. Ray Whittern of the Business and Professional Women's Club presented a number of suggestions. Among them were: sufficiently large, well-landscaped, and well-marked entrances to the city; a public comfort station; restoration of The Circle; restoration of the old community center, primarily for adults; temporary enlargement of the City Hall; licensing only of quality businesses; no destruction of established homes and business places in securing project sites; and neighboring stores with architecture matching homes in the district.

The Rev. Paul V. Frykman, representing the Ministerial Association, spoke of the difficulties involved in the problem of locating churches in new areas.

Local artist Cloyd Sweigert, speaking from the audience, called for a room or wall space where work of local artists can be hung when library improvements are made. Groups interested in art raised funds for such a room in the present library but crowded conditions have forced its use for other purposes, he said.

This story was in my clips, though I'm not sure who wrote it. I include it because it gives a good listing of Palo Alto concerns on the eve of the city's great growth surge. David Packard, who hadn't been on the school board long, already had defined the huge school-building task of the 1950s.

New gadgets at P.A. Hospital make life easy for infants

By WARDELL WINSLOW

On the third floor of the Palo Alto Hospital are a number of very young babies, most of them bawling loudly in the manner of young babies.

Why the newcomers should carry on with this noise is a mystery to the hospital staff, since the babies are being cared for with some of the neatest equipment known to maternity wards.

The equipment is rolling stock, and was pushed into the hospital recently in the form of 40 portable bassinet units and seven mobile incubator outfits.

The new bassinets are of the type developed at Stanford Hospital in San Francisco. They function as complete units in themselves. All the baby's equipment, from diapers to eyewash, is kept in a cupboard below the baby's crib. The cupboard and a table atop it, which can be used for washing and changing, pull out from the bassinet frame and crib, making for greater convenience.

The bassinets greatly decrease the danger of disease being transmitted from one baby to another by keeping everything used by each baby separate. They also save time since the nurse can work with the baby right by his crib.

"They're just like a single hotel room," said Dr. William R. Duden, director of the hospital. Dr. Duden was delighted, though surprised, when the new bassinets, made mainly of metal, arrived shortly after they were ordered.

Along with the 40 bassinets were five new model incubators. Paneled with roomy glass windows, they look a little like the cockpit of a pursuit plane. In them premature babies are kept comfortable with automatic heat and humidity controls, and arrangements for administering oxygen, if needed.

Dr. Duden claims the babies got wind of the arrival of the incubators. "We had them full in no time," he said.

With the installation of the new equipment, the maternity ward can handle about 50 babies and 40 mothers. There are the 40 bassinets for full-term babies, seven incubators for premature babies, and room for three in isolation units.

Business is booming, according to Dr. Duden. The ward is full most of the time, and Dr. Duden has no complaints about Palo Alto's birth rate.

In fact he is busy trying to figure out a way to change the layout of the maternity wards without shooing the stork away for a couple of weeks. The movable bassinets will help, since they can be placed anywhere while the changes are being made.

The hospital staff is also particularly proud of some other improvements recently made. The lobby assumed its full size again when the record room was moved. Separate telephone switchboard and admittance offices were constructed, and the business office was shut off from the lobby by a panel and glass wall.

A new record room and a new nurses' room both afford more space.

In the kitchen a new range, steam table, and ventilating system better the culinary operations.

The baby boom was on.

MISSING STANFORD AX IS FOUND BESIDE TREE ON UNIVERSITY CAMPUS

Famed trophy stolen from case at UC

The Stanford Ax, mysteriously missing from its case on the University of California campus in Berkeley since last week end, was found yesterday afternoon propped against a tree in an isolated section of the Stanford campus.

Leonard A. Sagan, an upper division student who is not enrolled for summer quarter, discovered the famous trophy while horseback riding with two children on an unpaved road on the campus.

Plans were made this morning for the return of the Ax this afternoon to the University of California student body, which won temporary possession of it last fall when the Cal football team won the "Big Game," 21-18.

Stolen at week end

The Daily Californian, student newspaper at UC, reported today that the Ax had been stolen under mysterious circumstances from its case in the Men's Club room of the ASUC Union sometime between Friday night and Monday morning.

Sagan found the Ax, mounted on its plaque and still shiny and bright, leaning against a eucalyptus tree just beyond the intersection of Searsville Rd. and the road leading to the Stanford Riding School, near the Carnegie Biological Laboratories.

He was riding with his 13-year-old sister, Terrye, and Larry Bacon, 9-year-old son of Mr. and Mrs. Robert Bacon of San Francisco, who are living in Manzanita Hall on the campus this summer. Sagan lives at 410 Lake St., San Francisco.

"We were riding down the road from the Old Red Barn," Sagan said this morning, "and saw the Ax gleaming in the sun, leaning against the first tree we came to, in plain sight. After we recovered from our amazement, I tried to mount with the heavy plaque, but my horse wouldn't let me. So I hailed a woman driving by and asked her take take it to the riding school."

The passing driver was Mrs. Wallace Carlisle of Menlo Park. She took the Ax to the stable and Sagan took it from there to Gordon Davis, Stanford chief of police and veteran of many "Ax thefts."

Davis locked the Ax in a safe and informed Lawrence A. Kimpton, dean of students, of the discovery. Dean Kimpton informed UC authorities and made arrangements for the return of the traditional "Big Game" trophy to the Cal student body this afternoon by Don Davies, Stanford summer session student body president.

Stanford authorities said today they believe there is no possibility of Sagan having been connected with the theft. They had no inkling of any circumstances of the theft, but conceded the possibility of a "student job." They speculated the thieves might have got "cold feet" or felt that pursuing Cal students were too hot on their trail, and planted the Ax on the campus where it could be easily found by the first passer-by.

University of California officials said they had no idea how or when the Ax was taken from its case over the week end.

The Ax was last stolen in April, 1946, allegedly by Cal students who carried it out of the Stanford Union in broad daylight. It was recovered in October, 1946.

This year's short-lived theft marked the sixth time the Ax had been stolen in its 52-year history. It was purchased in 1896 and first captured by a group of Cal students during the 1899 "Big Game" in San Francisco.

From then until 1930 it was kept in the vaults of Berkeley banks. In that year it was recovered by the famous "Immortal 21" with a daring plot that made headlines across the nation.

This Stanford Ax swiping may not have matched the earlier ones for high drama, but it was fun to write anyway. Leonard Sagan became a physician specializing in industrial and environmental medicine at the Palo Alto Medical Clinic, and I wrote often about his wife Ginetta, a West Coast leader of Amnesty International. Ax security provisions later were tightened, thwarting raiders.

TELEVISION GROWING RAPIDLY

New techniques for theatre obtained by Mrs. Robertson

Mrs. Hazel Glaister Robertson is back in the midst of Children's Theatre summer activities putting into practice a number of ideas she picked up in the East on a leave of absence this spring and early summer.

"It is desirable to keep abreast of current developments in drama and other fields connected with it elsewhere in the country, and I feel that a look from a different perspective gives better insight into current trends," she said. "Comparing values with those of others gives you goals to shoot for." And that's what she did with her leave of abscence.

One of the most interesting developments on which the local director had a look-in this spring was television—which is growing like Jack's famous beanstalk, she said.

Television's growth is without parallel. Its limited field has resulted in terrific competition —a wild scramble to get licenses," Mrs. Robertson explained. "It is still in a formative stage, and at present the techniques used are a cross between radio and the movies. People who have any idea of writing for television will have to do a big amount of research and a lot of thinking."

The field is still wide open for being developed into a distinctive communication medium, Mrs. Robertson said. One reason is that broadcasting companies leaped to secure channels before planning how to fill their time, and they must broadcast four hours of public service programs a day.

"Television costs are still very high, and it's a good thing the broadcasting companies have the capital to back experimentation," she said.

Mrs. Robertson also found some new radio twists in the East. One was a chain of stations experimenting with a day's schedule of programs beamed to farm audiences. Programs are timed to correspond with the farmer's day. Dr. Miller McClintock, a Stanford graduate, is directing their operation.

She has no sympathy for people who criticize radio techniques without making any constructive suggestions. There are some good children's radio programs being broadcast, but people won't take the trouble to look for them, Mrs. Robertson said.

The local director managed to visit most of the children's theatres in the East, and came home convinced that Palo Alto still has advantages over them. The Palo Alto Children's Theatre is the only one in the nation which operates the year round on taxes, and its meager 15 cent admission fee is also almost unique. Most of the theatres charge admission and laboratory fees, and thus tend to limit the number and type of children in their programs. Many have only summer programs, and some of these are tax supported, she said.

Several places in the East are considering starting community centers modeled after Palo Alto's, Mrs. Robertson found.

One of the children's theatre trends she observed was the production of better plays—well-tested ones in spite of higher royalties. Schools are finally realizing the importance of dramatic training, she said, and are putting some money into scripts. "They've been doing it with music all along," she commented.

Another trend, partly carried out at the Children's Theatre Conference at Denver, is the setting of standards of judgment for productions and creative techniques.

Mrs. Robertson was able to look over a number of youngsters' books in galley form. She plans to adapt one of these, "Oak Chest" by Kate Seredy, for a production this fall. Another production here will be the prize-winning play "Papa Papino and the Prizefighter," scheduled for the end of the summer.

The state department claimed some of Mrs. Robertson's leave time. There she helped prepare an exhibit on the working techniques of the Palo Alto Children's Theatre. It has been sent abroad along with exhibits from four other leading American children's theatres, for practical application in other countries.

Yes, Virginia, there was a time before television. Here Hazel Glaister Robertson, longtime director of the Palo Alto Children's Theatre, looks ahead to TV. My recollection is that I first saw football televised early in 1952 at Rickey's Studio Inn.

2-acre Palo Alto Bird Sanctuary is dedicated in formal ceremony

A small crowd of city officials, honored guests, and other interested Palo Altans gathered yesterday afternoon at the Yacht Harbor for formal ceremonies dedicating the Palo Alto Bird Sanctuary.

The two-acre retreat, a gift of the late Mrs. Louis Stern, was presented to the city by Walter A. Haas, executor of Mrs. Stern's estate.

"Mrs. Stern would have been happy to see the completion of this project because of her great love for, Palo Alto," Haas said.

Mayor Walter Gaspar accepted the refuge on behalf of Palo Alto, commenting that, because of Mrs. Stern's generosity, "all our lives are richer and fuller."

Then Mayor Gaspar presented Reinhold John Jungermann, naturalist and teacher of biology at the high school, to whom the sanctuary was dedicated at Mrs. Stern's request.

Jungermann described how the project had begun when he and Mark Nesbit, harbormaster, had been called in by Mrs. Stern to find what might be done to provide better protection of wild life in Palo Alto.

He and Nesbit studied the Lake Merritt preserve in Oakland, and then drew plans in cooperation with I. T. Johnson, city streets and parks engineer, Jungermann said. After a few changes Mrs. Stern approved the plans—one of her last acts before her death in 1946.

There are three things, Jungermann pointed out, that wild fowl need: a protected place away from animals of prey, fresh water, and food. The fenced-in sanctuary with a fresh water pool and feed provided by the city satisfies all these needs.

Prof. James B. Wells, chairman of the board of public works, accepted the refuge from the city for maintenance and preservation.

James Rigby, committee chairman of Boy Scout troop 50, told the audience that America has been prodigal with her wild life in the past but is finally coming to a realization of its importance.

Rigby said he believed the sanctuary and others like it on national, state, and municipal scales would bring America the following dividends: More wild life, a greater knowledge of the natural controls which make wild life economically important, and a greater appreciation of our natural environment.

Arthur James, city planning engineer, told of a few of the city's dreams concerning possible future developments of the Yacht Harbor area.

He paid tribute to those among the city fathers who "long ago dreamed of a wonderful recreation area" there — Councilmen E. C. Thoits, and E. P. Cashel and others not here now—Prof. C. D. (Daddy) Marx, Prof. Charles B. Wing, and J. F. Byxbee, former city engineer who was pioneer in planning the Yacht Harbor area.

James described a few of the dreams for the area: trees instead of vacant marshland . . . a swimming pool . . . a widened harbor channel suitable for yacht races, crew races, and even possible future Olympic Games. . . . a massive stadium . . . barbecue and picnic areas . . . development of the airport with skip-stop connections to major airports . . . all kinds of recreational activities. . . .

The city planning commission is making a detailed study of the area in connection with the board of public works, and L. Deming Tilton, city planning consultant, is assisting in putting it on paper, James said.

How soon the area will be further developed depends on how fast population grows, on finances available, and on the need, James stated.

Reinhold John Jungermann.

"I like to think that this bird sanctuary will perhaps be a cornerstone for great developments 10, 15, 25, or possibly 50 years from now," James concluded.

Mr. and Mrs. Jungermann and Mr. and Mrs. Haas were guests of honor at a luncheon at Sky Cafe preceding the program. The program was planned by a committee composed of D. Walter McLellan, chairman, Mrs. Frances Merner, I. T. Johnson, Mark Nesbit, and Jerry Ryan.

Although dedicated as a bird sanctuary, this Palo Alto facility became best known as the duck pond. R.J. Jungermann had been one of my teachers at Palo Alto High School, so I had a good "in" for this story — and then went on to write a profile of Harbormaster Mark Nesbit. Establishing the bird sanctuary proved to be a vital step toward saving the baylands.

HARBORMASTER

Mark Nesbit's activity list is just as long as your arm

If you'd like to meet one of Palo Alto's top outdoorsmen — a man with a list of sporting activities as long as your arm — drop out to the Palo Alto Yacht Harbor some day and say hello to Mark Nesbit.

Nesbit is listed among city officials as harbormaster, and he is in every sense of the word. But that's far from all. He is also well known for his weekly column on the Times' sports page, "Outdoors with Mark Nesbit," active participation in youth work, and membership in a number of clubs and associations.

When he's working around the yacht harbor clad in his skipper's cap and dungerees or khakis, Nesbit is the perfect picture of the old salt in natural habitat. Slicked up for a gathering of city officials, his silvering hair and mustache make him the local man of distinction. His deeply tanned face shows his love of the out-of-doors.

Nesbit became harbormaster in 1940 when he moved his insurance business out to the city-owned harbormaster's house close by the harbor. Before that he had been particularly active in Boy Scout and Sea Scout work. His insurance selling days are over, but his writing about outdoor life has taken their place.

The harbormaster-columnist-sportsman was born in Saratoga, Calif., and spent a number of years living in Lodi. He moved to Palo Alto in 1926 and has lived here ever since.

Mark was active in Boy Scout work for many years, both as a volunteer and professional worker. He was a camp director at camps in the Santa Cruz Mountains and near Yosemite, and also has traveled the Sierras with Scouts. He was formerly skipper of Sea Scout ship 58.

On his own camping expeditions Mark has combed the Sierras on pack trips. He prefers deer hunting and trout fishing, but keeps tabs on hunting and fishing of all forms.

This summer Nesbit and his wife, Mae, who is superintendent of schools in Belmont, packed 90 miles in 12 days with burros in the Sierras.

Mark wrote his columns as scheduled and hung them to a tree for the next person returning to civilization to mail. The system proved to be only moderately successful, and several of his columns turned up missing. The Nesbits went on to Canada later, where another of Mark's

Mark Nesbit, Popular Palo Alto harbormaster.

columns was lost when he placed U.S. airmail stamps on it by mistake.

Yachting is his "long suit," Mark says. He is secretary of the Palo Alto Yacht Club, a member of the Pacific Interclub Yacht Association, a director of the California Marine Parks and Harbors Association, and edits a monthly bulletin for the Coyote Point, Palo Alto, Sequoia, and South Bay Yacht Clubs which reaches 400 members.

Nesbit is also on the Palo Alto Red Cross water safety committee, and still takes an active interest in the Sea Scouts and the Girl Mariners. During the war he was an ensign in the coast guard temporary reserve and served one day a week aboard a 38-foot picket boat which patroled the bay.

The local harbor, Nesbit thinks, has a great future. He looks forward particularly to increased interest in crew racing there next spring when the road now being built to the point has been completed.

As harbormaster, Nesbit must register all the boats in the harbor and provide berthing space for them. The harbor, operated under the board of public works, is home to about 35 boats — divided about 50-50 between cruisers and sailboats. In his various duties Nesbit is as complete a master of it as a captain is of his ship.

Membership in the Redwood City Sportsmen, the Peninsula Sportsmen, the Associated Sportsmen of California, and the Sierra Club help Nesbit keep in touch with hunting, fishing, hiking, camping, and riding activities. He makes at least two trips a year to winter sports centers to gather information.

The Nesbits' vacation plans for the next few years include trips to get a look at sporting activities in Hawaii and Alaska. They will make the Alaska trip through the inland passage.

Nesbit's knowledge of wildlife is being increased now by his chore of feeding the ducks at the newly-dedicated Palo Alto Bird Sanctuary near the yacht harbor. He aided R. J. Jungermann in the planning of the refuge.

P.A. draft signup slow
★ ★ ★ ★ ★ ★ ★
Woman 'pickets' booth

Registration for the draft opened slowly this morning at Palo Alto High School, but a woman "picket" appeared outside the high school building distributing an antidraft broadside smearing soldiers.

Draft officials said the small, elderly woman was handing cards to men on their way to register. George Stewart, high school vice principal and army reserve officer, was sent to warn the woman that distribution of literature on the high school grounds is illegal, but found she had disappeared.

The franked post cards given out bear the same text as those distributed to passers-by outside the telephone building last Thursday, also by an elderly woman. The woman's description coincides with that given Thursday by two irate veterans who were handed the cards.

"The lowest aim in life is to become a soldier," the card said. It went on to describe "a good soldier" as "a blind, heartless, murderous machine."

A spokesman for the firm which printed the cards refused to name his client Thursday, but said "she is a very well-known Palo Alto woman."

Registration this morning was spotty, officials reported, with the largest groups coming in at 8 a.m. and at noontime. A small rush just before closing time is expected. Similar reports were given by Sequoia Union High School and Mountain View Union High School draft officials.

Mrs. A. E. Fagan, chief registrar, estimated that about 300 of between 3,400 and 4,000 men expected to register here would sign up today. Today's registration will be small, she explained, because only men born in 1922 after Aug. 30 are required to sign up today. A large percentage of those registering are veterans, Mrs. Fagan said.

The remainder of the registration schedule is:

Sept. 2-3—Men born in 1924.
Sept. 4-7—Men born in 1925.
Sept. 8-9—Men born in 1926.
Sept. 10-11—Men born in 1927.
Sept. 13-14—Men born in 1928.
Sept. 15-16—Men born in 1929.
Sept. 17-18—Men born in 1930 prior to Sept. 19.

Registration is taking place in room 104 of the high school between 8 a.m. and 5 p.m. Veterans must bring some proof of service—discharge papers or photostats. Nonveterans must bring some proof of identification—a birth certificate or driver's license.

Men registered under the previous Selective Service Act should know the number of their draft board.

Some 110 volunteers are working in shifts on the registration. Employers have been asked to grant their employes sufficient time for registration.

———— •◆• ————

A draft signup in August 1948 was instituted to remedy the too-rapid demobilization after World War II. Veterans and previous registrants had to check in, and you can bet a lot of them groused about it. As for the "picket," a fair guess is that it was Alice Park, for decades Palo Alto's most ardent peace agitator.

Portion of cash from Youth Fund will build new gymnasium for 'Y'

Palo Alto's Young Men's Christian Association, one of the seven agencies included in the 1948 Community Youth Fund, could more accurately be called YM&WCA. For, among the thousand youngsters using the facilities of the "Y" are 81 girls— members of five clubs which meet regularly in the "Y" building at 657 Cowper St.

And, in addition, there are usually a few girls among the 90-odd children who daily use the club's playground or craft rooms or participate in one of the other recreational or educational activities carried on by the "Y".

The YMCA has an impressive record of activities for Palo Alto young people. In addition to the 81 girls, 725 boys between 9 and 19 were served last year in some way by the "Y". Of these, 377 were enrolled in regular groups.

These youngsters find the "Y" provides 20 "Y" clubs for school g r o u p s — clubs which meet at the "Y" building as well as at homes, schools, and churches. Volunteers direct the four craft and hobby groups which the "Y" conducts. And then, the "Y" program includes facilities for basketball, volleyball, softball, and tether ball as well as educational and recreational trips to near-by areas.

Last year, 100 boys, regardless of race or color, camped out at the YMCA camp at La Honda.

The work being done by the YMCA is considered so necessary by the directors of the Community Youth Fund drive that a little less than one-third of the total fund sought will go toward financing the activities of the organization next year. Together all seven agencies of the drive are asking $57,729 as a minimum figure for 1949.

All funds over this figure will go into the YMCA building fund —eventual purpose of which is to construct the first unit of a long-range improvement plan. This first unit, a gymnasium, is expected to cost approximately $85,000.

Present plans call for the construction of the gymnasium on the present site of the "Y's" tennis courts, next to the club building on Cowper St. The present building, though originally designed as a residence almost 50 years ago, will continue to be used until subsequent units of the project are erected.

The proposed gymnasium will include an indoor gym floor which could also be used for an auditorium, workout rooms, supply and equipment rooms, locker and shower facilities, boxing and wrestling rooms, and other rooms for group activities.

YMCA officials point out that there are approximately 500 youths in the Palo Alto area between 17 and 21 who have no access to school-sponsored clubs or groups. No semipublic youth agency is giving any organized attention to this group, according to the "Y", although other communities the size of Palo Alto have provided YMCA facilities to serve these young men. Nor are there any private athletic or recreational clubs in this area, the officials say.

The YMCA's long-range planning committee has said that the first and most necessary step in providing service for these youths is the erection of the proposed gymnasium.

Eventually, the "Y" hopes to construct a plant which will include resident facilities, food service facilities, adequately designed club and craft rooms, an indoor swimming pool, gymnasium, and auditorium, showers and lockers, and suitable offices.

Members of the long-range planning committee, all members of the "Y" board of directors, include J. Knight Allen, Herman Bercu, W. C. Cobb, Everett Dean, Cliff Giffin, Glenn C. Kenyon, William H. Carr, Ralph Cressman, Edwin Gerth, Paul Meyer, Charles Means, Robert Richards, J. Earle May, Oscar Maddaus, Perry Moerdyke Jr., Linn Winterbotham, Dallas E. Wood. Everett Runyan, John Santana, John Schwafel, Myron Sprague, R. Marvin Stuart, and Guy O. Wathen.

In addition to the "Y," other service groups which have combined their appeals into the Community Youth Fund drive are the Boy Scouts, the Girl Scouts, the Youth Coordinating Council, the Stanford YWCA, the Veteran Employment S e r v i c e Council, and the United Veterans Council.

The drive begins Friday and lasts throughout October.

The YMCA, with another "Who's Who" committee list of 1948 Palo Alto, began a campaign to enlarge its downtown headquarters but ended up moving to a then outlying location.

PAGING THE PREPS

Leave us face it: In PAL Vikes are the team to beat

By DODE WINSLOW

In preface to this new Times sports column, we'd like to say that it will be about and for the prep athletes on the Peninsula. If you high school athletes, students, fans, and parents have any comments, criticism, or good tales out of school, we'd like to hear from you.

* * * *

Might as well face it: The showings of the Paly High Viking footballers in their first three games have put them, temporarily at least, in the embarrassing position of being the team to beat in the PAL.

A poll of preseason forecasters last week picked Lincoln, San Mateo, Sequoia, and Palo Alto, in that order, as upper division finishers. Play last Friday immediately put their choices under fire. The Norsemen came through with the only clean-cut win of the day, thumping Jefferson 32-6. But Lincoln was lucky to squeeze by Burlingame, 7-6, and San Mateo needed a freak pass interception in the closing minutes of their battle wih Sequoia to remain untied and undefeated.

Sequoia outyardsticked the Bearcats on nearly everything but "times goal line crossed." To get back to the Vikes, they have rolled up 56 big points while giving up only six. They have a hot pair of backs in Skip Crist and Hod Ray Jr., who are both Mr. Outside-Inside's. They have a fairly experienced line. Until someone proves otherwise, they're the team to beat.

Lincoln was not too impressive in its warmups, and just snuck by Blingum Friday under the lights. It may well be that the Panthers, rated sixth by the swamis, will turn out to be the giant-killers of the league. Paly will find out Friday when the Norsemen go Panther hunting up north.

Lincoln draws Jefferson, and Sequoia goes up against a South City team that drew a 6-6 tie with San Jose last Friday. San Mateo's large Bearcats tangle with the Bulldogs in the south. Paly's test should be the toughest of the week; the other rated clubs look like winners.

* * * *

Ballyhoo boys doing all right

In two practice tilts and the league openers, the most-ballyhooed pilayers of the loop have fairly well lived up to their preseason reputations. A representative list of these might include Backs Sal Campagna and Duane Eckert (SM), Jim Whitney (B), Skip Crist (PA), and Conrad Mendenhall (L); Ends Phil Casaroli and Grant Spaeth (PA). Bill McMichael (SM); Tackles Joe Ramona (L), Ernie Rossi and Ray Kraochak (SSF), Al Lopez (S); Guards Dick Borda (L), Bob Barnes (S), Bill Saia (SJ); and Center Jack Pitts (SSF) and John Bland (SM).

These touted boys by no means have the loop all-star positions sewed up. Plenty of unrated players already have shown that the competition will be fierce. Examples are Hod Ray Jr., Bob Peterson, Sequoia's sticky-fingered end; Bob Hamilton, Blingum halfback, and a number of others. Fullback Gale Dimick of the Cherokees has gained plenty of ground, and his teammate, QB Don McNeil, looks good too.

* * * *

Sequoia's Barnes is player of week

Bob Barnes, Sequoia's speedy left guard, was the first PAL player to be awarded the PALO Club's silver acorn in the 1948 season for being "player of the week."

While the Cherokees were dropping the 13-7 thriller to San Mateo, the rugged little lineman stood out on both offense and defense. Coach Al Terremere agreed with the judges in the selection of Barnes for the honors. "I don't think I've ever seen a prep lineman have a better day," he said.

Barnes was in the Bearcat backfield all afternoon, made an uncounted number of tackles, and hauled down a pass intercepter from behind to save the Cherokees from having another touchdown scored on them.

* * * *

OOPS!! WE MISSED 'EM DEPT.: We overlooked that dazzling 25-0 win turned in by the Paly High Sophs last Thursday in their PAL opener vs. Jefferson. They tell us End Buddy Brown caught two touchdown passes and Halfback Jack Bully speared one. Don Reeves ran one marker over and threw for another. Quarterback Pete Pederson also tossed two TD spirals for the winners. Leading the way up front was Guard Bob Armstrong, with Halfback Dale Hendrickson looking good in the backfield.

Also lost in the shuffle was the 13-6 triumph of Coach Ernie Lydecker's Jorday gridders over the Paly Soph reserves last week. For the Dolphins' scores credit Center Jerry Williams' for falling on a fumble in the end zone and Jim (Crazy Legs) Farrell for skirting end for 15 yards to paydirt. QB Frankie Mills hit on seven of nine passes to lead the attack.

* * * *

Eagle-Fremont 'traditional' Friday

Coach Stan Anderson's Mountain View Eagles threaten to make trouble in the Santa Clara Valley League in the remaining games on their schedule. After losing their curtain-raiser to Santa Clara, the Eagles rebounded to knock the stuffing out of the Gilroy Mustangs, 25-0, last week.

This Friday the Mountain View eleven entertains Fremont in the Big Game for both teams. The Indians from Sunnyvale bumped Washington of Centerville 13-6 last week.

* * * *

In watching Sequoia play two tilts, we've been greatly bothered by the Cherokee practice of sending subs on the field without helmets. In several cases boys have had to go through plays without headgear because there wasn't time to get into the helmet of the boy leaving the field.

It's not only dangerous, but with the free substitution rule, the practice frequently fouls up a crucial play for the team. The Purple Indians have only enough helmets for two strings, but they should make full use of those until enough are obtained to go around — and more are in order right away.

SPORT SHOTS
by Walt Gamage

We would like to call your attention to the new weekly column on high school sports by Dode Winslow appearing here for the first time today. This is part of a plan to print more news about local prep sportsters and we know its going to be a popular feature. . . . Talk about spotlighting Peninsula high school athletes, have you noticed that two radio stations (KEEN and KVSM) will now broadcast the remaining Paly High football

---

Walt Gamage, a great promoter, latched onto part of my work time for prep sports coverage, and had me launch a column. "Paging the Preps" ran for nearly four years under my byline, and lifted our attention to high school sports to a new level. As secondary schools multiplied in the '50s and '60s, this reporting task became very involved and earned the *Times* a reputation for quality and depth that extended far beyond our circulation area. Others shouldered that burden — in my day the beat was quite manageable.

Bettencourt intercepts pass, runs 75 yards for winning T.D.

By DODE WINSLOW

Paly High's Viking footballers came home with a 19-12 win over San Jose last night after the Bulldogs threw one pass too many.

The game had a sudden death ending. San Jose was on the Norse 25 with a little more than a minute to go and the score was 12-12 when Bulldog Quarterback Chris Pappas faded and pitched a pass to the flat. Palo Alto's Johnny Bettencourt came roaring out of the secondary, gathered the ball in, and raced 75 yards down the sidelines for the winning score. He had a large mass of jubilant interference with him.

Bettencourt's interception was something that had been building up all night. Many of the 15 pitches Pappas threw were the short and naked flat passes.

For the Vikings, the interception was a welcome break, and snatched an almost certain tie or defeat from the fire. Early in the first quarter the Raymen had discovered they weren't going to get far running a stubborn Bulldog line, and took to the air for all their major gains thereafter.

Lossers were good on ground

San Jose had more success on the ground and also did some neat passing up until the sudden death flip. The Bulldogs won statistically, but . . .

Paly had San Jose in the hole during the opening 10 minutes, but lost two good chances to score against stiff opposition from the SJ forward wall.

Shortly before the quarter ended End Phil Casaroli faded on a play originating on the 50 and pitched to End Grant Spaeth out in the clear. Spaeth was dragged down on the 2. The quarter ended and two plays later Hod Ray skirted right end, helped along by a beautiful block by Skip Crist, and scored. Crist's kick was wide.

The Bulldogs took over on their own 43 with about three minutes left in the half. Two short gains and a 20-yard jaunt by Stan Gavel took them to the PA 30. A flat pass lost four yards, and Pappas flipped one to Right Half Johnny Leal, who took it over his shoulder a step ahead of the Vike secondary on the 15 and raced on over. Al Johnson's place kick was blocked.

A minute and a half was left in the half after John Anderson recovered an attempted onside kickoff on the 33. Bettencourt pitched a short pass to Ray, who shook off three tacklers and churned to the San Jose 28.

One pass fell incomplete and another netted no gain. Then Bettencourt ran to his right and threw to Grant Spaeth, who was waiting flat-footed with a San Jose defensive back by his side in the end zone. Spaeth faked with his body and made a little jump to easily take the touchdown toss.

Crist's conversion attempt was blocked, and the half's wild and wooly ending was over.

The Bulldogs returned the second half kickoff to the 30, and marched the remaining 70 in 11 plays to score. Paydirt was reached when Pappas snapped a pass to End Mac Morris who made a neat catch and went over standing up. Johnson's kick was wide.

Paly got as far as the SJ 30 in the fourth quarter, but an interception broke up their drive. In the closing minutes San Jose End Sheldon Onstead recovered a fumble on the PA 33 to set the stage for the ill-fated flat pass.

Crist passes to Spaeth

After Bettencourt had gone over, Crist threw to Spaeth for the extra point. Four desperation San Jose passes ended the tilt.

San Jose had nine first downs to Palo Alto's eight. The Bulldogs gained 144 net on the ground and 94 passing for 238 total yards gained. Palo Alto gained a net of 49 yards running and passed for 162 for a 211 total.

Pappas did all the SJ chucking, completing eight of 16 and having two intercepted. Bettencourt, Casaroli, Crist, and Denny Lucas threw Paly's 17 aerials, completing nine and losing one on an interception.

Rudy Feldman was again the Paly line standout. Bill Saia did a bang up job of linebacking for the Bulldogs, and Onstead played a nice defensive game. Edgar Buchanan and Gavel did their best ball packing. Pappas gets his passes off nicely but is not too accurate.

There's nothing like a great turnaround play near the end of a game to set up a lively sports story. The Crist-to-Spaeth extra point deserves a niche in the annals of the Palo Alto bar as both later became prominent law practitioners here.

Vikings looked mighty keen beating the Indians, 40-14

By DODE WINSLOW

The tale of the '48 Thanksgiving Day
is one that was written by Crist and by Ray,
by Heraty, Spaeth, and Casaroli too,
plus Feldman and Taafee, who had something to do
with walloping Sequoia—as seldom is seen—
by the powerful score of 40 to 14.

Anderson, Norman, and John Bettencourt
helped prove that football's a top Paly sport;
Lozano was the other Viking first-stringer
who helped put the Indians through the wringer
again and again, as they ran up the score
on Stanford Stadium's turf-covered floor.

Beginning by land and repeating by air,
the Viking attack was something quite rare;
they shook off some bobbles, then softened the line
until they could score almost any old time.
There were few who could doubt, while the Cherokees fell,
that the Norse were the hottest in the PAL.

But their rampage was late — it should have begun
five weeks before, versus old Blingum
and continued against South City, two weeks after that
on the day their title was knocked to a cocked hat;
The Panthers cinched their flag Thursday with a six up tie
with Sal Campagna and company from San Mateo High.

But in spite of the title, fans will long rave
about Skip's touchdown running to "Dig 'em a Grave,"
about Heraty passing those guided missiles
that racked up points amid shrieks and whistles.
Sequoia wasn't happy—their comment we hear
was "just wait a while, we'll get 'em next year."

You can't please all the people . . .

That's all of that stuff; it just ain't good enough.
The PAL teams announced yesterday have doubtless caused a unhappy talk around here. No one ever picks an all-star team good deal of talk in prep circles already, and likely most of it is without having 90 per cent of those who see it say "They picked that jerk? Why so-and-so made a punk out of him in the such-and-such game and why didn't they pick our man?"

We sat in on the meeting last week at which the prep all-star clubs were picked, and found out the pickers have a tough job. There are scores of things which enter into the considerations. Probably the most disrupting is the fact that some pickers may have seen a top player on an "offday." You can argue that an all-league player doesn't deserve an offday, but it doesn't hold water. For instance, those who only saw Paly in action against South City rated Skip Crist below some other players who put in flashier performances against the Warriors. But no one in his right mind could say Crist didn't play all-league ball in the over-all season.

Then you run into cases like those of Mike Heraty, Bob Barnes, and Conrad Mendenhall. When they were hot, they were very, very hot—Heraty put on the best passing performance we've seen by a prep player against Sequoia—but injuries kept them out of competition for several games.

The all-PAL team is picked on the basis of individual performances and with no thought of providing a balanced team. It's a distinct possibility that the second team might beat the first if the two lined up and played (we can safely say that on the premise that they probably never will).

On the first team for instance, there are five linebackers—Crist, Whitney, Sala, Pitts, and Abelar. There's one defensive halfback—Campagna. The ends, Peterson and Kahler, are the only players on the team who have caught any passes to speak of during the season. There is no expert safety man in the crew. If they could compromise on who would back the line, the all-star team would probably be one of the roughest clubs on ground defense ever seen in action. On offense, we don't know.

The ends were really a toss-up. In Peterson, Kahler, Spaeth, Casaroli, Degan, and Morris the loop had six ends of about equal caliber—and one of the best crops of flankmen ever seen in these parts. All were expert receivers. Most of them were good defensively. Peterson was the PAL's top punter. Spaeth turned in the most amazing catches, and was defensive murder when the Vikings were in a 6-2-2-1, though he had some lapses in the 5-3-2-1. They were all good. Whadda ya gonna to do about picking the two best?

Here's a three-ended all-PAL

We missed seeing Burlingame and Jefferson play this season. We can, however, pick a mythical team we think would work well together based on the outstanding performances we've seen. At center, we'd use Abelar, thereby getting advantage of his defensive ability and blocking while sacrificing his running to get a faster backfield. At guards would be Barnes and Sala, who both get all over the field. At one tackle would be Feldman, of course, and at the other we'd use Al Lopez of Sequoia.

We'd have to have three ends—Peterson, Spaeth, and Casaroli. At quarterback we'd use Heraty on the basis of his passing and ballhandling against Sequoia and his defensive performance against San Mateo. At one half we'd have Ray, for his play-calling, defensive work, and running. At the other would be Campagna, who looked good even in defeat, and who is a defensive ace. And Crist, the guy who can do everything, would be our fullback. If we needed another back, it would be a scatback like, say, Edger Buchanan of San Jose.

It's pretty heavy on Paly. But bear in mind that we missed seeing Blingum and Jefferson, and saw most of the Vike's games, particularly their inspired ones against San Mateo, Lincoln, and Sequoia.

* * *

Next year? The situation looks glum at Palo Alto where Johnny Bettencourt will be the one returning regular. Sequoia will have a seasoned team with players like Blackmer, Schott, Crawford, and several others, plus the material from a championship frosh-soph team. San Jose ought to really have the club, though. The luckless Bulldogs, who outplayed most of the teams on their schedule and lost to most, will have a corps of fleet backs and some good linemen. But it's hard to tell how high school teams will pan out. Players turn from boys to men in a summer, and, as the well-worn phrase goes, a football bounces funny. The so-called experts rated San Mateo and Lincoln, the teams that tied for third, in top spots in their preseason predictions. And Burlingame, the winner, was tabbed for sixth place.

That's finis to 1948's prep football.

The Times had a strong rule against poetry or verse in its news or letters columns. Somehow I wangled permission to celebrate Paly's 1948 Little Big Game victory over Sequoia in doggerel. I swear I was not aware of Dr. Seuss, who cashed in much bigger on such rhymes.

Local fans will get their first taste of high school football a la 1950 this Friday and Saturday—and there may well be some spitbacks.

The deal which may leave a bad taste in some fans' mouths is the new set of rules the preps will use. For as long as most Peninsula Athletic League spectators can remember, high schools have been playing with the same rules the colleges use, with just a few minor modifications.

All that's changed now. This season the PAL and the neighboring San Francisco and Santa Clara Valley leagues and the Catholic schools in this area will conform with most of the other California high schools by using rules of the National Federation of State High School Associations.

These rules differ from the college rules in about 40 particulars. Last week we quoted PAL Commissioner G e o r g e Stewart as saying you won't recognize the game.

This week Jack Dyas of Palo Alto, who's been a PAL football official for seven years, has some fuel to add to the fire. Every year for the past several years Dyas has offered to visit PAL and SCVAL schools before the season starts to talk to players about rules.

Here's how he opened his talk at Palo Alto High:

"This year you'll be playing under a new set of rules nobody knows—not even the officials."

He asked the players to bear with the men in the striped shirts through what may be some trying games. That is, not to fly off the handle over a ruling, even though the player may be sure it's wrong. He pleaded for calm discussion until the new rules become familiar.

Stewart made the same plea to fans last week: Don't throw any abuse at the refs until you're sure you know what's going on.

In an effort to simplify the complicated rules for players, Dyas has formulated a cardinal principal—"Any time you pick up the ball, run with it. The ref will stop you if the ball's dead."

Here are some of the major changes he talked about:

1. Any player may recover and advance a backward pass or fumble.

2. Any kick is dead when it touches or crosses the goal line.

3. Any player in legal position and not in the line may receive a forward pass (this makes the T quarterback eligible).

4. An unlimited number of forward passes may be thrown behind the scrimmage line, but only one may cross the line of scrimmage.

5. A punt may be downed at any point on the field, even within the 10-yard line.

6. If a free kick or kickoff goes out of bounds, the ball goes to the receiving team 10 yards behind that team's restraining line, or closer to the kicking team's goal if it goes out of bounds there. This means a kickoff which goes out of bounds behind the receiving team's 40 comes out to that team's 40-yard line.

7. Two substitutes may enter while the clock is running or during the 25-second rhythm.

8. A punt may not be used on a free kick, such as after a safety. The fair catch is still in effect.

"You can't imagine how confusing, how tough it's going to be," Dyas told us. The lean Palo Alto Post Officer worker with the biting midwestern accent used himself as an example.

Dyas has been officiating 27 years. For 20 years in the midwest he worked both university and high school games (the lat-ter with the new rules which are to be used here). In this area he has worked prep and junior college tilts—35 to 40 a fall.

His hobby is keeping up on football rules. He gives talks about them to coaches, fellow officials, and players of about 15 schools a year. Ordinarily when fall rolls around he can take a quick look at any changes, lecture at a rules meeting, and scarcely ever make a mistake though he hasn't looked over the old rules for nearly a year.

This season he studied the new rules again and again. Then he talked about them at a coaches' meeting and was caught making six mistakes.

Most high school game officials don't study the rules as hard as he does, Dyas pointed out with justifable pride. Those who do also work junior college games and will be trying to use one set of rules in the afternoon and another at night. Pity the poor ump.

It seems to us rule changes in high school ball should make the game safer, more interesting, and simpler, in that order. How about these?

Safety? Can't see much improvement. Almost c e r t a i n l y some players will get hurt trying to scoop up fumbles on the run instead of falling on them.

More interest? The forward pass change and punt-downing change will add a bit. On the other hand, you'll no longer see players gambling on running kickoffs back out of the end zone.

Simplicity? Uh-uh. It appears that these rules are different just to be different, just to sell another rule book, just to satisfy the thirst for power of another set of rulesmakers.

Spectators, players, and officials will be confused. And even if they ever learn the new rules, players will have to unlearn them if they go on to play college ball.

How about that fancy column heading!

... he needs no introduction – Hod Ray, veteran Paly coach

By DODE WINSLOW

. . . he needs no introduction— Hod Ray.

The man probably known person-to-person by more Palo Altans than any other individual is Howard C. (Hod) Ray.

Thousands of present and former students have made his acquaintance during the 30 years he has coached athletics at Palo Alto High School. Many of them played on his teams.

Hundreds of teachers know Hod as the city school system's supervisor of physical education. Other hundreds of residents have met him at his popular night school badminton and businessmen's volleyball classes.

And anyone who doesn't fall into one of those categories and who has lived here very long has probably met Hod somewhere around town.

Practically all these people, soon after meeting the friendly coach, instinctively address him as "Hod." And it's a tribute to his remarkable memory that he can answer most of them by name.

Palo Alto is taking a little time out this year to express its appreciation of his 30 years of service to the community's youth. At the traditional Paly-Sequoia game Thanksgiving Day the PALO Sports Club presented him with a gold watch. It was an impressive sight as hundreds of Hod's former athletes gathered around while he received the gift. His gridders won the game especially for him and carried him across the field on their shoulders afterward.

Wednesday will be Hod Ray Day at the Palo Alto Chamber of Commerce's luncheon at Wilson's. The guest of honor will show color movies of the Turkey Day game and is in for another gift.

That Hod is a durable and popular coach is evident from his 30-year record—one of the longest stretches of service to a single school in the west. And he's here because he likes it. His close friends will tell you that Hod has turned down some attractive offers from colleges and other high schools.

Hod came up the hard way. He was born 56 years ago in Roslyn, Wash., a town about 100 miles east of Seattle, where his father, an immigrant from England, was a coal miner.

At Roslyn High School Hod was one of 18 boys enrolled and began collecting letters in sports. His basketball team—with only seven men on the squad and no coach—won the state championship.

"We just learned by playing night and day," he explained.

He played more football and basketball at Olympia High School as a senior, and then worked a year before starting college. Hod was all set to go to the University of Washington when he heard from a Roslyn friend who had become athletic director at Oregon State College.

The friend convinced Hod that he should seek higher education at Corvallis with the offer of a 1914 equivalent of an athletic scholarship—a promise of a part-time job (involving plenty of work) and a chance to eat at the training table if he made the team.

There was no degree offered in physical education and Hod studied animal husbandry.

Basketball was his top sport. He made the Beaver first team as running guard while a freshman and nothing dislodged him for four years. OSC won the Northwest Conference championship in 1915 and again in 1917 when he was a senior. Hod was chosen on the all-conference teams his junior and senior seasons, and captained the team both years.

OSC's cage coach left for the army in 1917 and Hod was elected to coach the team. The job paid nothing and he lost money by having to drop some of his work to handle it, but it's not every college boy who can coach the team he plays on to a title.

Though not too big, Hod was an all-around athlete. He broad-jumped 22 feet consistently—a winning mark then—but couldn't practice daily because he was working. The coach didn't see it that way, so Hod got in only a few meets. He was a starting halfback the one season he played football, and did some third-sacking for the baseball nine.

His sweetheart from Roslyn became Frances Ray early in 1918 and in April Hod entered the machinegun battalion of the 91st division. His outfit hit the front lines in France in August and fought at St. Mihel, Argonne, and Lyscheldt, Belgium.

The next May Hod was home and went to work, managing a sheep ranch in eastern Washington for 18 months. In 1921 Dr. A. D. Brown of Oregon State started a coaching school at Stanford and recruited Hod as a pupil.

During the summer the fledgling coach was offered jobs at Bakersfield High, San Francisco Polytechnic, and Paly High. He wasn't going to have his teaching credential until the end of the summer but the late Walter H. Nichols, then Paly's principal, waived the requirement and Hod went to work.

That 1921 outfit, his first, gets Hod's vote as his favorite team and provided him with his biggest coaching thrill by going to the North Coast Section finals.

"There were 18 men on the squad and they played on guts," he said. The team whipped strong Mountain View and San Jose elevens for the Peninsula title and squeezed past Salinas and Lick-Wilmerding for the right to meet Berkeley High for the NCS title.

"Husky Hunt was coaching there then," said Hod, "and they had a wonder team. Our 18 kids were out on Edwards Field warming up when a gate opened and six Berkeley teams poured in."

It was too much for the Vikings. They tightened up and fumbled so much that Berkeley

COACH HOD RAY

rolled up a 42-0 score.

"We played the unbalanced line with the single wing for the first time on the Peninsula that year; no one ever shifted to meet it," said Hod.

In later seasons Hod gradually shifted to the double wing and sometimes to a short punt formation. Since 1946 his teams have used the T.

"I always tried to adapt the formation to the players, and sometimes we switched back to the single wing from the double. But I like the T best. It's more romantic and you can do so many things from it. You can also simplify the blocks."

Hod considers his 1928 team, a single-wing outfit that won the NCS title, and this year's unbeaten team his two outstanding elevens.

Every Paly football team since 1921 has been trademarked "Ray." In practice games his gridders have won 52, tied 7, and lost 22. In league play the record shows 98 wins, 17 ties, and 41 losses. Paly has won seven PAL championships, 17 second places, three thirds, and three fourths. That's an overall everage of .703, one any coach would be proud of.

Hod's basketball teams from 1921-1946 compiled a league rec-

ord of 108 wins, 45 losses, and 12 championships. Twice the Vikes won the NCS. In league baseball from 1921-1926 Hod's team won 63, lost 41, and took six PAL crowns. His track teams in 1921 and from 1940 through 1950 won 42 dual meets and lost 16. The unlimiteds won four PAL titles and the 130s were NCS champs in 1944 and PAL champs in 1950.

His one disaster was the year he tried coaching swimming. The Palywogs lost both their meets.

Hod's three main goals in coaching are to give as many boys a chance to play as possible, to try to fit the system to the material, and to see that players have a lot of fun.

Asked whether he thinks football is still fun for the boys, Hod answered:

"High school ball is becoming too much of a business. There's too much pressure on high school as well as college players. Fortunately for me at Palo Alto the people have been more realistic and considerate."

Emphasis at Paly has been on a well-rounded program and some years there have been as many as 21 teams in competition. But, Hod pointed out, high schools don't have enough coaches to carry on all activities and must depend on volunteers in many instances.

In picking future champions Hod looks for natural ability and speed, along with the desire to compete.

"The biggest thing is the spirit of the kid himself. If he doesn't like contact in football, he isn't going to do very well."

As supervisor of physical education Hod, who took his master's degree at Louisiana State in 1937, sets up programs for PE work in city schools and visits each school nearly every week to confer with principals and demonstrate teaching methods. Here again the emphasis is on maximum participation and development.

With principals and administrators, Hod planned Palo Alto's distinctive program of turf playfields for elementary schools several years ago.

During World War II Hod wrote and received hundreds of letters from former Paly athletes in the services. He also taught first aid and trained many women who later enlisted in the Wacs and Waves to march at night school classes, and with Col. J. Fletcher set up a high school cadet corps.

The years have grayed and thinned Hod's hair, added power to his booming bass voice, and boosted his golf scores from the 70s to the 80s, but they haven't changed the twinkle in his blue eyes or his jaunty walk.

His hobbies, besides golf, include movie and still photography, furniture finishing, and bridge. He is a member of the Exchange Club and was in Sigma Alpha Epsilon fraternity at Oregon State.

With Madilyn and Marilyn Wood, twins from Palo Alto who are "Bugs Bunny" animators and artists for Warner Bros., Hod brought out a booklet called "Football Facts and Fun" last year. Its clever drawings and text on football from the average spectator's point of view won it a writeup in Life magazine. It's still selling.

Mr. and Mrs. Ray have a daughter, Patricia, who is Mrs. John Hess of Stockton; a son, Howard Jr., better known as Bud, who is studying construction engineering at Oregon State; and a granddaughter, 8-year-old Susie Hess. Bud was a Paly sports star in 1948. He attended Glendale Junior College last year and is considered a promising fullback at OSC.

Hod's dog, Mickey, is a frequent visitor at Paly, but Hod says the Irish terrier isn't the sports nut his first Mickey, an airdale, was. Mickey I rooted vociferously for Paly athletes until a poisoner killed her. She was buried under the oaks near the first Paly football field and honored by a poem in the Madrono, student yearbook.

That field, by the way, was built by Hod and his players in 1929. Two students, Phil Christiansen and Dean Stanley, put in the piping and found just one leak when they tried it out. In 1937 the WPA put in the present Hod Ray Field and the baseball field.

A high school coach gives practically his whole time to his job, Hod points out. During the season he's busy coaching on the field and organizing, planning, scheduling, scouting, and making public appearances off the field. There is also a constant bombardment of requests to write recommendations or to help Johnny over some rough spots.

"I wouldn't trade my years here for any other work," Hod concluded. "I've enjoyed it, and having a home here, one of the best places a person can live."

Don Edwards named head of Young GOP

DON EDWARDS

Don Edwards, Palo Alto businessman, is the new president of the California Young Republicans.

Edwards, executive vice president of the San Jose Abstract & Title Company who spends most of his time in the Palo Alto office, defeated Dr. Harold Graves of Sacramento for the office at the final session of the convention held in Bakersfield yesterday. He succeeds Joseph F. Holt of Los Angeles.

"The Young Republicans of California have a program that is aggressive, progressive, and dynamic. We seek the support of all of the people, no favored groups," Edwards told the Times today.

He said a platform, now being put into final shape, was worked out at the convention. It encompasses changes for the betterment of the party and a positive approach to politics, Edwards declared.

Edwards is a graduate of San Jose High School and Stanford University, where he was a golf team standout. He is well-known in California golfing circles.

Before World War II he served for a time in the Federal Bureau of Investigation, and during the war he served in the navy, rising to the rank of lieutenant.

He and his wife now live at Woodside and Canada Rds., Woodside.

Rep. Douglas swoops down on Menlo Park in helicopter

Rep. Helen Gahagan Douglas swooped into Menlo Park for a campaign chat yesterday and established herself as a notable "first" — the first campaigner ever to stump in these parts by helicopter.

Her red, white, and blue Hiller 360, its long, thin fuselage emblazoned with "Douglas for Senator" slogans, dropped down like a high fly ball to the grass just inside the Nealon Park diamond's left field foul line.

About 100 persons — mostly saucer-eyed children and their mothers — watched the 'copter land shortly after 3:30 p.m. Police held the crowd back and the fire department was on hand.

The Los Angeles congresswoman, wearing a blue suit and hat, a red coat, and dark glasses, climbed out and stretched her legs while Dr. Natalye C. Hall, assistant professor of government at Mills College, introduced her over the campaign craft's public address system.

Mrs. Douglas then described some of her political background and explained why she seeks the Democratic nomination for senator. She talked particularly of her support for the Central Valley Project.

After concluding her talk, the attractive former movie star answered questions, including some by youngsters on how it feels to ride in the 'copter.

"No," she said, "I'm afraid we can't give any rides. But I bet by the time you're grown up every one of you will have one of these."

Then she and her pilot and campaign manager got back into their flying machine built for three and pulled in the microphone.

Boys who had gone back to their pepper game in the infield looked around as the helicopter zoomed off the ground, dodging light tower wires. Candidate Douglas gave a merry wave as the ship flew off crabwise toward Redwood City.

Black gnats on the prod

But measures being taken to beat 'em

Biting gnats beware!

That warning was posted today by the Santa Clara County Health Department's vector control bureau, which is both studying and waging a war against the mysterious black, or valley, gnat in cooperation with the State Health Department.

Doug Gould, state entomologist, reported these developments in the joint project:

1. Gnat watchers are being lined up throughout the Santa Clara Valley. These observers will report occurrence of the insect.

2. Two light traps have been set up, one in Cupertino and one in Evergreen.

3. The weather stations have been established. They have automatic recording equipment for temperature and humidity. Instruments for r e c o r d i n g wind velocity and direction are to be added.

Gould said he will spend full time as the season advances actually observing the gnawing gnats and studying possible breeding areas. Investigators believe the problem is now confined to the west half of the valley.

The county health department would appreciate hearing reports from unofficial gnat watchers of the location and time of any appearance of the biting gnat. The telephone number is CYpress 5-6816.

Meanwhile, San Mateo County residents of various areas along Portola-Alpine Rd. reported that their annual battle with the pests is on.

One Westridge resident, Mrs. J. E. Hayes, said the gnats arrived—like the swallows returning to Capistrano—promptly on June 1 as usual.

They aren't as bad as last year, Mrs. Hayes declared, but they definitely are a nipping nuisance. Portola-Alpine Rd. gnats seem to appear only in the sunlight, she said, and evidently have no fondness for water. Neither do they like citronella, she added, although chemical sprays have not eliminated them.

Last year, Mrs. Hayes said, was the worst in recent history of gnats in the area. They stayed on into September. Residents are hoping this year that the winged marauders will be gone—also on schedule—at the end of June.

Ravenswood 'Follies' show draws plaudits

By WARDELL WINSLOW

"Fathers' Follies," the Ravenswood Parent-Teacher Association review with an all-male cast which opened last night, shows how good a variety show a group of determined amateurs can get together.

With a few top-flight guest entertainers and local talent ranging from a teen-age trampoline team to a beefy chorus line, the fathers manage to provide fun for all in their Gay '90's review at Ravenswood School auditorium.

It's a shame that all the tickets for tonight, tomorrow, and Saturday are sold out. The fathers are discussing further performances for those who couldn't get tickets.

Johnny Molinari, "Wizard of the Accordion," and Lester Bode, "The Master Juggler," provided high spots in the guest entertainment last night.

Molinari, a professioanl entertainer and record artist who got his start in Redwood City, used both trick effects and straight musical brilliance to fascinate his audience.

Tonight and Friday D i c k Penna will fill the accordion spot, and Saturday Don Langone will perform.

Bode, who performed on the Orpheum circuit for 30 years, put on a graceful and amusing exhibition the likes of which the small fry in the audience had never seen. The Menlo Park man is one of the best anywhere.

Among the best of the local acts is that of Jack Farrell's "Sensational High Divers," the trampoline team from Ravenswood playground.

Don Harper and Gordon Otter, both high school diving champions, lead them through intricate routines, and Harper and Rodney Anderson add comedy. In his final routine, Harper passes his body completely through a 24-inch hoop he holds while doing a series of back somersaults.

The "Fathers' Follies Dollies" chorus line performs twice with enthusiasm, if not finesse, and is especially funny if you know the dainty 200-pounders doing the can can.

Varian Associates may soon move to Palo Alto

Being named winners of the Franklin Institute's coveted John Price Wetherill Medal was a thrill for the klystron-developing Varian brothers—Russell and Sigurd—but it comes second to their bride in parenthood of a flourishing young Peninsula industry.

Varian Associates at 99 Washington St., San Carlos, formed two years ago in the realization of the brothers' long-time dream, has grown beyond their wildest expectations for its early development. Plans are underway to move the lusty infant plant to a larger site south of Palo Alto.

Since it set up shop with a staff of six in the late summer of 1948, Varian Associates has grown until it now has 100 employes. It began operation in one small building and has sprawled since then through a number of neighboring structures.

The company engages in research, development, and manufacture of microwave tubes and associated equipment, and in other types of development in the general field of applied physics.

Varian Associates is an unusual company in many ways. In its highly technical but rapidly expanding field it has little competition.

Much of its work is done for government agencies on cost-plus jobs, and because of the importance of its research and products to national defense orders have been flowing fast since the Korean war developed. Its staff "couldn't be duplicated," according to Mrs. Russell Varian, treasurer. About half the employes are engineers—skilled in an extremely technical field and hand-picked.

The nucleus of the staff is composed of men who worked as klystron engineers in the Sperry Gyroscope Company's pre-war laboratory in San Carlos. Many staffers were lured here by the promise of pioneering work and of living in California. There's a collection of no less than eight Ph.D.'s on the staff, not to mention special consultants.

Aside from its own experts, Varian Associates can draw on the knowledge of directors and engineering consultants — many of them at Stanford—representing the top brains in the company's field.

At the outset it was decided that major decisions would be made by men who had the technical knowledge to make them, and the management and directors were chosen accordingly.

"The company is about as close to a cooperative as it can be," said Mrs. Varian. The bulk of its stock is owned by company workers, and even the lowest-paid employes are buying shares.

There's a friendly, informal atmosphere in the Varian Associates' offices, where crowded quarters reflect the tremendous growth of the staff and facilities. Government officials have commented on high morale and efficiency, according to Mrs. Varian.

Latest victim to the plant's expansion was the horseshoe pit, where spirited noon-hour tournaments were held until equipment pushed into its place.

The basic manufactured item is currently the klystron—the radio tube utilizing very short wave lengths on ultra high frequencies which was invented by the Varian brothers.

Though the klystron is best known as the gadget which made possible rapid development of radar during World War II, it has a multitude of other uses. In radar its uses include marine and air navigation, searchlight control, gunlaying, air navigation traffic control, and instrument landing systems.

But the klystron is also finding many uses in the booming commercial communications field. Present television transmitters and relay links are built around microwave equipment.

Wireless long distance telephone calls are also being sent on point-to-point microwave relays. One recently put in service beams messages from mountain top to mountain top between San Francisco and Los Angeles. A number of other forms of microwave relay communications systems are being experimented with.

Five klystron models for various uses are now being produced by the company. Three have been developed since Varian Associates set up shop, and two are improvements of older models.

Both business connections and the know-how of company engineers promise to put Varian Associates on the ground floor when pulsed klystrons and magnetron traveling wave tubes are further developed.

Microwave measuring equipment is also being produced and sold in the same expanding market that wolfs up klystrons.

The company foresees a large future market in nuclear induction apparatus based on work done at Stanford by the late Dr. William W. Hansen and Dr. Felix Block. The process promises to extend magnetic field measurement and control, geophysical exploration and other forms of detection, and a broad field of chemical analysis.

A nuclear fluxmeter to stabilize and control magnetic fields —the first commercial application of the nuclear induction process—is now being produced at San Carlos.

One of the firm's new contracts is for construction of an installation on Cheyenne Mountain in Colorado which the bureau of standards will use for high wave research, particularly on high, fast planes. The project will provide information which will eventually be used in establishing air navigation controls.

Dr. Russell H. Varian, whose myriad ideas have resulted in more than 100 patents issued or pending in the microwave and applied physics fields, is president of the company and director of research. Sigurd F. Varian is chairman of the board of directors and director of the tube development laboratory.

Both Varian brothers still are affiliated with Stanford as research associates.

H. Myrl Stearns, who played a big part in radar development while employed by Sperry Gyroscope Company, is vice president and general manager.

— Dr. Russell H. Varian, left, and Sigurd F. Varian

Russell and Sigurd Varian chosen to receive Wetherill Medal award

Russell and Sigurd Varian soon will receive a new honor for their invention of the klystron radio tube at Stanford University in the late 1930s and their subsequent development of it.

The Franklin Institute of Philadelphia, Pa., has announced that the brothers will be awarded the John Price Wetherill Medal Oct. 18. Both expect to be present to receive the medal and the following citation which accompanies it:

"In recognition of their foresight in anticipating the need for a converter of electromagnetic energy in a hitherto unexplored high frequency region of the spectrum, their energy and technical insight in developing for this purpose a practical device, the klystron, which has opened up new fields in communications applications and research."

Dr. Henry B. Allen, executive vice president of the institute, who made the announcement, pointed out that microwave radar development during World War II would have been quite different and much slower if the klystron had not been invented.

It is doubtful, he said, that very short wave radio bands— known as the X and K bands— could have been made useful soon enough to be of military value without the klystron. The new radio tube has made possible much peacetime exploratory work in the electromagnetic spectrum.

Main development of the klystron took place at Stanford between 1937 and 1939, when the Varians worked as research associates with the late Dr. William W. Hansen, professor of physics. Dr. David L. Webster, then head of the physics department, was their adviser.

Dr. Russell Varian had, after taking bachelor's and master's degrees at Stanford, worked as a research physicist with an oil company and as a research engineer with a television development firm. In 1934 he returned to Stanford to engage in research in applied physics.

Sigurd Varian, after . . . studying two years at . . . California Polytechnic College, first barnstormed in old World War I aircraft and later became a Pan American Airways pilot, pioneering that company's Mexican and South American services.

He saw the need for a device to increase the safety of blind flying and to warn of the approach of enemy aircraft.

The brothers left their jobs and set up a small laboratory at their family home in Halcyon, near San Luis Obispo, where they began research work. But after starting on the microwave project they found they needed a well-equipped lab and shop and technical help.

So they returned to Stanford and, during three years in which they lived on slim savings, developed the klystron. In 1940 both brothers joined the Sperry Gyroscope Company, which took over the commercial and military development of the new radio tube.

In 1946 Russell Varian returned to Stanford as a research associate. In the fall of 1948 Sigurd joined him here and the brothers put a long-dreamed-of plan into action by setting up their own company, Varian Associates, in San Carlos. The firm is doing both development and production work.

In addition to its uses in military and civilian radar, the klystron has opened up development of microwave relay systems for wireless telephone, television, and radio transmission, as well as ordinary television transmission.

The Wetherill Medal is one of eight medal awards made annually by the Franklin Institute. Other Wetherill Medal award winners this year are Kenneth C. D. Hickman of Rochester, N.Y., for his developments of high vacuum pumps, and Dr. Donald W. Kerst of the University of Illinois, developer of the betatron.

INJUNS ON THE WARPATH

Menlo Park boys 'get in training' by joining class in athletic rhythm

For years Palo Alto boys panting after a long touchdown run or finishing a victory smile as they climbed dripping from the swimming tank have said modestly, "I owe my success to Harry Maloney's gym class."

A few years from now Menlo Park boys in the same situations may be commenting, with a blush, "I got my start in Mrs. Kreutzmann's athletic rhythm fundamentals class."

At least that's one way of saying an interesting project is now under way in Menlo Park. Taught by Mrs. William Kreutzmann and sponsored by the parent-teacher association, a weekly class is giving young boys a chance to "get in training" for future sports enjoyment.

In the class the boys, from 5 to 9 years old, play games designed to "develop thorough enjoyment of rhythmic activities and promote development and efficient use of the body."

Mrs. Kreutzmann, who designed the course and conducts the classes, is the modern dance teacher at Palo Alto High School and the adult evening school. She has had extensive experience in both dancing and the teaching of modern dance.

Daughter of grid coach

Before her marriage, Mrs. Kreutzmann was Janice Shaughnessy, daughter of Clark Shaughnessy, former Stanford football coach. Her father steered her toward the idea that is being developed in the Menlo Park class, though accidentally. Mrs. Kreutzmann tells it this way:

She was teaching a dance class at Stanford while Shaughnessy was coaching there, and told him to come and look it over some day. He did, and after he had watched some shapely coeds go through the modern dance gyrations for awhile, his daughter asked him how he liked it.

"I thought," she explained, "that he'd tell me how well my class was doing, how well taught they were, or something like that."

Instead the Wow Boys' mentor said, "There's a perfect set of calisthenics for my football team." As good as his word, Shaughnessy soon adapted the modern dance figures to routines to develop the coordination and agility of his grid stars.

When a group of Menlo Park mothers wanted some kind of dance training for their sons last fall, they called on Mrs. Kreutz-

mann. She agreed to teach the class on Saturday mornings. Then she put the course together.

Small boys, Mrs. Kreutzmann explained, stand in mortal fear of being tagged as "sissies" by their classmates if they're caught in a dance class. Consequently the course was designed so that the boys can be put "in training" for the various sports, just like Jack Armstrong.

Boys go for it

This idea has proved quite a drawing card — the kids really go for it. Of course, they're eventually supposed to realize that the stuff some people call dancing can be valuable and enjoyable, even to boys.

In their games, the boys are taught how to run, walk, hop, gallop, skip, slide, prance, leap, and jump correctly, and get plenty of practice at it. They also learn to bounce, stretch, flex, extend, swing, turn, fall, and contract—fundamental axial movements.

All the games are played to music. During their one-hour session the boys are football, basketball, and baseball players; firemen putting out a blaze; Indians on the warpath; cheerleaders; and even Captain Jinks of the Horse Marines — so it takes a bit of play acting, too.

Specific objectives of the course are to develop an accurate response to rhythmic stimuli, to provide experience in the various forms of movement, and to give the boys experience in and improve the quality of the traditional forms of dance movement.

In short, they get the "feel" of the various sports long before they participate in most of them. Naturally every boy in the class isn't expected to become a record-smashing athlete; the idea is rather to give them self-confidence in their ability for natural, fluent movement, balance, and coordination.

The Menlo Park PTA also sponsors four modern dance classes for girls, one of which is taught by Mrs. Kreutzmann, and a number of folk and ballroom dancing classes. The girls also go for the training in a big way, and they're happy to have it called just plain dancing.

$250,000 Sunset Magazine building now being erected in Menlo Park

Work started today on the ranch-type building in Menlo Park which will house business and editorial offices of Sunset Magazine.

Contract for the $250,000 building was awarded to Howard White of Palo Alto whose men today were digging trenches for the forms. The 30,000-foot building will be completed about Sept. 1 of next year, according to L. W. Lane, president of the Lane Publishing Company of San Francisco, which publishes Sunset and also operates a book publishing business.

Overall investment in the building, land, and landscaping will be about $400,000, Lane said.

The building will be situated on part of a seven-acre piece of property in the Linfield Oaks tract, part of the old Hopkins estate adjacent to Stanford Village. It is bounded by Middlefield Rd., Willow Rd., and San Francisquito Creek.

Higgins and Root of San Jose are architects for the structure, which was designed by Cliff May of Los Angeles as consulting architect. May is regarded as an authority on ranch-type buildings. Thomas Church of San Francisco is the landscape architect.

Approximately 100 Sunset employes now working in the company's San Francisco office will work in the new building, which will house advertising, editorial, circulation, and general offices of the magazine. The San Francisco building at 576 Sacramento St. will be sold, said Lane. The advertising sales department will remain in San Francisco.

All employes in the Menlo Park office will reside in this area.

"We are giving our employes a choice," Lane said today. "They may move down the Peninsula and we will help them find housing. Or they may choose to remain in San Francisco and we will help them find jobs."

Lane said it is likely that some residents of this area will be hired to work for the company.

"Some of the San Francisco employes who own their homes and who have members of the family working for San Francisco firms may not want to move," he said. "In those cases we will help them find jobs in San Francisco and find people from this area to take their places."

Inside and outside the building will typify ranch-house construction—on a large scale. The outside will be of stucco and redwood except for the center portion, which will be adobe, inside and out.

The central part will contain an entrance and reception room 56 feet in length, with a big plate glass window overlooking a wide lawn. On the Middlefield Rd. side the building will be set back 75 feet, with lawns and landscaping in front.

Most of the lawn and landscaping, however, will be on the creek side.

The building will rest on a solid concrete slab. Radiant heating will be used.

No printing work will be done at the offices. Sunset Magazine is printed in the Los Angeles plant of the Time and Life corporation.

Test gardens of Sunset will be maintained on other property in the area.

Sunset is distributed only in Pacific Coast states and is edited for homes in this region. It has a circulation of 500,000. This year coast and national advertisers bought more than $2 million worth of space in the 52-year-old magazine.

Sunset books are known as guides to western living in the fields of cooking, gardening, building, and travel.

Floyd Lowe, Palo Alto real estate broker who handled sale of the site to Sunset, pointed out that the unique professional zoning in part of the Linfield Oaks tract is now being studied in many communities. Allstate Insurance Company also occupies a professional zone site.

"We of course are very proud to have the origin of the zoning here," said Lowe. "Announcements will be made very soon of some other organizations that will be located in this same development, all of which will soon be assimilated and become a part of the outstanding growth of this part of the community.

"We are especially proud of the civic pride and interest these new companies are taking, and have noticed already that most of the new employment is from local people. Our merchants are already becoming aware of the increased trade that it will bring to the community."

VA hospital provides training as well as treatment

(This is the second of three articles on Palo Alto Veterans Administration Hospital in Menlo Park written in connection with Mental Health Week, May 2-8).

By WARDELL WINSLOW

You may not think of Palo Alto Veterans Administration Hospital as a campus, but that's exactly what it is for students learning to treat and prevent mental illness.

And it's the second biggest training center of its kind in the country.

Its students are on their way to becoming psychiatrists, clinical psychologists, psychiatric nurses, physiotherapists, psychiatric social workers, and recreation specialists.

The training program formally started in 1946 but actually was in effect long before that. In addition to teaching students, it trains the hospital's professionals on an in-service basis.

"VA U." has ties with colleges and universities all over the nation, and with a host of Bay Area clinics and hospitals. Actually the students, whose training is on the practical side, do part of the work of the hospital. They also have formal classroom work.

Why spend money for this training? First, the VA must have skilled professional people to treat patients, and there's a national shortage. Secondly, every citizen has a stake in the nation's mental health, and the VA has facilities to train workers to improve it.

Dr. Martha W. MacDonald, director of professional education, is in charge of training, particularly of resident physicians in a program supervised by the dean's subcommittee of the University of California and Stanford Medical Schools.

The "residents" entering the three-year course to become psychiatrists already have earned their medical degrees and served internships. Some have practiced for years. They rank as part-time workers and draw annual salaries ranging from $2400 to $3300.

At present the hospital has 32 residents working with and learning from its 26 staff physicians and 37 consultants, who cover many specialties.

They study on a rotation basis, spending periods from three to six months in various services at the Menlo Park hospital and at some of the following:

For Miley Hospital, UC's Langley Porter Clinic, Stanford Lane Hospital, Mount Zion Hospital, Children's Hospital, and the VA Mental Hygiene Clinic, all in San Francisco; Oakland VA Hospital; San Quentin; and the State Mental Hygiene Clinic at Berkeley.

They also attended seminars, lectures, and courses here, at Langley Porter, and at San Mateo Child Guidance Clinic. Services in the third year are mainly elective.

While the VA here is home base for the residents, it is a field training station for 21 intern psychologists — 15 from Stanford and six from Cal— under the staff's six clinical psychologists and seven consultants.

These interns are employed part-time during the four years they work for their Ph.D. degrees. In their first year they begin to apply psychodiagnostic procedures. Second-year students do much of the psychological testing and evaluating. Advanced interns help supervise work of those in the first two years, enter into psychotherapy work with patients, and plan and implement research.

John R. Schlosser is acting psychological service chief and Louis S. Levine is supervisor of training. Since 1946, 75 interns have had part or all of their field training at Menlo Park. There have been 101 residents in all.

Six UC students are taking their second year of graduate social work at the VA under supervision of the 12 staff psychiatric social workers.

Twenty students from affiliated nursing schools are learning psychiatric nursing with the help of the 79 regular nurses.

Dr. Maurice Grossman's 50-man medicine department helps train Stanford physical therapy students, and will have occupational therapy trainees starting in July. Some recreation majors from San Jose State are also getting five weeks of training at the hospital.

The program is still growing, too, and the hospital expects to have trainees soon in several other departments.

In addition to professional staffers mentioned above, those for whom the hospital runs its continuing in-service training program include 268 psychiatric aides, dietitians and helpers, dentists, pharmacists, and x-ray, laboratory, and dental technicians.

Importance of personal contact between patients and workers at the hospital is so great that administrative and business personnel get some in-service training too, and twice a year some of the 100 volunteer workers attend orientation courses.

Extent of the in-service training was exemplified this week at a showing of "The Quiet One," a film depicting causes and handling of the mental problems of a young Negro boy.

In the audience were staff and resident psychiatrists, staff and student nurses, occupational and educational therapists, volunteers, secretaries from the treatment services, psychiatric aides, an electroencyphalographer, social workers, and psychologists.

We often wrote three-part series in this era, usually about school or city bond measures. This is the middle part of a series about the Palo Alto Veterans Administration Hospital, then entirely in Menlo Park.

COMMENCEMENT EXERCISES ARE HELD OUT-OF-DOORS HERE

249 High School Seniors graduate

Two hundred and forty-nine members of the Palo Alto High School class of 1951 climaxed their local public school careers last night at outdoor commencement exercises at the high school.

In cap and gown — white for girls and dark blue for boys— the graduates filed across the outdoor auditorium stage before a large audience to receive diplomas that represent their tickets to employment, further education, or military service.

Sixteen graduates received diplomas bearing both the California Scholarship Federation's gold seal and the high school's silver seal for citizenship and service. There were 11 other gold seals and 26 other silver seals awarded.

It was something of a family affair. Diploma presentations made by Mrs. Arnold Brown, trustee, included one to her daughter Joyce, and Dr. Henry M. Gunn, superintendent of schools, awarded a diploma to his daughter, Mary Elizabeth.

Two students spoke for their class. Robert Smith, considering "The Challenge of the Years Ahead," said the class faces a great challenge in moving into a troubled world.

The graduates' first responsibility is to themselves, he said, to develop their individual talents to the highest degree. They must also work as parts of a whole in wiping out crime, poverty, and sickness.

Smith declared the entire free world is depending on the graduating class and others like it across the nation to guide America's immense power with its spirit, and to prevent the entire world from going under the cloud of tyranny and oppression that now covers part of it.

"If we work together and treasure our American ideals, we shall win through," he pledged. "Over a billion free men depend on us."

Gerry Kelly, talking on the topic "From Experience Comes Faith," said that when the class of 1951 left Jordan Junior High School it was "rated one of the least promising" ever to enter Paly High.

"The class has proved over and over again its ability to match criticism with success," Kelly said, pointing to its record in scholarship, student government, relations with the community, athletics, and special skills.

"Each of you," he told those in the audience, "owns a share in this class. You have helped mold it and will feel its impact in the future." He asked parents, teachers, and friends to "retain faith in the fruits of your labors."

"We don't leave you tonight —we join you," Kelly concluded. "We light our lamp of experience from your lamp of faith."

President Niles Elwood presented the class gift, a large redwood sign with gold lettering which will identify Paly from the corner of Embarcadero Rd. and Ed Camino Real.

In presenting the class for diplomas, Principal Ivan H. Linder said that 76 per cent of the 129 young women and 120 young men plan to go on to college —55 to state colleges, 25 to junior colleges, 55 to private four-year colleges including 34 to Stanford, and 35 to out-of-state schools.

Linder said '51 has received more scholarships than any preceding class—16 college and regional awards and 14 local scholarships totaling about $6000 in value.

Two members are already in the navy, two in the army, and one—Jim McGuy, who was present for the ceremony—in the air force, Linder said. Six graduates intend to go into nursing, six into business college, and 30 directly into employment.

Next year, he told the graduates, he would like to have them think of Paly High as their home base and report back on their activities, achievements, and problems.

Dr. Gunn, just completing his first year as superintendent, said in accepting the class, "I can say without qualification that this is the very best class ever graduated here under my administration."

He reported that a testing program showed that the class stands a year beyond achievements on the national norm.

Robert Littler, retiring school board vice president, assisted Mrs. Brown in awarding diplomas.

Winners of both the gold and silver seals are Gretchen Andersen, Lynn Atterbury, Turner Bledsoe, Betty Bolon, Delia Callander, Barbara Drysdale, Marta Field, Sara Fry, Mary Elizabeth Gunn, Alan Helgesson, Chuck Kashima, Gerry Kelly, Betty Krone, John Paciulli, Marianne Reeder, and Robert Smith.

Other gold seal winners are Alan Brown, Carolyn Cowan, Virginia Hafner, Ned Harrold, Erland Jacobsen, Lauren Johnson, Janet Kathary, John McCann, Ben Morgan, John Petersen, and Priscilla Simms.

Other silver seals went to Bob Armstrong, Mike Arnstein, Robert Brand, Mark Farmer, Fay Ferandin, Merle Flattley, Jack Frazer, John Hanley, Peter Hoss, Audrey Hurley, Dodo Kirkpatrick, Ronald Klein, Ann Knoles, Rod McDaniel, Bob McDowell, Heather Maclean, Jane Nakata, Sutton Parks, Cathy Phillips, Ron Plough, Barbara Sloan, Nort Thornton Jr., Earl Van Wagoner, Willie Wan, Richard Wylie, and Sue Ziegler.

AROUND THE BEATS:

Tyro's anguish told by expectant father

By WARD WINSLOW

THE EXPECTANT FATHER'S WATCH & Wait Society meets night and day at Palo Alto Hospital. Third floor, first door to the right, please.

You move at top speed till you get there. But the pace slows when you're steered into what the hospital coyly calls the "Heir Port." Dad-to-be isn't fooled. Only "waiting room" describes it.

YOU SET DOWN YOUR WIFE'S SUITCASE, murmur howdy and quickly type your brethren. There's Fourth-Timer, asleep. Journeyman, awake but fairly calm about his second. And you, Tyro.

After a minor eternity you notice the magazine you grabbed is "The American Girl." Your eyes twitch whenever anyone walks near the door. Buzzers make you jump.

The doctors and nurses do their best to keep you posted. They phone from behind a door marked "No Admittance." Or come out to talk. They let you visit your wife if they can. But sooner or later you're evicted.

It's Jan. 2. Conversation turns to why the crowd's assembling. Perhaps, the society agrees, the Ladies' Auxiliary relaxed when the New Year rang in — and the last-minute tax deductions were lost and the Baby Derby was won.

SOME HOSPITALS USE PINK AND BLUE lights to signal girl or boy to anxious fathers. But not Palo Alto's. Suspense is their specialty.

She who totes the newborn to the nursery is sworn to secrecy. Only when Father is standing by the glass booth marked "The Best Show in Town" will she unwrap Offspring and reveal the sex. And while Pop gapes at Baby, Nursie peeks at Pop. Both get a kick out of what they see. Baby yawns.

Now the routine shatters as a nurse bustles in with Fourth-Timer's newest. Soon he's back to say: "Third boy. My wife had it figured but my daughter will be disappointed."

The maternity staff kids a lot. "They've got to stay gay," an old hand remarks, "or they'd go crazy." Work can get hectic where life begins.

Here's the delivery room nurse with another baby. Her scanning eyes settle on Journeyman. "You'll do," she says. He grins. Everyone files out to look. Then the nurse corners the society. "Yours'll be next," she says, "then yours and yours and yours." Daybreak and B-hour are near. Statistics favor 4 to 8 a.m.

THE ANCHOR MAN LEAVES FOR breakfast. The timetable changes and he barely returns soon enough. A pooped tyro, after 26 hours, gets a chance to sigh "finally."

Dawn finds you alone. You pace, breaking the unwritten code. It feels better than tense sitting. Here's a new man. You can't type him. In 45 minutes the next baby appears. Yours? Nope, his. He beams. You glower. Now you know—he's Johnny-Come-Lately.

You add the score—four boys, three girls. Will the law of averages hold? More waiting. "No Admittance" finally swings open. The nurse signals you. Your heart thumps.

IT'S A GIRL! A TINY BEAUTY WELL worth the wait. Your wife's fine, the nurse answers. You wait to see her.

Then, departing, you realize part of the gnawing in your stomach was hunger. You're limp, yet too keyed up to sleep. It takes some time to unwind.

Reporter-written "Around the Beats" columns were a fixture on the editorial page for a number of years. In this, one of the early ones, I wait out the birth of my daughter, Lynne.

AROUND THE BEATS:

Bayshore shows cross-section of county

By WARD WINSLOW

BAYSHORE HIGHWAY FROM PALO ALTO to San Jose is far from being Santa Clara County's most scenic route. But perhaps better than any other road, it cuts a cross-section of the county, laying bare our prides and problems.

Along Bayshore lies a jumble of diversity. Agricultural, residential, commercial and industrial zones—it has them all. In placid pastures cows slowly munch the grass. Not far away supersonic jets streak in to land at Moffett Field. Our county's fruit-basket past and manufacturing future meet by the roadside.

Turning south from Embarcadero Road, you move past the vast Palo Alto drainage basin. After last winter's flood it was a shimmering lake, barely discernable from the bay itself.

INDUSTRY AND TRUCKERS' STOPS BEgin to pinch the highway in the Mountain View area. Then comes the expanse of the naval air station, the valley's biggest military base. Sleek jets and lumbering transports glide across the highway before your eyes and coast smoothly past the huge, humped hangars that once held dirigibles and blimps.

Sometimes you hold your breath for fear one of the aircraft is too low to clear the highway. Sometimes a jet bolts out of the southwest so fast its screaming roar startles you as it goes over your car.

Now and again you pass a field of corn, perhaps, or lettuce or cabbage or tomatoes. Almost anything will grow here. Another sort of row crop sprouts easily, too. Row after row of subdivision houses march inexorably from the foothill side near Sunnyvale, up to the ever-flowing river of traffic and beyond to the bay side.

Nearby lie the oat fields, soon to be covered by an industrial colossus, the General Motors assembly plant. And as you move into the Santa Clara area, you pass the smoke-belching Pittsburgh-Des Moines Steel, and Fiberglas plants.

Another mile along you find yourself in the Agnew pear groves. Their fruit collects blue ribbons annually. The orchards are now protected—at least until industrial pressures mount—by a new zoning weapon, the agricultural greenbelt.

ON A CLEAR DAY, YOUR VIEW OF OUR beautiful valley is superb. Sometimes just after rain has washed the air, the foothills can be seen in close detail and life across the bay is drawn near. But clear days are becoming scarce. Usually smog leaves the mountains as a hazy outline. When the "lid" —a temperature inversion layer—is on the valley, you can see the line where smog stops and crests of the Mt. Hamilton range poke through.

SOMEHOW YOU'RE ALWAYS KEYED UP driving Bayshore—maybe because death lurks at every intersection. It's a heavily traveled, high-speed highway, and any mistake could be your last.

At rush hours traffic becomes vicious. Vehicles pour northward from the San Jose area, southward from the upper Peninsula and onto Bayshore from the Ford plant in Milpitas, from the industries of Santa Clara and Sunnyvale, from Ames Laboratory and Moffett Field in Mountain View, from Palo Alto's electronics complex. Jams at intersections get a mile long.

Freeway construction is sorely needed right now on our "main stem" highway. There's no doubt about that.

P.A. planners vote 4-2 to uphold permit

A million-dollar, five-story hotel building can be built at Rickey's Studio Inn, the Palo Alto Planning Commission decided last night at a meeting attended by a standing-room-only gathering of 150.

Commissioners voted 4-2 to uphold the decision made earlier by acting city zoning administrator Louis Fourcroy to grant a use permit for the multistory hotel.

The commission met to hear appeals from both sides on Fourcroy's decision.

More than 130 neighboring residents didn't want the tall structure built toward the rear of Rickey's layout at all, while the inn management objected mildly to two conditions imposed by Acting Zoning Administrator Louis Fourcroy.

IN EFFECT, it was a victory for the restaurateur. Those protesting what they called the "five-story hatchet blade" lost the battle but not necessarily the war.

The appeals will go automatically to the city council.

Commissioners voted after hearing 18 persons testify and after taking a brief recess.

Mrs. Philip Towle put the motion upholding Fourcroy,

who had warned that the permit might be a precedent for other tall hotels in the area. Ray K. Linsley seconded, remarking that Rickey could build a six-story, 65-foot apartment house—as distinguished from a hotel—without a use permit.

Chairman William Brophy and Adm. John Ball joined them in voting for it.

• **ED ARBUCKLE** and Roland Sharpe opposed the motion. "It is a pretty broad step and I'm not satisfied all the facts are before me," Arbuckle said. Commissioner Stanley R. Evans, law partner of Rickey's attorney, William E. Anderson Jr., disqualified himself.

Anderson accepted Fourcroy's limitation of the 64-unit addition to five stories instead of the six requested. But he urged against a strict 47-foot height maximum.

He asked that the 85-foot setback from Wilkie Way be amended to 75. The original request was for 55 feet, but Fourcroy explained that the shadow effect of the building on homes northeast of it could be lessened by trimming the height and increasing the setback.

Foremost of the neighbors' objections apparently was what architect A. C. Prentice of 370 Charleston Rd. called the "visual intrusiveness of the building." The broad-sided, narrow-edged hotel would be out of character in the neighborhood, Prentice said.

THE PROTEST group, led by teacher Daniel Alcala, summarized its case through five speakers.

Joseph Ehrlich, 4225 Francisco Way, read a statement prepared by 10 area residents who work in the architectural and engineering professions.

"We seriously question the premise that catering to transients as a motel town is progress as the citizens of Palo Alto would like to see it," it said.

"We submit that this structure would create an undesirable neighborhood," it continued, and ". . . a spreading blight that could turn this area and adjacent areas into a tough and disreputable 'south side' of town."

They praised the city hall "as an integral part of the residential area nearby" and said "we expect similar concern will be shown for our area."

A PRECEDENT in the Rickey's case might lead to other multistory hotels behind Dinah's Shack and Hal's Restaurant, at Embarcadero Road just off Bayshore Highway and perhaps in the southern Middlefield Road area, they warned.

This news story about a disputed development presaged even hotter arguments in the years to come. Somewhat modified from the initial proposal, the tower at Rickey's Studio Inn was built and seemed not to be as visually intrusive as some had feared.

War waged against area mosquitoes

Swarms hatching in P.A. borrow pit driving neighbors nearly crazy

Crews from two abatement districts are waging all-out war on swarms of tule mosquitoes hatching in old Bayshore Highway "borrow" pits at Palo Alto's city dump.

Residents of Palo Alto Gardens and the Donohoe Street section in East Palo Alto, and Crescent Park, Green Gables and other subdivisions near Bayshore in Palo Alto, say bites have been driving them nearly crazy of an evening.

They've lodged "a heavy run of complaints," district authorities say.

The object of their ire is Culex erythrothorax, a small to medium-sized mosquito with a reddish thorax, described as a Tom Lauret.

Lauret said "relief should be felt in a few days" from the San Mateo County Mosquito Abatement District's last larvacide treatment of the pits, finished yesterday. The entomologist works also for the Matadero Mosquito Abatement District, which covers Palo Alto, Mountain View, Stanford and parts of Los Altos, and which has been helping in the battle.

BUT LAURET added that the "bad problem" won't be permanently eliminated until dumping operations fill the pits, "probably next spring."

The pits on the former Geng property were created when Bayshore was built in 1932 but haven't caused a crisis until now.

This year dense growths of tulles, some 12 feet high, have made it more difficult to move over rough ground through the large group of small ponds to apply chemicals where they'll do the most good.

"We have to take a boat in and induce the material as best we can," Lauret explained. "All trails must be cut through by hand."

Palo Alto officials agreed to move the city dump northeast across Embarcadero Road this year to fill the borrow pits.

THE TULE mosquito prefers to bite outdoors in the evening and early morning, Lauret said, but on occasion will fly indoors. "It is a most annoying mosquito there," he added.

Range of the pesty insects is a mile or two. They ride the prevailing wind off the bay.

As cooler fall weather sets in the hatch will slow down, Lauret said.

Most of the abatement work has been done by the San Mateo County district, in which jurisdiction the pits lie. However, the Matadero district stepped in to help because its residents were being stung.

BOTH AGENCIES have suggested ways to fill the pits faster.

Gordon W. Mapes, Matadero district manager, praised the neighboring agency for its efforts. His district had similar major problems in 1932 and 1949, he said, adding that "they take a certain amount of forbearance and understanding on the part of the public."

Mapes said mosquito-eating fish patrolled the ponds effectively until the tulles grew high. Since then the both districts have pumped the ponds, but subsoil water just runs into refill them.

Large number of birds visiting area

Bands of hungry robins and their berry-picking partners, the cedar waxwings, are larger than usual on the Midpeninsula this winter, authorities said today.

Robert C. Wood of Portola Valley, Palo Alto Junior Museum orinthologist and science teacher, said the birds "come down here from the north and from the Sierra."

THEY'RE attracted by the berries of such popular ornamental shrubs as pyracantha, cotoneaster and toyon, as many a resident whose bushes have been picked clean within a week or less can testify.

"They roost by the thousands up in the foothills, in the general direction of Woodside," Wood explained. In the mornings they fan out over the lowlands in search of food.

"Then in the afternoon they fly directly back to the hills in large flocks—a dozen, 50, 100 or more. You can see them any time after 3," Wood said.

How hungry are they? Two years ago, Wood said, an injured waxwing was brought into the Junior Museum. Its appetite wasn't hurt, for it consumed 249 pyracantha berries in a day.

The more numerous robins begin to disappear in the late winter, except for some that stay to nest, according to Wood. The waxwings stay longer, and some of them also remain to nest.

Robins are time-honored winter visitors to the Bay Area, but have nested here commonly for only the last 40 years.

P.A. woman's poem wins top Japan honor

A Palo Alto educator, Miss Lucille M. Nixon, today scored a notable "first" with a poem written for the emperor of Japan.

Her poem was chosen among the 15 best to be sung in the traditional New Year's Imperial Court Poetry Occasion, the Associated Press reported from Tokyo. It was the first time in history that a poem composed by an American had received the honor.

THE IMPERIAL household office announced that Miss Nixon was included among the authors of the 15 best waka (31-syllable, 5-line Japanese poems) chosen by the poet laureates from among 13,000 entries.

Miss Nixon, who lives at 1155 Ramona St., is consultant in elementary education for the Palo Alto Unified School District and president of the district's principals' association.

Another resident of the United States, Miss Fumiko Ogawa of Los Angeles, also won the honor.

Their poems will be made public Jan. 11 when the court poetry occasion is held. They are on "Writing," the subject designated by the emperor this year.

ALL 15 winners were invited to attend the court occasion in person and share the seats with the emperor, empress and all princes and princesses as well as the poet lauriates.

Miss Nixon was spending the Christmas noliday with her mother in Alhambra and could not be reached to learn if she would fly to Tokyo for the occasion.

Dr. Henry M. Gunn, superintendent of schools, indicated that leave will be granted if she wishes to do so.

MRS. DAISHO Tana of 4170 Coulombe Dr., Palo Alto, Miss Nixon's Japanese language coach, was overjoyed at the news.

"I was so happy for her I cried," she said, her face shining.

Mrs. Tana herself is a past

LUCILLE NIXON
Poem for emperor

winner in the competition. It is the only poetry event of its sort and attracts entries from all over the world, she explained, but it is extremely rare for a non-Japanese to receive the high praise from the emperor.

Dr. Robert H. Brower, assistant professor of Japanese at Stanford, commented that the waka, also called the "tanka" or "uta," is very short and appears deceptively simple.

BUT ITS technique is really very difficult, he added, because over 13 or 14 centuries the poem form has developed "a great deal of sophistication of technique, diction and imagery."

Friends said Miss Nixon became enchanted by Japan during a brief visit there while traveling around the world in 1955.

Upon returning home, she contacted Mrs. Tana, to whom she had been referred by Elizabeth Gray Vining, former English tutor to the Japanese crown prince, and a friend of Miss Nixon's.

While studying Japanese with Mrs. Tana, Miss Nixon got the idea of entering the poetry competition. Last year she wrote on "Early Spring" in English and Mrs. Tana translated the poem. It won a letter of thanks from the imperial household and notice in the Tokyo press.

THIS YEAR Miss Nixon concentrated her attention on the waka and penned her winning entry herself in Japanese script, Mrs. Tana said. The tutor made only one minor correction.

Actually, Miss Nixon does not yet speak or write Japanese with great fluency, which makes her mastery of the poem form the more remarkable, Mrs. Tana said.

Miss Nixon also is learning to play the 13-string Japanese harp under Mrs. Tana's tutelage, and is studying Japanese flower arranging.

Mrs. Tana was named a winner in the imperial poetry occasion in 1940 while she was living in Richmond. She did not hear of her award, however, until after the occasion was held. Later she received Nipponese newspapers bearing the news.

SHE SAID about half a dozen Japanese living in the United States have been honored in the past. Mrs. Tana submits an entry every year and contributes to poetry collections published in Japan.

Her husband, the Rev. Daisho Tana, a Buddhist priest, is also a scholar. He currently is working on textbooks for use in Buddhist churches in America.

The Tanas have lived in the United States for 18 years.

P.A. woman will go to poetry party

Lucille Nixon today cabled the emperor of Japan that she plans to be at his poetry party Jan. 11.

The Palo Alto education consultant won an invitation last week when her waka (a 31-syllable verse in Japanese) was chosen one of the 15 best in the annual imperial court poetry occasion.

NIPPON was astonished by the honor to Miss Nixon, the first American not of Japanese ancestry ever to win in the world-wide competition.

She said she will make the trip to Tokyo with Mrs. Sumiko Ogawa of Los Angeles, another of the 15 top poets this year. Mrs. Ogawa became a naturalized American citizen 2½ years ago.

Miss Nixon had said earlier she did not expect to attend the colorful court event at which the short, stylized poems are chanted by Japan's five poets lauriate.

However, in reversing that decision today she indicated there is a possibility she and Mrs. Ogawa may receive some government help as American "cultural ambassadors."

THE TIMES called on President Eisenhower editorially last week to make funds available for her trip as a good will gesture to the poetry-loving Japanese people.

Miss Nixon and Mrs. Ogawa have airplane reservations Saturday for the long trans-Pacific flight.

MISS NIXON won the famed contest on her second try, after a year of concentrated study of the mechanics and calligraphy necessary to compose a waka.

URGES HER TO CONTINUE COMPOSING

P.A. poetess hears her 'waka' chanted to Emperor Hirohito

By FRED SAITO

TOKYO (AP)— Ships' lanterns in the night, a Buddhist temple "where the soul's light glows eternally" and nostalgia for lost territories were leading subjects today at the annual Imperial Court poetry occasion.

Emperor Hirohito, Empress Nagako and members of the royal family listened to the 15

Lucille Nixon will broadcast from Japan for 10 minutes starting at 9:15 tonight, the Times was informed by cable today.

Radio Japan will air her remarks by short wave at frequencies of 11705 and 9525 kilocycles.

---

winning "waka"—31 syllable verses—chanted by five court officials in medieval s t y l e chorus.

HE THEN personally congratulated each of the poets who included two Americans this year for the first time in Japan's history.

"His Majesty urged me to continue composing poetry . . . and to become a bridge between Japan and America," beamed Miss Lucille Nixon of Palo Alto, to reporters.

"He also said to be careful of the flu now prevalent in Japan . . . he's a very nice gentleman and the empress a very beautiful lady."

Miss Nixon is consultant in elementary education for the Palo Alto Unified School District. She lives at 1155 Ramona St.

SHE SPENT a year learning how to write Japanese characters with a brush and studying the waka intensely before composing her verse. It says:

"Akogare no U r u w a s h i k i Nippon Horyuji hiru no Mia-kashi itsu mata towan."

Translated, it means:

"I am longing to return to beautiful Japan, but even more to Horyuji temple, where the soul's light glows eternally."

MRS. FUMIKO Ogawa of Los Angeles, a naturalized American, also carried out the general theme of "light" or "lamp." Her verse, in translation, said:

"Lights of ships, homeward bound for Japan, shine on the waves, and bring homesickness to one who remains."

The entire occasion was staged in strict accordance with 1,000-year-old pageantry.

It is the lifetime ambition of every Japanese poet to have his entry selected for reading. Some 13,000 were submitted this year.

(**THE WAKA** is written in five lines with a 5-7-5-7-7 syllable pattern. Prof. Robert H. Brower of Stanford said it "is very short and doesn't seem to require any sustained effort, but it's a form which has been practiced in Japan for roughly 1,300 or 1,400 years and has developed in the course of time a great sophistication of technique, diction and imagery."

(Mrs. Daisho Tana, Miss Nixon's tutor in Palo Alto, delightedly wished her pupil "millions of congratulations" today).

Lucille Nixon lived on our block, which gave me instant rapport when this amazing story broke. The paper helped get the support of Sen. Tom Kuchel and the U.S. State Department for her trip to the emperor's poetry party. The Associated Press report from Japan is included so I can tell about renting a wire (not tape) recorder to capture her short-wave broadcast at the home of an amateur radio enthusiast. In rewinding the wire, I somehow erased it all, and had to write the follow-up story from memory. It was a great broadcast but not so great a story. Tomoe Tana, Miss Nixon's teacher, became a lifelong friend.

MEMO from the Editor

By ALEXANDER BODI

ELSEWHERE ON THIS PAGE WARD WINS-low, our political reporter and someone who probably knows more about the Peninsula political picture than anyone else, has written an excellent analysis of the way the election looks hereabouts.

Winslow, incidentally, has covered all of our political news, both local and state, for several years. He's also dipped his feet into national politics by covering the various candidates and politicos on their tours through California, and by heading the crew of reporters that covered the Republican National Convention here two years ago.

The current election is his last assignment here for a while. After wrapping up next week's election news, he's headed for Washington to broaden his background. He'll be there studying the federal government and working on congressional staffs for nine months, as a result of winning a congressional fellowship from the American Political Science Association. He'll return to us next September with a more intimate knowledge of what makes the wheels of government go around.

AROUND THE BEATS:

Triumph seen for 'Pat' Brown in election

By WARD WINSLOW

HOW WILL THE CALIFORNIA VOTING go Tuesday?

As what is perhaps the most unusual campaign in California annals nears its climax, this reporter, frankly, is not sure.

But from all the straws in the wind, indications are that the question could be boiled down to: How deep will the Democratic trend be?

It appears that Attorney General Edmund G. (Pat) Brown will lead his party to its biggest 20th Century triumph in California.

Brown will undoubtedly run ahead of his ticket mates. But how long are his coattails? How great is the swing to the Bourbons?

It would not surprise me at all to see the Democrats—well organized and pulling together for once—take every one of the six state offices at stake plus the U.S. Senate seat. And analysts are nearly unanimous in expecting the GOP to lose control of both houses of the State Legislature.

THE STATEWIDE REPUBLICANS WHO seem to have the best chance are, in descending order, Controller Robert C. Kirkwood, Secretary of State Frank C. Jordan, Treasurer A. Ronald Button and Goodwin J. Knight. Kirkwood, by the way, is making no bones about the fact that he expects Brown to win and is willing to work with Brown.

On the Peninsula, the situation is not so bleak for the Republicans.

Contrary to Democratic inroads elsewhere in recent years, San Mateo and Santa Clara counties have preserved their tradition of all-GOP legislative delegations—congressmen, state senators, assemblymen.

All the incumbents seek re-election. Democrats hold voter registration edges in both counties, but not by such great margins as in other areas. Local Republican precinct teams remain capable of getting the high percentage of party members to the polls that has helped account for GOP supremacy in past years.

Still, I'd say the Democrats have at least an even chance of grabbing one or more of the seats in the two counties.

LEO RYAN, THE HIGH SCHOOL TEACHER from South San Francisco running against Assemblyman Louis Francis in San Mateo County's northern district is the most likely man to turn this trick. That district, the 25th, has a fat Democratic registration bulge and Ryan has campaigned hard.

Privately, Democratic campaigners aren't optimistic about ousting either Rep. J. Arthur Younger of San Mateo or Assemblyman Carl (Ike) Britschgi of Redwood City.

One of the Bourbons put it this way: "To beat Younger we needed a lion and we got a lamb." Elma Oddstad, Redwood City businesswoman, opposes Younger.

Britschgi is regarded as a sure bet. So is Assemblyman Bruce Allen of Los Gatos.

IN THREE SANTA CLARA COUNTY CON-tests, challengers claim to have almost an even chance. My guess is that Rep. Charles Gubser, State Sen. Jack Thompson and Assemblyman Clark Bradley all will be shaken but still in office when the results are known. But a Democratic tidal wave could engulf all three.

Gubser has said several times he might be beaten. He knows he's been in a race after his intellectual but hard-hitting debate series with Democrat Russell Bryan.

However, Gubser has an ace in the hole if the Santa Clara County contest is tight. He's sure to build up vote cushions in the other counties of his district—San Benito (where Gubser won both party primaries) and Santa Cruz.

EDITORIALS

The reason for being of a research institute

Some people have trouble understanding Stanford Research Institute.

When a Russian scientist inspected the Menlo Park facility during Premier Khrushchev's visit, he had difficulty grasping the capitalistic concept that SRI "sells" some of its research.

More recently, Lewis E. Harris, vice president of the American Council of Independent Laboratories, an organization of profit-making research companies, attacked SRI's tax-exempt status. Essentially his complaint was of unfair competition.

Harris accused SRI also of trading on the name of Stanford University, "with which," he said, "it has no real connection." He was so badly mistaken on this point that we will skip it except to note that although SRI is not under Stanford's direct operational control it does do many jobs for the university. The connection is close.

SRI is chartered as a nonprofit corporation by the state. It does both pure and applied research—on its own, for the federal government or for industrial and other clients.

Clients pay the cost of their project—including the time of personnel, materials and other expenses—plus overhead costs, plus additional amounts that are plowed back into SRI-supported research and new equipment and buildings. There are no profits, no stockholders. The institute pays property taxes but is exempt from federal corporate income taxes.

This form of organization has enabled SRI to take a broad approach to research problems and to build a staff and facilities of very considerable value to the nation. In effect, applied research for clients pays for other research that no one ordinarily would sponsor and that therefore would not be undertaken by a laboratory operating strictly for profit.

SRI, a strong contract research organization, had less and less interaction with the university and in 1971 became independent. It is now called SRI International. At this stage I had begun writing editorials full-time, plus an occasional column.

AROUND THE BEATS:

Yes, switch to journalism WAS right

By WARD WINSLOW

NEWSMEN ARE INCURABLE SECOND guessers—that's my excuse for wondering now and then if my college days decision to switch from electrical engineering to journalism was the right one for me.

Now more than a decade is in evidence. True enough, electronics opportunities on the Peninsula have been remarkable. But after thinking back over my high points of the 1950s as a Times reporter, I'll argue journalism's case with anyone.

When the decade dawned, barely more than a year as a cub lay behind and I was doubling in news and sports. A young Whittier congressman named Richard Nixon was running for the senate, but the story of that campaign that sticks in my head was the then-revolutionary stunt of his opponent, Helen Gahagan Douglas, of landing in Menlo Park in a helicopter.

PALO ALTO HIGH SCHOOL'S FOOTBALLers became invincible that fall. For two seasons they galloped undefeated through all opposition. Then as they basked in triumph at the end of their thrill-strewn path, tragedy struck — a heart attack took the life of beloved Coach Hod Ray.

My last sports fling was in 1952, broiling for two days in the Tulare sun while the incredible Bob Mathias won the Olympic decathalon tryouts.

Quite possibly San Francisco will never again in my lifetime be overrun by crowds like those that greeted Gen. Douglas MacArthur in April, 1951, after President Truman stripped him of his command. It was a stirring story to write.

Later that year came my first assignment in covering a president when Truman came west to address the Japanese Peace Treaty Conference. In following years there were interviews with two former presidents — Truman and, at one of his annual pre-birthday press sessions, Herbert C. Hoover.

IN THE COURSE OF THE 1956 REPUBLIcan National Convention, I found myself standing on a table in a St. Francis Hotel room-turned-madhouse during what must have been the wildest and wooliest press conference Dwight D. Eisenhower ever gave as president.

There also have been question-and-answer sessions, formal and informal, with almost all the leading White House aspirants on the scene today. Surely there's a future chief executive or two among them. Or is there?

Meetings of local governing bodies can be long and dull, but sometimes they amply reward a reporter's wait. The tipoff that it's happening is an outburst of frenzied scribbling at the press table.

A dramatic example was provided in 1956 when, in the course of what seemed an ordinary if acrimonious argument, the three-man majority of the Santa Clara County Board of Supervisors suddenly voted Sam Della Maggiore right out of his office as chairman. It was unprecedented, and I'm told the supervisors have matured enough since then so that it won't happen again.

NEWSPAPER WORK GOT ME A RINGSIDE seat in congress last spring when the usually ponderous House of Representatives rolled rapidly and with an air of great excitement to an historic vote for Hawaii statehood. Some say it completed the American Union.

And then there was a day of dogging Nikita Khrushchev's footsteps.

These peaks may be clearest in hindsight. My memories are fuzzier yet even warmer of day-to-day working relationships with some outstanding people in local government, where the reporter's performance counts most. I'm thinking of people such as the late, great Menlo Park councilman, Charles P. Burgess, in the early '50s; Dr. Henry M. Gunn and the remarkable mid-decade Palo Alto Board of Education; and Howard W. Campen, a man in a hurry to regain lost ground after he became Santa Clara County executive.

No, I'd not swap my copy pencil back for a slide rule.

AROUND THE BEATS:

5th grader's paper recalls earlier one

By WARD WINSLOW

ONE OF THE CASUALTIES OF SUMMER, along with school classes and new episodes of your favorite TV show, is a worthy rival of the Palo Alto Times in the part of town where I live—the Neighborhood Gazette.

The last item in the most recent issue told the tale of its temporary demise. Here, unedited, is the item:

"Notice: With this issue we close the paper for the summer. Because the present dito machine will not be available later than this issue. However we will start your present subscriptions as they are again next fall. WISHING YOU ALL A VERY FINE SUMMER, Sincerely, THE EDITOR."

THE EDITOR, NOW HAVING A VERY FINE summer, let's hope, is one Laddie Carefoot, lately a fifth grader at Palo Alto's Loma Vista school.

There's a soft spot in my heart for Laddie for I, too, once put out a neighborhood paper as a fifth grader. What's more, I figure there's a fair chance he may be my boss some day. The boy has a head for the publishing business.

It all shows in his one-page paper. The format calls for neighborhood news, school news, a joke, advertisements, and the Thought for Today. The makeup is routine.

Mostly the news is about birthday parties, trips, visitors, awards, club meetings. It leans heavily to fifth graders and their families.

But at top left, up in the masthead, it says: "Circulation 110." At bottom right, the price lists appear: "Subscription — 15c per month. Ads—3c a line." The advertising linage is respectable.

TO THE BEST OF MY RECOLLECTION, the Saratoga News of the mid-1930s had a peak circulation of 23. It was a weekly, priced at a penny a copy, and any subscriber was welcome.

A friend had had the original idea, and printed the first issue laboriously with a pencil before enlisting me. He was the editor, naturally. I was assistant editor. And publisher too after a marvelous Christmas present revolutionized our means of production (and gave me full control of same). The present was a hand mimeograph set—a pan of jelly and the messiest indelible pencils, typewriter ribbon and carbon paper imaginable. Plus a nifty book of illustrations to fit almost any occasion. Cartoons of pitchers throwing fast curves, and such.

Despite my sonorous title—assistant editor and publisher—there was never any doubt who was top dog on the Saratoga News. The editor. For we were editorial types, and lacked the enterprising Laddie's circulation and rate-setting talents.

WE PUT OUT A LIVELY SHEET. SOME weeks it ran several pages, complete with sketches, and in several colors, too. Some weeks guest columnists were featured. The spelling was typical fifth grade.

Ads were hard to come by then. To fill space, I must confess, we gave away more than we sold. The grocer, the barber, the druggist got free plugs and probably never knew it.

Once I paid a debt with a series of ads. The debt grew from the collision of a batted ball and a window. The aggrieved owner of the broken glass was building a house to sell. So for months the News extolled the virtues of that fast-rising residence.

WELL, I LOOK FOR PROMPT DELIVERY of the Neighborhood Gazette, come fall— and prompt collection of the monthly 15 cents. And this will serve as warning to the Times Circulation Department to look to its laurels if young Carefoot, full of vim after a fine summer, concentrates on extending his subscription list.

EDITORIALS

Prop. 14: No, no, 1,000 times no!

Proposition 14, a deceptive initiative drafted to aid only those who wish to exercise their prejudices at will, would add a new section to California's constitution. Its central provision says:

"Neither the state nor any subdivision or agency thereof shall deny, limit or abridge, directly or indirectly, the right of any person, who is willing or desires to sell, lease or rent any part or all of his real property, to decline to sell, lease or rent such property to such person or persons as he, in his absolute discretion, chooses."

The existing Unruh Civil Rights Act requires California businesses to treat all persons on an equal basis no matter what their race, color, religion, ancestry, or national origin. The existing Rumford Housing Act bans discrimination based on race, religion or ancestry (but not on other grounds, such as financial capability) in the sale or rental of certain classes of housing.

Proposition 14 would cloak with constitutional immunity those who discriminate in the sale or rental of their residential property. It would exempt them from the laws noted above and from future laws related to housing bias.

Put more bluntly, it would write into our constitution a statement that racial discrimination in housing (aimed, no doubt, mainly at Negroes) is acceptable.

Beyond single family home owners (only one in four of whom is now covered by the Rumford Act), Proposition 14 would grant the power to discriminate as a special privilege of a limited g r o u p of businessmen: land developers and apartment owners.

Real estate agents could discriminate only when acting on the specific authority of a property owner.

Governmentally, Proposition 14 would shake a dose of anarchy into the orderly procedures of representative government. It would put discrimination by a property owner beyond all reach by our state legislature, county boards of supervisors and city councils — and of state courts.

To those who find fault with the Unruh and Rumford Acts, we suggest that this remedy is as drastic as burning down a house because you don't like the kitchen wallpaper. If our elected representatives and judges are not left free to adjust housing problems in our crowded communities, is it not likely that federal lawmakers or federal judges will take over?

Historically, Proposition 14 departs from California tradition. Since 1849 our state constitution has recognized the inalienable right to acquire property — but not a right to refuse to rent or sell solely because of race or religion (no state's constitution now protects such discrimination). It has always been against the common law of our state for certain businessmen to exclude citizens from the market solely because of race or religion.

Educationally, the adoption of t h i s amendment would teach every school child that arbitrary acts of racial bias are privileged. Moreover, passage of Proposition 14 would say to every Negro, "California's white majority considers you inferior and asserts the right to refuse to sell or rent you a home on equal terms." Headlines throughout the world would say, with accuracy, "California legalizes housing segregation."

Morally, Proposition 14 affronts Christian and Jewish principles of equality under God, and the simple belief that humans should treat one another fairly.

Proposition 14's poisons already are polluting California's blood stream. We regard its defeat as the most imperative task voters must accomplish Nov. 3. The leaders of an unprecedented array of responsible state and local organizations agree. Vote NO on Proposition 14!

I was proud of our bold stand against Prop. 14, and of Palo Alto voters for resolutely rejecting it.

Navy's newest sub carries proud name

By WARD WINSLOW

MARE ISLAND — The USS Mariano G. Vallejo (SSBN 658), 40th and next-to-last of the Polaris nuclear submarines to join the fleet, was commissioned here Friday afternoon with full naval ceremony.

A chill wind knifed at the bellbottoms of the sub's crews, paraded on deck aft of the sleek metal sail, and kept the Stars and Stripes, once the ensign was hoisted, standing straight out from its staff.

Band ruffles hailed the arrival of four admirals and a commodore, and a cannon boomed out a salute that was echoed by the low hills of Vallejo across the channel. The ship, like the city, is named for the best-known native Californian of the Mexican - American and early statehood eras, Gen. Mariano Castro, diplomat, legislator, patriot and promoter.

Cmdr. John K. Nunneley, who grew up in Saratoga, took command of the Vallejo and its Gold crew, while Cmdr. Douglas B. Guthe did likewise for the Blue crew. The youngish skippers, both holders of master's degrees in nuclear physics, will hold the power to take the nation into war, as Rear Adm. J. H. McQuilkin, commander of the San Francisco Bay Naval Shipyard, noted.

Along with the traditional reading of their orders, the captains spoke of the human element in the operation of their awesome vessel — a weapons system designed to keep the peace by deterring nuclear attack through the ability of obliterating any spot on earth by firing, while submerged, the main battery of 16 Lockheed-built Polaris missiles.

Even amid the precision mechanisms, Guthe said, the individual still plays the vital role — just as he did in Gen. Vallejo's Indian-fighting days.

Nunneley told the assembled wives and families that their support is essential to the success of the crews, which will keep the sub on patrol almost constantly, alternating about every three months.

The main speaker, Rear Adm. John H. Maurer, commander of the Submarine Force, Pacific Fleet, paid tribute to the shipyard workers who built the series of Polaris submarines (the Vallejo is the last Mare Island will turn out) and to the crews.

He told the ship's company each man will be responsible for an average of half a million dollars' worth of government property — but stressed that each really is responsible not only for the safety of the whole ship and crew but also for the success of its deterrent mission.

My boyhood schoolmate, Jack Nunneley, skipper of one of the two crews manning the Mariano Vallejo, invited my wife and me to this commissioning. The day was very cold. Chilled during the ceremony, we passed up a chance to tour the boat and went right to the "wetting down" reception. The next morning, a Saturday, I told News Editor Thad Spinola about it. Knowing the interest of many readers who worked for Lockheed, he insisted I write an account, which I did despite a painful hangover.

NOT EVERYONE IS

Are you suited to the Skyline life?

By WARD WINSLOW

DO YOU LONG TO LIVE IN THE HILLS, flatlander?

Kathryn Stedman has some advice for you: Trees and views and open space are genuine joys, but drawbacks go with them. It's not a life for everyone; some are better off admiring the fog-fall from afar.

Mrs. Stedman is a hill dweller herself—a Woodsider. Being both a landscape architect and the wife of architect Morgan Stedman, she has a special sensitivity to the pleasures and problems of Peninsula uplands life.

The attractions, she says, can offset longer commuting and less f r e q u e n t attendance at theaters, lectures, church or city social attractions. "The arrival at a hillside home at the end of a busy day can be a moment of high enjoyment, a relief from the traffic and confusions of the city. On the way, the ever-changing views of the mountains give a sense of weather, seasons and the natural world.

"However, the higher the location, the more driving for the mother. . .Children around the corner may not be readily available, and thus responsibility for creative play may fall more frequently upon the parents. . . The teen-ager, the most gregarious of creatures, finds little to keep him happy without a car or motorcycle. . . Two cars, at the very least, are a family requirement.

"Maintenance of property in the hills absorbs much time . . . and there is a smaller supply of handymen or gardening help. Service calls cost more . . . Nature moves in swiftly, and people to whom this becomes a frustration move away as swiftly."

Settlers begin by seeking privacy and open space, but "inevitably a need for neighborli-ness arises as well." Yet there may be no easy path to the place next door.

THESE OBSERVATIONS ARE JUST ONE small part of a stunning booklet Mrs. Stedman has prepared for The Committee for Green Foothills, titled "Skyline Landscape," subtitled "A Look at Environmental Quality." Striking photographs by local cameramen illustrate it. Experts have contributed facts about foothills geology, weather, biological zones and history.

After the essay quoted above, the author offers engineering ABCs and landscaping considerations for homes on slopes. Then she distills what planners have evolved in the way of controls and policies for subdivisions and for preserving open space. County planners of both Santa Clara and San Mateo win thanks for work begun in the 1930s to guard the Skyline and the hillsides below it from despoliation.

HER MESSAGE IS SUMMED UP IN A chapter title: "Cooperation—A Regional Necessity." Mrs. Stedman writes: "Agreement on basic goals, consistent controls and regional organization are needed to preserve mountain character and hillside beauty in this Peninsula region. The park-like splendor of trees, ridges and canyons provides an inspirational setting for each city along the Bay. Common problems and common benefits lead toward formalizing cooperation by means of a legal district. This is possible. In fact, substantial federal and state aid programs are predicated on district (or regional) planning."

She stresses the need for a planning team drawn from the various specialties—"a skilled reservoir of unbiased advice and technical assistance"—and offers a model program.

"Skyline Landscape" is a booklet every local hill dweller, and many a baysider, would enjoy. It maps the route we must take if future Peninsulans are to be uplifted by the Skyline as we are today.

AROUND THE BEATS

Herman Dekker—yeasty philosopher

By WARD WINSLOW

HERMAN E. DEKKER WAS A LAND-scape architect by profession and a philosopher with both practical and poetic streaks by nature. He probably would not have changed the purpose of his trip last week, which was to view desert wildflowers, had he known it would prove his last one.

Mr. Dekker designed plantings for Stanford Stadium, the Palo Alto schools and Golden Gate Park. And after retiring, he wrote yeasty thoughts in a series of letters to the Times. One needed not agree with all his comments to enjoy them.

Though he was a half-century older than the collegians who mounted the Free Speech Movement at Berkeley in 1964, he remarked that, after reflection, "I find it much more satisfying to try to understand than to condemn."

"THE WORLD IS IN A MESS," HE added. "All around us we see war and the threat of wars more horrible than any so far fought, riots of race against race. . . . Buddhists fighting Catholics, Marxists against peaceful-coexistence Communists, cannibals eating missionaries, the few very rich exploiting the many abjectly poor, and everybody against us, the rich Americans who are desperately trying to buy their way into the favor of governments and the hearts of peoples of less well-endowed nations.

. . . No wonder thinking young people are disgusted and determined to change the world. They may not always think straight, nor always choose the right means to achieve their ends but, by God, they know that things are not as they ought to be or could be, and they're damn well going to try to make changes."

He once put up a good argument for granting zoning variances not for churches but for neighborhood stores, saying: "Church-going is a planned, dress-up, family affair, and the family can get the car out for that. But to be short an egg becomes frustrating, and borrowing is embarrassing. So the citizen walks two or three blocks and feels the better for it."

OPPOSING STANFORD UNIVERSITY'S development of a rolling hill near his longtime College Terrace home, he wrote:

"Changing from emerald green to golden brown as the seasons progressed, often a pasture for horses, sometimes for a small herd of Herefords, this hill was a joy and comfort to contemplate, a delightful contrast to the concrete and stucco facing us in all directions but south. Campus quail and their little broods visited our gardens in the morning. Little nocturnal beasts, such as possums and coons, rummaged around our home at night. Snowy white egrets even came from the Bay land in the pasture hoping to spear a gopher.

"Our children in turn roamed the hill, hunting mushrooms, picking the first poppies, flying kites . . ."

Piqued by teen-agers' pleas for a recreation center of their own, he delivered a lecture:

"These young people, who do not know the difference between a pine and a redwood, a sparrow and a finch, a shovel and a spade; who do not know how to properly wash a window, sew a seam or prepare a simple meal; these young people who have not accomplished anything yet in life to make them deserving of special consideration, beg for wet-nursing and insipid entertainment at the expense of their elders.

"Why aren't they made to realize that any rights they crave, even those of life, liberty and the pursuit of happiness, must be earned by the willing performance of duties, and that the problem of entertainment will be solved automatically . . .?"

RECENTLY, INDIGNANT ABOUT "THE pink-faced jockeys at Dinah's Shack," he declared:

"Instead of helping the Negro to find himself and to realize that he must be encouraged to take pride in his blackness, instead of making him feel that he was and is an important part of total African-American history, we paint him pink and say: 'You see, it's alright now, your folks never really were slaves.' The dishonor in slavery is not the slave's but the master's."

Two years ago in April he reported on a drive through the desert in wildflower season, concluding:

". . . to Borrego Valley where ocotillo, indigo bush, creosote and desert lily, all in flower, stand on varicolored rugs in pastel shades.

"Really, you must have noted an allergy of some sort which will make it absolutely necessary to take a few days off, away from your desk. It would be balm for your soul . . ."

AT THE DEDICATION

Out, says Menlo's landlord

By Ward Winslow

"AS THE IRISH WOULD SAY, 'IT'S A great day for a dedication,' " City Manager Mike Bedwell declared Saturday to a sun-drenched crowd arrayed on the plaza of the newly completed Menlo Park Civic Center. Soon afterward, San Mateo County Superior Court Judge James T. O'Keefe Jr. remarked that he thought the Irish would say, "It's a great day for a picnic." They were both right.

The city's evident affinity for the Irish must have played a part. There was a fine mood of celebration as hundreds of townspeople and friends attended the ceremonies, then swarmed through the new City Council Chambers and Administration Building, and also through the not-so-new Recreation Center, Library, Police Station and Municipal Service Center. My impression was that most went home pleased by what they'd seen.

With bobtailed oratory, the 10-event formal program was over in about half an hour. One insider confided that a snappy pace was planned after a hindsight look at the Palo Alto Civic Center dedication last April.

JUDGE O'KEEFE DELIGHTED THOSE who remembered his wit from his many years as city attorney. He spoke as president of the board of the nonprofit Civic Center Corporation, which financed the construction by selling tax-exempt bonds that will be retired with the rent the city pays. And he was well into intoning a notice of eviction giving officials three days to quit their new quarters before he said, "Oops, picked up the wrong document."

Other Menlo Park old-timers serving with him on the board took bows: John M. Black, John Gertridge, Warren (Kip) Morey and Larry Johnston.

The lengthiest applause went to the St. John Baptist Church Choir, directed by Nathaniel Wilson.

Bedwell introduced the architects, Kingsford Jones and his associate, Raymond Smith, and landscape architect Arthur Cobbledick, himself a former Menlo councilman. Mayor Ira Bonde presented his council colleagues—former mayors Bill Lawson and Mike Belangie, Mayor Pro Tem James Calloway and Donald Horstkorta—and a string of honored guests. Among them were two retired officials, City Manager Cecil Longson and Treasurer Frances Maloney, who worked for the city when it bought the 26-acre Civic Center from Uncle Sam for $99,000. It was a real bargain, but one speaker recalled that federal surplus property disposers were tough to deal with.

AS THE TOURS BEGAN, ATTENTION centered on the well-appointed Council Chambers. Roomy, upholstered seats are a big change from the metal folding chairs on which council-watchers of yore spent many a numbing hour. And the closed-circuit TV system is a modern touch. But what really got the older visitors talking was the watercolors by Rachel Bentley on the walls. A posthumous gift of Miss Susan Gale, the former city historian, they depict memory-stirring old homes, stores, churches and other buildings of the Menlo-Atherton area of a quieter day.

The startling aspect of the Administration Building to me was the space—an astounding proliferation since 1948 when a small barracks building amply housed the city's whole full-time staff. On its main floor and basement, the new building goes on and on in carpeted comfort. And there's a second story in reserve.

When the plantings leaf out, the landscaping will add to the showplace qualities inherent in the design, which is cohesive, yet employs a variety of levels to add interest and a feeling of spaciousness.

MOST VISITORS ENDED UP IN THE Recreation Center and partook of refreshments provided by the city's service clubs. There Menlo Park showed off a lively asset—the senior citizens of Little House, which stands on land the city rents it for $12 a year. Grayheads of the Little House TNT Band made swinging music.

Meanwhile, top officials and honored guests were hosted at an elegant luncheon in the SRI International dining room by two public-spirited Menlo Park "industries"—Stanford Research Institute and Lane Publishing Company (Sunset).

ADVISER THINKS NOT

Worse smog spells ahead?

By Ward Winslow

HOT WEATHER EARLIER THIS WEEK plunged the Bay Area into its first official smog alert, a crisis that one student of air pollution and its control thinks might never be exceeded.

Edward (Ned) Groth III of Menlo Park, a doctoral candidate in the Department of Biological Sciences at Stanford University, has turned more optimistic in recent months about the region's outlook in battling smog.

As a scientist and control procedures analyst with an activist approach, and as a leader of a Stanford study group, Groth stung the Bay Area Air Pollution Control District so severely last year that he ended up on its advisory board.

He was at a meeting in district headquarters Wednesday, in fact, when the smog alert was called off. It was ended, he explained, because the weather forecasts for the coming 12 hours did not indicate that the oxidant level would remain above the alert threshold, .10 parts per million.

Actually, Groth said, there were no 12-hour periods during the alert when that level stayed consistently above the trigger point. But the alert m u s t be called when meteorological predictions make such conditions likely, which is the case when the Bay Region is becalmed in a high pressure area with little or no air moving and the temperature exceeding 100 degrees.

REGIONALLY, IT WAS O N E OF THE most prolonged periods of hot, stagnant air conditions on record, Groth noted, very much like a spell in the fall of 1969 that produced severe smog.

Are there worse smog crises yet to come here? Maybe not, Groth says, pinning his guess on the evidence that emissions have been reduced and that the general pollution trend is downward.

However, he can readily conjure up situations that would be more miserable. If the weather situations were much worse, say in terms of higher temperatures or of more prolonged air stagnation. Or if especially bad conditions prevailed near the oil refineries, smelters and other factories clustered in Contra Costa County that pour heavy tonnages of contaminants into the air. Or if smoke from forest fires collected in the Bay Area.

BUT GROTH SEES A FAIR CHANCE that the region's natural air conditioning, coupled with the gradual reduction of emitted pollutants, may leave the Combined Pollutant Index reading of 147 recorded in the San Francisco-Oakland zone Monday the blackest mark on the BAAPCD books.

Automobiles generally are blamed for 80 per cent of the Bay Area's pollutants, industries for 12 per cent, power plants for 2 per cent and other sources for the rest.

But there's a fallacy in those figures, Groth says. It is best grasped by considering that cars pour out large volumes of carbon monoxide (CO), which in most situations is not the worst part of the pollutant mix. Sulfur dioxide, present in most industrial emissions, is 20 times as toxic as CO.

ONE OF GROTH'S ENDEAVORS HAS been to develop a weighted scale of the Bay Area's pollutant sources to correct for that fallacy. On this scale, he attributes 43 per cent of the air pollution to automobiles, 30 per cent to industry and 18.8 per cent to power plants.

But in hot, still air, photochemical smog resulting from auto emissions grows worse, Groth pointed out.

Midpeninsula students ex

By WARD WINSLOW
Times Associate Editor

Punch the Palo Alto button on the data processing unit listing the University of California at Berkeley's 27,500 students and the print-out

FROM PALO ALTO
Emy Chan

FROM PALO ALTO
John Carefoot

runs to 312 names. From Abbott to Zamvil, 234 are undergraduates.

Los Altos adds 127 undergraduates and 29 grad students. The Midpeninsula is well represented across the Bay, even to 26 graduate scholars and 16 undergrads who call Stanford home.

At Berkeley, students exist under distinctive pressures— of academic competition at America's top-ranked state university, of the squeeze left by a run of tight budgets, of bureaucracy it takes to make the campus function, of political and social waves that often crash first near Sather Gate.

BOMB THREAT

A visiting editor, invited by the UC public information office, recently had an instant sample. No sooner had I met four Palo Alto-area scholars than a Student Union staffer popped in to say there'd been another bomb threat. The building is just across from where Telegraph Avenue empties onto the campus, and some Cal types think it has become a target as a result of quiet efforts to limit use of the Union by nonstudents, often seeking a free pad for the night.

Left to decide for ourselves whether to evacuate, we debated, with no one showing anxiety, then went outdoors. Searchers found nothing.

Three of the student hosts were seniors: Tina Lyman of Los Altos, a tennis player of note; Gary Bankhead, also of Los Altos; and John Carefoot of Palo Alto. The fourth was a junior, Emy Chan of Palo Alto.

Both women had entered Berkeley as freshmen, and said they adjusted easily to its bigness. Bankhead transferred from Foothill College.

Carefoot, who started at UC Santa Barbara, felt the average Midpeninsula high school graduate might find the direct jump to Berkeley unsettling.

(Chancellor Roger Heyns said later that certain freshmen can profit from being in a large institution with many graduate students—freshmen capable of moving along intellectually, independently, without a lot of nurturing.)

MARATHON RUN

The three seniors want to go on to graduate work, but must scramble like marathon runners for a place near the head of the pack. Bankhead is a good example: An environmental design and architecture major, he wants to become an architect, probably doing commercial buildings. He has a 3.8-point (A) grade average but he's very worried about getting into graduate school. Why? Because 400 students are vying for the 30 places at UC.

It's much the same in other departments—particularly in such popular fields as history, sociology (in which Carefoot hopes to teach at the college level) and anthropology (Miss Lyman's major, although she plans on graduate work in education and psychology to qualify as a school counselor).

Sociology Prof. Neil Smelser later confirmed Carefoot's claim that UC lags in gearing for rapid enrollment growth in these social sciences. But while Carefoot sees it as a result of former UC President Clark Kerr's conception of the university as a training ground for industry, Smelser explains the inequity in relation to, say, engineering or law as more of a budget problem.

My hosts remarked that the old antipathies between the

Section III

physical and social sciences are softening, as concern for protecting living things grows.

ECOLOGY BUFF

Emy Chan attended Cubberley High in part of the period chronicled in the recent Sylvia Berry Williams book, "Hassling." An ecology buff, she is studying in a new field, environmental sciences.

In company with many others, Miss Chan got gooey cleaning wild birds after the big Bay oil spill. She grasps, though, that meeting conservation needs takes more than tender care—it requires the preparation to use scientific knowledge.

Miss Chan applied a standard solution to one personal environmental problem. When tear gas wafted into her room too often during the People's Park struggle in May, 1969, she moved away from the South Side.

What might happen this spring—"the time of the sap run," public affairs officer Dick Hafner calls it—is a favorite campus topic just now. Apparently no one has done a thesis documenting that spring is UC's prime period of crisis. But most Cal denizens believe it, though Chancellor Heyns remembers fall tensions as just as bad.

Only half joking, Emy Chan says that science majors slate their hardest courses for spring, thinking they may re-

This was a special opportunity to visit Cal and talk with students from our area. After this feature ran, retired magazine editor Bruce Bliven sent compliments on what "a pencil and pad reporter" can do.

plain pressures of UC life

Alto Times

AN INDEPENDENT NEWSPAPER

FRIDAY, MARCH 12, 1971   Page 25

ceive automatic completes if turmoil halts classes.

PEACEFUL UNITY

Carefoot bristled at the idea that weather is the trigger. Last spring it was the Cambodia incursion, plus Kent State. Cal people recall that as an extraordinary time when the unity behind peaceful protest was the highest ever. Violent activists were overridden by the great outpouring of volunteer effort (Tina Lyman worked a midnight shift for days, organizing it). Some believe this spirit would dominate again in a new crisis.

"Nothing could be as big as Cambodia," Carefoot said, musing on possible action this spring. Yet the result of that left him down about the chances of winning significant change. Berkeley's mass society, campus bureaucracy and large scale of action channel activity through associations, not individuals. They go "on the street" but often don't get much done, he said.

Miss Lyman and Carefoot, both over 21, are registered and plan to vote in the April 6 Berkeley election, which figures to be one of Cal's spring things. On the day I visited, the student-published Daily Californian reprinted a Berkeley Gazette editorial calling "the 'seize the city' threat made by radical forces . . . a palpable possibility." The Gazette, the DailyCal commented, "draws a bright picture of

Berkeley's future. . . . The domination of city politics by the real estate and business interests may well be drawing to a close."

DOOR RAFFLED

Propped against Sather Gate was the door from the former business office of Councilman John DeBonis, a conservative mayoral candidate, salvaged from a Bank of America building being razed. Enterprising activists were selling raffle chances on it.

What else might blaze up? Perhaps a joint UC workers-students' protest. Or the state budget crisis, which bears hard on UC students.

"In anthro," said Tina Lyman, "the faculty is asking students for volunteer help with clerical work. . . . We're losing a traveling professor, one of the best on the faculty."

Emy Chan noted that enrollment cutoffs in required courses are common, so that half those requesting the class—often meaning hundreds—can't schedule it. Some TAs (teaching assistants) are volunteering to take on extra papers, she said.

Carefoot reported the halting of a sociology statistics course because funds for computer time ran out. Students passed a hat to pay for more. Professor Smelser recalled once when enrollment in a specialty course quadrupled

his expectations. What's more, nearly every student took up his offer to give anyone who wanted it an individual oral examination rather than a written final. He had to let a lot of other activities go that term.

Chancellor Heyns, questioned about faculty workloads, said emphatically that "there is plenty of time to do both" teaching and research. One student, told of Heyns's stand, retorted huffily that that's not true for the prof or TA who's voluntarily doing heavy extra duty.

When a coffee break was suggested, Carefoot insisted that the group not patronize the university-subsidized Dining Commons. It is the target of a boycott aimed to force it to buy only lettuce harvested by Cesar Chavez's agricultural workers, and Commons business is hurting.

Cal is not all mass pressures and politics, of course. There's some spillover of the freaky between the end of Telegraph Avenue and Sather Gate, in the transitional zone where political argument and literature handouts are hot and heavy and aspiring entertainers test their styles on passersby.

On a bright, calm day, even after a bomb threat, it is hard to remember the ferocity of all the past action on that strip.

Beyond the gate the foot traffic thins down mostly to staff and students in myriad forms of garb, much of it lumpy looking. Minorities are much in evidence—Heyns is proud of UC's gains in that.

In the gorgeous glades along Strawberry Creek and the buildings a bit off the axis of action, an open, peaceful spirit blossoms, giving off occasional whiffs of a bygone

era of college life and some new aromas of its own.

Many of the academic buildings throb with such creative activity as to make the visitor envy the students, pressures and all.

FROM LOS ALTOS
Tina Lyman

FROM LOS ALTOS
Gary Bankhead

OPINIONS *Ours*
...yours
...others

It's Valentine's Day and hardly a mouse
Seems stirring in our haunted House
On the vaunted heights of Capitol Hill.
What's come of that impeachment bill?

Green Eyes

Angelina, cara mia,
How'd you like to come and be a
Democratic cand. for guv?
That'd show him good—your luv!

No. 2 Doesn't Try Harder

Jerry, Jerry, you're the guy,
Apple of the country's eye,
Lots of folks would like to witness
A coaching change, and test your
   fitness.

Just Plain Bill

Simon is the energy czar,
Simon says don't use your car
Unless you want this wheely nation
To founder on the shoal of ration.

Simon says that he believes we can
Get by (if states push the Oregon plan).
Simon says that oil is tight;
Simon says it'll be all right.

Simon gives us lots of chatter
Explaining just what is the matter.
How come when his turn is used
We always come away confused?

Sugar's Sour

Roses are red,
Violets are blue,
Dick's in the pot,
It's Watergate stew!

Mother, O Mother
Come Home With Me Now

Glamorous Gloria ("call me Ms."),
You've filled her mind with heady fizz;
She's out to be the people's choice,
She wants her thoughts to boldly voice.

Her promise she means to fulfill,
She'd like to pay the grocery bill,
She'd like to own the biz, or make
A corporate prince's weekly take.

Why not? Who wouldn't? But the rubby
Is what must then be done with hubby,
Kids and cats and dogs and chores,
Opening eyes and closing doors.

You've led us to an awful hassle,
A man's home is no more HIS castle;
It's hers and his, or maybe their,
—Or hers, if strain splits up the pair.

You've triggered quite a revolution.
Next we'd welcome a solution
That would no further families render,
That would curb this gender bender.

Two-Timer

Handsome Ronald, golden Pop,
Your citizens do wish you'd stop
Winging off to Dixie dinners,
Meet the Press, and Saints and Sinners.

Sometimes, Guv, we feel that maybe
You deceived us, Ronnie baby,
When you said no woo you'd pitch
Toward a presidential hitch.

Confession's good, come let it out,
Don't you aim to be mahout
Of an elephant that's in a fix
Due to end in Seventy-Six?

These political comic Valentines are ancient enough to require some identification. They ran while the House of Representatives was supposed to be considering a bill of impeachment against President Nixon. San Francisco Mayor Joseph Alioto's wife Angelina was talking of running for governor. Jerry is Gerald Ford, then vice president.

"Glamorous Gloria" is Steinem of Ms. magazine.

TIMES UNDER ATTACK

About the all-male ticket

By Ward Winslow

THE TIMES IS UNDER FEMINIST attack today for coming out with "men only" recommendations for the Palo Alto City Council. Our womanless list presents a political target of opportunity, too, and some of the shots at it seem more demagogic than equal rightist.

—The Palo Alto chapter of the National Organization of Women (NOW) has expressed "considerable disappointment" with our "sexist endorsements."

—Plans to picket our office this noon were announced by Alice Smith, an organizer whose supporting documentation identifies her with the ABC slate.

—Our stand is the subject of a scathing tongue-lashing from one of the last female Palo Alto council candidates we did back, Councilwoman Enid Pearson. "This list refutes all those past equal rights pronouncements," she says. And her last word is that "a woman editor is desperately needed to lead the Times into the current era. Any of the five woman candidates would do an outstanding job."

(We think we were led into the current equal-rights era by a woman editor, Elinor V. Cogswell, now retired.)

RECOMMENDATIONS — AND WE INtentionally call them that rather than endorsements — are touchy. The concept is simple enough: In a contest the voter must make a choice, in this case among 16 contenders for the five four-year terms and two for the one short term. If the Times, as a newspaper that covers the council and the campaign, wishes to advise readers which candidates we prefer, we too must choose.

Such a selection has the potential of pleasing six candidates and riling 12, though a few far-out officeseekers might consider our blessing an establishment "kiss of death."

Whatever we do — whether it's to back all incumbents, call for a fresh start, support one slate in toto, or try to offer a ticket balanced by age, sex, neighborhood, religious affiliation, ethnic background or whatnot — is likely to be assailed by those who feel we're wrong or who can make political hay by yowling.

WHAT WE DID THIS TIME, AND almost always do, was to select the individuals we considered best qualified, giving preference to incumbents. For the full terms, we felt that the four elected incumbents had earned re-election. All happened to be men.

That left one opening and a dozen other candidates. Among them were Sylvia Seman, who under the charter could hold her appointed term only until this election and who chose to try for a full term rather than the remaining two years, and three other women — all with good credentials plus real verve as campaigners. Also Prof. Byron Sher, a former councilman. It was a close decision, but we rated Sher first.

That made five men, plus a sixth, Roy Clay for the short term. It seems to me that people truly liberated from sexist thinking could accept that as a judgment from our viewpoint (subjective, to be sure) of the best qualified.

Two years ago we rated three women among the four best-qualified.

It just adds outrage to injury to say why we pass over candidates, except for elected incumbents, so we don't. Because Mrs. Seman was an appointee, we skipped any rationale.

For the record, she has worked exceptionally hard, is well informed on city business and is a very pleasant person. Like any other incumbent contender, she has a council record and a platform, which voters can judge for themselves.

THE IDEA THAT EACH COUNCIL class should have quotas of men and women is distorted. Sure, variety is great. But there could be as much variety among nine women — if those nine were the best people for the council — as among five men and four women, say.

Women have played key roles on the Palo Alto council since the 1920s. The election of a woman is no novelty here, and the city is beyond the need for gender tokenism.

I claim we didn't offer "sexist endorsements," just plain recommendations.

OPINIONS *Ours ...yours ...others*

EDITORIALS

Tighter reins on 'massage'

Three just-enacted Palo Alto ordinances will not, unfortunately, put an end to the smutty business being done by prostitutes operating at the city's too-numerous massage parlors.

But the new rules adopted by the City Council should at least rub the masseuses who go beyond massage, and their pimps, the wrong way.

Henceforth massage parlor hours must be confined to the 13 hours between 9 a.m. and 11 p.m. Massage "technicians" — the Bicentennial-era nice-Nellyism for whores (always excepting the victimized legitimate staffers at the few genuine therapeutic massage establishments)—must get their permits renewed annually. And any new "adult-oriented" enterprises—which is to say sex-pandering shops—must get use permits from the city.

Possibly this tightening of regulations will have the same effect a regulatory ordinance enacted about 1½ years ago had—it may drive some of the massage parlors out of business. That would be good, but it might not be a total plus. The customers stimulated at these places might simply take their trade to the surviving studios, making them so profitable as to attract big-time criminals who feed on vice.

Anyway, the new ordinances may afford some respite to nearby businesses and residents pestered and embarrassed by these shameless titillators and their carousing clienteles.

There is another avenue of suppression open to the city: vigorous policing, and prosecution of the state laws regulating illegal sexual conduct. But criminal court proceedings can be dragged out for months, even years. City authorities also have found that police crackdowns tend to work at cross-purposes to the pressures that can be brought through business licensing.

Licensing—that is, requiring use permits and setting up standards for massage technicians and the like—is the city's only path of legislative approach. The state government has pre-empted law-making in the field of sexual conduct. And it is past time for the California Legislature to take a new look at the loopholes in these laws.

Won't some able legislator help rid us of this plague of rubdown perverters, this torrent of tarts with turkish towels?

OPINIONS *Ours ...yours ...others*

EDITORIALS

Child care merits full funding

Palo Alto Community Child Care (PACCC) deserves recognition for what it has built up since 1973. No recognition would be more fitting than for the City Council to fund its 1976-77 program fully.

Like other city services facing budget pinches even before the city undertook to pay $7.5 million cash to settle the Arastra Ltd. foothills suit, child care is threatened with cutbacks. But as a people-serving program that was running on a shoestring to begin with, it is very vulnerable. Any substantial cuts would mean serious losses of quality or capacity laboriously built up.

Not everyone is clear on what child care is. It's not nursery school and not just babysitting, though it has some elements of both. It is care given at a set of places where working parents leave children during job hours, meaning the centers must be open for up to 10½ hours a day. More than half the children come from single-parent families and are at the centers so long daily that it's vital for them to receive good "parenting" there. The caring is done—and done well—by trained, dedicated staffers who toil for very minimal pay.

Child care is a big thing in the lives of the parents using it, and they volunteer a lot of effort to make it better. Most of them pay from 10 cents to $1.70 per child-hour, on a sliding scale based on income, with the city subsidizing almost all the difference.

PACCC contracts with the city to deliver the service. In 1975-76 it served 169 families and 186 children—all Palo Alto residents, by the way (and there's a waiting list). The subsidy averaged $1,177 a child. Stated another way, it cost less than $5 a resident, mostly paid by sales taxes and property taxes on business and industry.

The benefits dwarf the cost. It enables many young divorced mothers, for instance, to work rather than live on welfare. It gives quality care in the formative years to children who, lacking it, would be prone to grow up with "problems." It helps a hard-pressed, locally underrepresented age and income group whose members are a valued part of the community.

It is an enlighted investment, well worth some sacrifices in less tender areas to avert damaging cuts.

OPINIONS *Ours ...yours ...others*

EDITORIALS

Belt-tightening time is here

Palo Alto city officials this week are finishing off one of the more traumatic of city budgets in the past couple of decades, at least.

Palo Alto, with its image (and self-image) of being the affluent, tree-lined community, has suddenly found itself overextended on the fiscal front.

For just too many years, citizens have demanded (and gotten) more and more city facilities and services, in addition to the basic high level of traditional civic hardware like sewers, streets, parks and public buildings.

But for each new nature interpretive center, or cultural center, or park and library expansion has come an ongoing operating cost — the cost of the manpower needed to care for the facility and run the program located there.

Palo Alto's citizen taxpayers have tended to forget (if they ever knew) that the reason for Palo Alto's affluence has been that the city owns its own utility systems and makes a "profit" off most of them. In addition, it has a healthy industrial, business and commercial community that kicks in about two-thirds of the property tax revenue the city gets.

Palo Alto is nowhere near broke. It has virtually untapped bonding capacities, since it has used the pay-as-you-go philosophy for many years.

The recent $7.5 million settlement of a major foothills zoning law suit was a financial blow, but the city has money left over.

The suit settlement isn't the major problem, even though it has impacted many planned city projects. The main problem is that the growth of revenues just hasn't kept up with the growth rate of city expenditures in the past decade.

So what's the proper solution? The staff and council this year are responding with close to $1 million in cuts and about that much in new revenues, from a 6% telephone and electricity users tax and an increase in the transient occupancy tax (motel and hotel users). But this is just another stopgap measure, a holding action for another year. Public officials (and employes) everywhere must begin to realize that there is only one proper and long-term response to budget-balancing dilemmas. It is to cut, trim, hack, chop, squeeze and bleed the public budgets so the government lives within its means — just as the rest of us have to.

New and newer revenue sources, ad infinitum, are an intolerable burden to ask taxpayers to carry in the face of continuing cost-of-living inflation.

This means that for the Palo Alto citizens who have historically demanded higher and higher service levels there will have to be some soul-searching. There must be at least as much citizen demand to "hold that budget" as for new or better services for the city officials to be able to make their new-found austerity policies stick.

There comes a time when the piper must be paid — and also the firefighter, police officer, gardener, maintenance worker, street sweeper, tree trimmer, naturalist, ranger, recreation leader, librarian, administrator, paramedic and parking monitor, too.

School officials, who run their separate domain, please copy.

OPINIONS *Ours ...yours ...others*

EDITORIALS

Did you see a burglar today?

Many Midpeninsulans have felt the dismaying, angering, frustrating impact of "hits" at their homes by burglars. Our institutions get hit often, too.

When these impacts are added up — when the frequency and range and dollar loss involved in a string of crimes by a habitual burglar is exposed by an arrest — the result can be astounding. Unfortunately, the dismay, anger and frustration do not mount proportionally; we've become too accepting of this cancer on our culture unless it chews directly on us. Not that good citizens condone burglary — it's just that it has become so commonplace that we tend to accept it as something we can do nothing about.

That, of course, is not so. Police agencies do nab droves of burglary suspects, and the courts convict a good many of them. But the point is that a lot more one- or two-burglar crime waves could be stopped if people just bore down harder on the task of catching the thieves.

Ask any patrol officer and he or she will tell you that the "cat burglar" image — the idea of a burglar being a smart, agile, never-seen wraith who's a wizard at opening locks — hardly ever fits an actual case.

Burglars generally are clumsy and stupid. They often are seen. In apartment units, indeed, they often are seen lugging their swag away. Even in posh estate districts their vehicles must often be noticed.

When they get away despite being observed, perhaps with the goods, it may be because the witness whose suspicions are aroused is too worried about making an unfounded report to police and not concerned enough about protecting the neighbors' property — and his or her own — from ripoff.

When schools or other institutions are entered and looted, applied thinking by the people responsible for building security can usually give the police a list of possible suspects among whom the culprits will be found.

Helping to "bust" one burglar, or a pair, or a ring, can stop an amazing number of crimes and save possessions worth many thousands of dollars over the course of, say, a year. It truly is the kind of stitch in time that saves nine.

Judges ought to think more about this factor when setting bail for accused persons. Wouldn't it be worth the community's while in losses averted and police services not required to keep the more obvious narcotics addicts and repeater burglars locked up while awaiting trial? All too often the burglar suspect arrested turns out to have been freed, not long before, on his own recognizance (without bail), whereupon, facing escalated costs, he quickly resumes his customary way of getting quick cash.

LETTERS IN THE TIMES
A community art form

By Ward Winslow

FORUM LETTERS IN THE PALO Alto Times have developed as a community art form. That's my contention in an article in the fall issue of The Masthead, quarterly publication of the National Conference of Editorial Writers.

Here, slightly shortened, is how I portrayed our Forum and its "artists" to colleagues across the continent:

Some contributors lay on textured colors with a palette knife; others use bold Chinese brush strokes, or paint wispy watercolors. We have our cartoonists, our finger painters, our monochromists, our primitives, our stark black-and-whitists. Styles run the range—flowery Latin, ponderous German, blunt Anglo-Saxon, awkward English-as-a-second-language.

In a community having a large proportion of residents engaged in high technology or academic work—and one that is home base for many political and commercial organizations—we have an articulate readership. The Forum does serve as their primary means of access to the Times from the opinion standpoint, although occasionally we will devote op-ed space to commentary that cries for more than a 350-word letter. (Overstroking that "canvas" is the most common problem, but we are strict about the limit.)

THE WRITER'S NAME AND ADdress are required in every case. Lacking addresses—expecially in our fairly compact circulation area—readers would understand a lot less about the writers; without names—well, we have too many phonies and pranksters wanting to fool us now, along with a few correspondents with good reasons for wanting not to be identified.

This requirement is held against mounting objections. I think these are fed by trends toward the anonymous society, nudged along not only by cranks, con men and literate thieves but also by police stop-burglary clinics, anti-rape advisers, consumers fighting the telephone company, etc. To date, we never have heard of a case of a Times letterwriter's person or property being attacked, although some do get phone calls or letters after their letters are published.

LETTERS ARE A POLITICAL art. Ours run heaviest during hot election campaigns, even though we require that they hew to issues and not be endorsements of individual candidates.

During the spring campaign on Proposition 15, the nuclear power plants initiative that Californians defeated almost 2 to 1, we probably ran more letters on the measure than any other paper in the state. It was an illuminating debate, drawing in prominent authorities along with foot soldiers in the pro-and-con ranks.

We do print some "regulars" whose basic message remains the same, but to get published (once a month is the informal limit) they cannot merely repeat—they must cite fresh news developments or construct a new argument. Letters meant primarily to publicize a cause rather than to state an individual opinion are not accepted. Loony letters are for the loony bin.

We do not print letters that, in effect, report news or criticize arts events, but we will accept specific commentary on our reporting and reviews.

Letters telling the editor how to run the paper are noted as free advice, considered and filed. Letters that raise precise, legitimate questions (in our judgment) about coverage and commentary are published. We usually respond to direct questions on coverage in an editor's note, either admitting error or defending the reporting.

EDITING LETTERS IS AN ART form, too—sculupture, perhaps, what with the hacking, whittling, flaw removal, fine polishing and titling. It's a nonpartisan, professional art, but one in the practice of which the editor must be sensitive to the politics involved.

THE COMMUTING CYCLIST

Pedaling to work pleasant

By Ward Winslow

The bicycle commuter crowd keeps growing, despite the lack of any through-ways comparable to freeways or express-ways for autos.

Students form the bulk of this corps, from small fry on small bikes to collegians on 10-speeds bearing heavy rucksacks toward the campus. But there are plenty of workaway types, young and old, run-ning the gamut from craftsmen to of-ficeworkers.

Now and then, especially when the weather is fine, I join this set, cycling from north Los Altos to downtown Palo Alto and back. It takes roughly twice as long as driving, but — barring rain or stiff headwinds or awful heat — it is much more enjoyable. More lathery, too.

Others must similarly feel my smug self-satisfaction while and after pedaling. I have exercised, and get to work invigor-ated. I have saved fuel and money. I haven't poured any significant fumes into the atmosphere. And I have had a good look at what is going on, at a pace slow enough to savor the subtler signs of the seasons changing, even the shifting moods of the day.

THE OTHER DAY IT WAS REVEALED to me that one can get too smug and ride for a fall. Nearing Embarcadero Road on the Alma Street sidewalk, I turned to ad-mire an industrious householder's vegeta-ble garden. Looked too long and ran off the pavement into an ivy patch. Then hit a chunk of cement in a driveway, blowing the front tire. Still out of control, but mer-cifully slowing, crossed driveway, hit curbing, pitched over handlebars, landed on hands and, softly, nose. Walked the rest of the way, pushing crippled bike.

Not long ago, my sister was less lucky. While bicycling and delivering papers for her son, she watched a toss too long, cracked up and had to have a head cut stitched. Not without reason are bikes high on the hazards list.

EVEN IF THERE WERE SEPARATED bikeways, they'd probably be less fun than my route. It goes through variegated types of housing along Park Boulevard and in Southgate, as well as past industrial and commercial sections. Mostly, the traf-fic's light and it's quite peaceful.

In the morning the air often is balmy and bath-like. Mornings one notices that most everyone is going somewhere — those who aren't bound for work or school, such as early tennis players, stand out as if out of place. I watch family clus-ters parting for the school day, commer-cial gardeners, other churning cyclists. There's the pressure to get there on time, and any stop is begrudged.

EVENINGS ARE SOMETHING ELSE. The weather usually is less comfortable, though nice if a little breeze arises. Why do things look so different going the op-posite way? In the evenings I look more at shrubbery, house shapes, what homes are being reroofed. Cooking smells hang in the air. Many cats are out to be spotted sitting in the westering sun, but rarely is a cat seen in the morning.

Even the pavement seems more notice-able while homeward-bound. What is it that makes some paving so slow to ride on, while on other sorts the cyclist really glides and swoops? Most of the ramped curbs are too steep and bumpy. But there's one at Kingsley and Alma that's perfect.

The uphill stretch at day's end is felt more deeply, and getting home is a most welcome event.

INMATES FAVOR IT
An unobtrusive jail

By Ward Winslow

THE NORTH COUNTY JAIL is a secure lockup. Its entry ports clang shut with indisputable authority. No inmate has ever broken out.

It is located unobtrusively in the basement of the North Santa Clara County Office Building, 270 Grant Ave., Palo Alto. From outside, you might not guess that up to 60 men can be held there — waiting to be bailed out or released on their own recognizance (O.R.), waiting arraignment or trial in the Municipal Courts upstairs, or serving sentences. No women, except a few transported in by day for court appearances.

Capt. Don Tamm, the Sheriff's Office detention division commander, invited me for a look-see the other day while he tested the building's auxiliary power for use in case of blackouts.

INSIDE, IT'S CLOSE-QUARtered, like a Navy ship. Inmates rate North County a good one as jails go, Tamm said. The main County Jail in San Jose holds 600 — with many more than 10 times the problems of 60. North County's layout and small cells make it flexible.

State law requires jailers to separate various classes of prisoners, but Tamm's bunch goes beyond that by evaluating "criminal sophistication" in assigning cells. North County affords the jailers secure "housing" for men, such as child molesters, who might be attacked by other inmates, and for homosexuals and transvestites. It has several close-observation cells for disturbed prisoners, and specialists from the mental health office upstairs can be called in quickly if needed.

One booking-area cell is handy for lawyers, bailbondsmen and O.R. interviewers, who are mostly Stanford students.

There's a small galley but no mess hall — lunch was spicy ravioli. Each side of the visiting area seats three, with glass between, and phones to talk through.

A nurse comes in to run "pill call" three days a week. Prisoners taken ill are sent to the Main Jail infirmary. In a medical emergency, such as a stroke, an ambulance is called and the victim goes to Stanford University Hospital or Valley Medical Center.

LT. C.C. (CARL) MOORE, the jail commander, operates with three deputies on each watch — custody, identification and control officers. At night, when a sergeant is one of the three, they're understaffed, but not as badly as the Main Jail.

Six inmates are trustees, called stewards. Moore assigns others who are nearing release to pre-steward duties.

Because the jail has no day room, Moore began a new program yesterday of letting those in each of seven "general housing" cells out into a larger space for an hour a day, free to use the telephone, showers and library. Everyone can exercise at least three times a week at the enclosed sundeck across the driveway.

The inmates' compact law library doubles as a classroom, with 10 to 14 usually turning out. Luisa Priddy, director of the Stanford Prison Information Center, has arranged self-awareness and rap sessions. Dr. Grace Brown of Palo Alto, a retired San Francisco State professor, has added a second weekly reading class by inmate request. Moore and deputies talk about practical matters, such as how to apply for a job. Valerie Patton of Stanford teaches art. There's a Bible class, too.

FRIENDS OUTSIDE, WHICH helps inmates' families, has spawned an offshoot, the Palo Alto Criminal Justice Committee, that works to improve North County jail conditions. Sometimes it pleads with county and state officials, sometimes it stages workshops, or raises funds for law books and other extras.

It's confining to run an editorial page almost single-handedly. For a while I tried to spend one day a week visiting a community institution. This column stemmed from one such visit.

OPINIONS *Ours*
... *yours*
... *others*

EDITORIALS

Illicit massage finally rousted

At last public authorities have found a way to take effective action against places of prostitution masquerading as massage parlors. All 17 such sex shops in Palo Alto were closed down in one fell swoop Friday, for a good long time if not forever. Bravo!

This unique legal approach was charted and executed by the Palo Alto Police Department and the Santa Clara County District Attorney's Office. Three cheers for them!

What makes it doubly admirable is that besides seizing and shutting the illicit massage studios, the legal action figures to create so much trouble for their operators and the owners of the buildings housing the studios that they will be discouraged from doing any more pandering, directly or indirectly. Indeed, there could be heavy fines, and sex-for-sale operations in other California communities could be dislodged because of the terms of the court order.

Unitl now, attempts to suppress this disgraceful traffic have created heavy workloads for law enforcement authorities without much lasting success. This attempt has turned the tables; the burden of expense, delay and lost business henceforth will weigh much more heavily on those who have been profiting from illicit operations.

What's more, Palo Alto, whose people have never considered their hometown any sort of an "open city," finally has shed its unwanted reputation as the Peninsula's largest sex-shop center. It is poetic justice for a city of rather conservative social tastes not only to find the means of brushing off these leeches, but also to show the way to other cities that dislike being victimized by procurers, pimps, prostitutes and shadowy profiteers.

Although the massage studios were seized under court order, fitted with new locks and closed tight, presumably for one year, in coordinated raids early Friday morning, Palo Alto police and Deputy Dist. Atty. Dennis Lempert had been preparing for the action for more than two months.

Plainclothes investigators had gathered evidence that employes of the massage parlors and nude dance studios actually were soliciting for acts of prostitution. When the lawmen had accumulated more than 100 sworn statements alleging the illegal acts, they put the evidence before Superior Judge Peter Anello in a civil (rather than criminal) proceeding. He issued an order based on the state's Red Light Abatement Act and laws dealing with unfair business practices.

Thus the phony massage parlors were put out of business, and those who lease or own the premises where they had operated were put under court order not to run similar operations anywhere in the state.

All in all, then, we can score one—a very big one—for the good guys. As for the massage parlors, good riddance!

So that's '30,' Times; hello, Times Tribune!

This is the swan song of the Palo Alto Times, a farewell and hail in the 77th and final issue of our 87th year. But the metaphor does not fit well — there is no mood of sadness at the Times. Let's say instead that this is our last day in a chrysalis form. Monday we emerge fully from the cocoon and spread new butterfly wings as the Peninsula Times Tribune.

Writing "30" is my honor as the senior active editorial staffer. (Photographer Gene Tupper never took leave and has served longer continuously).

Most people think of their community newspaper as what they read. We who work for the paper see other dimensions, too. It's a team of people, a building, machinery, processes and procedures — all in continual change. It's also a place with tone, and the Times always has had high spirits, high principles and a high standard of performance.

When I was hired in 1948, the plant was at Hamilton and Ramona. The newsroom was all one chamber with a dozen editors and reporters. It was close

Ward Winslow

and hot, but not as bad as the composing room, which was stifling on sunny days. One vivid memory is of waiting by the teletype (then the fastest news source) for a thrilling sports story from London — Bob Mathias, 17, winning the Olympic decathlon.

The next summer we moved two blocks to a new building — Publisher Gene Bishop's delight — fronting on Lytton halfway from Ramona to Emerson, once Parkey Sharkey's taxi park. The post-war rush was coming, and the Times was ready for it.

The city room was much more commodious, and there were separate cubicles for the editor, Elinor V. Cogswell (as fine a writer as ever we've had), for sports editor Walt Gamage and others. The staff still was small and close-knit. Harold Stevens covered the City Hall and then made up Page 1. Gamage, who doubled as Menlo Park reporter for a time, later recruited me to cover Paly High sports and write the first preps column. In 1950 and '51 Paly had unbeaten

years; never since has one school had such coverage. Sequoia stringer Dave Wik lacked the teams to vie.

Clanking linotypes filled the backshop; most of today's older printers bear scars from their "squirts" of molten lead. It seemed a long time before Teletypesetter, the first semi-automated step, came in.

Back from Navy duty in 1954, I found the top lineup changed: Harry Millet was publisher, Charlie Tyler business manager, Al Bodi editor. Growth was upon us. Soon I was doubling in politics and the San Jose bureau, and during '56 ran PNI's Cow Palace bureau for the Republican Convention. Election nights were exciting at the Times — the ballot bags were delivered at the office; semi-official results were chalked up inside for the public. TV election centrals and electronic vote counters weren't yet born.

By the early '60s, the Times had outgrown its shell again, plus several old houses nearby. Construction began on an addition that swallowed up the gas station next door and tripled our floor space. On a run of proud nights we held open house and showed off Publisher Tyler's pride: a big Goss Headliner press.

At first we rattled around in the new building, but the late-'60s were boom years. Huge papers took all the copy news editor Jack Silvey could find. Al Bodi, who fiercely protected editorial integrity, opened many new fields of coverage. Glenn Brown, now managing editor, pioneered business; Harold Stevens and the late Paul Emerson, the arts.

The printing revolution of the '70s took us first to paper or "cold" type, and finally to writing "on the tube." The Times Tribune will be based in the Times building, and we're expanding greatly internally. The other day workmen sawed a hole in the back wall and I carried my terminal through to a new spot. Soon I'll press a key and set this column in type.

David Burgin, our new editorial director, has opened multiple areas of new excellence. All of us, including many staffers coming south from the Redwood City Tribune, are excited. You'll recognize the markings of the butterfly you see starting Monday — a familiar paper, renewed and expanded. So, so long, Times. Hello, Times Tribune.

This sign-off was well received by our staff and former staffers except for one department that truly was shorted. What once was "Society" or "Women's Pages" had grown and changed through "Tempo" and "Lifestyles" to "Peninsula Living."

Comment

The Times Tribune credo

The Peninsula Times Tribune, born today, is a new newspaper — but one built on tested traditions. For 60 years, its parent company, Peninsula Newspapers Incorporated, has published papers with the highest standards of local journalism.

The Times Tribune combines the Palo Alto Times and the Redwood City Tribune, local newspapers renowned for their service to Peninsulans. The merged publication is designed to serve residents even better. How? Here is our credo. This we believe:

Our prime purpose is public service.

Our role is to be a local newspaper, edited for the information, enjoyment and guidance of all readers, and to help them make wise decisions about their lives and their government in times of rapid change.

We exist to deliver timely and accurate news, thought-provoking commentary and trustworthy advertising.

We intend to be a strong local institution in the area from the Skyline to the Bay, and from Belmont to Sunnyvale and Cupertino. Our special devotion is to making the Peninsula and each section within it a better place in which to live, work and play.

These are no new aims. In the first Palo Alto Times, Jan. 5, 1893, the editor wrote: "We feel honored in having a voice in matters of the town, and a home among its estimable citizens." The Times pledged "to support those measures which will best subserve the interests of this community."

We renew that pledge.

In its first issue, on May 1, 1923, the Redwood City Tribune said editorially: "The advancement of community improvements, community institutions and all else that contributes to the greater enjoyment of life in Redwood City and environs will be a leading editorial policy...."

We renew that pledge, too. And we bring new resources to fulfilling it. Our reporting staffs have been combined and enlarged. They will cover Peninsula news more thoroughly than ever before. Advanced communications and technical means will aid them. Our local coverage and commentary will be of a caliber that no competing medium can match.

"Local" news has an expanded meaning today. The Peninsula long since has seen how its developments can influence the whole world — electronics, for example. Peninsulans are interested in what goes on throughout the Bay Area, in Sacramento, in Washington and elsewhere. We will bend our efforts to covering those "local" interests, which well may be at the cutting edge of national or world progress.

We are editorially free. We will be enterprising, vigorous and editorially militant. A newspaper has great power to exercise leadership, stimulate achievement and right wrongs. We mean to use that power in the community's interest.

We also will have a heart. We will take care not let a newspaper's unique power to damage be used for passing thrills or chuckles or other insignificant purposes.

We hope our readers will speak up, telling telling us of news or concerns, praising or criticizing, commenting on the issues. In a very real sense, a newspaper belongs not only to its owners but to its community — in our case, the Peninsula's people.

Don't sell public schools short

Superintendent Newman Walker might justifiably have been more assertive last week in answering a critic who said the Palo Alto Unified School District shouldn't rent vacant classrooms to private schools.

The Board of Education approved leases involving three closed school plants, Garland and De Anza to 180-student private school operations for about $27,000 each per year, and portions of Ross Road School to smaller private setups for $13,400.

The critic, Tom Smith, a former Los Altos High School science teacher, suggested that leasing to private schools could actually cost the district money in the long run. His reasoning was that if 10 students switched from public schools to one of the private schools, attendance-based state grants adding up to more than the lease revenue would be lost.

"There is a distinct intent on the board's part to commit suicide," Smith said, "but it lacks the courage so it is handing the knife over to its competitors."

Walker's response was that zoning regulations limited the potential uses of the surplus schools. He conceded that "It is legitimate to say we are subsidizing private school operations."

Well, we have no quibble with Smith's accountancy on the penny-wise level. Yet from a public standpoint, aren't the trustees duty-bound to rent to any appropriate takers, private schools included? To reject bids in order to squelch competition would be impolitic and improper.

For Smith to rate the small, individualized private schools as life-threatening competitors of the Palo Alto Unified School District is, however, to say that a few little exotic fish may swallow a porpoise.

That was Walker's cue, in our book, to say that the trendiness of knocking the public schools evidently has made a lot of people lose sight of what a superb educational job a school system like Palo Alto's does. Private schools are, in fact, a good safety valve for a community to have, and families may find sound educational or social reasons for sending a student to one sort of private school or another. To believe that, however, is not to say that private schools do a better job overall than a vaunted school system like Palo Alto's. The district is rich in master teachers, in finely honed curricula, in facilities and in special services. While there certainly is room for further perfection of program and personnel (and pupils and parents, too), it offers students a remarkably good education. This, too, is subsidized by the public — and the results reward the public.

Though parents may have cause to consider private school for their young, they'd do well to take a long look at what public schools offer before selling it short.

U.S. can cut 'parental kidnaps'

If someone steals your car and drives it to another state, you can get the Federal Bureau of Investigation on the case right away. If someone kidnaps your child and flees across a state line, the FBI will comb the country — unless the culprit is the child's other parent, even though he or she may have no legal right to custody.

"Parental kidnapping" is a tough subject from the word "split." It brings into play many varied emotions of broken partnerships, immature and insecure children, and anxious families and guardians. Nowadays it is complicated by jet travel, substantial differences in state laws, refusals to respect another state's jurisdiction, the grey areas of "domestic affairs" when it comes to standards of evidence and, finally, by the lack of a law making it a federal offense.

Bills to create such a law are pending in both the House (H.R. 1290) and the Senate (S. 105). We hope that Congress will mark the Year of the Child by enacting one of these two similar bills. The very existence of a federal law would do much to discourage parents from snatching their youngsters illegally, as they do now in between 25,000 to 100,000 cases a year, mostly because they can get away with it easily.

Besides setting a federal standard, the bill would write three main practical points into the law:

1. It would require state authorities to give full faith and credit to a child custody determination by a court of another state which has jurisdiction and meets specified conditions. It authorizes a state court with jurisdiction to modify a custody determination of another state court which no longer has jurisdiction or which has declined to exercise jurisdiction.

2. It makes it possible for authorized persons to get information about any absent child or parent through the federal Parent Locator Service. This service, established to track parents who have reneged on child support, has collected more than $1 billion a year in lost support payments. Its use in locating missing parents who have absconded with children will close a big loophole, making it much harder to hide out without going totally underground.

3. It will make parental kidnapping a federal offense, punishable by a fine of up to $10,000 and as long as six months in jail. Thus the FBI may enter the picture. While the FBI says it recognizes the seriousness of the act as "an injurious, sometimes violent activity that causes grievous hurt to all parties concerned, particularly the children," it is no keener than other law-enforcement agencies to take on "domestic" cases by the thousands. So a delay of at least 60 days is specified before the FBI can enter a case. Its budget will need bolstering, too, and Congress should see to that.

As things stand now, it is too easy for a parent who does not have custody — and who has no respect for the law — to snatch his or her child (or children), whisk him away on an airliner and have friends in the courts of another state issue a contradictory custody ruling. The bereft parent then has a tangle of jurisdictions to deal with and legal and travel expenses to shoulder, if the missing child can be located at all. Even if custody is recovered, the experience may harm the youngster severely. Almost incredible injustices are being done.

States have edged toward handling these cases better, but in these times of nationwide computer setups and rapid travel they are still in the slow bus stage. A federal law is needed. For the kids' sake, let's have it in this Year of the Child.

Waverley Street is a good cross-section

An bicycle ride along Waverley Street cuts as good a cross-section as any of residential Palo Alto.

At its southeast end, at Charleston Road, Waverley begins as the most boulevard-like alley in town. Toward the foothills, homes that face on Redwood Circle and South Court have back gates or unhookable fence sections for trash removal or children's shortcuts to the schools across the paving — Ohlone, Wilbur Middle School and, beyond Wilbur, Fair-

Ward Winslow

meadow. During summer vacation, there's little but recreational traffic, but the Besse Bolton Children's Center remains busy with day-care youngsters.

Across East Meadow, Waverley is a genuine street with homes facing it. A number of VW vans are seen, and some boats and auto repair jobs in the driveways. Some yards are ultra neat, others less so.

Most of the soil is adobe and gardening takes persistence, though even in the space of a block or so there may be rich alluvial deposits that make some land dramatically more fertile. Squash grows in a few front yards or parking strips. On one lawn an overgrown zucchini lay by a sign saying "Free." (Do "boat people" like zucchini? Let's hope so!)

Once past Loma Verde, there's a pronounced change in the houses — probably traceable to a different builder, though all through the area so many alterations have been made that the tract origins are well masked. The downtown-bound cyclist is getting into one of Palo Alto's intensive upkeep areas. Passing 2525 Waverley, which suffers from neglect, you see why neighbors fought a rezoning.

A few pre-1950s homes, usually swathed in shrubbery, are relics of the era when Oregon Avenue was town's end and farms lay scattered beyond.

North of Oregon, there's another marked change. The homes are older, larger, more elegant. The trees are mature — some olives go almost 30 feet — and

their canopies create plentiful shade and give the air a delicious freshness that even fumes from the buses that ply Waverley cannot spoil.

The curvy section always stirs a memory. Henry Martin, a master teacher at Palo Alto High School, used to let physics students deliver reports to his door there up until midnight on the due date.

At about Seale Avenue, a change in the paving from asphalt to cement becomes noticeable. Some walnut trees grow streetside, and a squirrel carcass may be visible. Walnuts make a mess as their nuts ripen. But they aren't as big a nuisance as magnolias, which must be among the least biodegradable of local leaves and pods.

Passing Miss Elizabeth Gamble's house and large garden — fields, in fact — between Kellogg and Embarcadero, one wonders if this holdover from the days when Palo Alto homes were country estates will be divided up some day.

Across Embarcadero is Professorville and another change of tone. A few blocks on it becomes evident that some places have multiple renters. Apartments begin to mix in. Opposite the Palo Alto Medical Clinic a jacked-up house waits, probably for a new foundation. Adjoining it, the yards of Creative Initiative Foundation leaders sport flowers galore.

By the corner of Homer stands St. Thomas Aquinas Church, certainly one of the finest wooden structures in the city, given world renown in "Harold and Maude" — and darned if that movie isn't still playing in Palo Alto. Thence into the mixed, senior-heavy residential and commercial district, although somehow business never has hit Waverley too hard.

A block or so on, bungalows from the '20s — or was it before that? — show restorers' care. Unfortunately, the area must bear a heavy daytime load of cars parked by downtown workers. Near San Francisquito Creek, the ride is uphill. At Ruthven an old house with a porch is wreathed by what could be the Peninsula's largest wisteria vine. At Palo Alto Avenue, a sign points left to the bicycle/pedestrian bridge, in case you want to sample the Waverley on Menlo Park's side — a much newer street.

Was inflation bad in your youth?

The question jolted me. "Dad," my 18-year-old son had asked, "was inflation this bad when you were a kid?"

Certainly the answer was no. Inflation was not a bogeyman during the Depression years of my boyhood, though a lot of citizens would have swapped their lack-of-income problems for some of it. It put a few tooth marks in us during the early stages of World War II, but for most people it was no great wound then, because pay was inflating too.

Edward has done grocery shopping now and then for a couple of years. In preparing to go to college he has been hit by how tuition and room and board charges are rising. He has shared the harrowing experience of the past year at the gasoline pumps. He reads the papers and has noted the reports of double-digit inflation, the worst in a long time.

He says he can remember when candy bars were a dime. Candy bars by rights sell for a nickel, my generation knows. And big ones. You could get fairly delectable nibblies for a penny.

Even before candy bars, however, I thought of postage stamps. A first class letter, weighing not more than an ounce, remains recorded in my mind as

Ward Winslow

costing 3 cents. When ordering stamps at the post office window now, I almost misspeak every time: "A book of threes, please." Or sometimes 13s.

Stamps aren't any accurate measure of inflation, of course, because for many years the government subsidized first class postage and even now there are political peculiarities in the Postal Service charges.

Still, the fact that our basic letter-mail stamp was a 3-center from 1932 until 1958 says something about stability in that era. Even as late as 1970, the rate was only 6 cents. Then 8 cents in 1971, 10 in 1974, 13 in 1975 and, since January '78, 15 cents.

Saturday afternoon movies cost a dime in the '30s,

if memory serves. The first haircuts I recall cost a quarter. Remember, though, a dime and a quarter were worth a lot more then. The buying power of a dollar in 1940 was something like five times what it is now. But incomes were teeny in today's terms.

It is sometimes hard for those of us whose heads are filled with all these ancient benchmarks to grasp that there has been a terrific onrush in the 1970s — markedly since the 1973-74 Arab oil boycott levered our whole price structure upward. The government's Consumer Price Index shows it. Using 1967 as the base, or 100, it reads 116.3 in 1970, 133.1 in 1973, 161.2 in 1975, 193.2 in 1978 and 216.6 in June, 1979.

One of the figures Uncle Sam puts out as part of "Statistics in Brief" is the price of a pound of hamburger. It is given in adjusted dollars, with the 1967 dollar worth $1.00, to provide a basis for comparison. In 1952, hamburger was 52 cents a pound (adjusted — the price would have been less at the butcher's counter). In 1970, it was 66 cents; 1975, 88; 1977, 85; 1978, $1.20. The other day I bought some for $1.69 a pound (unadjusted).

Peninsula housing is exceptional, admittedly, but its dizzying climb in recent years has run gasoline price inflation a good race. When my parents moved to Palo Alto in 1941, they were not in a position to buy, having tied up their savings in a house in Saratoga. The four-bedroom, two-bath house we rented, a bungalow built by an early professor, could have been purchased for about $7,000. But the terms for buying a house were sterner then than they were in the '50s and '60s — it took a relatively large down payment. (Buyers today tend to face a similar problem, and it must break young couples' hearts.) Anyway, instead of buying, my folks rented for more than 20 years. Doubtless that house would sell now for $107,000 and then some.

Edward and his cohort are pretty resilient young people, inured to inflation in their formative years, and as they go to work, they'll have a fighting chance to cope with it. But inflation is doing ferocious things to older people on fixed incomes. It doesn't help that they remember an era of more stable prices as well as I do, and probably better.

The biggest profiteers operate close to home

Question: What regional business netted $30 billion in profits last year, more than twice the profits — sometimes called "obscene" — of the nation's 15 largest oil companies? Hint: You may be a partner in it.

Answer: Richard Carlson, SRI International senior economist, calls the enterprise Bay Area Inc., though it isn't really incorporated. You are a partner if you are one of the 2 million "speculators" who own a local residential property that grew fabulously in value.

This gimmick is Carlson's lead-in to make the point that California has the world's eighth largest economy, the Bay area is its financial and high technology leader and the Peninsula is "the center of the center" — America's wealthiest, fastest-growing economy.

Ward Winslow

Speaking at SRI's recent forums on "Community Options for the '80s," Carlson said the area between Redwood City's south border and San Jose's north edge already has reached employment levels that, in 1975, were projected for 1990. Pressures for growth are expanding, he added. "The information society" is just beginning and energy troubles mean faster growth here in computerville because they signal the need for more complex controls. Beyond that lies biological engineering. Renewed emphasis on national security means more defense jobs for an area that in the early '70s switched mainly to civilian work.

Naturally, there is trouble in paradise — limits to growth. But Carlson and colleagues who also spoke — Thomas W. Fletcher, former San Jose city manager, and Roger Mack — are not scared by the physical limits cited in such studies as the recent report of the Santa Clara County Industry and Housing Management Task Force. They see air quality as better than 10 years ago and due to be much better by 1990. They note that the major use of water — agricultural processing — is declining. As for land scarcity, Fletcher says that, physically, every Californian could be housed with an ocean view if we wanted to do that.

The menacing limits, Carlson said, are those no community has faced before. They can only be met by identifying the crucial problems and creating the will and the structures to put solutions to work.

Listing problems, he used some gag titles:

The Bubble Theory of the Environment — Many measures that improve things locally, such as freezing industrial expansion, make matters worse in other parts of the region, for example, by accelerating sprawl in Sonoma, Solano and Sacramento counties.

OPEC (the "C" is for charities) — Making people drive farther and farther makes them use more costly energy, and relocates air pollution.

The Policy of the Vanishing Commuter, also known as the Mary Poppins Theory of Transport — Carlson asked how many reached the meetings by motor vehicle; about 535 hands went up. Then he asked how many rode the bus; two responded.

The Man from Mountain View Theory of Labor — This is the belief that we can expand employment and someone else, hopefully Mountain View, will build the requisite housing. Mountain View, for its part, believes in the man from Sunnyvale.

For all that, Carlson said, it is surprising how well local systems worked in the '70s. Confounding predictions, the net in-commuting remained roughly constant, a fact that puzzled the researchers until they found that the number of workers per household had gone up from 1.2 to more than 1.6. This enlarged the Santa Clara County labor pool by 70,000 to 80,000.

Mark said, however, that this source of new workers has been pretty much tapped, and that the in-commuting from southern Alameda County of new workers needed by the tight high technology labor market is due to start in earnest. He forecast that the new Dumbarton Bridge and improved Highway 237 will move the traffic choke points to Bayshore Freeway and the laterals connecting it to I-280.

Many policies of cities, counties and industry are mutually contradictory. Fletcher stressed that new units to solve the problems can be created by the public, private and non-profit sectors if they will it.

Palo Alto will wrestle with its jobs-housing monster soon. Its officials might harken to what the SRI men told one Palo Alto woman who asked how the city could keep a no-growth status: "No way."

Opera's brief fling in Stanford Stadium

"The first" and "the only" ought to be red-flag words for editors. When a newspaper writer applies these distinctions to some happening, it's a fair bet that something was overlooked. Perhaps our motto should be taken from Ecclesiastes: "...and there is no new thing under the sun."

All this is by way of apologizing for not knowing that opera had come to Stanford Stadium in 1922.

The error of omission crept into our editorial columns on Dec. 5, when a short piece ran, commenting on the idea that is under discussion at the university of moving commencement ceremonies from Frost Amphitheater to the stadium. Returning the ceremonies to the stadium, rather, for they had been held there in 1935, with former President Herbert Clark Hoover as

Ward Winslow

the speaker. That information was derived with the help of Donald T. Carlson, Stanford's director of university relations, backstopped by the research staff of university archivist Roxanne Nilan.

It fit in with a tidbit from my own memory banks of political history: that Hoover had given his speech accepting the Republican Party's nomination for president in the stadium in 1928. So I mentioned it, as "Only one other memorable non-athletic event" that had taken place in the giant bowl.

The night the editorial ran, one eagle-eyed reader with a long memory, Marvin O. Adams of Los Altos, wrote saying, "There were several operas one year."

The next morning Mrs. Dell Theodore Lundquist of Palo Alto telephoned. Her recollection of the operas was detailed — she named the productions as "Carmen," "Faust" and "I Pagliacci." It also was romantic, for she and the late Dr. Lundquist had been engaged then and she said one performance had been lighted by a great full moon. But theirs had been a long engagement, and she was not certain of the opera year.

The year was 1922, the archivist verified. The stadium had been built in 1921 (although thousands of its present seats were added in 1927). Maestro Gaetano Merola of the San Francisco Opera had conceived the idea of using it for open-air opera. The performances were fund-raisers to benefit the Stanford University endowment and the Memorial Church organ fund. They took place in June, ending at graduation time — "I Pagliacci" on June 3, followed the same night by three ballets; "Carmen" June 7 and repeated June 16; and "Faust" on June 10 and again June 17.

A large portable stage had been constructed facing the north end zone. Judging from the remarks of Palo Alto Times reviewer Dorothy Nichols, it gave not only the opera cast but the corps de ballet ample room.

The reviews lacked crowd estimates. But the repeat performances, which were tied in with commencement, were reported to have drawn the best.

Reviewer Nichols, after hearing all three productions, pronounced "Faust" the finest. She noted that the claims of perfect acoustics had been justified out, although one soloist in "Carmen" had had to sing louder. She spoke appreciatively of "seeing the best without coming home with the milk" — a reference to riding the "milk train" home from shows in The City — and pronounced the stadium "the logical center for an annual season of open-air music."

A few days after the last aria, however, the Times reprinted a San Francisco Journal editorial saying that "the distance of Stanford from San Francisco and the newness of the project were factors that seriously interfered with the financial success of the performances." Put more bluntly, they were something of a box-office flop, albeit artistically good.

In 1924, at mid-afternoon on June 8, Mendelssohn's oratorio "Elijah" was presented in the stadium. Louis Graveure sang the title role, and university organist Warren Allen directed a 500-voice orchestra, accompanied by 65 members of the San Francisco Symphony Orchestra. The archivists pointed out that "Elijah" had been underwritten in advance, with financial help from Timothy Hopkins. Dorothy Nichols wrote a glowing review, but at one point remarked that the wind had robbed some of the sections of their fullness. The crowd was reported at 5,000, which meant that more than 66,000 seats were empty.

From then on, musical events on the Farm have been afforded more sheltered and intimate settings.

June Fleming praises the YWCA

By Ward Winslow
Times Tribune staff

When it comes to being on the cutting edge of social action, June Fleming, Palo Alto's assistant city manager, thinks of the YWCA.

The Young Women's Christian Association is the world's oldest and largest multi-racial women's organization, she points out. "The Y has always taken up causes before they were even labeled 'causes' and before they attracted groups of celebrity followers and promoters."

What sort of causes? Women's rights, for one. Housing for single women. Special counseling needs — before psychology and psychiatry became big and profitable business. Racial injustice. Student support on college campuses. Child care. Fair employment opportunities. Rape crisis counseling.

Part of Mrs. Fleming's admiration of the Y arises from her own experiences. Addressing a dinner audience of 86 persons last week at the Mid-Peninsula YWCA's 30th annual meeting in Palo Alto, she recalled her girlhood in Little Rock, Ark.

"As a young black girl in a small Southern town where all the discrimination practices that there ever were were in full force, your life can be very restricted and you can be dehumanized. Where do you turn for recreation? Where do you turn for the typical teen-age involvements? Years ago, for me and hundreds of other black teens, it was the Y.

"The Y was the only — the only — organization that actively and productively addressed those needs in a constructive way for young blacks," Fleming said.

"The Y fought with and got commitment from other agencies to lease that camp on the lake so that black women in my home town could have an away-from-home, two-week camping experience. The Y organized counseling groups — and social activities. As I now look back I see that for the Y the future was then. The Y dealt with issues before they were issues ..."

Again, in college and later as a young graduate librarian in New York City, Fleming found the Y a mainstay. "In many of the larger cities of this country the Y provided the only viable place a young woman could find housing as she entered the job market."

A week after June Fleming became Palo Alto's director of libraries, the YWCA sought her help. First, she recalled, Marguerite Anderson asked her to serve on the board, and, remembering her mother's advice never to turn her back on her past, she agreed. Before long, two long-time local Y leaders, Elizabeth Payne and Helen Flack, tapped her to go to a national meeting in Houston. They prevailed on Gerald Morgan, then city manager, to consent to the trip, and he did readily, Fleming reported, although in those days "he said no a lot." And Helen Flack personally took care of the Flemings' child.

In Houston, the mid-Peninsula's delegate played a key role in the hard-fought convention caucuses that led to "the elimination of racism" being adopted as the YWCA's imperative.

"The future has never been to-

In 1993, June Fleming became Palo Alto's city manager. This speech she made at the YWCA reveals influences that shaped her character. I was irked that the news side did not get the story in right away — it was at a time when a very large staff, created by the merger, was competing fiercely for all available space.

for championing social issues

morrow for the Y, but has always been now," Fleming said.

"The great women's liberation movement as we know it now is a 'Johnny come lately' when you compare it to the Y's active and persistent involvement and support in women's rights issues. Think about it: The Y might not have packaged it up in a Madison Avenue-type campaign attack, but the Y was there when it was crucially important and not an organized national issue — in the trenches, so to speak — taking steps that made a difference."

As for racial injustice, she said, "Long before the present black movement, the black support organizations, the Chicano organizations — long before minorities were appropriately organized into their own support networks (especially in this country) — the Y was there ... not waiting for the future."

It showed concern and perceptiveness in the women's rights area, she said, not only in housing but in forming rape crisis centers, working with employers to encourage the hiring of women in non-tradi-

tional jobs, making women's place in our society's decision-making areas a public topic and exemplifying that women are capable administrators.

At colleges, Fleming said, "in the earlier years the Y stood alone as a campus organization. It was only after its success in touching students' lives and (demonstrating the role of a support group) that other organizations came to college campuses."

"Farsightedness has been the modus operandi of the Y," she said. Delving into projections of the future in her talk, the assistant city manager noted the recent rise of a new pragmatic view of the value of forecasting. "Although our control over the future ... is mainly marginal, we have learned that small marginal adjustments in planning can make all the difference between misery and contentedness for large segments of people.

"This newly acquired realization of our power to affect our own destiny through long-range planning brings with it a new social responsibility for scientists, analysts and

Times Tribune file photo
June Fleming

social organizations, such as the Y. If falls upon them to provide the kind of comprehensive analysis of the future in which the process of influencing the future must rest. It also calls for facing the future today and not waiting for tomorrow."

Comment

The American way of drinking

Thanksgiving Day tomorrow is the first slosh of the year-end holiday season. It's a marvelous, distinctively American holiday, but it is marred more and more by another distinctive national trait: the American way of drinking.

It is cruelly reasonable to predict that Thanksgiving Day and the ensuing long weekend will exact a cruel price. There will be terrible automobile accidents involving drivers who had been drinking. There will be booze-triggered domestic altercations ranging from arguments to murder. There will be people young and old who, in the stress or the peer pressure or the loneliness of what for most folks are convivial times, will cross some invisible boundary on their journey into alcoholism.

The year-end holidays are not so different from the rest of the year, of course. The football-season tailgate parties, the workweek "happy hours," the campus beer busts, the stage-show cast parties, even the church-group supper sherry hours — all these border on binges, regular binges, for numbers of people. What is mainly different about the winter holidays is the seasonal emotion.

Of the recent Peninsula events relating to this subject, none seemed to catch the public's attention more vividly than the deaths late in October of two gifted Stanford students in a car crash after a night of partying. The driver, who survived, faces prosecution for vehicular manslaughter and felony drunken driving.

In the aftermath of the tragedy, there were suggestions that a place where they'd gone for cut-rate drinks was partly to blame, and that boozing on the Stanford campus was exceptional and excessive.

The comments that stick with us, however, are quite different. They were made by Stephanie Brown, director of the Alcohol Clinic in the Psychiatry Department at the Stanford University Medical Center.

"The reality that makes that accident such a tragedy is that this (drinking) is the norm of our culture . . . ," Brown said. "Not drinking is deviant behavior for us. People are more likely to be asked why they don't drink rather than why they do."

The clinic director noted that because Americans tend to look upon alcohol as a solution, it can't ever be labeled the problem — indeed, the whole culture is involved in denial of the real extent of alcoholic problems. "With that kind of baseline, any easy answer isn't going to work," she said. First the culture must change.

She longs for a climate in which people are freer to choose one way or the other about drinking. But some who intend to be "moderate" drinkers aren't able to be.

The issue is complicated, Brown says, by the American ideal of the strong, self-made man who can control any situation and take care of his own problems, " . . .so there is no room for the people who cannot. (They are) deviant, weak, a failure."

Adolescents say, "I can handle this," as a mark of adulthood. Teen-agers go on to college, where heavy drinking has become "the norm all over the country" — certainly not just at Stanford.

Stephanie Brown says the only hope for change is that "at some point people will get horrified enough at these tragedies . . .to make them recognize that the culture is going to have to look at its beliefs and values." In families where parents are concerned about coping with their sons' and daughters' drinking, she suggests, that might well begin with some honest discussion of how both teen-agers and parents are using alcohol.

America's drinking problem will be plainly visible for the next six weeks, as it actually is at any time. Some year perhaps we'll see it.

Toward a kinglier El Camino

Long live The King's Highway! El Camino Real has been cleared for a widening and beautifying project through Mountain View that will conform it to the more elegant sections in Palo Alto and Sunnyvale.

The Mountain View City Council gave unanimous approval to the project Monday night after hearing protests from about one-seventh of the property owners involved. Approval was no small matter, for the city is going to invest $6.7 million in the work. Property owners will be assessed $6 million, and the state government will pay $5 million, for a total of $17 million plus.

It has been five years since the Mountain View council first approved the concept of widening El Camino — the Peninsula's intercity main stem — to six lanes from Showers Drive to Highway 85 at the Sunnyvale line. In those five years the cost estimates have almost doubled. Right now may not seem the most propitious time for the work, with the economy in a slump, but by the time the construction is completed, all that may have changed, and anyway, such projects give some lift to employment and money circulation in hard times.

Along with the widening there will be sidewalks constructed, a median divider built and landscaped and utility lines put underground. El Camino Real should be a graceful and attractive boulevard all up and down the Peninsula, and it's a fair guess that the frontage owners who feel pressed now by what may seem staggering assessments will make out like prospectors with claims along a major gold vein.

Giving this key local roadway adequate capacity and accouterments that keep traffic flowing smoothly produces varied rewards. One noted earlier in 1981, after tests in the stretch of El Camino extending from Atherton to San Antonio Road in Mountain View, was that the air quality had improved. Carbon monoxide levels, a measure of pollution from automobile exhausts, had dropped dramatically below the national median for such routes in 11 U.S. cities, and slightly below what the federal government considers the threshold danger level.

El Camino Real sometimes has been the butt of ridicule by professional planners, who speak of it as "the largest strip commercial zone in captivity" and lampoon the oversized signs, kitschy structures and jumbled development that have blighted parts of it. For all their criticisms, the route has many eye-pleasing vistas and locally beloved landmarks, and if Peninsulans keep working to upgrade it to a high standard, its elegance will reward us.

It should be a highway that both serves well and delights us commoners who are today's kings. Mountain View's widening work will advance progress toward that end. Other cities that have not yet projected their improvements, please copy.

Elinor Cogswell, editor

ELINOR V. COGSWELL, who died Saturday at age 90, gave a great deal to Palo Alto in a 41-year career as a reporter and editor for its newspaper.

After taking a master's degree in English from Stanford and trying teaching, Miss Cogswell in 1918 chanced upon a job with the Palo Alto Times, a tottery little daily with an editorial staff of two.

New owners the next year bolstered the paper, and the cub reporter mastered her craft in a college and commuter town that gave the nation a president.

The staff grew and she moved up, in 1938 becoming one of the few women editors of a U.S. daily newspaper. She hated being pointed out as a freak — "California's only woman editor" — but she loved her work and did it well.

She stood for crisp, correct writing. And her own reporting, research and writing were marked by a compassion that readily communicated to readers.

After giving up the editor's chair in 1952, she plied her editorial-writing skills for all the Peninsula Newspapers and continued her "EVC at Bat" column in the Times. When she retired in 1959, Miss Cogswell listed as causes she and the paper had fought for:

Offstreet parking, master planning, clean government, a new Santa Clara County jail, humane treatment of animals, smog control, preservation of open space and historic values, civil rights for minorities, freedom of speech and of the press, "and whatever seemed to us to contribute to ... world peace."

The list sounds trite today, but in many of those fields she and her colleagues were plowing hard-baked adobe.

She added her "small pet causes: the spring wildflowers, public toilets in the business districts, stray puppies and lost kittens, curbside benches for old people, landmarks and reminiscences of early days, the ideals built into Palo Alto."

Many of those ideals were built in at the instance of EVC, a keenly interested yet critical citizen, a Stanford alumna who savored town-and-gown struggle.

A sense of humor was not the least of her attributes, and, anticipating her obituary, she once wrote: "NOT an estimable person or an esteemed citizen or noble Christian character." Yet we can say Elinor Cogswell was an editor who made her words count and a person who made a lasting impact on her city.

Not only is her name perpetuated in Cogswell Plaza, the park catty-corner from the Times Tribune plant; her spirit lives on in Palo Alto and its press.

When I was job-hunting, Naomi Gill, our high school journalism teacher, sent me to see Elinor Cogswell. Her columns and editorials were sparkling pieces of writing, and she was a delightful person.

Five-dot adventure: covering the heart of the Peninsula

Ward Winslow

HERE BEGINNETH an adventure in three-dot journalism. Not exactly Herb Caen's three-dot stuff (invented by Walter Winchell, wasn't it?) or even the style of my first professional column mentor, **Walt Gamage**, whose copy rivaled Morse Code in its dots and dashes. Three dots meaning the designation for the Times Tribune edition covering Palo Alto, Stanford, Los Altos and Los Altos Hills (and I'll sneak in Mountain View, another favorite of mine). Also two dots, for the zone covering East Palo Alto, Menlo Park, Atherton, Portola Valley and Woodside.

This five-dot combo is the very heart of the mid-Peninsula. It deserves to be addressed as a unity, with minor variations for certain items landing north or south of San Francisquito Creek, a dividing line only at flood stage and tax/election time.

On the column menu will be some news fragments, or sidelights too brief for separate stories. Advance flashes on big events that'll rate stand-alone coverage later. Personal-insight vignettes. Recognition of local persons whose excellence has gone too long unsung. Oddities, funny happenings, Our Town tragedies. Poetic or polemic pokes into why we love this place and its people. A shot now and then at the shoddy, the scandalous, the scalawags. What's salty and what's sacred in our little hub of the high tech world. Grabber capsule quotes (and let's have yours) on the current Topic A.

Great and influential as our area has grown, there persists a unifying spirit here to be spoken of and spoken to. It's a choice assignment for a former staffer, now strictly a once-a-week columnist. So here goes: ... .

PALO ALTO's JUNIOR MUSEUM, still the only show of its sort around and heavily patronized by kids from towns nearby, has opened a new exhibit: "Butcher, Baker, Candlestick Maker." The title jobs are snubbed, but youngsters will find thrilling props for trying their hands at being a helicopter pilot in a cockpit designed by **Mearl Carson**, Junior Museum supervisor for 15 years, or a police officer, with red lights and siren set up by **Gale Bruce**. Or they can pretend to be a circus performer, **Ted Chandik**'s creation, or a computer programmer, programmed by **John Walton**. Or play doctor (under close watch), **Judy Eaton**'s production. And more.

Exhibits like this one run for about six months and often draw 1,000 or so visitors a weekend. It's a tad like staging a play to get them ready. The planning starts early but, as office specialist **Laura Dayharsh** puts it, "Everything that has to be done always takes immediate priority until *it* becomes the immediate priority." Dayharsh's Law.

HIGHLY RECOMMENDED for grownup kids who want to let their fantasies loose is the NASA-Ames exhibit at the California History Center at De Anza College, Cupertino, in the Petit Trianon replica. It has superb photos and text, plus identified flying objects and artifacts used in perfecting same. For example, the little balsa-wood models **R.T. Jones**, the intuitive genius from Los Altos, used to show how swept wings outflew straight ones.

Dr. Seonaid (say "Shona") **McArthur**, the History Center's outgoing director, deserves great credit. She persuaded Ames people, whose heads usually are in the clouds or outer space, to turn their focus from the future to the past for long enough to save stuff destined otherwise to gather dust in family attics. She recruited **C.A. "Sy" Syvertson**, Ames boss from 1978-84, to pull the facts and showpieces together and also to give a series of lectures at the History Center, where the exhibit will be up through June.

At the opening, **Smith J. "Smitty" De France** of Los Altos, Ames Research Center director from 1940-65, was present in his wheelchair, no longer biting his cigar, indeed, unable to speak.

WHEN ARE EAST PALO ALTO's kids going to have Head Start classes again? After a locally based program was folded last year owing to operational irregularities, the Feds took over. Since fall, it was all going to begin again next month, then the next month, then the next month. Despite an $800,000 budget which a federally chosen agency evidently is consuming, there are no Head Start classes going in EPA. Some head start.

THE CELEBRATION FRIDAY of San Jose's new United States Courthouse, wherein a full-time federal District Court operation with all the trimmings is now ensconced, went on without participation by the federal judges who sit only in San Francisco. It wasn't lingering opposition to the San Jose setup — the dinner tickets at $40 scared them off.

GOV. GEORGE DEUKMEJIAN's criticisms of President Ronald Reagan on two symbolic human rights stands called to mind an offbeat question thrown at the Duke when he met with the Times Trib editorial board in 1982. Asked if he thought he could be a better governor than Reagan was, Deukmejian flushed, then gave a modest response. But all present sensed his real answer: Yes.

Nearly a year after I retired as managing editor of the *Peninsula Times Tribune*, I was invited to write a local column – at the suggestion of Bill Harke, who later became the last editor. City Editor Bill Shilstone usually wrote the headlines – and did it very well indeed. This is the first column. Toward the end, they ran in the *Palo Alto Times* tabloid section of the *Times Tribune*.

All is not tranquillity in the Peninsula's horse belt

THE FOOTHILLS ARE starting to go tawny. Before long they'll be clad in summer khaki. But let's not forget all the green months we've had, while most of America wore dun. On a breezy day of late, you could drive up Page Mill Road, stop at the light at Foothill Expressway, look west and see the grass on a hilly corner of the Stanford lands rippling in giant waves. No football rooting section could do it so smoothly.

A furlong or so to the south, you saw horses, some frolicking, some grazing, some grouped for a stand-up siesta under an oak. Their turf remained high-spring verdant. But whose horses, anyway?

It took a few minutes' wandering on Coyote Hill Road, then up Hillview and Arastradero to Deer Creek Road and back toward Page Mill to find out. It's the Ramos Ranch, covering about 600 acres between I-280 and the expressway, Page Mill and Hillview-Arastradero, with five or six folds of hills. No ordinary ranch in at least one respect, the Ramos spread boards horses for people all around the mid-Peninsula, and boards them where they can run free. No stables, no steeds for rent, just tender loving care (when needed) and leg room. Locally, a horse's paradise. At $80 a month.

Katherine Ramos came out through a gate to tell about it, while a flock of pigeons, more industrious and disciplined than their downtown cousins, climbed and wheeled and dove over a corral.

Horse people mostly aren't rich — Katherine was emphatic about that. It's that they have a passion, like sports car buffs. They're not all cowboy boots or jodhpurs wearers, either.

As she spoke of the land and her family's hope to keep it in its present use, she mentioned other old family names associated with open-uplands and four-legged mounts — Piers and Webb and Zwierlein — and it struck me that here's another unseen strand running through our region, the horse belt.

Tranquil as the day was, all is not calm in the horse belt, if Katherine is any indicator. Her mind was much on politics — trails that other interests are loath to share and the clash over Coe Park usage; people who find horse manure repulsive; and, horror of horrors, the attempt to run horsemen out of Huddart Park in Woodside where decades of hoofprints have hallowed the riding ring. Under it all lay a trace of paranoia. It's a fear of being overrun by the forces of growth. Those forces press in on the ranch: traffic on Page Mill and 280, beautiful but land-eating buildings of Syntex, Xerox, Hewlett-Packard and the like on two sides.

In departing I delved for an encouraging word. It turned out to be an initial thought — that more folks than she knows delight in seeing those horses.

HOW DO YOU WRITE A FIGHT SONG for a direct-sales dress company? Charlotte Best of Los Altos was one of 45 Doncaster, Inc., agents to solve that mystery — and won first prize, $1,000!

She took a ditty everyone knows, the Notre Dame fight song, and applied sales pep. Here's a sample:

We've got the spirit, we've got the class,
We've got the duds if they've got the cash;
Even if they're broke right now
We will arrange a deal somehow ...

Then she and her neighbor-partner, Carol Proffitt, rounded up Carol's spouse, Norman Proffitt, their son Norman Jr. and Charlotte's daughter's fiance, Mitchel Short of Sunnyvale. With the composer at the piano, Proffitt Jr. on the banjo, the senior Proffitt whistling and singing and Short singing too, they made a tape. That background laughing was Gordon Best's.

THE BIG SURPRISE in Palo Alto Educators Association internal politics this spring is the decision of Dave Struthers of Los Altos Hills to run for vice president. Apparently while he was on the 1984-85 negotiating team Struthers saw problems he wants solved — likely on both sides of the table.

Struthers is on the Gunn High math faculty, whose students scored a coup by edging their Paly rivals out of the top regional math spot in test scores. He's one of those teachers who could earn more in private industry, yet remain dedicated to education. In the negotiations it was he who demonstrated the erosion of faculty salaries in living-cost terms, a critical factor at the Struthers home, what with collegians to support.

IT'LL BE A FIESTA May 22 honoring Jesus Sanchez, who is retiring as principal of Los Altos High School. Sanchez, who was principal at the old Mountain View High School earlier, will be feted by the LAHS Parents Group and Community Advisory Council at the home of Roy and Penny Lave. For information, call Lou Ann Walker at 941-9637.

WIN A FEW ... Leonard Wittlinger found it in the listing for an Old Palo Alto house built 47 years back — a condition that a dwelling worth at least $6,000 go on the lot. And, a covenant said, occupied only by "members of the Caucasian Race or their colored servants." Ugly, and now illegal.

LOSE A FEW ... Rixford Snyder, one of Stanford's great resident emeriti, won a rousing ovation for reminding Palo Alto Rotarians that back in the '20s you could ride from San Jose to downtown Palo Alto on the Santa Clara interurban street car in 35 minutes. Try that some workday at 4:30 p.m.

Why you don't get your mail delivery until late afternoon

POSTAL DELIVERY VEHICLE ENVY — who would have thought five years ago that our neighborhood would develop that syndrome? We have it, and bad. Once you have it, the symptoms can strike anytime. Say you are going to pick up a youngster at a school. Or to the store, or out to lunch, or to the dentist. You see a mail carrier's vehicle, note that it's only 2:30 p.m., or maybe 1:15, or *even morning!* And presto: PDVE, also called Junk Mail Jeep Jealousy.

Our neighborhood must be last on the list. Mail deliveries here occur in the morning only if they're a day late, in the evenings only if there's little mail that day. Regularly the mail comes after 4, indeed, after 5 now with DST, after 6 about twice a week.

So we go green-eyed at seeing other postal patrons getting their checks before the banks close, their bills in time to phone before the end of the business day if there's some problem, their personal letters soon enough to dash off a response and mail it that very afternoon if need be.

Have we protested? You bet! **Carol M. Powell** tried the blowtorch approach — a withering blast by phone. So did others. In December, I wrote to Palo Alto Postmaster **Johnny Y. Maeda** with copies to the postmaster general, consumer advocate and two congressmen, co-signed by 18 neighbors. We didn't blame our carrier, by the way.

Maeda's response was prompt. "Under normal circumstances, all deliveries in Palo Alto are scheduled for completion by 3 p.m. Due to recent shortstaffing and extremely heavy volume conditions, instances of late delivery have occurred and I sincerely regret the inconvenience . . . "

He promised "a significant improvement in the immediate future," and we got it for a while. Then backsliding began, and now it's worse than ever.

The postmaster politely rejected my contention that we should not *always* be last, and that " 'business' residents do through the mail is no less important than that of commerce and industry."

Business gets more mail and more accountable mail, making security a factor, he said. "The cost of periodic adjustments to rotate who was served last on a route would be prohibitive and . . . detrimental to efficiency."

We are not alone in postal problems, of course. There's a flap over 94022, which while living in Los Altos I rated tops. And others, no doubt.

There are bright spots, too. For instance, Mountain View's downtown post office has great front-counter teamwork, and at least one clerk there, **Maureen Bones,** would make a perfect national model of patience and helpfulness.

Still, isn't the Postal Service spiraling downward like the other "service" agencies of our time?

SALLY SIEGEL'S 75TH BIRTHDAY party comes off today in Palo Alto's Mitchell Park Community Center, a gala being run along lines like those of a campaign event. About 150 folks attuned to school politics, from high state officers to lowly precinct workers, will share the fun with superactivist Sally. Not invited: Gov. **George Deukmejian.** He missed his chance when he didn't name the birthday girl to the lottery commission.

ANOTHER BIRTHDAY CELEBRATION today is the Midpeninsula Citizens for Fair Housing's 20th. The drop-in party will run from 5 to 8 p.m. at the Stanford Museum. President **Diana Diamond** will talk about how MCFH had hoped to be out of business by its 20th. The rest will be what ExecDir **Mary Davey** calls "fun-raising." **Pete McCloskey** and other longtime fair-housing advocates will be there, perhaps including **Francis B. Duveneck.**

FRANK DUVENECK, AT 97, is the area's patriarch. His schedule would tax a tad — grand marshaling the Los Altos Pet Parade; last weekend accepting waves and serenades as he sat in the picture window of his Los Altos ranch, Hidden Villa, while the Country Fair went on on the grass outside; joining in weekly luncheons of the Friends of Hidden Villa. He uses a walker now but is alert and witty. A bon mot from under his mustache: "The best crop at Hidden Villa is the kids."

FOR VIGOR, HE HAS nothing on **Marie Louise Laudereau** of Southgate, the neighborhood across Churchill Avenue from Palo Alto High School. At 101, this French-born lady needs no spectacles and usually outpoints her friends in a Thursday night bridge game. Recently she had a mastectomy at Stanford University Hospital, was home after two nights and missed only one evening of bridge.

SHIRLEY COBB of Portola Valley, whose downtown Palo Alto book store has gone out of business, wants mid-Peninsulans to know she appreciates the "many complimentary and gracious statements" about the store. It was extremely fortunate, she adds, "in having staffs which were efficient, courteous, knowledgeable and loyal."

After she suffered a crippling stroke in 1971, Miss Cobb added, the book store would have closed had it not been for **Bern Ann Abbaduska** of Menlo Park, who then ran it. Ty Cobb's daughter says of Miss Abbaduska: "She has done a superb job!"

AUTHOR YVONNE JACOBSON of Los Altos, whose "Passing Farms, Enduring Values" belongs in thousands of local waiting rooms, told her dentist about the book one day. He suggested she give it to him. She was about to part with an author's copy when a thought came: Hey, when has a dentist given *me* anything free? (A toothbrush?)

Where airline pilots end up when they quit the skies

WHILE ITS PILOTS STRIKE lasts, United Airlines must be casting baleful glances in the general direction of Los Altos.

More than 400 retired airline pilots live in a cluster in Los Altos, Los Altos Hills and Mountain View, according to Roy Eckert of Los Altos, who points out that they could live anywhere but like the local weather and lifestyle.

Eckert counts 23 assorted ex-jet jockeys within two blocks of his house, and 17 retired Pan American pilots like himself within three blocks.

In general, he says, they break about half and half into those who had all the traveling they wanted during their careers, and now stay close to home, seldom going farther than Tahoe, and those still gnawed by wanderlust. Eckert is one of the latter; he flies often to overseas points on Boy Scouts of America projects. He's also an ardent bicycle tourer, off for a month in Iceland and Finland.

Present and ex-pilots are sprinkled across the mid-Peninsula. Woodside, Portola Valley, Atherton, Menlo Park and Palo Alto have their share, but Eckert claims the thickest cluster.

IF YOU THINK YOU'VE BEEN SEEING more squirrels than usual this spring, you're right, according to Wildlife Rescue specialist **Marilyn ——**, who begged not to have her last name used because she'd get too many (pardon the expression) nut calls. Our squirrel population is growing, and so is the proportion of black squirrels in it, she says. Eastern grays remain dominant, but the blacks — once isolated at Stanford — now are all about. Indeed, Wildlife Rescue has been releasing foundlings from Sunnyvale, Mountain View, Los Altos, Palo Alto, Portola Valley and Woodside in the hills.

The babies, born furless and blind, usually end up at Wildlife Rescue after pruning of oaks, pines, palms and other trees brings down their nests. Others are injured by dogs, usually fatally, or collected by cats, as gently as kittens, or hit by cars. After being tended by volunteers until they are fit, and are 12 or 13 weeks old, they are freed in appropriate terrain.

It's safe to handle the babies, Marilyn says. No rabies has afflicted local tree squirrels for at least 40 years. Squirrels are territorial, but do move on. Some have shared the yards of local residents for five or six years. They live 8 to 10 years in the wild, 16 to 20 if domesticated.

Mama Squirrel may bear two litters a year, spring and fall, usually three or four kits, sometimes six. Tree squirrels are protected by law, by the way. They like people and prefer living in a residential area, Marilyn says. If you like squirrels, try feeding them sunflower seeds, nuts and vegetables. If you like the idea of Wildlife Rescue, now based at Cubberley High School, volunteer — help is sorely needed. Dial 494-7283.

WHAT MAKES FOOTHILL-DE ANZA Community College District a winner? Consider Chancellor **Tom Fryer's** approach to his state association's recent "Day in Sacramento."

Most districts sent their chief executive and a couple of trustees. Fryer and Trustee **Robert C. Smithwick** took along more than a dozen others — Fryer calls it the "leadership nucleus": the presidents of both campuses and all major organizations such as the faculty senate, classified staff unions and the student bodies.

In turn, this aggregation prompted State Sen. **Becky Morgan** and Assemblymen **Byron Sher, Ernie Konnyu** and **Dan McCorquodale** to show up at lunch, and **John Vasconcellos** to drop in.

"We're trying here to deal a lot more people in on the important affairs of the district," Fryer explained. That not only gives them a broader perspective and deeper knowledge, it forestalls collective bargaining trouble that might ari if people thought their group was being left out.

Foothill-De Anza's good reputation has led to Fryer and now De Anza President **A. Robert De Hart** being called in to counsel the troubled Compton Community College District near Los Angeles.

DOROTHY GRAY of Los Altos and her students at the University of Santa Clara School of Law are running up quite a score in their Criminal Appeals Program, which provides legal representation for low-income people appealing misdemeanor convictions. So far they've won five of seven decisions, including a right-to-a-speedy-trial case that could shake up the misdemeanor processing system.

Students argue the cases and prepare the briefs in appealing Municipal Court midemeanor convictions to the three-judge Appellate Department of the Superior Court. A third of the program is funded by a U.S. Department of Education grant.

OUR ITEM LAST SUNDAY made Sally Siegel's 75th birthday bash sound overly political. Its spirit was written on one of the two sheet cakes: "A Toast to Our Educators." Sally has been praising and thanking teachers since the days when her father, a great admirer of learning, sent her to school with candy for her teachers.

Her party drew a rare reunion of Palo Alto Unified superintendents, including **Henry M. Gunn, Harold Santee** and **Newman Walker.** Walker will join Gunn and Santee in retirement next month; a party honoring him is set for June 23 at Tresidder Union, Stanford. Also present were **Wilson Riles,** former state super, and most of the PAUSD and Foothill-De Anza brass.

Sentimental tales of Jordan Middle School, 1937-1985

JORDAN MIDDLE SCHOOL's 47-year life span will be hailed and farewelled at the school Wednesday from 4:30 p.m. to 6:30 p.m. in what promises to be a sentimental gathering. (See the preceding page for details.)

As an investment, the Palo Alto Unified School District may be deemed to have gotten its money's worth out of Jordan. Its original construction cost in 1936-37 was $322,550, plus $14,000 for the 16-acre site. In 1965 a reconstruction of the locker rooms and library was completed and new buildings on the Middlefield Road side of the campus were added. That cost $757,000. Let's call it amortized, without even grappling with residual value.

The architect for both jobs was — guess who? Birge M. Clark, of course, Palo Alto's all-time all-timer. The contractor in 1965 was Vance M. Brown & Sons, and one of the sons, Robert V. Brown, later mayor of Portola Valley, had been in the first class to go all the way through Jordan — the class finishing in 1940. Bob Brown was touring Russia at last report, but his brother Allan F. Brown of Menlo Park, recalls that it was the firm's last school job, "also the best," even though a lot of unexpected dry rot turned up in the stucco walls.

For that matter, Birge Clark had more than a passing interest in the school. His son Richard Clark, of Menlo Park, was in the first ninth grade (Jordan was a junior high school for many years), and another son, Dean T. Clark, of Los Altos, was in the first three-year class. Dick, who became an attorney, had gone to the old Channing School in the seventh and eighth grades, and remembers the new Jordan as greatly innovative. For example, it had a two-way speaker system the teacher could turn on before leaving the classroom and monitor what happened afteward. By using the speaker system, Jordan also could hold assemblies without ordering all the students to one place. All its lockers had built-in combination locks, too. And there was parking for students' cars!

Dean Clark, a surgeon, remembers something different: There were cows next door, along with flies. That figured. Oregon Avenue was the end of town. Dean also remembers that discipline consisted of being sent out to pull weeds from the turf. The puller of the longest dandelion root got an award.

ROBERT A. KREUTZMANN, now a Palo Alto insurance broker, said it was nice getting into a brand clean school. It had a cafeteria, the first its students had used. Bob still recalls with pleasure his election as ninth-grade class president of that pioneer three-year class. And why not? The school was then the newest pride of the unified district, the seminal junior high of the area, and its first waves of students produced some locally noted people, and some nationally famed ones, too. Such

as? Such as UC Med's Dr. Philip R. Lee and his brother Dr. R. Hewlett Lee, executive director of Palo Alto Medical Clinic, auto dealer Leonard Ely, internist Frank Wheeler, office builder William R. "Bob" Cobb and real property developer Ryland Kelley. And legions of others.

Rye Kelley still echoes the excitement he felt at seeing Jordan's interior design and great buildings. It prompts him to speak of euthenics, the notion of benefitting man through the influence of his environment. Jordan's glass-walled hallways changed the feeling of being in a building, Rye says, and also changed people's attitudes about education.

ALL PALO ALTO STUDENTS WENT to Jordan until Wilbur was built in 1953 — for $1.6 million. And now all will go to Wilbur, but it won't be Wilbur, it'll be Jane Lathrop Stanford Middle School. Palo Alto City Council Member Gail Woolley, who teaches at Jordan, says her students already are talking about "the Janes." Mary Ann Somerville, who has done an outstanding job as principal at Wilbur, will head the new school.

It takes some depth in the district to remember it, but there used to be another Stanford School — the Stanford Elementary School near the heart of the university campus, on a site now covered by faculty housing. Stanford Elementary, which was small and reputedly very brainy, closed when Lucille Nixon School opened in the late 1960s.

Meredith Duncan Whitaker of Palo Alto, a Stanford Elementary alumna and now the Walter Hays School "lunch lady," says the idea of a new Stanford School is fine with her. Meredith went to Jordan, of course, a couple of years after its first three-year class, and remembers the shocked feeling of moving from a very small school to a (locally speaking) large one. She also remembers the long bus ride from the campus out to Los Altos and on to Jordan, taking about an hour. Sewing was not a Stanford Elementary specialty, and Meredith still can feel her frustration at being unable to sew a straight seam at Jordan.

JUST ONE MORE TALE out of school: (By the way, more women would be quoted here but for ((a)) the difficulty of tracing them, and ((b)), the fact that so many didn't answer — they must all be working these days.)

In 1949, while doing duty as the Palo Alto Times preps columnist, I was handed a long letter from Bill Farr, who later became an ace investigative reporter in Los Angeles. Farr, in collaboration with Gary Williams, now a Menlo Park public relations executive, predicted that their Jordan class would produce some of Palo Alto High School's greatest teams ever. Sure enough, they did.

Losing 405 years of teaching know-how in one jolt

WHAT HAPPENS WHEN an area's top-rated high school loses nearly 20 percent of its teachers to retirement in one fell swoop?

No one is certain, but Palo Alto High School's standing in the standard test scores during the next few years will bear watching. Retirement is sidelining 16 Paly teachers, most of them grizzled veterans with 25 to 35 years of local service.

Losing 405 years of teaching know-how in one jolt figures to be felt in some way. If no other, the Palo Alto Unified School District should save salary money for a while.

Paly High's retirees are George Truscott, 35 years; Leonard McCord, Kenneth E. White and Bernard Tanner, 31 years each; Walter White, 30 years; Frank Barr, 29; Dow Huskey, 28; Robert Starkey, 27; Anne Dreyfuss, 26; Harriet Auxler, 24; Gerald Kelly and Jack "Sandy" Snodgrass, 23 years each; Geraldine Meyer, 20; Walter Buhler and Lou Anne Large, 17 years each; and Barbara Melosh, 13 years.

The Paly cadre was the biggest single one among the 37 teachers and 11 non-certificated employees of the unified district who are bowing out. The aggregate service of the whole gang is 1,040 years, an average of 22 years each, Pat Einfalt, assistant to the superintendent, reported. Ten had service of 30 years or more.

One other surprising figure came out when the departing were honored June 7 at a reception jointly sponsored by the Board of Education, the district cabinet, PAEA, CSEA and the management team.

That was that 12 of those retiring finished their hitches at the same school site where they'd been ever since being hired. Somehow this durable dozen missed being caught in closures.

On the other hand, consider Queenie Dauler, secretary at Duveneck School. In 25½ years with the district she had worked at seven elementary schools, two of which, Mayfield and Lytton, soon will be forgotten by all but the archivists — and a handful of hardy old boys and old girls.

A short-timer in the retirees bunch is Newman Walker, who is leaving the superintendency after 10 years. Some wag said it seemed like 35.

JULIAN CROCKER, WALKER'S RELIEF man, already has huddled with the teachers union leaders, and they listened attentively as he presented his philosophy of "win-win" bargaining.

What made even more of an impression, however, was a matter of personal rather than high-level policy. Crocker announced that it's his practice to spend five days a year calling in for random assignment as a substitute teacher. What's more, he wants other administrators to do likewise. So teachers who sicken may feel even worse if their lesson plans aren't ready. And Jan Parker, who assigns substitutes, could feel a touch of extra power.

IT HAS NO DIRECT RELEVANCE, but for some reason we are reminded of the days when Harry Reynolds was Sequoia's new superintendent. He made an unannounced visit one noon to Ravenswood High, then being touted as a magnet school. In the course of opening a set of classroom doors to look inside, Reynolds caught two amorous teachers in *flagrante delicto*. The ensuing remarks were not, unfortunately, recorded for posterity.

IT HAPPENED IN LOS ALTOS, but commercial names and denominations are being changed to protect the culpable.

A minister's wife reached the head of a supermarket checkout line. The clerk proffered a bit of pasteboard, saying "Here's your bingo card." Scrutinizing the card, the woman announced, "I don't like the idea." "Neither do I," the clerk shot back. "I think people should keep bingo in church where it belongs."

MORT LEVINE, PUBLISHER of the Country Almanac, expects to move the weekly's production facilities from Woodside to Menlo Park soon. But that's not the item. On a trip to China last month, Levine was struck by the newly blossoming entrepreneurial activity of the people. It reminded him a little of Silicon Valley, especially when chip sales are hotter.

The policy switch that's allowing private enterprise ventures, sometimes with state funding, has the Chinese "ebullient," Levine says. And, he adds, the atmosphere in China is in tremendous contrast to that in the Soviet Union, where he has traveled a couple of times.

IT'S NEWS TO ME, THE STORY former NASA Ames director Clarence "Sy" Syvertson tells about the first Ames director, Smith J. "Smitty" De France, who died last month. While De France was a young aeronautical engineer at Langley Field in Virginia in the 1920s, he was severely injured when a pilot he was flying with froze at the stick of an open cockpit plane and they crashed offshore. It took De France a year to recuperate.

In the aftermath, he promised his wife never to fly again. Though he guided Ames into the jet age and then the space age from 1940 to 1965, Smitty De France never took off again. He rode trains.

DIANA BOS, ADMINISTRATOR of the Oak Creek Apartments in Palo Alto on Willow (soon to be Sand Hill) Road, wants Peninsulans to know Oak Creek's name is not going to change, no matter what feeble quips you read here last week. Same goes, no doubt, for the Willow Bend Apartments and Willow Pond Apartments, both in Sunnyvale.

Railriders jury still out on new CalTrain commute cars

THOSE SLEEK CALTRAIN CARS have been rolling on the Peninsula long enough now to be part of a commuter's humdrum routine, but for one fact. A lot of the real heavy-duty commuters haven't ridden one yet.

California Avenue, my station for about six months a while back, buzzes with activity every morning roughly from 7 to 7:30. Well, not constantly — swarms appear near every train time. People materialize out of the morning mists, up from the subway, through broken fences, down the tracks, out of parked autos where they were listening to radios, and also on the run out of cars that have just screeched to a stop.

Train 37 from Calif. Ave. to The City leaves at 7:15 (no wonder it pulled away without me so often — I thought it was 7:17) and makes just four stops, reaching San Francisco in 48 minutes, if all goes well. Its homeward-bound counterpart is true express — SF to Calif. Ave. non-stop in 36 minutes (again, if all goes well), 5:15 to 5:51 p.m.

So, I asked some former fellow travelers, how are the new cars? Allan Wentworth of Los Altos said he hadn't been on one yet. But he'd heard of a good: Their steps are four or five inches higher than on the older double-deckers (and in Menlo Park the pavement has been built up to compensate).

Carol Casey Gelatt of Mountain View, who was taking the 7:29, hadn't ridden one either. She pronounced commuting unchanged this year.

Then came the San Jose-bound 7:31 and, voila, it was all made up of the magic cars. One young woman who declined to be named, evidently because she felt she wasn't a thoroughly qualified commuter yet, said they weren't quite as leg-roomy as the other double deckers.

The northbound morning stop-at-every-station runs begin with the No. 43, which reaches California Avenue at 7:40. By then most of the commuter crush is over; the later passengers are students, part-time workers, shoppers, people with special business. For now, they're the experts on the new cars, they and those who work late. Technological innovation takes time to filter down to the masses.

AT THE MENLO PARK CHAMBER of Commerce, which is the flip side of the Menlo Park train depot, strong opinions were pronounced by a couple of non-riders. Mary Martin and Estelle Tobias of the chamber staff say the whistles on the new locomotives are about 10 decibels louder, and are blown more often. Perhaps the engineers are behaving like kids with new toys; folks awakening angry will scold them, 'cause mama don't allow no whistling where there ain't a grade crossing 'round here. Hey, could the Air Pollution Control District get us those 10 decibels back?

Commuters are connoisseurs of light baggage — attache cases, brief cases, umbrellas, backpacks, shoulder bags. Carrying two such pieces is common, and three not rare, particularly for women in rainy season. Sometimes you see interesting special cargoes: art work in outsize portfolios, bulging file boxes, folding bicycles.

MOST RAILRIDERS SEEM TO have found a niche they want to fill time after time. They always want to be near the front, or in a middle car, or in the smoker, traditionally the car nearest San Jose. But only on the older double-deckers, for smoking isn't permitted on the new, carpeted Sumitomos. This may never rate a special symbol on the timetables, for all the older cars are scheduled to go out of regular service by next spring.

Bob Halligan at Caltrans says they're getting some flack from heavy-habit smokers, who'd been squeezed down to half a car, and some favorable comment from smokers who say they can do without for the length of a ride, along with praise from the non-smokers who almost suffocated in the other halves of the smoking cars.

Getting back to commuter behavior, some clearly are strategists, engineering their choice of seats for efficiency and a place near the head of the bus line. Others tend more to comfort, and seek a place to be warm or cool or to snooze undisturbed. All in all, they are a patient lot.

Newspapers should love commuters; they read as thoroughly as the ride allows. Some favor books, usually paperbacks; others, magazines. Scholars keep their noses in tedious-looking tomes.

THE SINGLE-DECK CARS that the Sumitomos replaced are, Halligan says, finding a ready market as museum and collectors' items. Amazing! Anyone who has had to ride them through the hot and cold seasons could only say good riddance. In the winter their doors blew open, admitting icy drafts; in the shortest days, six months from where we are now, their lights dimmed off at every station stop. In summer, they could be stifling. Harrimans and Coolidges, they're called, and Halligan says train buffs who missed the sentimental last ride a week ago are clamoring for another.

While rolling, the commuter's world is a narrow one. But perhaps split vision fits better than tunnel vision, for the commuter lives as a citizen of two cities, but takes part less than fully in either one.

The Rev. Canon Roswell O. Moore told me he used to chide some members of the flock at Holy Trinity, Menlo Park, when he was rector there because as commuters they failed to pay enough heed to local affairs. Ros is a commuter himself these days, plying the skyways from Los Angeles to Spokane in a new ecclesiastical assignment. Somewhat sheepishly, he concedes that he has lost a lot of his local focus.

Ours just may be the best set of libraries in the U.S.

WHAT SMALL CITIES CLUSTERED within a 12-mile radius have the best, and best-used, set of public libraries in the nation? Answer: The mid-Peninsula's.

Unhappily, this claimant can't prove it, even quantitatively; too many apples and oranges mess up the statistics. Quality calls are subjective — and I'm biased. But it's still true, whether you take a tight circle from Mountain View to Woodside, or one encompassing Sunnyvale, with its patent section, and San Mateo, with its business specialty.

Before shutting out the neighbors and focusing on Santa Clara County's fine city and county branch libraries, let's mark the fact that south San Mateo County has thriving libraries too, obviously in Menlo Park and Redwood City but also in East Palo Alto, Atherton, Portola Valley and Woodside, where the branches boast special materials, respectively, on black studies, gardening and local history, travel, and horsemanship.

The Menlo Park and Palo Alto libraries have what **Janet Rafferty**, chairperson of the Menlo Park Library Commission, says is the only inter-county arrangement she knows of. Palo Alto library card holders may obtain Menlo Park cards, and vice versa.

Karen Fredrickson, Menlo Park city librarian, said the cooperation with Palo Alto is "not unbalanced." Some Palo Altans who live near San Francisquito Creek find the Menlo Park library closer for them. Others are "library junkies."

What's the attraction? For one thing, Menlo pioneered bringing in microcomputers and software, and offering introductory computer classes.

THE PALO ALTO AND MOUNTAIN VIEW libraries offer a study in contrasts of two routes to excellence. Palo Alto's impressive system grew up decentralized, with a Main Library and five branches: Children's, Downtown, College Terrace, Mitchell Park and Terman. Mountain View, by policy, maintains a strong central library and uses a bookmobile to serve neighborhoods (and a new one will be on the road in a few months).

Ruth Stilwell, Mountain View city librarian, says library usage is "exceedingly high" in Santa Clara County. Past patronage levels have been lifted, she explained, by people going to school year-around and by the high proportion of adult professionals who continually pursue interests such as computers, hobbies, music and art.

Stilwell considers Mountain View strong all around, but when pressed for specialties she named American history, cooking, auto repair, office management and classical music.

In an experiment under way for a month, a terminal is available for the public to access the automated circulation system.

MARY JO LEVY, Palo Alto director of libraries, pointed out that the Peninsula has no lock on good libraries. The Pike's Peak Regional Library System in Colorado was the first to computerize fully, has transit and class schedules hooked in and won an expansion OK from voters. Iowa City's system is famed for audio-visual and cable TV activity.

Palo Alto has been in the process of computerizing its catalog since 1978. Circulation operations are automated, and usage is "really phenomenal" (12 items per capita per year circulated, as against 7 in 1920), which Levy attributes to the high educational level. The Main Library staff gets a question a minute.

She regards branches as important in affording public access, especially for kids. She believes Terman area youngsters used the libraries less than peers in other neighborhoods until their branch opened four months ago.

The Main Library houses the Palo Alto Historical Association's collection. Other than that, Palo Alto claims no specialties, but will admit to having good periodicals and back files, and a very fine program for children. Many users are men and women who work but do not live in Palo Alto.

Microcomputers have been available at the Main and Children's libraries for four years now. An IBM PC-XT has just gone in at Mitchell Park.

Levy said candidates for staff posts are being judged more and more on interpersonal as well as library skills. The old "Shhhh!" image is out.

Stilwell noted that the perception of a library as a place where housewives checked out light reading is dead. Libraries are viewed today as information centers, and users expect — nay, demand — data bases and up-to-date resources.

THE ONE LIBRARY up against it right now is the Los Altos Regional Library, a county branch which **Carol Tefft** supervises. Starting in August, the Main Library on San Antonio Road will be closed Fridays and Sundays, and the Woodland branch will cut back to 26 hours a week. Tefft hopes a measure will go on the November ballot to give Los Altos and Los Altos Hills voters a chance to bail the library out with a five-year special tax.

Los Altos has "very heavy" usage, according to Tefft — 18 items per capita per year, the highest of eight Santa Clara County branches. Its strong suits are travel, business and investments (including newsletters), consumer information and mysteries.

Children make up one-third of the use by gate count, children's librarian **Molly Wright** said. Kids in the Summer Reading Club who read any 10 books attend a party and are given a new paperback, courtesy of Friends of the Library. And there'll be contests with bubblegum, peanuts and (market conditions permitting) watermelons.

Active Peninsula retirees will take on new territory

SIRs, THE PENINSULA's gift to retired men, is about to bust out of Northern California. Next stop: Lacey, Wash. (near Olympia): Soon: Southern California, Oregon and Nevada.

The full name is Sons In Retirement Inc. So far, that name is being protected by the Northern California organization, which extends to Redding, Placerville and Fresno but mainly is concentrated in the greater Bay Area. Lacey will be Branch 1, Sons In Retirement-Washington, according to **Park Learned** of Menlo Park, area governor (and state board member) for Area 16, the Peninsula.

Learned expects SIRs to go national, and its growth record supports his view.

It all began in San Mateo in spring 1958 with four guys at the Elks Club. When they had eight, they formed what's now known as Branch 1.

IN THE 27 YEARS SINCE, SIRs has grown to 28,127 members and 127 branches, up 4 percent in the past two years — not bad for a gang averaging age 75 and subject to attrition. Branch 5 (Palo Alto) has 500 members; Branch 35 (Los Altos, Mountain View and Sunnyvale), 400 members; Branch 51 (Menlo Park, Atherton, Portola Valley), 250 members, and the larger two have waiting lists.

To join, a man must be fully retired and have a member-sponsor. There is no initiation fee and no dues, although a hat, pitcher or bucket is passed at the monthly luncheon and everyone puts in $1. Most SIRs were middle managers, executives or professionals, but the occupational range is broad and the outfit is democratic, unless you deem Area 16's dress code (shirt, tie and jacket) autocratic.

Area 16 branches hold lunch on various Wednesdays at the Palo Alto Hyatt (still the Cabana to them). The presidents, titled "Big Sir," are **Thomas McElwrath** of Palo Alto, Branch 5; **Ed Gravenhorst**, who recently moved to The Villages in San Jose (where there are two branches), Branch 35; and **George Simpson** of Menlo Park, Branch 51.

WHY SIRs? Dr. **Elmar Siegel** of Palo Alto quotes a noted physiologist: "There are two types of retired people — the active and the dead."

"You've got to be active," Siegel adds, "but you should be doing what you enjoy doing."

Stan Chernack of Los Altos, who belongs to a dozen organizations, says he enjoys this one most — it has no cause, it just helps its members have fun and relish "the dignity of retirement."

The SIRs enjoy a lot of things. A branch may have activity groups for golf, bowling (indoor and lawn), bridge, dominoes, photography, computers, history, travel, fishing, gardening or singing.

Golf brings up a SIRs joke **Al Condon** of Los Altos tells. A good, older golfer is having eye trouble and keeps losing the ball. The club pro hears about it and says to him, "Hey, here's an old-time SIRs member who has the eyes of a hawk. Take him around and he'll follow the ball for you, and you can help him with his game."

Off they go and at the first tee, the ace makes a long drive. "Great hit," his companion says. "Where'd it go?" the weak-eyed one asks. His buddy hangs his head and answers, "I forget."

SOME ACTIVITY GROUPS span several areas. For instance, the Civil War Roundtable of SIRs meets in San Carlos, pulling from the Peninsula and the East Bay. It started, says **Paul Beveridge** of Palo Alto, its president, back in the early '70s when the San Francisco Presidio Civil War Roundtable (not an SIRs unit) "got overstocked with Confederate sympathizers."

Sometimes the talk is of Civil War events. In June, secretary-treasurer **Fielding McDermon** of Portola Valley covered battles in Missouri, and a while back **John Beahrs** of Palo Alto (an Iwo Jima beachmaster in World War II) showed slides of visits to Civil War battlefields. One member with strong credentials is **Ed Guilford** of Belmont, grandson of Gen. George G. Meade, the victor at Gettysburg.

CHERNACK IS IN HIS eighth year as Branch 35 program chairman. A big carrot he dangles in attracting speakers is an audience of at least 300, a crowd that can put out a rousing standing ovation. He tries to keep the schedule open so he can exploit hot new topics. Sports, business, Stanford Medical School, the Hoover Institution, SRI International and the Veterans Administration Hospital are heavy providers. **Leonard Koppett**, Times Tribune editor emeritus, is a SIRs favorite, Chernack said.

No-nos are speeches on politics, religion or investment or other sales pitches. "If they (the members) don't have those things taken care of now, they'll never do it," Learned says. Congressmen may be invited if they pledge not to breathe a word of partisan politics. A nun addressed Branch 35 once, but it was on the odds in gambling.

One more SIRs joke, this one from Siegel:

A retiree is given a dinner party and a gold watch. "We have one more thing for you," his company's president says. "It's a thorough physical exam. Be sure and take it — it's well worthwhile."

So the he takes the physical. Then the doctor asks, "How old are you?" The answer is 73. "You're in wonderful shape," the doctor says. "Your vital signs are those of a man in his late 50s or early 60s. What'd your father die of?"

"Who said my father died? He's 94 and in great shape, in fact he's getting married next week."

"Why would a man 94 want to get married?"

"Who said he *wanted* to get married?"

How Doni Hubbard became an expert on horse trails

Ward Winslow

HORSE PEOPLE THROUGHOUT the mid-Peninsula will be interested to know that **Doni Hubbard** of Los Altos Hills has published a new trails book, her second. It is titled "New Trail Adventures for California Horsemen."

For the region at large, the book's main dish is its rundown on the not-yet-completed Lake Tahoe Rim Trail in California and Nevada, a 10-day ride that Hubbard has broken into one-day chunks. There also are fine sections on trails in the Wine Country, the Gold Country and the East Bay. But for Peninsulans, the central attractions have to be her accounts of four San Mateo County trails (Skyline, from Wunderlich to Huddart County Park; Pescadero Creek County Park; and two in permit-required San Francisco Water Department lands, Ridge Trail and Filoli Trail) and eight in the Mid-Peninsula Regional Open Space District, plus four more nearby in the Santa Cruz Mountains.

Excellent maps by **Deborah Young** detail each trail, and in the back of the book, a second copy of each map comes with a perforation, so the rider — or hiker — can tear it out to take along. (Credit that good idea to Hubbard's husband, **Sid**.) The book itself is enhanced by the outstanding craftsmanship of editor **Walt Peterson** of Los Altos Hills, the retired Stanford University publications ace.

"New Trail Adventures" is dedicated to the memory of Doni Hubbard's father-in-law, **Wesley L. "Bud" Hubbard**, with the words: "He blazed the most important trail of all, the example of a good life." Bud was the Hubbard of Hubbard and Johnson, a lumber and hardware firm no longer in the family, and served, like his father before him, as a Santa Clara County supervisor. His widow, **Bea**, one of Palo Alto's great ladies, is spending a busy summer keeping her eye on 13 grandchildren.

HOW DONI HUBBARD CAME TO BE the region's leading authority on trails is as good a story as her books. Like many girls, she was horse crazy, and her father, who traveled a lot, once promised her a steed. When she was big enough, she demanded that he pony up. It was a big family and times were tough, so he gave her a library card instead and told her to read all about horses. Disappointed but game, Doni devoured every book on horses in the Palm Springs library. It got so the librarian called her when a new one came in.

Years later, Doni was serving on the Mountain View Environmental Planning Commission when her daughters, **Vallee** and **Audrey**, reached the horse-struck age. That rekindled Doni's own old ardor. So the three of them joined 4-H and later were given a horse. Doni, who had been a history teacher and remained library conscious, then searched for books about trails — and found none. So she did field research for a couple of years, then wrote the book herself. In the course of publishing "Favorite Trails of Northern California Horsemen" in 1980, she set up her own "one-horse" publishing company, Hoofprints, in Redwood City.

SELF-PUBLISHING IS A TRIAL as stiff as any trail competition, Doni found. In doing an advance sale on the first book, she promised it by June 15, 1980 — a pledge that turned Peterson pale when he heard of it. In the end, they missed by only three days. Doni had half the book written when she realized she was indulging herself in flowery prose, so she cut back the description to the basic information a busy horseman would want. She spent hours in the saddle, checking and rechecking.

This time she was cannier. When Doni discovered printing costs had gone up by 250 percent since 1980, she sold a few pages of advertisng. To cover more ground more thoroughly and save wear and tear on herself, she hired six "research riders" and used a questionnaire to be sure she got the information she needed. She also studied photography at Foothill College to improve the many pictures she took herself. **Charlotte MacDonald** of the open space district contributed numerous photos, too.

THE FIRST BOOK featured personalities related to the trails described. There's also no lack of sketches this time — one nifty one is on **Lewis Reed**, mayor of Woodside and trail boss for San Mateo County horsemen; another is on **Carolyn Lekburg** of Sunnyvale, president of the Midpeninsula Trails Council. However, in the new book the accent is on organizations active in the field — and their number is amazing. Doni salutes as "trail patrons" the San Mateo County Parks Department, Los Altos Hills Horsemen's Association, Los Altos Trails Club, Palo Alto Horsemen for Trail Preservation, the Horsemen's Associations of San Mateo and Santa Clara counties, six other Woodside-based trail users' groups (Los Viajeros Riding Club, Happy Hoofers, Woodside Trail Club, Mounted Patrol of SM County, Los Altos Hunt Pony Club and Woodside Pony Club), Midpeninsula Trails Council, Peninsula Open Space Trust, the Midpeninsula Regional Open Space District, Sempervirens Fund and lots of others.

There's also emphasis on overnight trips and on something old that has become something new — carriage driving. Not every trail is wide enough for carriages, but many are. Antique lovers are after buggies these days. There's a Peninsula Carriage Driving Club, based (where else?) in Woodside.

One more feature of the book ($19.95 at saddle shops, Kepler's and Printers Inc.) is a listing of "fun, sport and public service" trail-riding outfits. There you can learn that some Triathlon fans are substituting an 18-mile horseback riding course for the swimming portion of their grueling pastime.

The 'Japanese Legacy'

HEART MOUNTAIN, WYO., is a place few Americans remember ever having heard of. It takes a long time to find it on a map, as far north as Yellowstone National Park but to the east, a bit north of Cody, Buffalo Bill's town.

To a select group of Santa Clara Valley people, mention of Heart Mountain must stir bitter memories, perhaps accompanied by a few pleasant personal recollections, for even in a horrible place some of life's sweeter side persists. Heart Mountain was the relocation center where the Valley's Japanese-Americans were sent in 1942. Despite the desolation, heat, cold (the mountain tops 8,100 feet) and wind, they managed to farm the place, and — most of them — to survive.

During the Labor Day holiday weekend, there will be a Heart Mountain Reunion at the Red Lion Inn in San Jose.

ALL THIS IS PRELUDE to some news about a book due for fall publication. "Japanese Legacy: Farming and Community Life in California's Santa Clara Valley" is the title. **Timothy J. Lukes** and **Gary Y. Okihiro**, both professors at the University of Santa Clara, are the authors. A significant feature of the book will be its photographs, drawn from the collections of leading Japanese-American families with deep roots in the San Jose area.

The California History Center at De Anza College in Cupertino instigated the writing of "Japanese Legacy." While Lukes and Okihiro were raising funds, the project grew in scope to include a photographic archive, a 20-minute videotape and a curriculum package for use in schools. So quick-on-the-uptake school systems soon will be able to give their students a fascinating glimpse of the past, and with it, let's hope, some sense of the gross injustice committed when those hard-working folks, nearly three-quarters of them United States citizens, were shipped off to Tanforan or Salinas, and thence to Heart Mountain, or another bleak, guarded camp.

I remember going down to the California Avenue district, probably to the **Page Mill Methodist Church** (which had to be put in mothballs, so to speak, when its Japanese congregation left) to see a busload of Paly High classmates and their families off for Tanforan. The sadness was acute, and is easily revisited. The shame did not come until much later, with the realization that I'd never traced what happened to good friends like **James Saito**, a senior who played lightweight basketball and sang in the choir and wrote wildly patriotic letters to the editor of the Palo Alto Times.

PUBLICATION OF THE BOOK was made possible by grants of $3,000 for research from the American Association for State and Local History, an agency of the National Endowment for the Humanities (NEH); $1,000 from the Sourisseau Academy at San Jose State University for manuscript preparation; and $7,500 for the dissemination of information generated by the project; and $4,250 in challenge match funds from the California Council for the Humanities and the aforementioned NEH.

At a luncheon at SCU in June, arranged by the History Center, additional funds were raised from Japanese-American societies. (More funds are needed, and more photos are sought.) Rep. **Norman Y. Mineta**, D-San Jose, a superlative public man, took the lead by plunking in $500 from his own pocket. Mineta has written the foreword. I suppose it echoes his luncheon remarks — that "if history is not recorded, it serves no one's benefit."

THE HISTORY PRESERVED mainly spans the era from 1895-1907 when Japanese migrant labor first reached California, to 1945, when the first groups returned to the Valley from the detention camps. In '45, by the way, a low-key fight took place that should have occurred in '42. Several governing boards, including the Santa Clara County Board of Supervisors and the San Jose City Council, passed resolutions opposing the return of the Japanese-Americans. But the newspapers — the Palo Alto Times, San Jose Mercury and San Jose News — backed the returnees, who got most of their aid from citizens who had long supported them quietly. Some helped to the extent of serving as owners of record of Japanese-Americans' land.

The first workers were men and formed bachelor societies. San Jose's Nihonmachi (Japantown) developed as the place where they gathered in the winter; until about 1920, it was dominated by boarding houses, pool halls and bathhouses.

Then came the women, either as immigrants accompanying their husbands or "picture brides," and with them, civilization. Families put down roots as farm tenants, and produced children who were born American citizens. The Issei were denied citizenship by alien exclusion laws.

Many of the immigrants, by the way, came from the Hiroshima district. Whatever their talents, they were likely to work in agriculture. Farm clusters began springing up around the Valley, each with a Japanese language school, picnics and festivals. They shared wells, tools, horses and laborers, formed buying and marketing cooperatives, and experimented with crops and farming techniques and inventions.

World War II halted their progress. Yet when they could, they returned, only to find their homes, farms and businesses in disrepair or stolen.

About as far north as Mountain View, Japanese-Americans looked to San Jose's Nihonmachi. However, Palo Alto was the center for another cluster. About that, more another time, if the right sources make themselves known.

Council's tune: 'Oh Willow, zip Willow, no Willow'

CREDIT THE PALO ALTO City Council with a final solution to the Willow Road problem: Its days are numbered. Come July 1, kaput!

There should be ceremonies — a burial, or at least a wake. With a chorus of "Willow, zip Willow, no Willow" (and apologies to Gilbert & Sullivan), or a rousing rendition of "They Shall Not Pass."

Willow has a been a public issue for nigh onto 60 years. In the great bygone era of local boosterism, it was to be the Yosemite-to-the-ocean route. Later on a more modest local expressway was planned, but its backers barely escaped lynching.

In more recent years Willow succeeded in tying the City Council in conflict-of-interest knots and has made official Menlo Park-Palo Alto relations about as cordial as those across the Berlin Wall.

The new name has a familiar ring: Sand Hill Road. And it could start a new fight. Until now, Sand Hill has been the exclusive property of Menlo Park and San Mateo County. Lately it has been publicized by Tom Ford's collection of world-class venture capitalists at 3000 Sand Hill.

There is a tradeoff, however. Though it may have to share Sand Hill, Menlo gets an excloo on Willow, save for the stretch shared with East Palo Alto. Let's pronounce Willow tamed. You can ride it from Bayshore in to Sunset, but not much farther.

Along with a few institutions on Sand Hill nee Willow that'll have to change letterheads, this thorny rose by another name will leave many an apartment dweller in nomenclatural limbo. Would you believe the Sand Hill Creek Apts.?

THEY ARE MADE OF STERNER STUFF in Menlo Park, evidently. At the age of 103, Lu Luhrmann, a retired Army nurse living at the Veterans Administration hospital, is celebrating the addition of two new members of the clan. Her nephew, Ken Malevos of Los Altos, and his wife, Madeleine (Molly to almost everyone), have two newborn grandchildren.

A COUPLE OF GUYS WHO STAYED AWAY from the Jordan Middle School farewell party Wednesday, if they knew what was good for them, are Bruce Emmons and Mike Barry. These two recently were honored by the Palo Alto PTA Council for their years of tracking demographics in the PAUSD. Splendid as their work has been, they are regarded as bad news in certain neighborhoods.

One time Bruce joshed a woman who was concerned about selling schools when the future might hold a big new baby crop. Bruce told her that if that happened, it'd be easy to put second stories on the remaining schools. She put him down as a high-rise advocate. Score his a fallen arch remark.

IF ANY REVIEWERS WERE AT FOOTHILL College last Sunday afternoon to see the curtain-raiser of the Summer Festival '85 of the Performing Arts Alliance of Foothill College (pause for breath), they must have missed a crucial note on the back of a news release — a PR sin. The California Coast Opera, which was to do "The Silent Wife" June 2, had to cancel, so the festival didn't open until Friday night's twin bill.

Hey, what's this? Not only has Foothill swallowed up most of the old Cubberley High School campus (and why don't they have a field class in gopher-trapping?) but now the Foothill Festival is grabbing the Jordan School Amphitheater for a set of Sunday twilight Palo Alto Chamber Orchestra concerts in July and August. Actually, William Whitson's PACO has played Jordan often before, but it sure helps to fill out the festival events calendar.

"AN EVENING WITH MARK TWAIN" will be presented by Ray Reinhardt as part of the festival on June 29, and it's a fair bet Mildred Nelson of Palo Alto will be there. The 150th anniversary of Twain's birth (or Samuel Clemens', if you're persnickety) is this year, and Millie, an almost lifelong Twain buff, went to his hometown, Hannibal, Mo., last month to see the raft launched.

She liked the new Visitors Center, featuring Norman Rockwell paintings of episodes from Tom Sawyer and Huck Finn stories, but was disappointed not to see Clemens' "Letters from the Sandwich Islands" among the first editions. Millie is a Hawaii buff, too, and favors her hero's reports from the Islands to his Sacramento newspaper editor.

HOW MANY EDITORS DOES IT TAKE to cut your best prose to shreds? The Rev. Jeffrey Patnaude of Holy Trinity Episcopal Church, Menlo Park, may find out. His article, "Being Parents to Your Parent," is going to make some magazine happy, he figures, if only he can get it trimmed from 5,000 to 3,000 words. There are five editors in his parish, and he asked them to help. Have five editors ever agreed on anything?

ACTUALLY, FIVE EDITORS MIGHT AGREE that students turned out by Barney Tanner, the peerless Palo Alto High School (and before that, Cubberley) English teacher, really know how to write. Barney, the most recent winner of the Palo Alto Educators Association's Sally Siegel Award for excellence in teaching, is retiring this month.

One of his prize products, Sharon Noguchi, who broke in with the Palo Alto Times and the Times Tribune, then went to Japan to work, now is home and deskpersoning for the San Jose Mercury.

'Ghost businesses' can conjure up pleasant memories

MAYBE THERE'S A NAME for them in the terminology of real estate or sociology; if so, that name is unknown to me. I just call 'em ghost businesses.

What are they? You go by the place where they used to be, realize the business isn't there any more and either wish that it still were or experience a gush of pleasant memories.

Take a few recent examples. Mayfield Mall (the whole thing). Werry's Electric Shop and Shirley Cobb Books and the Starlite Super in Palo Alto. Bullock's at Stanford Shopping Center (though Nordstrom is OK by me, and a good place for a quick lunch, according to one dental hygienist who misses the Stanford Barn eateries). Peninsula Building Materials in Menlo Park, a place to go for bricks. Rick's Swiss Chalet. These are just to get you in the ballpark.

SOME OLD-TIME REALTORS around here must be able to cruise down University Avenue in Palo Alto, or Santa Cruz Avenue in Menlo Park, or maybe Main Street in Los Altos or Castro Street in Mountain View, or certainly El Camino Real in almost any town, and look at a particular spot and tell you what used to be there for generations back.

For the rest of us, it's a more subjective experience. What I remember best, for instance, are the landmarks on University Avenue during my World War II high school days. T.C. Christy Co., for one, was where we bought letter sweaters and Levi's and gym clothes, except that for basketball shoes we went to Smith's On the Circle. My mother favored Roos Bros. for style in sport coats and suits. There were two good shoe stores, Zwierlein's and Thoits. Some of the businesses that proved to be survivors — Walgreen Drug, Wideman's, Congdon & Crome and others — were in locations other than they occupy now. F.W. Woolworth Co. is about the only big one that's stayed put.

J.C. Penney Co. used to be at 300 University, where Walgreen's is now. In those pre-plastic days they emphasized James Cash Penney's middle name. It was cash and carry, and your sales slip and the money you presented went in a conveyor capsule up to an office high above the main floor, and change came back. Mothers outfitted their school kids with underwear and knockabout clothes there. Monkey Ward's — uh, Montgomery Ward & Co. was at the corner of Emerson and University, where Cornish & Carey is now, with what seemed like a huge basement. And Palo Alto Hardware — there's one I really miss from young householder days in the '50s and '60s, not only on University but at the San Antonio Center. Eyerly's, too. And the Homewear Store, which was a few doors off the main drag.

LET'S NOT EVEN MENTION grocery stores — it makes Palo Altans too sad. Suffice it to say a flock of good ones existed downtown for decades. And we'd better be careful with restaurants, too, or there'll be tears in some eyes at the sound of Longbarn, John Barnes, Sticky Wilson's, Bennington's, The Old Plantation, Sakura Gardens, The New Orpheum Cafe, Bishop's Creamery, Marquardt's, Bertrand's. Back in the '30s there was an all-you-can-eat place on El Camino in Mountain View, where a squad of Stanford trenchermen held the record for prodigious consumption. Bet you could name a dozen of your favorites that are gone, too. But don't forget, a lot of good new ones have come in.

A look at the Mountain View City Directory for 1955-56 shows that there weren't too many eating places on Castro Street, and of those only two, Andy's Chinese Restaurant and Qui Hing Low, were of Asian ancestry. Andy's is a survivor, and it sure has plenty of company now.

Time was when every town around had a Sprouse-Reitz Co. variety store; those in Mountain View and Los Altos held on quite a while.

THE THING ABOUT A GHOST BUSINESS is that you rarely like what took its place better than your old favorite. The new establishments may be very fine outfits, but they usually happen not to speak to your needs like the old one did.

Apartment houses replaced the Home Garden Nursery at an offbeat location in Palo Alto, on Tennyson off Alma, if memory serves. Home Garden was great for bedding plants and advice delivered in rich Scots brogue. Another in an unusual place, Schmidt Nursery on Lambert, was a favorite for fans of hybridized pelargoniums and other specialties, and what's there now escapes me. Maybe it's that great vegetable stand — or is that gone too?

We'd better cherish places like the Furuichis' Los Altos Nursery and Woolworth's Garden Center and the retreated Roger Reynolds. Why not say a kind word to the proprietors of all the businesses you deem special? — they may vanish before you know it.

It's hard to realize how quickly and how much our demographics change. Mature gardens don't need as many plants as those being pioneered. Grown people generally require new clothes less often than growing people. Remodeling seems to use up less in the way of building supplies than yesteryear's do-it-yourselfing, or is it just that fewer folks remodel?

Times change. Proprietors retire or die. The tides of commerce and merchandising ebb and flow, leaving us staring wistfully at places — institutions, really — that are gone but not forgotten.

Hang in there, Hoot 'n Toot Carhop Cleaners on Santa Cruz Avenue — it won't be the same after you've split.

On the end of summer

SEPTEMBER'S QUICKENING on the Peninsula seems to march right on no matter whether the days are chilly or torrid, and without too much regard for how Labor Day and the almost-forgotten Admission Day (except among public employees who get the day off) happen to fall on the calendar.

The year shifts gears and surges ahead at a revved-up pace. Yet there's a gentling about it, too — a moderation of the harsher ways of summer.

If you are a garden watcher (and one I know tries to count the blades of new grass daily), you see it very plainly. A growth cycle you thought had exhausted itself in the heat of late August suddenly is off on another go-around, with new leaves unfurling and blossoms budding. It doesn't take Indian summer — that's for the harvest in October. All it takes is the shortening days and a faint weather turn to the milder, presumably calculated on a balance of calories.

THE START OF SCHOOL signals everyone to buckle down to the academic-year routine, even if they have no personal stake in school. All is reorganized, schedules are made, the new television shows appear, pro football gets serious. In a way, some of it is crazy. Nowadays, when many people have the option of going on vacation at any time of year, and around here where the summer Coast Range fog keeps most of our days bearable, the summer routine hardly is necessary. No longer do many of us have prunes to pick, hay to mow, grapes to crush or cucumbers to pickle at an unalterable time nature insists upon. Events and activities could be spread more evenly through the year. But tradition rules, summer is for a change of pace, and most of us like that.

The length of the September transition caught me by surprise this year. Having converted to a more demand-driven occupation, I figured the tail end of Labor Day week would be a wipeout, with everyone scurrying to get caught up both personally and on the job. But the next week, the one just ended, seemed to promise fast forward motion. Wrong! Organizing still is in progress; the complexity of today's infrastructures must create a need for more fine tuning. The big thrust is yet to come.

SUMMER'S END SHOWS at the Parcourses too. The gang of regulars changes. Are they there earlier, maybe in order to get to school jobs on time? Or are they just too busy to work out, or to keep doing it at their favored morning time? The day after the first rains, when it almost always gets colder, really drove them away. We who live in the region Redwood City used to boast of in a sign arching across El Camino Real — "Climate Best By Government Test" — are supersensitive to small variations in the weather. Six months in Wyoming would cure us.

Four or five years ago Parcourses, Gamefields and other exercise courses, patented or no, were the rage. Now they are more the province of middle-aged folks worried about keeping their hearts in shape or their weight down. Oh, sometimes a couple will show up — one pair I see tether their two dachshunds to a fence and leg it a turn or two around the track. But the young bloods, the damsels and the guys in the self-conscious grip of early womanhood and manhood, all seem to have taken to spas and indoor fitness centers and the like. Doubtless they look, meet and confer there, but how can they track the clouds and the birds and the squirrel action in those enclosed sweathouses?

Can the outdoor courses be dying? Where I strive to work up to par some of the signs are partly or entirely gone, and a few original parts of the course are missing entirely. What's more, only us obedient types tend to heed what instructions remain. Lots of exercisers simply run. A few find charging up and down the bleachers all the workout they need. Some folks run time after time around the big field but never on the track; others favor the track and shun the field. Still others jog by on the streets or sidewalks.

Herewith, a secret: At that stage in life where the flesh and the willpower keep locking in groaning combat, one may suffer the tortures of certain exercise stations and enjoy the ease of others, but some stops there are that one slyly skips. After all, when you know one pull-up is your absolute limit, why humiliate yourself at the chinning bar?

EVEN AT A CLOSED SCHOOL, or one changed from its original purpose, the playfields get a lot of use. One of the scandals of our time is the trashing of these fine amenities. Sure, some people use the garbage cans provided, while others are littering the place with pop tops, bottle caps, bags, adhesive tape and broken glass. But then vandals dump the garbage cans out. If you've been a good citizen and have done some policing up, the wanton undoing of your labors can infuriate you.

IS THE STANFORD SINGLES Club, sponsored by the Stanford Alumni Association, going in for homewrecking? Recently the flier for their 11th "On Being Single" conference Oct. 11-13 at Fallen Leaf Lake turned up on our refrigerator door, its label addressed to me, with a note from my wife: "Something you forgot to tell me?"

The Singles' headliners are Mel and Pat Krantzler, Mel being the "Creative Divorce" author. Activities include hiking, tennis, boating and volleyball, plus dancing, sing-alongs, bridge and backgammon. The club is rashly promising Indian summer weather. Nevertheless, I'm not going.

Astronaut's show for the home folks

PALO ALTO'S OWN ASTRONAUT, Dr. Loren Acton, will report on his Spacelab 2 mission to the folks at home on Tuesday, Oct. 29, and the 1,000 seats at Spangenberg Auditorium, Gunn High School, may not be enough to hold the crowd.

Acton, a solar physicist and senior staff scientist at Lockheed's research and development unit in Palo Alto, not only will talk about his ventures into weightless telescopy; he's bringing movies and slides of the superheated action on the sun's surface, too. He'll present flares with a flair.

Speaking of flares, Acton has said in a classic mini-science lesson:

"When the sun produces a flare, it is one of the grandest shows in the solar system. A flare can release the equivalent energy of 1 million erupting Mount St. Helenses in a single instant, and produces measurable effects well beyond the orbit of Jupiter. It is, in fact, enough energy to supply the energy need of the United States for 100,000 years."

Acton's appearance at the free program is being sponsored by the Palo Alto Unified School District, the PTA Council and the city of Palo Alto. The fact that the astronaut's wife, Evelyn, was secretary to former PAUSD Superintendent Newman Walker has much to with the school system's involvement.

During the seven years Dr. Acton was training and waiting for his launch, Mrs. Acton left the PAUSD, went with him to Washington, D.C., and worked in U.S. Sen. Alan Cranston's office, and then came back West to help organize the 1984 Democratic National Convention in San Francisco.

Teachers are being urged to invite their students to the program, which begins at 7:30 p.m., so those who want a seat had better be there early.

POLO BUFFS WHO FIND IT difficult to follow the action on the standard 300-yard-long field should be glad to know that a new variety of polo, touted as more congenial to spectators, is being introduced Saturday, Oct. 26, in the Woodside lowlands, alias the Menlo Park outback.

Arena polo, something new to the Bay Area, will make its debut that morning at the Combined Training Equestrian Team Alliance Horse Park, a large chunk of Stanford land known as the Guernsey Field, on Sand Hill Road between Interstate 280 and Whiskey Hill Road.

Vic Thompson of Portola Valley, who'll be one of its first practitioners, describes arena polo this way: It has three rather than four players on a side, is played in an arena 350 feet long by 150 wide, and has four-foot-high sideboards off which the players carom the ball. Spectators will watch while sitting on cars pulled up outside the sideboards. (Bring your own shield.) It's the six-man football of polo.

The maiden match will pit the resident Horse Park Polo Club against the Los Altos Hunt. Two guest stars will be Duncan Peters of Woodside and John Walworth of Pebble Beach. Dr. Tom Harris of Woodside, Wesley Linfoot of Portola Valley, Richard Arnold of San Francisco and Thompson will round out the thundering trios.

The polo action will precede the Saturday afternoon Los Altos Hunt

Ward
Winslow

Club hunter trials, which in turn will herald the opening of the Los Altos Hunt season on Sunday, Oct. 27, with a drag hunt. (It's not called drag because of those red coats but because imported eastern fox urine is dragged around to madden the hounds.)

Robert Smith, the enterprising president of Horse Park Club, has been the leading figure in the CTETA push to heighten the success of California riders in Olympic equestrian competition. On the leased land the club has constructed an outdoor hunt course, jumps, two dressage rings and other facilities. The arena is shared with a carriage driving group. Buggy whips may yet come back!

IN CASE YOU'RE WONDERING what that scaffolding is doing on 101 Alma, the high-rise residential building at Alma Street and Palo Alto Avenue, near El Palo Alto (the famous redwood) and Alma's junction with El Camino Real on the Menlo Park side, here's the scoop:

When 101 Alma was built 23 or 24 years ago, the cement grillwork was not waterproofed. Over the years water soaked in, rusting the iron reinforcing rods and causing the cement to spall. One set of owners found an epoxy injection they thought would fix it, but couldn't persuade enough co-owners.

The place has 99 condominiums, and if you've ever been involved with a residents' association, you can imagine the ferocity of the politics. Several factions were pressing their views. The situation called for a master statesman.

It happens One-Oh-One has one: Fred Eyerly, former Palo Alto councilman and mayor. Fred organized a committee, worked in all the factions, and step by step secured agreement. If you think that sounds easy, consider that the work is costing about $700,000, which means every owner has a four-figure assessment. Bill Bolton quoted more than $6,000 for his medium-sized apartment.

The architect they retained came up with a bronze glass facing that will change the looks of the building quite a bit. The work is running late, and it's feared that the scaffolding, which went up in July, won't be down by Christmas. Meanwhile, a project committee headed by George Swatch, the residents' association president, is eying the work.

Who was who in Professorville: a Palo Alto memory

PROFESSORVILLE, AS A Palo Alto neighborhood, is known nowadays for its restored old houses and its listing in the National Register of Historic Places. But I can't recall ever hearing the name while living there in my high school, college and cub reporter days.

My parents, **Edward T. and Roberta Winslow**, who are in their upper 80s and live in Saratoga now, remember the term from when they resided farther out Kingsley Avenue in the 1920s. And **Barbara Marx Givan**, a long-time resident, told a reporter in 1979 that "Professorville" was a jocular label first used around the turn of the century.

It regained vogue starting in 1969. Prof. **Robert Textor** bought a house there only to learn a week later that the Palo Alto Medical Clinic was planning to build a high-rise hospital nearby. Indignation didn't just nix the hospital — it sparked restorations, got the district's history dug up, and put it on the way to state and national recognition.

Professorville consists of 10 blocks between Addison Avenue and Embarcadero Road from Emerson Street to Cowper Street, and most of its shingle and clapboard houses look better today than they did 30 years ago. Lincoln and Kingsley avenues and Bryant Street are its main stems.

THE BLOCK OF RAMONA Street between Lincoln and Kingsley is the one I can tell about. We moved there in mid-1941, a few months before World War II began. Our house was an oversized bungalow that had been built by **Andrew Allen Browne**, a mechanical engineering professor, and his wife, **Marian**. Browne died in 1906, and in 1908 his widow married a widower, Prof. **Charles B. Wing**, who was famous both as an engineer and a Palo Alto city father, and who had built the first house in Professorville. (The professors chose their district in preference to campus sites with long-term leases, which some felt were unsound).

IT WAS AFTER THE WAR ended that the 1100 Ramona block really coalesced, in my mind, as a close-knit neighborhood.

Professors there were. **Karl Brandt**, who later served on President Eisenhower's Council of Economic Advisers, lived at one end in a large house facing on Kingsley and **Merrill Bennett** at the other, and both were with the Food Research Institute.

Around the corner across Kingsley Avenue lived **J. Pearce Mitchell**, Stanford registrar and professor of chemistry, and a 21-year member of the old 15-person City Council. I mention him only to remind people where Mitchell Park got its name. Actually, my memory picture is of him mounted on his bicycle, pedaling off to the campus.

The other residents weren't professors but they were distinguished. Next door to Prof. Starks lived the **Wilbur W. Boltons**. In fact, the Starkses and the Boltons had bought a lot between their houses and split it, giving each home a more spacious setting than other homes on the street. On our side, things were so close that we and the **Ernest Becker** family next door shared a common driveway which forked at the back and led to tiny one-car garages. Ernie was famous among Peninsula telephone people, for he'd begun as a teen-ager and gone through every system installation.

On the other side of us, after a few years, was **Howard Pease**, a renowned author of boys' books. **Stanley Blois**, who was connected with the Stanford Laundry, lived down the block, and at the corner of Kingsley, in the Marvins' house, **Lucille Nixon** had an apartment. Miss Nixon was the school curriculum coordinator who became big news as the first American not of Japanese ancestry whose haiku won her an invitation to Emperor Hirohito's poetry party. After her death in an auto-train crash, a new school at Stanford was named for her.

AT WILBUR BOLTON'S FUNERAL in April at the Methodist Church, Bishop **R. Marvin Stuart** finished his own remarks and asked if anyone had anything to add. As one of a parade of boys who'd cut Wilbur's lawn, I should have stood up and said it was the block barbecue at the Boltons every summer that really made the neighborhood. Everyone came, including students both foreign and domestic who occupied spare rooms or apartments during the great postwar housing crunch.

His widow, **Besse Bolton**, who in the 1940s established Palo Alto's pioneering preschool family education program, and later studied with Carl Jung, was at the funeral, looking sweet as ever. But a stroke had taken her memory.

All these people are gone from the block, but some are still around. **Lillian Russ**, who lived with us, and **Florence Becker**, the second of two sisters Ernie married, are downtown. **Mrs. Brandt** is at Channing House. My folks rented on the block 25 years before returning to a home they owned in Saratoga. In 1941 they could have bought the Ramona Street house for about $7,000, but loans weren't easy then.

IT WAS A COSMOPOLITAN BLOCK, and it's part of why Palo Alto never has seemed provincial to me. There are lots of other professor-impacted blocks around the mid-Peninsula today, and in those that enjoy the sort of neighborliness ours did, a healthy cultural cross-pollination is going on.

Renovation stirs memories of elegant Cardinal Hotel

IF YOU'D LIKE A PEEK at how Palo Alto's most elegant hostelry of 1925 looked, walk into the lobby of the Cardinal Hotel at Hamilton Avenue and Ramona Street. Use the better entrance at 235 Hamilton.

The Cardinal opened Dec. 13, 1924, marking the event with a banquet for about 250 guests, most of whom had their names published in the Palo Alto Times beforehand. Even before the first guest signed in, one of the seven stores then on the hotel's perimeter became home to the Palo Alto Chamber of Commerce. The Rotary and Kiwanis clubs soon made it their base, and athletic teams visiting to compete against Stanford were quartered there.

The plan for the hotel was conceived quickly, after a rival business group talked of building a hostelry at University Avenue and Waverley Street. Birge Clark, then the city's lone resident architect, tells about it in one of his priceless memoirs, "An Architect Grows Up in Palo Alto." Clark got a hurry-up request for a rendering of the Cardinal-to-be. He squirmed, and as a result, he was invited to join forces with W.H. Weeks, whose architectural firm then was based in San Francisco. Weeks had recently completed the Milias Hotel in Gilroy; the Cardinal was to resemble it, so his sketch of the Milias could be used.

Thus Weeks was the principal designer and Clark was the supervising or "local" architect. The arrangement did not work out to Birge's complete satisfaction, and he records that "I decided that never again would I be associated with another firm of architects unless I was the prime architect rather than the 'local' architect."

Whatever the problems of the association, the result was a good one. What Clark describes as the "Spanish Revival" style still possesses great charm, and the decorative touches — a specialty of Weeks and also of Clark and his father, Prof. A.B. Clark — are of lasting interest. (Even from outside, you can see the automobile coupes carved on the pillars.) The original dining room later became the present Adele's, an antique shop now run by Dennis Backlund, and its art deco ceiling lights and valances are proudly preserved.

The Cardinal opened an era in another respect: It was the first all-concrete hotel built in Palo Alto. In 1925, a hardwood spring dance floor accommodating 300 was installed in the basement, adding $10,000 to the original $250,000 investment.

IN 61 YEARS, A HOTEL endures a lot of wear and tear. Nevertheless, my opening statement about the Cardinal still showing its 1925 elegance is consciously made. Jack B. Power, who with his partner, the late Hugh Jackson, leased the hotel nearly a decade ago, gradually has been reconditioning its 64 rooms. His business plan called for the lobby to be redone in 1985.

Enter Marge Power, Jack's wife, an artist. Looking the lobby over, she saw the possibilities of recapturing its inaugural glory. It was a labor of love for her, and the hotel staff got excited, too, and pitched in. Marge and a long-time friend, Bea Hubbard, researched the Cardinal's history. Then the job of reconditioning its appointments began.

The lobby is very spacious, and the foyers leading in from both streets add to its roominess. A large tiled fireplace with a raised hearth and a hammered brass hood is the focal point. It has massive brass and copper andirons and is flanked by tall, free-standing torchiers of wrought iron, and fat ceramic jugs. A very large skylight is above the area in front of the fireplace, and wrought iron electrical fixtures styled like candle rings hang from the false-timbered ceiling.

The wrought-iron lamps are of special interest because they were designed by A.B. Peterson, in 1924 chief of Palo Alto Electric and head of the business group bankrolling the hotel. The lighting fixtures were made by John Otar, who styled himself The Lamp-Maker of Santa Cruz.

Mrs. Power's key strategic move was to uncover the beautiful small tile of the floor. Then came repainting. "I took the colors from the floor to put on the walls," she explained. Repairs presented a challenge, but in Tony Borgasano of Wrought Iron Specialties in Redwood City she found the man to restore the andiron finials. Getting broken stained glass in the torchiers replaced was easier — an artisan at nearby Wood and Windows did it.

WHEN ALL WAS MADE WHOLE ANEW and the lobby was gleaming, the Powers threw a private tea dance for 130, celebrating their 44½th wedding anniversary and the hotel's 61st. Power found in the city transportation office an understanding employee who provided "Temporary No Parking" signs for the Hamilton entrance.

For some of the guests, the occasion stirred vivid memories. Jeweler Art Gleim recalled that while he was in Palo Alto High School in the early '30s, the Trellis Room in the Cardinal's basement was THE no-alcohol night club in the area — a popular dancing spot. The Harry LeClaires of Atherton remembered using rooms there to dress for their wedding. Polly Hunt Bell harked back to a senior prom in the early '30s. Jean Clark also was ecstatic.

WHAT FIRST BUMPED the Cardinal out of its No. 1 spot was that only about half the rooms had private baths. The 40-cent merchant lunch and 85-cent Thanksgiving dinner of 1934 are gone, but the current room rates of $180 to $200 a week with private bath, and $23 to $23 a day without, make a place that's clean and interesting a bit of a bargain.

Mountain View High and the prolific talent of William H. Weeks

Ward Winslow

KAY PETERSON OF LOS ALTOS, who could do all right with a one-woman campaign if she chose to, is seeking some help in saving Mountain View High School. The school is just one example of the educational architecture of **William H. Weeks** and, as a history activist, Peterson would like to see it preserved after it is sold, even if it is devoted to a non-educational use.

Weeks, who lived in Palo Alto from 1914 until 1917, was exceptionally prolific when it came to schools. One reason he lived in Palo Alto was that he was designing Palo Alto High School, which was first occupied late in 1918. Weeks also was the architect for Burlingame High School though not for Sequoia High, which resembles some of his work. Later he did Fremont High School in Sunnyvale, completed in 1926. By then Weeks lived in Piedmont and had offices in Oakland.

The architect was no slouch at other buildings, either. Credit him with the Hotel De Anza and the Medico-Dental Building at Sixth and Santa Clara streets in San Jose; the Cardinal Hotel, Masonic Temple, First National Bank and the earlier First Methodist Church in Palo Alto; and the Leamington, Lake Merritt, Shattuck and Durant hotels in Oakland and Berkeley. He also designed all the original buildings for Cal Poly at San Luis Obispo.

WEEKS WAS "DISCOVERED" by Peterson some time ago. She is a former schoolteacher who is a headliner in Sunnyvale's history appreciation program. She leads adult tours, sends docents into elementary classrooms to talk about local heritage and can fill you in on any significant historical observations coming up in the region during the next six months. Her hobby is looking at real estate that's for sale. Despite her Scandinavian married name, she is of Yugoslav stock and perks up her ears at the mention of a Yugoslav name. That's how she found out that the Hotel Palomar in Santa Cruz, now a retirement residence, originally was the Hotel Balich, and was designed for its owner, Andy Balich, by none other than William Weeks.

That was trail enough to lead Kay Peterson to Watsonville, where Weeks was headquartered for 18 years up until he moved to Palo Alto in 1911. Watsonville is a treasure chest of Weeks' work. If you've been there you've surely seen the big red brick St. Patrick's Roman Catholic Church, one of his designs. He also did the First Christian Church, which burned to the ground in 1892 before it could be dedicated. Another church was built on the same site to the same plans, and it burned in 1902. For the third go-around, Weeks planned a church made of stone. Even so, fire gutted it a quarter-century later.

IN THE LAST COUPLE OF YEARS Peterson has led two tours to Watsonville to inspect Weeks' creations. The most recent one, with 65 persons in tow, included a stop in Santa Cruz to place portraits of Weeks and Balich in the Palomar's lobby.

At a reunion at Fremont High ten days ago, a group of her tour-goers met to admire the trimmings of the Wigwam Room, originally the library. Led by the principal, Jane Martin, they perused the outside of the stucco building, complete with bell tower and many other decorative touches that charactize Weeks' style: inlaid tiles, ornamental sculptures and wrought-iron lanterns and grilles.

Then the group saw color slides taken by Glenn Herreman of Palo Alto, a retired Hewlett-Packard mechanical measurement instrumentation specialist. Herreman and his wife, Clara, had made the tour. But Glenn also had some splendid photos of Paly High, which could be Weeks' finest school. They bring out design qualities I never paid any attention to while a student there, and the Herremans, both Paly graduates, admitted that they hadn't either.

ANOTHER PETERSON "FIND" joined in the reunion — Harold W. "Bill" Weeks of Los Altos, the grandson of the architect. Bill had lots of boyhood memories of his grandfather, and he explained that *his* dad, Harold H. Weeks, who worked for the firm, had been a painter and after a sojourn in Mexico in 1928-29 brought back many art ideas that were worked into later projects.

Bill Weeks and his brother, Ernest Weeks of San Mateo, originally had planned to work into the firm, but World War II changed all that. Although Bill did not know chapter and verse of his grandfather's projects, he is about to be enlightened the easy way. Betty Lewis of Watsonville, who lives in a Weeks-designed house, is bringing out a biography of the architect in November.

Bill Weeks did bring along a family-treasure rendering of the Medico-Dental Building in San Jose. One of the Sunnyvale history docents, Vaughn Wolffe, a retired airlines employee, was holding it up for the reunion group to see when suddenly he glanced at the sketch with intense interest. In his youth, he said with a grin, he was a steeplejack, and by golly he'd once painted the flagpole atop that building (a high-rise which has a good many floors) and had taken down the metal ball at the top to hammer gold leaf onto it.

Several oldtimers in the tour group took bows at the meeting: Herman Horn, who worked 42 years at Del Monte in Sunnyvale; Fern Ohrt, a docent who'll soon be 88 plus 2; and Catherine Gasich, who has lived in Cupertino since 1905 and was postmistress there for many years.

As for saving the old Mountain View High building, Kay would like to enlist its best-known grad, Sen. Alan Cranston. But she'd welcome leadership from any fellow preservationist.

No one should rely on purported facts in this column without reading the corrections on the opposite page.

Ward
Winslow

Setting the record straight

CONFESSION TIME: I've been gulled. Back in September one of these columns was devoted to the work of architect **William H. Weeks** and appreciation thereof by history docent **Kay Peterson** of Los Altos and numerous students of hers. It ran with some excellent photographs of the architecture of Palo Alto High School, taken by **Glenn Herreman** of Palo Alto, and it said Weeks had designed Paly, along with Mountain View, Fremont and Burlingame high schools and numerous other landmark buildings.

Wrong! Weeks did not design Paly. I have it on the excellent authority of **James H. Stone**, a retired San Francisco State University professor who has gone beyond researching the history of houses in Palo Alto's Professorville district to document the pedigrees of structures throughout the city.

The design of Palo Alto High was executed by a Los Angeles architectural firm, Allison & Allison. Indeed, the choice of a Southern California outfit prompted some local criticism at the time, Stone reported after refreshing his recollection of the record. The critics perhaps were justified. It was near the end of World War I, overlapping the time the United States was in that conflict, and building materials were in short supply. According to files I have checked (belatedly), the new high school might have been left incomplete but for the help of Stanford University President **Ray Lyman Wilbur**. The files don't say exactly what Dr. Wilbur did, but it's my guess he loaned or sold materials from the Stanford corporation yard. Earlier he had arranged for the leasing of Stanford land for the Paly site to the then new union high school district, a precursor of the present unified district.

IN SOME ERAS ARCHITECTS have received great credit, and in others they've been paid little notice, at least in the press. If one were to misname the original architect of Stanford or Foothill College or Palo Alto City Hall, one would hear about it post haste. But the World War I era evidently was more anonymous.

Professor Stone's catch might have been reported earlier, too, but a long trip intervened between his spotting of my goof and his first real opportunity to say something about it.

Other structures have been attributed mistakenly to Weeks, by the way. One of them is the Ste. Claire Hotel in San Jose. That fact is attested by **Betty Lewis** of Watsonville, author of the recently published "W.H. Weeks, Architect."

Stone's specialty at SF State was American studies, and he finds that his retirement pastime research often uproots some neat social history. Buildings usually had permits at the outset, but building permits do not convey the same quality information as, say, birth certificates. Information about a building is often missing, sketchy or inaccurate. The detective work to set the record straight can be fascinating, Stone says.

WHEN HIS REGISTRY of historic Palo Alto buildings is done, it may be kept by the city as a resource, Stone expects. Personally, I hope he'll find all the makings of a book in his research, whether fiction or fact. I hope the same for **Betty Rogaway's** oral history of the Palo Alto school district; ideally she or someone else should put it in book or pamphlet form, the form that will get the most use in the future. Same same for the Stanford oral histories which, **Fred Glover** says, focus on outstanding academic figures. "Profiles in Farmsmanship" — how's that for a title?

It's cause for cheers that **Clyde Arbuckle** has come out with a book about San Jose history in a most readable form, according to reporter **Harry Farrell's** story about it. Arbuckle has been one of those great local news sources that a reporter learns early on to cultivate. His San Mateo County counterpart was **Frank Stanger**. Palo Alto is indebted to people like **Guy Miller, Dallas Wood, Hugh Enochs, Dorothy Regnery** and **Ruth Wilson** for performing this function. **Steve Staiger**, the Palo Alto Historical Association's man at the Main Library two days a week, is coming along well as Wilson's successor, Stone says.

BACK IN THE '50s, both the San Mateo County Historical Association and the Palo Alto Historical Association published excellent pamphlets, usually zeroing in on a single subject and doing it in the round. Stanger was the mainspring for "La Peninsula," evidently, and Enochs for "The Tall Tree." The Chamber of Commerce footed the bill for publication of a memorable 1958 issue of the latter, titled "The First 50 Years of Electronics Research." Both chambers of commerce and historical units seem to have different energies working nowadays.

ANOTHER BOOK MENTIONED in an earlier column is out just in time for holiday gift-giving. It is titled "Japanese Legacy: Farming and Community Life in California's Santa Clara Valley." The authors are **Timothy J. Lukes** and **Gary Y. Okihiro**, both of Santa Clara University. Rep. **Norman Y. Mineta** of San Jose wrote the foreword.

The booksigning and authors' reception took place Saturday at the Wesley United Methodist Church in San Jose. The publisher is the California History Center Foundation at De Anza College and it sells, including tax and mailing, for $18.95 hardbound or $14.95 softbound.

Not yet having had time to read the book, I can't assess the text, but there's plenty of it plus what's likely to be the most celebrated part: fascinating photographs of the Japanese-American community's development in the Valley.

Will the tail-gaters survive a Stanford night game?

CREDIT ANDY GEIGER, Stanford University athletic director, with nerve. In setting the kickoff for the Oregon State game at Stanford Stadium next Saturday back to 5:15 p.m., he is tampering with Tradition in a very dangerous way.

Any trick-or-treater's mother can tell you it's quite dark at quarter past 5 since we returned to Standard Time and darker yet soon after that. Thus the home game will be played under lights — a first for Stanford football if not the stadium, which was lighted for the Super Bowl last January.

Leaving aside the issue of how well Jack Elway's Cardinal squad does under lights (remember the debacle at San Diego State?), Geiger is rescheduling umpteen thousand tailgate parties and probably dinners too. He is discommoding folks who like to go to the ball game to sit in the sun — the evening will call for much warmer garb. He is rearranging a lot of people's Saturday routines. And he'll be sending fans out in the dark to hunt for cars. Take flashlights and reflective vests.

Riskier still, there's a chance that the Stanford crews, unaccustomed to night football operations, will overlook some vital detail. After play ends, Geiger has promised, some of the light banks will be rotated to illuminate the stadium perimeter.

DESPITE HAVING EDITED BALES of letters to the editor over the years, I've written only one. It went, long ago, to the Stanford Daily, complaining of the chaos after a track meet because the athletic department had no one on hand to unlock the gates. Even little old ladies were climbing the fences, jeopardizing more than their dignity.

Why is the game time being moved? For $100,000, that's why. Turner Broadcasting System is paying to telecast the contest, and not only SU and OSC but every Pac-10

school will get a cut, Stanford's being about a hundred grand. Refunds are *not* being offered to the holders of Stanford's 22,000 season tickets, who presumably paid the university somewhere around $100,000 in anticipation of seeing an afternoon game.

Something worse could happen. Wasn't it raining the day Oregon State upset Washington?

EVEN IF IT PROVES COLD and rainy, the game has little chance of matching the Stanford-Army game of Nov. 18, 1950. Walt Gamage, then sports editor of the Palo Alto Times, got all the then-big name San Francisco sports writers to agree they'd never seen a game played under worse conditions. The press box leaked badly, Gamage reported, dousing even the father figure of sports writers, Grantland Rice. Thousands of cars parked around the stadium got stuck in the mud; tow truck operators grew rich pulling them out. Army won the mud bath, 7-0, and the Cadets' coach, Earl Blaik, told Gamage he hadn't seen the real Army team, which Walt took to mean Blaik thought they'd have won by four TDs on a dry field.

An illness later forced Gamage to retire from covering sports, but he's still a regular in the now-glorified Stanford press box, accompanied by his son-in-law, Phil Ferris. Walt and Crystal Gamage's three daughters, Crystal, Carol and Cynthia, who used to hand out hot dogs and soft drinks in the press box, have added three granddaughters and two grandsons to the tribe.

It was a fan of Walt's who suggested this update. Alan Winterbotham, the Dean Witter boss in Palo Alto, pointed out that Gamage was "a guy with tremendous influence on a lot of us at the time when we growing up during the war."

Walt reached Palo Alto in mid-1943 and signed on as the fourth person on the editorial staff in a "temporary" job, which was to last until 1971. At first he had only half a page a day for sports and doubled by cover-

ing the Menlo Park City Council, South Palo Alto Civic Club, fires and whatnot. He remembers going to Mountain View in June 1944 to hawk papers announcing the D-Day invasion.

Gamage played a key role in getting the PALO Club started, and for decades it provided a focus for area sports activity. He fostered intensive coverage of high school sports, too.

ONE NOTABLE CHAPTER in his sports editorship was a feud with the San Francisco 49ers' brother-owners, Tony and Vic Morabito. Walt was close to the players, who then practiced at Menlo College, and he broke the news that they were considering a strike, as his longtime assistant, then successor, Dave Wik, remembers it. The Morabitos blew up, and the good-natured Gamage was banned from practices, press releases, press box tickets — the whole bit. The Niners played at Kezar Stadium in San Francisco then, so Walt — along with another writer who was in the 49er doghouse, the late Prescott Sullivan of the Examiner — wangled press tickets through the S.F. Recreation Department. Wik thinks it wasn't until after both Tony and Vic died that the freeze-out ended.

Nowadays Palo Alto sports writers seem less chummy with Stanford and tighter with the 49ers. Walt was such a favorite on The Farm that he was given the first honorary Block S blanket ever awarded by the Athletic Department, Chuck Taylor then presiding. After all, Gamage originated the Stanford Hall of Fame in 1954 and finally, in 1971, fulfilled his ambition to see Stanford play in the Rose Bowl. Stanford beat Ohio State by 10 points — exactly the margin Walt had forecast.

After serving as a Santa Clara County United Way volunteer for many years, Mrs. Gamage has been working for the charity full time since 1976.

A tape recorder and an old-timer are all an oral historian needs

ORAL HISTORY IS THE NAME of the game and, valuable though it is, it seems to be pretty much an amateur sport.

To do oral history, you need a tape recorder, a source willing to be interviewed and, if you're lucky, the luxury of having someone transcribe the tapes into manuscript for you. If what your interviews produce is worth the effort, it may be edited and find a place in a local or state library.

Bancroft Library at the University of California, Berkeley, apparently has the most extensive collection hereabouts, a treasure trove of state and local history. Some of the Peninsula's libraries, too, are building up volumes of good reading, featuring people who, if they'd had to write it, might never have become authors.

The most concentrated local effort going on is at Stanford University. With Roxanne Nilan, curator of the university archives, and Fred Glover, emeritus secretary of the university, doing the steering, a team of volunteer oral historians is documenting Stanford's administrative history and growth, the effects of changes in the academic organization, and the development of science on The Farm.

As seems typical of oral histories, the Stanford project is skimpy on funding, long on material.

MORE OF A ONE-WOMAN SHOW is in progress in the Palo Alto Unified School District, where Betty Rogaway, retired director of the pre-school programs, is doing the district's oral history as a hobby. It's a good thing, too, because she already has taped conversations with some past leaders whose voices death later stilled.

Among her subjects have been Lois Hopper, Birge Clark, Esther Clark, Emmitt J. Bohne, Henry Gunn, Harold Santee, Besse Bolton, Ruth Squire Beaver, Ray Ruppel, Tully Knoles and Sally Siegel.

"Everybody has fascinating stories to tell, even if they think they don't," Rogaway said. One she specially likes came from Mrs. Hopper, a former school trustee and the daughter of Stanford's Ray Lyman Wilbur. When El Camino Real first was paved, it seems, the highway engineers wouldn't let cars on it right away. But kids were OK, and they roller-skated from Menlo Park to Mountain View.

The PAUSD is doing the transcribing, and well it might, for the only other records of any standing this remarkable local institution has are the board minutes. Someone needs to go through those and construct a time line, Betty said.

The Rogaway technique is to spend an hour or two talking to someone first, then return with a recorder and a list of questions and do a focused interview. She's been completing about one a week, and currently is looking for people who grew up in Palo Alto a long time ago.

IN ATHERTON, Barbara Norris and Sally Bush pioneered the taking of local oral histories 15 years or so ago and since have been spreading their know-how throughout the Peninsula.

Barbara became fascinated when she sat in on a Bancroft Library taping session with her father, the late Max Schmidt of Schmidt Lithograph. At Bancroft's regional oral history office, she related, Willa Baum has become celebrated for her thousands of interviews. There are series, for instance, on Earl Warren and Ansel Adams.

Whereas Betty Rogaway took a course at Berkeley, Barbara Norris taught herself — though she says with a chuckle that past experience as a PTA president helped her deal with cutting off windy diatribes and steering the conversation back to the subject. She and Sally Bush were involved in a Friends of the Atherton Library old-timers event in the late '60s. They expected 200, but 500 showed up. Taking the cue, they began taping. Among the first were Police Chief Leroy Hubbard and former Councilman Edward Eyre. Eyre's willingness to record some memories opened the door for many other proper Athertonians to join the fun. Still, some residents stood on their dignity and declined interviews.

Jeannette McDowell of Atherton, a former legal secretary, was a great transcriber, Norris said:

Usually library users are given access only to the edited transcripts, not to the tapes. Indeed, sometimes sources restrict the material for X years — that must be juicy stuff indeed. Norris agrees it would be interesting for posterity to be able to hear the voices of community old-timers, but she leaves it to audio wizards to do that work.

Later on Norris and Bush did about 20 interviews in Menlo Park. Norris went on to help Redwood City, and now is getting involved in Sunnyvale and may teach at De Anza College, Cupertino.

MOUNTAIN VIEW LIBRARY has a project titled "Bittersweet" that was carried out with CETA funds in the late '70s, said library supervisor Marjorie Kohn, who edited the transcriptions. Etsuko Uyeda interviewed key figures in the Japanese community, Mary Herrero in the Spanish community and Elena Robles in the Mexican community. Meanwhile, Antoinette Barrientos' talks with Filipino residents were consolidated as slide/tape presentation. A community advisory committee representing the ethnic groups helped select the interviewees.

IN EAST PALO ALTO, Councilwoman Barbara Mouton recalls that Canada College students taped some long-time residents a few years back. Apparently the tapes are at the college rather than in the city, however.

Contractors try to fill holes while the sun shines

IT'S THAT ANXIOUS TIME of year for contractors, developers, construction workers and others involved in building from the ground, or deep under the ground, up. They may be the most nervous weather watchers around.

Contractors are gamblers of a sort anyway. Sometimes they bet their boots in bidding a job; sometimes they face rewards for beating the elements and the disruptions of supplies and labor; sometimes they incur penalties for being late.

Snow, ice and hurricanes aren't big threats here. Presumably, every cautious contractor has an earthquake escape clause in his deal. So it's rain, heavy rain, fairly continuous rain that applies the drip treatment to their weathered brows.

EXCAVATIONS ARE WHAT try builders' souls most sorely, said **Doug Ross** of Ross-Wilson, a Palo Alto contracting firm. Excavations have long drying times. Excavations can turn into mud 2 feet deep after a soaking rain. That takes four days to dry, Ross said, and by that time, it may have rained again.

"Everybody in this business hates the weather, unless he's a skier," Ross said.

Yet, so far this season, it has been mostly Camelot weather, with next to no rain on work days, only on evenings and weekends, Ross said.

His firm is erecting the Garden Court Hotel in Cowper Square, behind the old President Hotel at University Avenue and Cowper Street in Palo Alto. Within days, the slate roof will be fairly complete, though there'll still be some flat sections to fret about, Ross said. The 61-room luxury hotel is being built with a modern steel skeleton. It'll have a Mediterranean exterior with wood siding and complex plaster work — Ross had to hunt up an old-time craftsman to handle the plastering. Prolonged soaking could bedevil that work.

The hotel is being built by a partnership made up of **Sam Webster** of Palo Alto, **Norm and Nan Rosenblatt** of San Francisco and **Irwin Kasle** of Woodside. The Rosenblatts run the Inn at Union Square and the Washington Square Inn, both winners among The City's little hotels. Innkeep Associates manages the properties, and **Mitch Miller** of Palo Alto, the company's project manager for the Garden Court, is sweating out the construction, too. He manages the money involved, and a key part of his mission is to save interest dollars. That takes praying against rain and for an early completion.

A bigger Palo Alto job that could suffer this winter is the 140-unit Stanford housing project at 1100 Welch Road, said **Fred Herman**, the city's chief building official. It is in the grading and foundation stage.

AN EXCAVATION IS nothing but a hole in the ground, of course, and Mountain View has the granddaddy of those. That would be rock promoter Bill Graham's amphitheater at 2400 Stierlin Road, near Shoreline park. **Ron Geary**, city building inspector, said the bowl hole will be 40 to 50 feet deep in most places, 70 at the deepest — and partly below sea level. Pumps already are at work. It is to be completed by spring.

Mountain View has several other winter biggies in the works or about to start. A couple on El Camino Real still are bare ground: Kulakoff-Sobrato's 12-story project at 2400 El Camino, which will have retail shops on the ground floor, offices above and two levels underground, and Hare, Brewer & Kelley, Inc.'s three-story office building at 800 El Camino, also with two basement levels.

Much further along are South Bay Construction's nine office buildings on the old Pacific Press site. An adjoining 250 apartments that Dividend Construction is building on another part of the same site are in the framing stage. Over at the old Cherry Chase golf course, 80 foundations are going in for what will ultimately be 180 townhouses, Geary said.

IN LOS ALTOS, **Al Woolworth** said his Woolworth Construction Co. is close to having the roof on a big wood-frame commercial complex at First Street and Edith Avenue for owner **George Korpontinos**. In the city building department, secretary **Norma Dennison** also is keeping an eye on a two-story office building at Lyell Street and San Antonio Road. Woolworth is doing that one, too, and has just completed the foundation walls. He's sweating out pouring of the basement floor now.

Much of the work in progress in Los Altos Hills involves rebuilding homes lightly or heavily damaged in the July 1 fire. **Dave Linebarger**, the Los Altos Hills building official, said most of the jobs under way remain open to the weather. It takes about three good rains to delaminate ordinary plywood, Linebarger said. Some years more heavy rains than that fall in November and December; in other years, there may be no late-fall storms at all. Let's hope the skies won't empty on the burned-out families. They've suffered too much already.

A drive along Arastradero Road through the fire area still is an eerie trip. Eucalyptus trees with charred trunks and browned leaves now show sprouts of dusty blue-green foliage. Some of the Los Altos Hills folks are unhappy, I hear, because more of the hot-burning eucalyptus have not been removed in a nearby row under Palo Alto's jurisdiction.

ATHERTON HAS JUST a couple of construction sites at risk in the Knoll Vista subdivision on Oak Knoll, off Walsh Road, Building Official **Don McPherson** said. The houses to go up there are in the $1.5 million class. Without landscaping.

Reflections on Christmas shopping on the Peninsula

Ward Winslow

CHRISTMAS is coming, the goose is getting fat; If you don't start shopping soon you're asking for a spat.

But first, a check with the stockbrokers, the investment folks who figure to be having more plums in 1985 than have come their way in many a year. Surely they are loaded with tales of merriment, stories of conspicuous consumption, reports of riotous office parties, glimpses of giddiness in the sedate enclaves of 3000 Sand Hill Road or the 500 block of University or maybe Sears near the plumbing department.

Would you believe it? Nothing but sincere explanations of the market's behavior, hedged guesses at what next, and deference to the whims of Congress and what if anything it decides on tax reform.

Pressed about the mood in the offices, **Malcolm Dudley** of Prudential Bache confessed it was good, that Santa's visit indeed had been noted. **Ric Mauricio** of Dean Witter one-upped Malcolm: The mood, he said, was excellent. Sutro folks weren't available; the next morning's business sections hinted they were on the merger block. **George Dunn** at Smith Barney finally thought of one lady who'd bought a new BMW, but he believed it was because her old BMW had broken down.

Betraying my tenbehindmanship I asked about the investors sitting around watching the action. Hey, there may be a ticker but there's no tape, not that kind of tape. Today it's videotape. You can watch two tickers at once on Channel 48; it's mesmerizing. Mauricio said when he was home sick a week ago he watched the market like a bleary-eyed bull through the wonders of television.

WELL, IF THE BULLS WERE pawing their turf and snorting, the bears clearly had taken over the stores. This is a nation not of free enterprisers, not of shopkeepers, not even of bureaucrats, but of teddy bears. Whole stores are devoted to them. Almost every shop seems to have a few on display.

Is there a companion revival in "Winnie the Pooh" and other A.A. Milne books? What could say it better than: "A bear, however hard he tries, grows chubby without exercise; my teddy bear is short and fat, which is not to be wondered at ... "

What's news to me about shopping doubtless is old hat to most people, for I'm a junior-grade Rip Van Winkle, revisiting haunts not seen in years. At noon of a day approaching the weekend, the action was hot in the food stores and bakeries — ah, those great smelling places — of Santa Cruz Avenue. Specialty shops were getting some play; unseasonal businesses were all but deserted. How many camera dealers can one street support? (The oldest of them, Menlo Camera Shop, still is in its old house, set back from the front line of stores, featuring pictures with Santa and loudspoke music to catch attention.)

The banner-bedecked avenue's lights were barely discernible in the bright sunshine, but it is ready for today's parade. The thought came that here was a little jewel of a place to shop, and that others somewhat like it, yet each with a discrete personality, dot the mid-Peninsula.

Stanford Shopping Center, Town & Country Village, University Avenue, Midtown, Charleston Plaza, California Avenue, downtown Los Altos, the San Antonio Shopping Center, Castro Street, Blossom Valley, Rancho Shopping Center, Woodside Village, Portola Valley — those and others overlooked or never discovered in a lifetime around here all stockpile treasures, delights and nice things that have grown too pricey. If you can't find it within 10 miles of Stanford Stadium, who can imagine it's worth having? The same places are staffed with nice people, prime hours and gridlocks perhaps excepted.

PEOPLE ARE FUNNY ABOUT shopping. Some love it; women in seemingly frail condition summon fantastic endurance for it. Others hate it, and if they can't avoid it are likely to find some refreshing place to lollygag. There are stores like that — places of sheer delight to certain beholders, oases in the rushing rivers of commerce. And then there are the big places that are understaffed with overworked yet uninformed personnel.

The aforementioned George Dunn has a favorite escape from the securities and retail markets. He retreats to Sunnyvale or Palo Alto Muni and dissolves the cares of the day in hitting a bucket of golf balls. When there's a sale in the pro shop he says he looks at the shiny clubs like a kid in a candy store. Maybe he buys a box of yellow golf balls and hands it over to his wife to wrap as what he wants for Christmas.

Certain others don't like to shop — except for selected items that really turn them on. **Eleanor Mead** of Mountain View, who once sold yardage, says she still has $500 worth of materials stored at home — fabrics whose look or texture or price she couldn't resist at one time or another. One suspects she is not alone.

WELL, THE GOOSE IS getting fatter, and I have to do my shopping one of these days. Tomorrow the mercados will be overrun with students home from a thousand, nay two thousand colleges and with workers furloughed from distressed electronics and semiconductor companies for the balance of the year.

Meanwhile, here's wishing you Joyeux Noel, Feliz Navidad, Mele Kalikimaka, and the same sentiment in scores of other tongues. Except, of course, in Los Altos, where one can only say: Merry Christmas! And, Yule Love It!

A father's perspective on Rajneeshpuram

HOLIDAYS ARE TIMES for family reunions, and they take on a special quality when all the family is home, or when someone who has been away for many years rejoins the circle. Both those conditions were met in our family, and Christmas indeed was special.

The return of Wendy, at 28 my second oldest daughter, provided our extra oomph. She had been away for about 10 holiday seasons, first in Poona, India, then in Antelope, Ore. And Antelope's down-in-the-valley sister city, Rajneeshpuram.

Her passport says **Wendy Pushman**, her married name. **Bhagwan Shree Rajneesh**, he of the mesmerizing eyes, flowing beard and, when federal marshals in North Carolina got his knit cap off, unexpectedly bald head, had given her the name **Ma Deva Parmita**, "river of the divine soul." For reasons beyond my ken, she had gone to court in Oregon and had her name legally changed to the *sannyasin* version, usually shortened to Parmita. Now she's going to have it changed back. Call it part of the mainstreaming of the Rajneeshees.

IF YOU HAVE NOT ALREADY taken warning, reader beware! This column is primarily a father's perspective, only secondarily a newsperson's. Hearsay, surmise and speculation are thick. Strain it through your own filter.

First, a disclaimer. I bear no brief for Rajneesh. Whatever allure he has does not move me. Intellectually, however, I could appreciate

Ward Winslow

the youngsters' Walden-style fascination with making Oregon's high desert bloom and building a Utopia of sorts.

Initially he seemed an eclectic guru, borrowing from many religious traditions, turning out poetic essays on assorted virtues for American magazine ads. Being mildly of missionary bent, I was irked by his promising (while comfy in his Rolls-Royces) his hard-toiling followers they'd live in luxury. The free-love bit, not far from what many younger Americans practiced if not preached for a decade or so, struck me as overplayed in the press.

Rajneesh is a true publicity hound, an egomaniac, albeit with a sense of humor. This flaw brought him down. His outrageous statements even after he copped out in a court case he well might have won made it harder for those he left behind. He then fled to Nepal, leaving the commune to collapse.

Perhaps some scholar will explain in time why Rajneesh was able to captivate our kids. I remember the Midpeninsula Free University, which mushroomed in Palo Alto during the 1966-71 protest era, warning: "We'll steal your child." They failed, pot, political passion and all (though many courses popularized at the Free U ended at Rajneeshpuram's university). But a strange guy in funny robes succeeded.

For what it's worth, Wendy was always a goer and a doer, restless as soon as she could toddle. At Los Altos High she was in the biggest baby boom class, and pulled a surprise by announcing scant weeks before graduation that she was finishing a year early. Then she wangled a long stretch of travel, came home, worked hard to buy the next ticket and was off to India. Without denying imperfect parenting, I can say some offspring take charge of their own lives sooner than others.

Strangely enough, the crash of Rancho Rajneesh didn't break the *sannyasins'* hearts, though the thought that they'll never harvest the fruit of trees they planted, or that the ranch's tame deer will be slain, can evoke sadness. Members of the commune, a group of about 200 among four classifications of thousands at the ranch, worked four years for just room and board and left with little but travel-home money. They aren't poor-mouthing, however, and consider this: They are starting out fresh and debt-free. And without any babies born at Rajneeshpuram.

Those who didn't already have marketable skills learned some at the ranch. Parmita, a highly artistic weaver by calling, supervised construction and laid enough carpet to get a piecework job doing that in Southern California. She wishes she'd learned to run heavy equipment: It pays better.

She also was mayor of Antelope when the Rajneeshee council resigned and left the dozen longtime residents to reclaim their ghost town.

It's likely they'll meet some prejudice on jobs and off, but hostility to them tends to melt in face-to-face situations. The commune evidently taught good lessons about getting along with people, though curiously the troublemaking potential of pistol-toting **Ma Anand Sheela** was more evident to us home televiewers than to those on the scene.

Books about it all will flood the market soon, a number of them sympathetic to the bhagwan. Perhaps they'll help us understand. Personally, I hope to see an independent weaver get set up with an eight-harness fly-shuttle loom before long.

The world's best garden

IT'S HIGH SEASON FOR tree watchers. With the leaves gone from most of our deciduous trees in January, their skeletons stand ready for admiration, some with old nests, mistletoe, or birds that perch hidden in more verdant months.

What's more, the saucer magnolia blooms are beginning to burst, acacias are unfolding their dazzling yellow display, and the flowering fruit trees are budding. One, in fact, is beginning to blossom in our neighborhood — it must be an almond.

Marmalade time is here, too. Citrus trees — oranges, lemons, tangerines, grapefruit and their hybrids — are heavy laden, apparently having come through December's long run of cold nights OK.

THE MID-PENINSULA IS a tree lover's paradise. As city arborist David Sandage put it when he arrived from San Mateo several years ago, "Palo Alto can be called an arboretum of the world." Let's add, before parochialism flares, that the neighbors — Menlo Park, Atherton, East Palo Alto, Portola Valley, Woodside, Los Altos, Los Altos Hills and certainly Stanford University — share most of the same tree species, with only fine distinctions.

In "Trees of Los Altos" (1970), editor **Ed Walker**, then Town Crier garden columnist, comments:

"The trees of Los Altos give the city great natural beauty. ... With a mild climate and soil unequalled in fertility, Los Altos is a veritable garden. In this garden is one of the widest selections of trees of any place in the world."

This old 'cot pruner did note one omission: Nowhere in the book are apricots mentioned, though the orchard outside City Hall is an identifying feature of Los Altos. And in the library copy of the book, a reader had caught the mislabeling of a Silk Oak, or Grevillea robusta. Yet the book is noteworthy for good pairing of text and photos.

NO LESS AN AUTHORITY than the editor of the Sunset Western Garden Book, 4th edition, 8th printing, **John R. "Dick" Dunmire** of Los Altos, says it with poetry, as a good editor should.

In the introduction, **Joseph F. Williamson**, Sunset garden editor, points out the special climate and geography of "this portion of the earth," referring to all Sunset's domain, and goes on to say:

" ... The result is a gardening region like none other in the world. For the most part, our climates allow us to grow a wider array of plants ... than is possible anywhere else."

Asked if this applied even more to mid-Peninsula trees, Dunmire recalled that in "Recessional" Rudyard Kipling spoke of Britain having "dominion over palm and pine." Our area, said Dunmire, not only has dominion over palm and pine and thinks nothing of it, but also has citrus and all sorts of other trees — native, introduced, exotic.

Indeed, he observed, we are in an area almost at the intersection between the temperate and subtropical zones, and enjoy the best of both.

BOOK DRILL ON TREES proved enlightening. Looking at "Trees of Palo Alto" (1976), "Trees of Menlo Park" (1972) and "Native Trees of the San Francisco Bay Region" and "Introduced Trees of Central California," the latter both by **Woodbridge Metcalf** of Berkeley, taught me how much I didn't know. For instance, that the Spanish padres had one name for the live oak, *encina*, and another for the valley or white oak, *roble*. Also that I didn't know how to spell albizzia, which shade our yard. (Still don't — Sunset prefers one "z.")

The Palo Alto book, which features color art and easily located specimens, lists 204 trees. Menlo Park's book is slightly less slick than the others, but the research behind it is impressive. Metcalf, a UC-Berkeley authority, did a census of Menlo Park trees, street by street. If you can't name the trees in your yard, you could look it up at the library.

DUNMIRE OBSERVED that local cities may have peaked on tree performance, owing to governmental economies. It's increasingly difficult to get money for maintenance. "The greater the initial effort, the greater the performance, the more shocking neglect will prove," he predicted.

Palo Alto is doing something about that. Arborist Sandage heads a new tree program. It calls for taking inventory of trees in 10 percent of the city each year, removing the poorer trees and replanting. In this, Year 3, the Embarcadero-Hamilton-Alma-Middlefield zone is under study.

After the first 10 years, two areas will be checked each year. New street trees will come from 35 species named in the plan. Magnolias, which have destructive roots, and liquidambars, which are in oversupply, are off the list.

(Tree descriptions dwell on the best features; they seldom say magnolia leaves are almost non-biodegradable or that liquidambars' spiny little mace-shaped pods fall off all year.)

The plan is fine reading, by the way. It should be; in addition to Gary Nauman, the city's urban forester, Sandage and administrative assistant Cathryn Clark, its authors include a set of old pros, members of the Tree Advisory Task Force: **Larry Booth, Joyce Duckstad, Nancy Hardesty, Jean Jones, Erica Prince, Allan Himes Reid,** "garden doctor" **Albert Wilson** and Williamson.

No trees column should skip the jeweled spires of our landscapes, the coast redwoods. Here's another book-drill tidbit: El Palo Alto, the city's namesake tree, originally was one of twins, as many know. One twin's trunk snapped in a storm about 100 years ago. What was new to me was that the Spanish explorers had written of *Dos Palos*. But for that storm, we might bear the name a Central Valley town incorporated in 1935 now sports.

A bough to trees, Part II

TREES MAKE NEWS HERE, as a look at the fat files the Times Tribune builds up attests. Often in this season it's a story and a photo about a venerable giant falling, usually an oak. But the choicest morsels in the file are not about crashes but rather the clashes trees engender, frequently ending in court.

Peninsulans have done battle over trees that cut off sunlight, trees that suffered mayhem, trees felled without authorization, trees they plain didn't like and did something mean to (like poisoning), trees they labored mightily to save.

Rest easy, old warriors, I'm not about to reopen any wounds, with the possible exception of one case with a new development.

So far this winter, storms haven't done much to blow trees down, but we're losing some nonetheless. Blue oaks out in the foothills are dying in large numbers, **Nancy Hardesty** of Menlo Park said. (She's the landscape architect who planned the plantings for Portola Valley Ranch and wrote a book about it.) And in Palo Alto, along Charleston Road, holly oaks are dying from sour soil and blight, Palo Alto city arborist **David Sandage** said.

STANFORD HAS SO MUCH LAND that it's hard to keep track of all the arboreal demises there, but they happen every year due to old age and neglect, according to **Herbert Fong**, the university's manager of operations and maintenance (grounds chief, some call him). Stanford, too, has been losing blue oaks, which are natives of the San Joaquin Valley foothills. Dead blue oaks are not removed when they're out in the boondocks, but are left standing for roosts and nesting, the idea being to leave the foothills as undisturbed as possible. Indeed, Stanford is very reluctant to remove a live tree anywhere. An oak, for instance, must be "a recognized danger to life, limb or property, or dead," Fong says, for Stanford to give it the ax.

Some tree people find Stanford pickier than they would be. **Jim McClenahan**, whose Portola Valley-based tree service is the largest private one around (city and PG&E line clearance crews actually do more), recalls being denied permission to cut what he deemed a dangerous oak hanging over a corral in which romped an extremely valuable horse. McClenahan also has lost some scrimmages over sick trees bordering parking lots.

IF YOU VISIT CITRUS COURTYARD on the east side of Memorial Court you'll get a clear look at the value Stanford places on certain trees. Avocados grow there — large, mature specimens. Seven of them once were doomed as part of a construction project on the Quad, but professors **Eric Hutchinson** and **Ronald Bracewell** defended the trees with great passion and won. The professors said the avocados were worth about $22,000 (in 1979 dollars). It cost Stanford $100,000 to $150,000 to revise the plans and save the trees, Fong said.

Currently Stanford is having trouble with *cryptocline diplodia*, a bacterial organism that is damaging some of its trees, Fong said. Guess where the Cardinal turned for help. To the University of California Extension Service, of course. Farm adviser **Larry Costello** and **Carl Taylor**, a Berkeley plant entomologist, are working on cause and cure.

Meanwhile, Stanford is planting acorns up along the foothills and protecting them with cages and fences from damage by cattle, deer and rodents. Oak trees in containers and acorns are being planted along Interstate 280 and the Foothill Expressway. Indeed, Fong said, Stanford is planting more trees than it loses. How many? A long pause ensued. Then Fong replied, "Probably close to 500 a year."

THE ARBORETUM started out as a very special collection, but it's no longer truly an arboretum like the Strybing Arboretum in San Francisco, Fong said. Just a planting of natives and escaped exotics extending from El Camino Real to the Quad, certainly featuring eucalyptus and palms and some fancy specimens around the Mausoleum.

What Stanford does have that's still very special is the Jasper Ridge Biological Preserve. The university took one neighboring property owner, **Ed Mendell,** to court for using his chain saw on some trees in the preserve where it borders his land, and it cost his insurers $5,000. Now another round with the same contestants is in the offing.

THE BLUE OAKS AND HOLLY OAKS are believed to be dying from weather stress. First there was the drought, then three wet years — two of them really flood years. Sandage, Palo Alto's arborist, gave the explanation I found easiest to grasp. Trees react a long time after the stressful events, he said. Trees do not like change; they prefer steady-as-you-grow. Trees like those holly oaks along Charleston grow vigorously in their adolescence, but when they reach maturity, adverse ground conditions, fungus, pathogens in the soil and the like take their toll.

In replanting street trees, Palo Alto is becoming more sophisticated; Varieties are to be alternated block by block, and account will be taken of the different exposures on each side of the block. Ultimately the city will have not more than 10 percent of any one kind in its street trees inventory.

Though I'm not yet stumped for material, not in our nature-endowed arboretum, here endeth a two-column bough to trees. Let's leaf it at that.

Living in retirement

AFTER THE REV. HAROLD BJORNSON retired in June 1981 as pastor of the First Baptist Church of Palo Alto, he painted his house. Then Pilgrim Haven, the American Baptist retirement home in Los Altos, hired him as chaplain. He's been plenty busy ever since.

Not entirely with the chaplaincy, though that involves preaching twice on Sunday and other tasks. Bjornson also took on denominational work, including visiting retired ministers and missionaries and their widows in Northern California and Nevada.

A 92-year-old Fresno widow taught him what staying active was all about, he said. She believed in remaining physically and mentally alert, so she was (1) learning a new language, (2) writing a book (and doing her own typing), (3) walking two miles a day and (4) playing the piano.

Pilgrim Haven is an excellent institution, Bjornson declares. He quotes his friend, **Rabbi Sidney Akselrad** of Temple Beth Am, as saying it's the best in the area. "It has the plus of compassion that I think grows out of religious expression," both from staff to residents and among 170 residents, he said.

Like most large retirement residences offering health care, Pilgrim Haven has three groups. There are 66 in its nursing home, and about 20 in a group requiring partial care. The rest are like people living in a typical condominium, Bjornson said.

THE SEQUOIAS in Portola Valley is looking ahead to marking its 25th anniversary May 31-June 1, according to **David Taxis**, president of its residents council. The 325 residents have 45 committees to guide their activities. Amazing!

Administrator **Dick Wiens** and Assistant Administrator **Alexa Knight** both are fairly new. Secretary **Marlene Short**, a five-year staffer, said it's noteworthy that residents serve as volunteer tour guides, show visitors their own living units, and talk frankly about how they like retirement-home living. The current waiting period is 8 to 10 years for a single unit and 10 to 12 for a two-bedroom.

Taxis, retired Los Angeles County vocational education director, pointed out that residents who wanted to swim raised the money to build and maintain a $250,000 indoor/outdoor lap pool. About 50 use it and the indoor, 102-degree spa. **Mary R. Gruetzman**, age 100, cut the ribbon Dec. 9.

On March 19, folks at The Sequoias have a date to go see a variety talent show by Corte Madera Middle School students, under **Barbara Schneidermann's** direction. Taxis is proud the seniors are the kids' first choice as an audience.

The Northern California Presbyterian Homes office plans a new Sequoias adjacent to Peninsula Hospital in Burlingame. Portola Valley residents reviewed the drawings and made suggestions.

IN PALO ALTO THERE'S AN unusual service club, the Kiwanis Club at the Senior Center. None other than **Frederic O. Glover**, retired secretary of Stanford University, organized it several years ago. The club meets Fridays from 10 to 11 a.m. **Gregory H. Davis** of Atherton, 80, a former San Francisco bank executive, and one of the few members not previously a Kiwanian, is currently president.

Glover says the regularity of the 24 members is extraordinary. At first, they took turns telling about their careers. Glover was so fascinated he has attended most of their meetings as an honorary member (he's a longtime Palo Alto Kiwanis Club member).

CHANNING HOUSE, Palo Alto's biggie with 265 residents, is in its 23rd year. It still has some original residents, **Mrs. Roscoe Maples** for one. Its council president, **Rolf Eliason**, Stanford professor emeritus of civil engineering, cited redecoration of the lobby, refurnishing of the infirmary and better food service (a big item) as recent improvements. Administrator **Fred Seal** is fairly new.

LYTTON GARDENS is the daytime stomping grounds of one fairly new Channing House resident, **Bishop R. Marvin Stuart**, who has come full circle back to Palo Alto, where he was minister of the First United Methodist Church in its great growth years. As chaplain at Lytton Gardens, Stuart "has helped many people in many ways," said **Lucy Cormick**, council president. He knows just how to deal with depression or grief. As for Dr. Stuart, he says he's having a ball being a pastor again.

WEBSTER HOUSE, next door, will use Lytton 3 at times. Opened in August, Webster House is an experiment in luxury retirement living, and guarantees residents lifetime health care and lifetime occupancy. It has 37 units and is almost full.

Administrator **Barbara Shaw** is assisted by **Bern Ann Abbaduska**, formerly of **Shirley Cobb's** No. 2.

Two residents, **Professor and Mrs. Paul Hanna**, formerly of Stanford, have loaned Webster House pieces from their extensive art collection.

ADLAI STEVENSON HOUSE on Charleston Road in Palo Alto is in some ways an opposite of Webster House, being a low-income housing project with 120 apartments and 136 residents. Its median age is 79 now, assistant administrator **Lisa Campbell** explained, so administrator **Christine Cooper** and the board, which includes two Stevenson House residents, **Grace Harter** and **Carl Law**, are looking for creative responses to "aging in place" problems. These may involve arrangements with community agencies providing middle level services, some perhaps done "in-house," Campbell said.

The Stanford fraternity

EDUCATORS PLAY A FOREMOST role in the community of Peninsula retirees, and Stanford University faculty and staff are perhaps chief among them.

On campus, the continued residence of retired university officers and emeriti professors in their own houses or in residential units sponsored by Stanford creates a close and active community. Former officers such as **H. Donald Winbigler, Harvey Hall, Pete Allen and Fred Glover** often are asked by President **Donald Kennedy** or other leaders to handle special tasks. Winbigler, for instance, heads the Centennial Committee. Glover in recent months has headed arrangements for two all-university funerals, first for former President and Chancellor Wallace Sterling, then for Dean and Mrs. Ernest Arbuckle, both killed in an auto crash.

Years ago, many Palo Altans attended Stanford events other than sports rather closely, the Tuesday Evening Series, for example. Growth on both the town and gown sides made it necessary for Stanford to make its welcome mat less visible, but at certain gatherings a substantial corps of Stanford followers still can be detected.

In quick looks at some of the larger local retirement residences last week, it was noted here that retired Professor **Rolf Eliason** heads the Channing House residents council, and by the way, he's still active as chairman of the board of a Boston-based engineering firm, Metcalf & Eddy. Just as important to Channing House people is the entertainment committee presided over by **Margarita Espinosa,** former principal of Castilleja School. Her unit arranges dances and music and lecture programs.

Academic figures and their spouses provide more than their share of the spice at various seniors' residences around the area.

ON THE CAMPUS, HOWEVER, there occasionally is some bumping and scraping as crowds from the groves of Academe struggle to resolve their varied interests. Put together retired and active faculty, owners and renters, all-U types and those interested in only one department and there's bound to be a little friction, maybe even more than the ordinary homeowners' association creates, which is a combustible mix in my experience. This is helped along, sources say, when Stanford or the Hoover Institution bends some rule for what no doubt seems very good purposes of its own.

The redoubtable Professor C. Northcote Parkinson told us there'd be times like this, with dispute usually centering on a $5 or $10 item. At the Pearce Mitchell housing units on campus, there is a rule that residents' curtains must be white or lined with white where they are visible from outside. It took diplomacy bordering on statesmanship to avert a nasty spat when someone noted that one denizen had put up non-white curtains years ago.

AT LYTTON GARDENS in Palo Alto, back in 1980, there was a lively tiff over stray cats a couple of residents had adopted. What do you know? **Lucy Cormick,** president of the residents council, reports that HUD, the federal department that oversees Lytton Gardens as an assisted low- and moderate-income senior housing project, now says small pets are to be allowed. At this point, only a few birds share space with the 352 Lytton 1 and 2 residents, about 50 of whom are in "community care" status — that is, they need some special assistance.

Lytton Gardens has developed a lot of character. **Janie Johnson,** who is fairly new as administrator of Lytton 1 and 2, says it's remarkable for the broad range of its programs. She is referring to such matters as social services, transportation, vesper services, a link with the Co-op markets, beauty and gift shops and an on-site emergency staff, partly composed of residents, which is first to respond if someone pulls the cord. Johnson also means activities of all sorts.

The adjoining Health Center, often called Lytton 3, takes seriously ill or recuperating seniors and has an excellent therapy department. **Patricia Sorensen** is its new director-administrator.

ONCE I HEARD IT FROM a couple of ladies in a good position to know that cliques sometimes form at large and rather fine retirement residences. "You're in or you're out," one woman remarked, summing it up.

That's a problem for staff and elected leaders to cope with, plainly. Most of the units have at least a monthly get-together, whether it is a mass birthday celebration, a bring-your-own-drinks "sundowner" or some other jolly-up activity. Good therapy, those.

WHILE THE LARGER COMMUNITY may think of seniors as needing help (and at times they do need not only traditional sorts of aid but some inventive new varieties), the larger community would be in real trouble without the help of senior citizens. They provide volunteer power for dozens of institutions: the Veterans Administration hospitals, senior centers, many programs with "volunteer" in the name, boards, churches and so on and on. They have plugged a gap resulting from changing labor patterns, more women working, more families needing two salaries — a considerable drying up of pools of younger volunteers.

Another aspect of this phenomenon, springing both from corporate nomadism and the separation of many occupations from a local community base, has led to a certain graying of organizations like service clubs. Without seniors' participation, some of them might fall apart.

A year with THE cello

MATT HAIMOVITZ DEPARTED Palo Alto for New York and the musical big time 2½ years ago, but his Palo Alto friends and admirers likely will go on claiming him as one of their own for the rest of his life. Duveneck School proudly hails him as an alumnus.

Now 15, Matt appears well on his way to fulfilling his career ambition: to be a cello soloist. He's a student at The Juilliard School, which he entered as a protege of the late Leonard Rose, and several of the world's leading cellists already have welcomed him to their inner circle.

Duveneck's news about Haimovitz is that he has been chosen to use the late maestro Pablo Casals' cello for a year. This honor is given only to the finest, most promising young cellists, as the instrument, now owned by a foundation, is perhaps the rarest and costliest in the world.

A second flash reached **William Ratliff**, Times Tribune music critic, from **Marlena Haimovitz**, the young artist's mother. Because of a cancellation in the New York Philharmonic series, she reported, Matt has been asked to solo with the orchestra with **Zubin Mehta** conducting. The concerts will take place Feb. 6, 7, 8 and 11.

Neither being entrusted with a famous cello nor soloing with a symphony orchestra is new to Matt, but these events represent steps up the ladder toward the top for him. Dr. **Tom Gray**, head of the also-honored Palo Alto schools music program, calls Matt "a real genius." A recital Matt played in 1983 with his friend, pianist **Navah Perlman**, daughter of renowned violinist **Itzhak Perlman**, earned funds to benefit the music program. His charm and poise matched his musicianship.

(Ratliff, who once played french horn, is doubling now as an editorial writer and reviewer.)

IN LOS ALTOS, Dr. **Roger Eng**, the mayor pro tem, is proving adept at catching spears hurled his way and zinging them back at his detractors.

Dentist Eng presided, as it happened, when the City Council took final action in December on a resolution adopting English as the official language of Los Altos. He pulled the item off the consent calendar to allow Dr. **Allan Seid** of Palo Alto, a psychiatrist and state president of Asian Pacific American Advocates of California, to speak for five minutes as an envoy of **Irvin Lai** of Los Angeles, grand lodge president of the Chinese American Citizens Alliance.

Two other minority group spokespersons, **Robin Wu** of Chinese for Affirmative Action and **Enrique Valenzuela** of the Mexican American Legal Defense and Education Fund, were not allowed to speak because they arrived at the meeting after the council had acted, according to Eng.

Seid discussed the episode at length in his group's newsletter, APAAC Alert, under the headline: "Language and Racial Intolerance on the Rise." The item upbraided Eng both for the way he ran the meeting and for his vote for the resolution. After printing Seid's full prepared statement, APAAC Alert said pointedly: "APAAC applauds City Councilpersons **Lily Lee Chen** (Monterey Park) and **Mike Woo** (Los Angeles), who have stood up against Language Intolerance exhibited by the 'official English' resolutions in their areas."

Eng, a founding member of CACA's Peninsula Lodge, wrote to Lai saying, "I hope that next time you select someone else to speak for the lodge," and branding the APAAC newsletter " 'yellow journalism' in its highest form."

"My conduct at the meeting was fair," Eng asserted, "and I deeply resent the APAAC article saying I showed an 'arrogant and indifferent attitude towards the populous (sic)."

Henry Der, executive director of Chinese for Affirmative Action in San Francisco, later wrote Eng saying the resolution and his vote "contradicts the efforts by ... CACA and other civil rights groups to promote and support a tolerant American society."

Eng's response said, "I have been fighting racial discrimination in the way which I feel is best, and that is by joining the establishment and changing the minds of people by examples and not threats. The only message ... Los Altos wishes to send to the minorities is that this is a racially tolerant city and the citizens proved it by voting twice for an Asian-American to be their leader and mayor. Can San Francisco say the same?"

MORE IS INVOLVED HERE than pyrotechnic minority group politics. Seid and his allies are well aware that **Dinesh Desai** of Los Altos, a naturalized U.S. citizen born in India, not only pushed for the Los Altos resolution but now is collecting signatures on petitions for a state proposition on making English California's official language.

The arguments in the Los Altos spat look like rehearsals for a state-level battle. Seid's key contention is that "official English" measures are unnecessary and divisive and won't help, but devoting more resources to language training will.

Seid formerly served, as a **Jerry Brown** appointee, on the state Board of Education, where he and Hispanic friends championed bilingual education.

Eng, a Republican, contends that the only thing divisive is the people yelling about official-English resolutions being divisive. He points out that Asian groups, especially, often have supported schools for training in their mother country's tongue and could as well support intensive training in English.

So a state's responsibility versus individual initiative argument may be shaping up for election year 1986. Some issues are double-edged, so be careful where you grab them.

Killing the carriage trade

Ward Winslow

THE DANCE SMALL BUSINESSES do along our main streets goes on and on. Sometimes it's a dancer dropping out for lack of energy or patience, sometimes a game of musical chairs or changing partners. And sometimes it's ongoing chin music in a sour key about the stupid and unfair things "they" — some power-that-is — are doing.

HOUSE OF TODAY, a longtime fixture on the main street of Palo Alto and, more recently, Menlo Park, will be House of Yesterday a month hence. **Valerie Briggs,** who began working for the store in the mid-1960s and has owned it since 1974, says she's tired of "genteel poverty." She's closing.

"It doesn't pay the rent," she said.

By Briggs' definition, House of Today is one of the last of the contemporary specialty stores. Design Research and McDermott's in San Francisco and Frasier's in Berkeley have folded, she pointed out, and Taylor & Ng is down to one store.

When House of Today left University Avenue in the late '70s, the building it was in had been sold and, Briggs said, the rent was "going up to astronomical fees. Here (on Santa Cruz Avenue) it's not that at all. It's just not making what the money invested in the business ought to earn.

"Times change. Discount stores come up. Department stores hold sales every week. Small stores can't afford to do that." Nor can they make up for loss leaders by what they charge for junky stuff.

So House of Today will be out by March 15. Briggs promised that its final sale, beginning March 1, will be "an absolute beaut."

"I want these ladies to grieve," she said, referring to a devoted clientele, one that demanded plenty of service such as gift wrapping and deliveries. "I hope they really miss us."

Briggs told her senior employees of her plan more than a year ago. They've been finding new niches. As for Val Briggs, she says she'd like to do something totally different.

IF THE STORE OWNER also owns the building, it's a huge advantage, Briggs observed. Frank Mills, who owns Mills the Florist in a two-front building on University Avenue at Ramona Street in Palo Alto, isn't so sure. Mills and other owners of 47 unreinforced masonry downtown buildings are sore at the City Council for ordering them to make costly earthquake-proofing surveys on their buildings by a relentlessly approaching deadline, or face a fine of $500 or a jail term.

Mills and his father, **Herbert Mills,** moved into their now-prime location in 1960, when Frank says the building had stood empty for a year and it was generally thought that downtown had been killed by the Stanford Shopping Center. They bought a few years later and remodeled extensively in 1970, just before earthquake standards of the 1973 building code, now deemed minimum, were enacted.

Frank Mills once wrote out a statement to the council that ended, "If you leave it alone it'll be here when we're dead and gone." He never made the speech — too many of the other 12 University Avenue owners involved got the floor first.

"Buster," as Frank was known in his Paly High days, when he was a devastating hitter in baseball and pound for pound as hard-charging a back as the Vikings ever had, speaks with a sense of history on the issue of downtown survival. Members of his family have been purveying plant materials to Palo Altans since his grandfather started in 1903.

In his souvenir-laden upstairs cubbyhole office Frank jokes about putting up a sign a friend gave him. It reads: "This Building is Not Earthquake-Approved. Enter at Your Own Risk."

Restaurateur **Fred Maddalena** is taking that risk, in a way. He's redoing the place next door, part of Mills' building, as Cenzo's Italian Family Restaurant. It'll open in March, and Maddalena promises inexpensive family-style meals.

CLOSING OUT SOON, like House of Today, is Agapanthus in Menlo Park's Sharon Heights shopping center. Owner **Marjorie Martin** wants a respite after 15 years at it — indeed, she's going skiing as soon as possible. Agapanthus specialized in fine china, crystal and antiques, almost all imported and very expensive. Martin found her location pretty quiet. Is the carriage trade's axle busted?

ON MAIN STREET in Los Altos, Expressions is preparing to close Feb. 28, but expecting to reopen in May across the street in the boys portion of Young Villagers.

The moving task of the three owners of Expressions — **Mary Bourquin, Pat Casterson** and **Claudia Davis** — is complicated because they rent display spaces to about 50 artists and craftspeople, who must store their own stuff for the nonce and move it later.

One artist-renter is **Pat Hayes,** an original owner who sold her share to Davis three years ago.

Expressions is moving, Davis said, because it lost its lease after almost 10 years. One advantage the owners see is that they'll have about the same space in the other building, but with skylights, and more Main Street display windows.

Moving toward assisted suicide

HAS IT EVER OCCURRED TO YOU that someday you might want to end your life for what to you are very compelling reasons, and to be assisted in carrying out that decision?

The issue clearly is not one most of us dwell upon often. But there are people who think about it, perhaps because of their own advancing age and ills, more likely because they have seen parents, spouses, friends and other kin endure the degrading fate of clinging to life as helpless "vegetables."

On Feb. 23, about 160 such thinkers gathered at the Palo Alto Unitarian Church to take the first mass step in forming the Peninsula Chapter of the Hemlock Society. **Derek Humphry**, executive director of the Los Angeles-based national society, was on hand to illumine the issue, encourage the organizers and sell memberships and books.

Jean Holmes Gillett of Palo Alto organized the meeting. She is temporarily heading the steering committee, for which 20 volunteers signed up.

RETURNING TO THE BIG CASINO question, the talk by Humphry spelled out where the Hemlock Society (named for the poison brew Socrates quaffed to kill himself) stands. It bills itself as "supporting the option of active voluntary euthanasia for the terminally ill."

Earlier, two New York-based societies led the way in promoting passive voluntary euthanasia through such devices as the living will and the durable power of attorney, both now widely accepted. The Hemlock Society believes in the passive way where appropriate, Humphry said, but goes beyond it to champion an individual's right to actively opt for death. The society's drive is to get assistance legally and morally for voluntary euthanasia.

Humphry, a former journalist, helped his terminally ill first wife, Jean, take her life in Britain a decade ago. He has written a book about that, "Jean's Way." Another called "Let Me Die Before I Wake," a how-to book on suicide, has sold 62,000 copies.

If anyone complains about the circumlocution in "option of active voluntary euthanasia for the terminally ill," Humphry grants the criticism is just. He doesn't mind saying "assisted suicide" or "accelerated death." But he sums up Hemlock's intent as "law reforming, not law breaking."

SUICIDE IS NOT AGAINST THE LAW in California and many other states. Assisting a suicide is. The society aims to remove the latter criminality.

Holland is the only country that has tackled the matter and made great progress, Humphry said. Dutch courts have evolved "a new way" in a series of family mercy killing cases in which very light punishments were meted out.

The parliament in The Netherlands is expected to pass a liberalized law this fall. Humphry says its key requirements are that the patient be verifiably terminal and asking for death, and the doctor agrees. Then the physician can upon request administer an oral overdose or a direct injection. The doctor is excused from criminal prosecution.

AS HUMPHRY SEES IT, the U.S. drive for reform is going well. There is a groundswell of interest that seemed to start in a big way last year, he reported. Support is strongest in California, with Florida, Arizona and New York coming along. He doubts that any legislator will dare push the requisite law changes through in California; it most likely will take an initiative measure, a petition with more than 600,000 signers, then a vote in favor of a state ballot proposition. The year to "put our foot on the accelerator" will be 1987, he said, and it'll take three to five years to get the law passed.

There are enough doctors who believe in the assisted-suicide option to make it work, once society wants it and once it is law, Humphry said. As for the general public, he quoted public opinion polls as showing 70 percent of all Americans believe in the propriety of doctor-assisted death, up from 30 percent in 1970.

Californians passed the first living will law in 1976. Now it's the worst and Louisiana's is best. Anyway, the durable power of attorney works far better, Humphry said. He advises those who can't get a doctor to disconnect artificial life support despite a patient's living will to threaten a lawsuit.

THE FIRST QUESTIONER declared that dying "is the process of transferring your assets to the medical community," and asked if there wouldn't be fierce resistance. Humphry replied that it is a very human issue, and doctors who are seen as opposing medically assisted suicide in terminal cases for financial reasons will be in trouble. The Hemlock Society is leery of Colorado Gov. **Richard Lamm** and his talk of doing in the terminally ill to save money, Humphry said. "We say the primary interest is ethical. Financial is secondary."

Dr. Walter Bortz, a Palo Alto Medical Clinic physician interested in gerontology, stood up to observe that there's a broad spectrum of opinion in the medical community. "The difficulty we face is malpractice," Bortz said, going on to suggest that in the medical profession there is "an immense ally out there waiting for some sort of action" — for sanction now blocked "by these anomalies in our legislative system." He was briskly applauded.

Most other seniors' groups shy away from the issue. Humphry quoted the advertising manager of Modern Maturity, the AARP magazine, as remarking, "We don't even like to remind our members of hemorrhoids." However, he expects the strongest opposition to come from the radical right.

Why froggy sings his song

PLEASE TELL ME ABOUT the frogs!," **Jean Horn** of Palo Alto implored the editor just after February's tropical rainstorms ended.

" ... They are bursting with song around us. We don't hear them in the summer.

"When the rains stop, do they turn into little dry froggy wafers, to be reconstituted with wet weather? And where are they, anyway? We have never seen one of the hundreds who must live here (by Dry Creek near Arastradero and Fremont roads).

"Bless their little froggy hearts — they remind us that nature still lives even in suburban back yards. Re-deep!"

Well, Jean Horn, those frogs were singing for their mates, and they may have stopped by now, unless the latest rains restored their ardor. Or so I am informed by **Judy Eaton**, a naturalist at the Palo Alto Junior Museum. She identifies the elusive amphibian as the Pacific tree frog, which, despite its name, usually is found on or near the ground, in shrubs and grass, fairly close to water. Posting a bounty with a few neighborhood kids doubtless would bring specimens to the Horn doorstep.

"They sing and scream all night," Eaton said.

Survivors among the frogs live more than one year, Eaton said. When the moist spots they favor dry up in summer or fall, they bury themselves in the mud and await a reviving wet spell.

One more thing. The Pacific tree frog is quoted by **Robert C. Stebbins**, professor emeritus at UC-Berkeley and the man who wrote the books about Bay Region herpatology, as singing "Kreck-ek." To Eaton, it sounds like "Cre-eek," high-pitched and loud. This song, by the way, is the one Hollywood moviemakers long have recorded and used to depict authentic outdoor nighttime sounds. If the frogs near the Horn home sing a different song, perhaps they represent two other varieties found in the area: the red-legged and yellow-legged frog.

THIS INQUIRY POINTED UP the fact that urban and suburban naturalism is an underdeveloped branch of science. **Ted Chandik**, who like **John Walton** does duty as a naturalist both at the Junior Museum and the Baylands Interpretive Center, said it's easily assumed that the creatures that live through the urban onslaught are common sorts studied long ago. However, he noted, the house sparrow has been in North America for only 135 years but already has evolved four subspecies.

Chandik is going to lead a Sea of Cortez Natural History Expedition April 26-May 4. Last year, a member of the first group he took to Baja California caught a rattleless rattlesnake on Santa Catalina Island.

Meanwhile, back at the Junior Museum, Eaton says the deluge must account for many museum critters ending their hibernation early.

AN ITEM ABOUT a Sunnyvale musical comedy director whose parents grew up in Palo Alto, work in Menlo Park and live in Los Altos Hills fits nicely into the scope of this column.

Scott Williams is the main subject. He's now in Tokyo, spending two months directing the inaugural show for the new Tokyo Children's Theater, a production called "The Phantom Tollbooth."

Scott is the son of **Gary and Elissa Williams**, and in departing, he left the Sunnyvale Community Players production of "Baby," which he directed, with four performances (last weekend) yet to go.

Scott's call to Tokyo was extended by another pair of longtime Palo Altans, **Jerry and Susan Inman**, both Stanford graduates. Jerry is serving as a ranking member of **Ambassador Mike Mansfield's** U.S. Embassy staff in Tokyo and completing a 30-year foreign service career. Susan, one of the founders of the Tokyo Children's Theater, teaches English and performs on camera and does voice-over work on Japanese radio and television.

The Inmans and the Williamses are old friends. Susan and Elissa went to elementary school together and Jerry and Gary played football and appeared in the Senior Play at Paly High.

Susan's parents, **George and Elma Evans**, now live in retirement in Carmel. Jerry's dad, **Louis Inman**, better known as **"Red,"** is an SRI retiree; he and his wife, **Geraldine**, recently moved from Palo Alto to the Santa Rosa area.

When the younger Inmans complete their second diplomatic tour in Japan, Jerry plans to retire, probably to Mariposa, near Yosemite. Other postings they've had were to Korea, the Philippines, Venezuela, Mexico and Washington, D.C.

Getting back to Scott, he'll stay at the Inmans' embassy apartment while directing "The Phantom Tollbooth," which is based on a popular children's book. The play will be performed by adults in English for child audiences, and will be taken to several Japanese cities outside Tokyo.

SCOTT, WHO RECENTLY completed his master's in dramatic literature at San Francisco State University, has an unusual collaborator in writing for musicals: his father. Scott writes the music while Gary, an adman by trade, is the lyrics wordsmithy. Together they've done an original show titled "House of Tomorrow" and based on adolescence, plus words and music for "The Grinch Who Stole Christmas," "Charlie and the Chocolate Factory," "Charlotte's Web" and the Tokyo inaugural, "The Phantom Tollbooth."

To date this father-and-son team hasn't made the charts, and Gary'll be lucky if they ever do, for Scott's directing pull is strong. When he returns in May, he'll start directing "Waiting for Godot" with **Doyne Mraz** at Los Altos Conservatory Theatre.

Suffrage on the Peninsula

THE EVENTS LEADING UP TO the vote by California men in 1911 granting women access to the polls were expertly detailed by historian **Yvonne Jacobson** of Los Altos Hills in a recent Women's History Week talk.

Jacobson began by relating how two celebrated suffragists, **Elizabeth Cady Stanton** and **Susan B. Anthony**, met in 1851 and for the next 50 years led the national movement. She quickly focused on California, the Bay Area and the Santa Clara Valley, and told fascinating tales about our foremost women's roles.

California women under Spanish and Mexican law enjoyed rights their U.S contemporaries did not have, Jacobson said. The community property concept, descended from Roman law, gave married women solid rights as matrimonial partners. Dona Juana Briones, using hers with inborn skill though she couldn't read, shed her husband in 1844 and bought a rancho now known as Los Altos Hills.

IF SANTA CLARA COUNTY IS justly famed now as a feminist capital, Jacobson said, it was true in the 1800s too. Its women were among the first to voice complaints about the rights they lacked.

Sarah Wallis missed a fortune when she sold, just too soon, the American River property where gold was found. But she went on to fame, settling in what later became Barron Park and becoming the first state Women's Suffrage Association president in 1870.

Part of the women's club movement that took shape in the latter 1800s campaigned directly for suffrage, but other parts were concerned with temperance, varied social or religious issues, or cultural attainment — those were the clubs that spent a year studying, say, France. There were interties and ultimately, Jacobson said, they formed the bridge that women marched across to the ballot box. Indeed, they became the precinct workers. Protestants were foremost in the church-affiliated groups, but Catholic and Hebrew benevolent groups also developed an interest in suffrage.

All this was given impetus by the educational opportunities Santa Clara County afforded, Jacobson said. What is now University of the Pacific in Stockton began in San Jose in 1851 as a female institute, and in 1862 went coed. The State Normal School, now San Jose State University, opened in the 1870s, Stanford two decades later.

JANE LATHROP STANFORD AND Phoebe Apperson Hearst won special tributes from Jacobson. Besides their respective roles in making Stanford and UC-Berkeley great, they pushed for suffrage. Mrs. Stanford carried on a correspondence with Susan B. Anthony, and Anthony, her era's version of a jet setter, turned up at meetings of the Century Club of California in San Francisco — a club Hearst helped form, along with Mrs. Aaron Sargent, whose daughter-in-law, **Cornelia Sargent**, also Mrs. Aaron, of Palo Alto, remains active in it.

For all their noble cause, the women's clubs were not above some bigotry, Jacobson pointed out. Some racial and religious bias was ill-concealed. However, Dr. Edith Eugenie Johnson, a Palo Alto physician who delivered 3,500 babies and lived past 90, was lauded by Jacobson for her care of poor Asians and Mexicans.

JUDY ADAMS OF MENLO PARK is embarking on a womanhunt. Her quarry is the politically active woman, the officeholder, the candidate, the woman who has lived in the public eye.

Adams, who holds a Ph.D. degree, is directing research for an exhibit to be mounted by the California History Center this fall, marking the 75th anniversary of women's suffrage in the state. She is in charge of a team of San Jose State and De Anza Community College students who will interview the women Adams lines up to record a look at their experiences in politics and stateswomanship. (The center is based in the Little Trianon on De Anza's Cupertino campus.) Willing subjects may call Adams at (415) 326-1235. Excerpts from the oral histories will appear in the CHC magazine, The Californian, edited by **Kathi Peregrin**, also of Menlo Park.

JUDY ADAMS FIRST GOT my attention with a letter protesting some ill-considered remarks in an earlier column to the effect that all you need for an oral history is an old-timer and a tape recorder. Adams had worked with Stanford University archivist **Roxanne Nilan** and others on the Women's Peace Oral History Project, and has taught oral history at San Jose State and Stanford. So she wrote:

"Preparations and research ... are quite extensive in the professionally done oral history — preparing biographies, reading written source materials and comparing with the interviews, etc., so that the interview gets at material unavailable in written sources and cross-checks a person's recall with other documentation."

The peace project, in its sixth year, is a story in itself. Former Times Tribune staffer **Mary Ann Seawell** told part of it last year.

66-year family residency ends

Final chapter to a bit of Palo Alto history

PERHAPS THE LONGEST continuous occupancy by one family of a house in Palo Alto ended when **Minerva King Green**, at 82, moved recently from the residence at 235 Melville Ave. which her family had occupied since 1920.

Castilleja School, across Melville, now owns the house. Two Castilleja tennis courts flank it, and, using the ground the courts and the house occupy, the school plans to add a playing field.

Eli King brought his young family from San Jose in 1904 when he became cashier of the new First National Bank of Palo Alto. The Kings first lived on Homer Avenue, but in 1920 moved clear across Embarcadero Road (their postal address was 234 Embarcadero, to save letter carriers a trip around to the front door). There were three sisters, Melissa, Frances and Minerva, and Minerva, the youngest, was in the first class to go entirely through "the new" Palo Alto High School, that is, the one at the present location. Times Tribune music and drama reviewer **Dorothy Nichols** — then the high school principal's daughter and Dot to the King girls — was a special friend of Frances'.

Minerva and an art school classmate, Jay S. Green, were married in the yard. They lived in the Montclair district of Oakland for 40 years, returning to Palo Alto in 1964, after the senior Kings died.

For the next 10 years, the three sisters and Minerva's husband shared the house, aided by some clever construction Green planned so each sister had her own space. Jay Green died two years ago, after the widowed sisters. Minerva is moving near a daughter, **Frances Barnsley**, in a new duplex at Murphys, in the Mother Lode. An-

other daughter, **Joan Ansell**, teaches graphics in Oakland.

Besides having been home to clan King for 66 years, the house sheltered generations of Stanford pre-med and medical students. The first was **William H. Clark**, the former city councilman, who was Melissa King Clark's stepson. Dr. Bill's stepmother taught at Castilleja and later was Mrs. Herbert Hoover's secretary. May King, Eli's wife, set a good table for boarders. Castilleja teachers were roomers, too.

J. Pearce Mitchell, a revered Stanford University and Palo Alto leader, lived across Embarcadero. Mrs. Green likes to tell about J.P.'s chicken flock, probably illegal after the city grew less rustic, being almost hidden in a vegetable garden alongside the Kings' lot. A devoted gardener, she took "a truckload" out of her doomed garden to transplant to Murphys. There's plenty left for Castilleja to have a benefit dig. She's also taking the leaded glass dining room doors, an oval china shelf, and a lifetime of memories.

Mrs. Green believes the house was built between 1908 and 1911. Though it will be gone, the Times Tribune is not losing a customer. Mrs. Green is having her paper mailed to Murphys.

If you're doing income taxes abou t now, you can appreciate the frustration that drove **William W. Palmer** of Los Altos, electrical engineer and former Navy pilot, to invent a new tax system.

"We're now in a vast and murky tax swamp, up to our eyeballs in IRS and special interest alligators," Bill says. "...We must insist that our government stop appeasing the alligators and start draining the swamp." He's engineer enough to try to start the pumps.

Palmer says the whole tax code should be written on one page, and

he has done it (though he used fairly small type). His idea is a flat-rate tax levied on every transaction, replacing all present taxes. It'd be simpler, he says, than a value-added tax, which involves complex calculations of the difference between buying and selling prices.

He'd restrict taxes to collecting money to pay for necessary government; other means would have to be used to encourage investing and saving, support worthy causes and redistribute wealth. Social Security could be treated as a retirement annuity, not a tax.

One big problem would be defining a transaction. Presumably a contribution to a church would be a gift, and not taxable.

Palmer thinks the transaction tax rate might run between 5 and 10 percent, but he's guessing. He'd need a computer model of the U.S. economy to test it out, and research centers with such models don't seem keen on humoring single-taxers.

Perhaps the toughest part would be getting our tiers of government to give up their separate taxing powers and team up on the complex task of apportioning revenues the transaction tax would raise.

But imagine the benefits for the citizen: no tax returns, no intricate record-keeping, no exemptions, no deductions, no eyeing tax effects in planning how to use your money. "The reduced accounting costs to businesses may more than pay their taxes," Palmer notes, adding dryly, "I'm sure the accountants and tax lawyers, who now live off the miseries of taxpayers, can find more satisfying work to do."

When does he think such an idea will be adopted? Not in his lifetime, says the white-haired Palmer. Still, he's a man of abiding hope. Did I mention that Bill Palmer also is a great fan of electric cars?

The night Sousa marched up San Juan Hill to Hoover

IF YOU PLAYED IN SOUSA'S Band, and especially if you played under John Philip Sousa's baton on Nov. 6, 1928, the Children's Health Council's Summer Symphony XXVII is looking for you. Even if you aren't musical but were present when the band serenaded President-elect Herbert Hoover that night, the CHC wants to talk to you.

Nov. 6, 1928, was election day. It was also Sousa's 74th birthday. As if magically, two of America's most popular men came together that night.

Hoover, home to vote, was relaxing in his campus residence on San Juan Hill. Sousa, the nation's leading popular music figure for many years, and as much a sensation in his heyday as the Beatles became in theirs, was playing two concerts at the Stanford Pavilion, where he received flowers and birthday letters from Palo Alto school children.

Election returns were announced during the concert, and by the time it ended Hoover's election was assured. (Palo Alto had gone almost 5 to 1 for its hero.) So Sousa & Co. marched up San Juan Hill, following a throng of Stanford students and townspeople, to join an impromptu victory rally.

WHERE DOES THE SUMMER SYMPHONY fit into all this? Well, on July 20, its program is going to be "Marching Along With Sousa," featuring Keith Brion, as John Philip himself, conducting the Oakland Symphony Orchestra. The gates of Frost Amphitheater on the Stanford campus will open at 3 p.m. for picnics and jazz music by Turk Murphy.

Brion was director of the Yale University Band when he had the idea of doing a replica of a Sousa concert as a Bicentennial observance. He has done it often since, dressed in a JPS uniform, made up to resemble the March King, and with Sousa's own baton leading a painstakingly researched program of music — marches, sure, but also tone poems, opera arias and other light classics — just as Sousa's Band used to play it.

Clearly the CHC Symphony is heading back to the full pops form it had when Arthur Fiedler conducted. And Carolyn Reller, the event chairman, and Ruth Kaplan, CHC fund development director, are looking for people with "I was there" recollections of that night on San Juan Hill.

Some already have been identified: Birge Clark, Dr. Esther Clark, Lillian Kirkbride, Carl McDowell and Mary Kennedy. Another avid spectator figures to be Tom Sousa of Palo Alto, the conductor-composer's grandson.

RETREAT, HELL — THEY'RE advancing in another direction, those CCHBs. That would be the Menlo Park Chamber of Commerce Has Beens, and they're heading toward a retreat replete with trivia

contests, matching games and a crossword puzzle, all Menlo-flavored.

The core of the group is 15 or so past chamber officers and other dedicated Menloites who gather now and then to party, golf, enjoy each other's company and keep the city's spirit warm.

Among the members are Lee Boucher, appliance store owner; Doug Dupen, SLAC official and former mayor; John Head, retired grocer; Neil Siciliano, co-owner of Phelps Terkel menswear; Liz Goldberg, who was the first woman CofC president and is the chamber's new hired hand; Marilyn Carrel, ex-CofC prez and wife of former chamber exec Bob Carrel; George Hirzel, jeweler; Tormey Ward, Wells Fargo bank manager; Eleanor Knight, a planning commissioner; Jeanne Betty Crumpler, former businesswoman and civic leader; Bill Weseloh, real estate dealer; Gary Williams and Bill Neylan, admen; Gordon Ingersoll, photographer; and Lou Godman, ex-CofC executive.

City Manager Mike Bedwell has been known to attend the annual outing, which for '86 will be in May at the Carrels' newly acquired home at Lake Wildwood, near Grass Valley-Nevada City.

One of their trivial delights is a game wherein the players may ask either the questions or the answers. The question might be, "What was Menlo Park's population in 1919, thanks to Camp Fremont?" Or, answer first, "Hamilton, Jefferson, Pierce and Van Buren." You can map that one out.

The toughest question, one in-grouper asserts, is: "Name California's first native-born governor. His heirs sold what is now Menlo Park to Oliver and McGlynn." (The two were worthies from Menlough, County Galway, Ireland). The answer: Don Luis Antonio Arguello. (Where's his MP street?)

There's a "They also serve ... " delegation of the CCHBs, too, the ride-along spouses. They are: Jenelle Boucher, JoAnn Dupen, Christina Head, Alicia Siciliano, Pete Goldberg, Doris Hirzel, Carol Ward, David Knight, Jeanne Weseloh, Elissa Williams, Peggy Neylan and Jewell Godman.

A SOURCE WITH IMPECCABLE credentials tells me a recent column was incorrect in saying John Philip Sousa's band marched up San Juan Hill to play for Herbert Hoover the night he was elected president in 1928. The band rode in a bus, Carl McDowell attests. He should know: He arranged the buses. A thrill awaited McDowell, then working in the Stanford concert series that brought Sousa to the campus. He had the honor of introducing Sousa and Hoover, who had never met. Their brief conversation wasn't memorable, but what happened next was: Sousa's band was the first to play "Hail to the Chief" for the freshly elected president.

The Ngo family's version of the American dream

THIS IS THE STORY OF how a family from Burma — the father 50 years old when he immigrated here with language problems and limited work skills — realized what he calls "90 percent of the American dream."

The family is headed by **Lyan Seng Ngo** and his wife, **Bee Hwa Ngo**. Their children, **Julia, Tony, San San** and **Benny**, are in their 20s now. Many readers have met the Ngos, but perhaps didn't know their name. The parents ran the 7 Seas Restaurant in Palo Alto, on Emerson between University and Lytton, from 1975 until a week ago.

The Ngos' odyssey began in Burma in the 1960s. Lyan Seng's family, originally from China's coastal Fukien province, had been in Burma for three generations. Lyan Seng and Bee Hwa, a handsome couple, were successful people. He owned a building supplies business. She operated a tailoring institute. Their children attended a good mission school.

All that crashed down after a coup in 1962 deposed U Nu's democratic government and set up the Socialist Republic of the Union of Burma. The businesses were nationalized; then the school was, too. For years the Ngos lived on savings; in 1971 they seized a chance to come to the United States.

Arriving in San Francisco, Lyan Seng decided to learn the restaurant business. He'd work for low wages if someone would teach him to cook and manage a kitchen. He hired on at a Chinese restaurant, but a problem cropped up. Lyan Seng spoke Fukienese, Mandarin, Burmese and a little English, but no Cantonese. Most San Francisco Chinese speak Cantonese. The newly hired kitchen helper and his manager found they couldn't communicate properly, so the job ended.

Bee Hwa had gone to work for Levi Strauss as a samplemaker, translating designers' ideas into garments. But they needed more income, so Lyan Seng read the want ads in a Chinatown newspaper. A Chinese restaurant in Billings, Mont., a thousand miles away, was looking for a kitchen helper. Talking to the owner in broken English, he got the job, though it meant leaving his family for a year.

HOME ON A WEEK'S VACATION, Lyan Seng decided to stay. Through the state employment service he got hired by Marin Joe's in Corte Madera and learned to make salads.

Part of the Ngos' dream was owning their own business again. So they lived frugally, saving $4,000 for a down payment in 1973 on a house in San Francisco. Still saving, they began looking for a restaurant. That led them to the 7 Seas.

Owner **Dom Yee** took a liking to Ngo. Yee was asking $59,000; the family had about $6,000. So Yee suggested Lyan Seng might qualify for a Small Business Administration loan, and sure enough, he did. The Bank of America made the loan with a 90 percent SBA guarantee, and the federal administrator decided the Ngos should have $4,000 extra in case of start-up financing problems.

The Ngo family, now living in Sunnyvale, has realized "90 percent of the American dream" since their arrival in this country from Burma about 15 years ago.

THINGS WENT WELL AT the 7 Seas, but Lyan Seng and Bee Hwa were working 14- or 15-hour days. "We got tired," he said reflectively, sipping ginseng water. The commute to and from The City was too much. What to do? He had the $4,000, so he put it down on a house in Santa Clara. He hired weekday help, but on weekends the children, then ages 10 to 16, worked with their parents, waiting table and washing dishes.

Earnings piled up during the late '70s, and the children did well in school. In 1981, an amazing thing happened. The family had acquired an Apple computer, and Tony and Benny wrote a video game program. They took their game, "Gamma Goblin," to the Computer Show in San Francisco and sold it for royalties. In the ensuing year, $80,000 poured in. The money was handed to Lyan Seng, for the Burmese custom is very family centered, children are obedient, and property is held in the name of all members of the family.

With the royalties and restaurant earnings, Lyan Seng invested in real estate. He traded their original SF house, plus cash, for a five-unit apartment in the Richmond district.

All the youngsters finished college (UC Berkeley, San Jose State or De Anza) and landed good jobs in medical or computer technology. The boys kept writing computer games, money kept flowing in, the Ngos kept buying real estate. Investing about $700,000, they have acquired scores of units, worth perhaps $2.5 million.

Lyan Seng is 64, though he looks younger. He and Bee Hwa decided to sell the 7 Seas, manage their property, and visit China, where Bee Hwa has never been. (Lyan Seng went once to meet a brother he hadn't seen for 50 years.) The whole family still lives together in a big house in Sunnyvale, with swimming pool. "Our customers helped us make the American dream come true," Lyan said. He states the 90 percent qualifier in a good-humored allusion to greed — "You get a hundred, then you want a thousand."

The Ngos took pride in modest prices, fresh food and a Cantonese-Mandarin-Burmese-American menu. Lyan Seng developed entrees such as Royal Burmese chicken. Foreign students at Stanford love the place.

Jesse Han is the buyer. Recently he has managed Grand China in Los Altos, previously China First in Palo Alto. The Ngos chose him carefully.

Peninsula's creeks – both idyllic and terrifying

OUR CREEKS ARE MAGICAL PLACES, fingers of wildlife that reach into suburban neighborhoods, winding pathways for furry, feathered and finny woodland creatures. Down beside them it's a different world; their high banks shut off the frantic throb of life in our culture.

That poetic appreciation is from Vicki Riley of Portola Valley, who has relished creeks since she was a child in Hayward. In attending Stanford on and off through a doctorate in organ music performance, and raising her family, Vicki has lived with her husband, Russ, by Matadero Creek in Barron Park and Corte Madera Creek in Portola Valley. Their daughter Kaiti, freshly graduated from Mills College in computer science, attended a nursery school at age 3 and 4 beside the one creek that makes a big mark on our map, San Francisquito.

Trickling water, pots of mud in the streambed, cool, verdant, buzzing with dragonflies, smelling of bay laurel and decaying duff and amphibian life — that's a creek in summer. In winter storms they're truly something else: wild, roaring, rising to unbelievable volumes of water, strewing boulders and trees and anything they catch full force.

THE MID-PENINSULA IS honeycombed by them: (reading up from Mountain View) Stevens Creek, Permanente, Adobe, Barron (Dry), Matadero, San Francisquito and its tributaries. Some, after flooding expanses of the lowlands in the 1950s, were concrete-lined to speed their runoff, and it cost them a lot of their natural charm. But deep San Francisquito flows where it will, with man's control limited to minimizing damage by removing trees and shoring up trouble spots.

Jim Abler, who retired three weeks ago as Palo Alto supervisor of engineering services, recalls that before Bayshore Freeway was built a hobo jungle of some size existed along the creek near University Avenue's "Whiskey Gulch." More recently shanties of street people and the homeless have mushroomed in the stream bed near El Palo Alto and the Southern Pacific tracks, he said.

Abler also remembers one time when a doe and her fawn moseyed down the creekbed to a ri-prapped portion, found they could not climb the banks, and were spooked by hollering kids. The deer had to be chased back up to Stanford Golf Course before they climbed out.

STANFORD GOLF COURSE has water hazards at the 3rd, 4th, 8th, 9th, 12th and 14th holes, thanks to the creek. Mallards are a biological hazard near the 12th tee. Longtime pro Bob Stevens says a golfer who loses a ball there had might as well take a penalty and drop a new ball. "You could break a leg down there," he said. "Some places are inaccessible." Kids sometimes gather the lost balls.

Upstream a way, almost to the confluence of Los Trancos and San Francisquito creeks, stand a home and the aforementioned nursery school in a creekside setting as beautiful as I have ever seen. Martin and Doris Errecca have lived there for 45 years, and Martin says there has always been water in SF Creek in that time. Right now, as many as 10 pairs of timid wood ducks are in residence in the Erreccas' vicinity. Martin says he's not much of a fisherman, but he has landed steelhead there. Doris tells of an agile young man who took trout of impressive dimensions.

BESIDES THE FISH AND FOWL, the Erreccas have seen the works when it comes to local wildlife: raccoon, opossum, fox, bobcat, coyote, deer, skunk.

Doris has operated her nursery school for 31 years, long enough so members of a second generation of the Webb Ranch Webb family are there now. Jim O'Connor, who was walking his dog when I met him nearby, also has had children and grandchildren in Doris Errecca's unstructured classes.

Idyllic as the place is on a fine spring afternoon, it can be terrifying in a storm. The worst was in 1955 — the creek rose so high that water came two feet deep into the house and school. Afterward, neighbors sold out, and an official, asked what he'd do, advised the Erreccas to leave, too. They mopped up instead. Again in '82 a few inches flooded into the house. After that, they erected a concrete wall to contain the flow somewhat. This February they sat up all night with a big flashlight; the high water mark was 10 inches from the top of their new wall.

"When I see people flooded on TV, I almost cry," Doris said. She knows what exhausting work the cleanup is, and how wrenching it is to lose your potted plants, school toys, even big picnic benches.

There's more to say about creeks — next week.

Adobe Creek next in line for flood control project

A NEW ROUND OF BIG DIGS for flood control is about to begin on Adobe Creek in Palo Alto. The Santa Clara Valley Water District aims to enlarge and fully concrete-line the channel in stages to make Adobe big enough to contain the epic 100-year flood. It may take 'til the 1990s.

Design division engineer **Mike McNeely** said segments of the lined channel will be reconfigured from the present trapezoidal shape (slanted sides) to a rectangular or U-shape (vertical sides).

McNeely said work will begin very soon on a $2,259,084 contract awarded to **William P. Young** of Redwood City for the Adobe Creek segment from Louis Road to the downstream side of Bayshore Freeway, near the Palo Alto flood basin. The lining between Louis and East Meadow Drive will be enlarged, and the earthen channel below East Meadow will be concrete-lined, too. Although Adobe has not flooded in the '80s, McNeely said, it has a higher priority than Matadero or Barron creeks, which did flood in 1982 and 1983, because its overall potential for causing damage is greater.

Dave Matson is Palo Alto's project monitor.

The SCVWD collects both an ad valorem tax and a benefit assessment authorized about five years ago that runs roughly $1 per month per home. Countywide, these levies raise $14 million a year for flood control. Flood problems in the bad winters of 1982 and 1983 are prompting the SCVWD board to ask in the November election for an increase in the benefit assessment, McNeely said.

SAN FRANCISQUITO CREEK, being a political problem, gets inspected yearly. It commands the obeisance of a flock of jurisdictions as the county line between Santa Clara and San Mateo and the city line between Palo Alto and Menlo Park. (Los Trancos Creek is the county line until it joins San Francisquito, but less attention is paid to that.)

Every year in late summer or early fall maintenance people and engineers from the Santa Clara Valley Water District, San Mateo County and the two cities get together and walk San Francisquito's course along the bottom, starting below the Stanford Golf Course and ending at Bayshore.

George Zinckgraf, associate SM County civil engineer, says about half a dozen make the hike, looking for trees that might fall and create blockage, and trying to spot severe erosion hazards. It's a warm outing, but worthwhile, he says.

Roldano Guerra, Menlo Park construction supervisor, remembers the engulfed feeling of being down about 30 feet below nearby street levels. In fact, Zinckgraf recalls, the banks look so much alike in various areas that the engineers must look for landmarks to be sure where they are, and aside from road and bike bridges, not many are visible.

THE VALLEY WATER DISTRICT'S part in the inspection is key because the district has tax money to spend. In the new fiscal year, $300,000 is in the budget for sack revetment work near Palo Alto Avenue, according to **Dan Kriege**, head of operations and maintenance at district headquarters in San Jose. Palo Alto is expected to share in that cost. **Roger Cwiak** usually is Palo Alto's trekker.

HONORS FOR THE MOST creative use of a local creek go to Portola Valley School District, particularly Ormondale School and science consultant **Margaret De Staebler**.

Corte Madera Creek runs by the school grounds. A couple of years ago, **Herb Dengler**, one of the region's foremost creek-watchers, designed a nature trail there, and Portola Valley people and school hands built it and now maintain it — no easy job, as a lot of poison oak must be grubbed out.

Every year fourth- and fifth-grade students are trained as science docents, and in the spring they take first- and second-graders out on the trail and teach them to look carefully at what kind of plants and animals are there and who's living where.

There are enough trees so the children feel very separate, De Staebler said. There's plenty to observe: squirrels, birds, mallard ducks that lay eggs in the sand, footprints of deer and raccoon.

On the bridge-builders of San Francisquito Creek

HAVE YOU EVER HANKERED to have your own private bridge across San Francisquito Creek, the Midpeninsula's misnamed river? Don't laugh — residents of Palo Alto's tony Crescent Park district went on a bridge-building spree about 50 years ago, and there's even one left.

It took the famous "garden doctor," **Albert Wilson,** who has lived on both the Menlo Park and Palo Alto sides of the creek, always close to it, to surface this bit of history. He also took me on an inspection tour, not even bothering to don the trademark beret seen on his television show. The gentleman, a survivor of the 1906 earthquake in San Francisco, is spry, and it's a delight to ride along with one having so keen a landscape architect's eye and a first-hand wealth of local history.

THE PRIVATE BRIDGE BOOM came after Hare, Brewer & Clark (Kelley wasn't in the title yet) subdivided Crescent Park in 1928, Wilson said, laying out wide and generous lots along the creek. The tract's name came from a big crescent traced by that reach of the creek. One Peter Middlecauff bought at the end of Lincoln Avenue, No. 1370; he also bought acreage on the San Mateo County side — a pear orchard. Middlecauff built himself a bridge, low slung and straight, in order to get to his property across Woodland Avenue, where he exercised mornings by hoeing and whatnot. Then, alarmed by a lawyer who warned there'd be trouble if the bridge washed out, Middlecauff replaced it with a high-arched, Japanese tea garden model.

Another Crescent Parker was a man named Carr, Gov. Young's appointee as president of the Railroad Commission. When Young left office so did Carr, and the splendid Spanish-style house he had built at 75 Crescent Drive was acquired by Albert Hooper. Hooper redid the garden, with Wilson's expert help, and built a magnificent high bridge of excellent design. He maintained terraces on both sides of the creek with cement walls and very secure paths, and his creekside gardens and bridge were lighted at night.

Finally there came Mrs. Anna Maskey, a candy maker then famed as "the sweetest lady in San Francisco," to build at 27 Crescent Drive. She wanted Wilson to build her a bridge to use when she entertained Mayor Angelo Rossi and other SF friends, but he knew his limits. So an engineer was hired and erected the strongest, best structure of them all. It has survived flows that immersed its top, more than 30 feet above the creek bed.

MRS. MASKEY, IN COLLUSION with Wilson, also had the lower creek banks of her property cleared, which meant grubbing out poison oak and clearing around a fine big bay tree. Well sir, came a flood in about '38. The cleared portion washed out and the full fury of the river aimed itself right at Mrs. Maskey's beautiful home. The bay tree went, the home fortunately escaped and all learned a lesson which Wilson puts this way: "YOU DON'T PUSH THE RIVER AROUND." The banks by 27 Crescent were soon clad in concrete, a foretaste of much reenforcement done since the mid-1950s.

The Middlecauff and Hooper bridges washed out in the '50s because of wood rot and the tons of high water pressure the creek brings to bear. But the Maskey bridge remains. Mr. and Mrs. **Bob Saldich,** who bought the property a couple of years ago, recently renovated this last private bridge.

ALBERT WILSON IS THE AUTHOR of "Distinctive Trees, Shrubs and Vines in the Gardens of the San Francisco Peninsula," a work that inspired all the later "Trees of ... " books and pamphlets around here. And he has contributed more than a few specimens to the list.

In 1929 Wilson built his first house at 654 Creek Drive on the Menlo Park side, then ran a water pipe in a ditch across the road to the creekside. There, with help from the U.S. Department of Agriculture's division of plant introductions, he shaped basins and planted some trees that still stand as fine specimens. One is *Eucalyptus evansii*, another the *Acacia farnesiana*, or African or sweet acacia, a thorny but fragrant tree used in perfume-making in France. Still another is *Abies vanusta*, the Santa Lucia fir. He also planted natives: Bishop pine, toyon, California bay, ceanothus, California buckeye and dwarf coyote bush. Once started with about a year of special attention, all have thrived.

Perhaps some luck has helped. Sidney Pay, an old Menlo hand, warned Wilson that in 1908 the area from the creek to Santa Cruz Avenue was a lake. That was before Searsville Dam impounded water upstream. Taking the cue, Wilson built a 7-foot cellar under his Creek Drive home. But, he says, it has never flooded.

Matadero Creek's toads missing for three years

A FANCIER OF CREEK DENIZENS is Mary Cordon of Palo Alto, who lives on Emerson Street near Matadero Creek. There used to be an influx of toads about one inch long into her neighborhood every spring, she said, and strings of tadpoles could be spotted in the channel.

"They climbed the concrete sides, moved into our gardens and were an absolute delight," she said of the toads. "When they were swarming we had to stop mowing the lawns."

Sometimes when she sprayed the garden at 4 or 5 p.m., from a tiny hole in row of bricks at a border as many as 14 little toads would struggle out.

For three years, the toads have been missing, Cordon said, Could Santa Clara Valley Water District channel maintenance have done them in?

The word given me by an SCVWD M&O spokesman is that no poisons are used to discourage toads. A herbicide is applied to check plant growth in the channel, but it should not harm amphibians. However, he raised another possibility: When residents drain swimming pools into Matadero, the chlorinated water could kill the toads. Illegal oil disposal could do likewise.

THE MAGIC OF A CREEK, which started this series a few weeks back, is well captured when seen through the eyes of a young mother who tends also to view it through her child's eyes.

Rebecca Vitale-Mardich and her husband, Mitchell Mardich, live on Creek Drive in Menlo Park with their son, Matthew, 2½, a dog and a cat. But let's let Rebecca tell about it:

"Every member of our group adores the creek (San Francisquito), but especially Matthew, who now uses it as an outdoor classroom (I am the teacher). We usually go early in the morning, sometimes before 7 a.m., and hope to find our two nesting mallards, the carrion beetles, and craydads, and spot a swallowtail or two, a cabbage butterfly and of course tadpoles! Also, inspired by Professor (John W.) Rick of the Stanford archeological dig (and being a closet archeologist myself), we dig for bones, relics, etc., and have found some things.

"THE CREEK ALSO HAS a special quality that no one really talks about. My husband and I have both noted that when we grew up as children (in the '50s) all the outdoor creatures — beetles, butterflies, etc. — were everywhere, even in one's own backyard. Now it seems one must go to a natural spot out in the undisturbed areas to find any abundance. But all these creatures can be seen and enjoyed in a natural spot in the midst of an urban area, which is quite unusual in this paved-over, butterflyless world.

"We also use the creek as a playground and roll up our pants and go wading and climbing. But my son enjoys most to bring down a wagonful of toys including the obligatory bucket, shovel, a small bulldozer and ditch digger, and camp ourselves down on a lovely sandbar formed by the winter storms. The sun streams down through the canopy of bays and buckeyes and the birds keep the air filled with song. We eat our picnic snack, watch the clouds puff overhead and tranquility is ours.

"IN THE EVENING THE CREEK creates a new magic. The symphony of crickets, frogs and assorted creatures break into their "creek litany." A visiting friend will always remark, 'I can't believe it — it reminds me of my childhood,' and a nostalgic contentment will pass over the face, and this special place has warmed another heart.

"Occasionally a large white majestic owl will swoop overhead and be seen in the full light of the moon. Perching itself in one of the large eucalyptus, it is ready for a night of hunting and hooting.

"And sometimes in the heat of the summer when all is hot and still, late in the night a scent peculiar only to that striped fellow will come wafting in an open window and wake us from our slumber ... "

ADOBE CREEK, WITH ITS headwaters up on Black Mountain, does more appearing and disappearing than any other creek hereabouts, according to Albert Wilson of Palo Alto. Wilson tells of a friend of the late Frank Duveneck, Dr. W.F. DeNiedman, a retired U.S. Army doctor who'd been born in Russia and learned medicine in Scotland. DeNiedman came to the Santa Clara Valley to retire, and lived on Moody Road by Adobe Creek, where he pursued his interest in exotic plants. A grove of California bay laurels stood on his property, Wilson said, and through the doctor's worldwide acquaintances and contacts with the U.S. Department of Agriculture, he was requested to gather California bay seeds to be shipped to Turkey and there planted along rivers.

Some new things in store for kids with disabilities

ONE BATCH OF MID-PENINSULA students who'll be going back to school in a fortnight haven't had a long summer off. Many kids with disabilities had only a brief break, if any. But for most of them school is vital, and they'll welcome the day-in, day-out fall routine.

Two clusters of these institutions in Palo Alto have farflung importance in San Mateo and Santa Clara counties, and beyond the Peninsula as pattern-setters for kindred care centers elsewhere.

One, on the southwest side of Middlefield Road between the Mitchell Park Recreation Center building and Charleston Road, consists of PCC Children and Youth Services Inc. (PCC stands for the old name, Peninsula Children's Center); Community Association for the Retarded Inc., commonly called C.A.R.; and Martin J. Spangler School for the Mentally Retarded and Physically Handicapped.

The other pair, Children's Hospital at Stanford and Children's Health Council, are across Sand Hill Road from Stanford Shopping Center.

Farther north, at Las Lomitas School in Atherton, the San Mateo County Office of Education provides a class for 12 children with severe language disorders.

C.A.R. DOESN'T HAVE A SCHOOL, but it's the linchpin operation not only for its flanking neighbors but also for other schools for children with disabilities, such as Juana Briones School across Palo Alto, which is partially devoted to educating orthopedically handicapped kids, and Morgan Center in Los Altos, a small private school that deals with youngsters with autism or other problems.

One big need filled by C.A.R. is after-school recreation for kids with disabilities. "These are kids who'll never make it in Boy Scouts, Girl Scouts, or the parks and recreation programs," said Ellen Corman, C.A.R. community education director. "They need a lot of attention. Without C.A.R., they'd probably go home and do nothing. Their physical and behavioral problems require a lot of structure."

Another C.A.R. forte is supplying swimming facilities for children and adults with any disability whatever. "Back-to-school means schools in the area will be bringing in kids by the busload for swimming," Corman said.

C.A.R. has six other programs, too. One of the most needed is its respite service — it supplies the only overnight care in the region. Families needing a break from the strain of constant care bring adults or children from as far away as Redding or Monterey.

PCC IS A PRIVATE, NON-PROFIT outfit, serving children with autism, mental retardation or behavioral problems, many with more than one difficulty. Its school, with 53 registered, runs year-around, although for three weeks in August it is mainly a recreation program. Twenty-three school districts in San Mateo and Santa Clara counties send PCC children who are unable to attend public school, along with some funding. However, private funding also must be raised.

On Sept. 3, when PCC kids resume classes, they're going to find a brand new lobby and entryway. A mural depicting lambs is being executed by Palo Alto artist Joan Hancock as a gift and will be the lobby centerpiece, said Patricia Gardner, PCC development director.

SPANGLER SCHOOL, WITH 45 enrolled, has a couple of changes in store, according to Michelle Burchfiel, speaking for vacationing Principal Barbara Ballard. It will begin an early intervention program for north county children 1½ to 3 years old. Until now they've had to go to San Jose. Santa Clara County operates the school.

THE CHILDREN'S HEALTH COUNCIL, a private, non-profit outfit, runs a school with two campuses, one near its headquarters at 700 Sand Hill Road, the other at the Fremont School site on Middle Avenue in Menlo Park. About 50 children come from the area between South San Francisco and San Jose for "whole child" treatment.

How dog Dustin's deposit revealed leak in leash law

THE DOG WHO WALKS ME when he comes to visit sometimes drags us into trouble. He looks fierce (call us Wolf & Walker), and from a cat's eye view he is. Flushing a cat makes his day. He's part lion dog — Rhodesian ridgeback — and holds any feline fair game.

His name is **Dustin**, and he's a pretty fair actor, baleful eyes, a guilty look if you almost catch him reclining on the furniture, and ears that spring to attention if you say "leash." In truth, he should be called "Le Nez," like a French winemaker, for olfactory analysis is his passion (after cats).

At this point Dustin is an East Palo Alto dog, though he has lived all over the mid-Peninsula. I don't know if East Palo Alto has adopted a city animal control ordinance, and if Dustin does he isn't saying. No matter. He's a pretty good citizen on a leash, save perhaps for, uh, calls of nature.

ONE DAY WE WERE NEARING the end of our jaunt when Dustin stopped to lift a leg on a fireplug, or maybe it was a shrub, outside a corner house. After we crossed the street a crabby guy at the house opposite saw fit to deliver a lecture, making it clear that he didn't want any leaking on his juniper hedge and declaring Palo Alto ordinance makes it a crime not to curb your dog. I thought at the time he must have been a refugee from San Francisco, where "Curb your dog" and "Post no bills" were the most ubiquitous signs 50 years ago. But months passed before I got a good chance to research the matter at the city attorney's office.

Well, sir, as I read the law, Dustin's walker is innocent, or not as guilty as feared. The "Nuisances by animals" section says, "It is unlawful for the owner or person having custody of any dog ... to permit, either willfully or through failure to exercise due care or control, any such dog or animal to commit any nuisance upon the *sidewalk* (emphasis mine) of any public street; or upon any walkway, path, grass or play area of any park or school," or in various other areas used in common by the public. No mention of off-the-sidewalk bushes, and no curbing requirement as such. Wet spots that drip onto the edge of the sidewalk are an offense, no doubt, but the evidence evaporates rapidly (unless you're a dog with a keen nose).

Bet our tormentor would like to see a pooper-scooper ordinance. His tactic has paid off, though.

Going past his juniper I drag Dustin to the curb, and that's the last place where this dog'd ever go.

JOSEPH EUGENE BEH OF ATHERTON is well known in Menlo Park where he has been a real estate broker for 36 years, but he may be even better known in Washington, D.C. Well, a part of Wash DC, to be more precise: the Georgetown University campus. He's one of four Hoya heroes to whom its Alumni Square was recently dedicated.

Dedication of the buildings took no fewer than five Jesuit priests, with two others handling the invocation and benediction and the Rev. **Timothy S. Healy** delivering the President's Address.

More than a few people around here are university trustees, but Joe Beh's dedication to Georgetown is something special. He practically commutes to the capital, serving first on the Alumni Council of the biz school, then on the Board of Regents, then also on the business school's Board of Visitors, next as a member of the National Campaign Council. Most recently he drew additional duty on the Northern California Campaign Council.

For all his jetting across the country, Joe's active in his home territory, too. He's known as a booster of youth baseball and served two terms as president the Herbert Hoover Boys' and Girls' Club.

Cry your eyes out, Notre Dame. Joe Beh was the first in his Iowa family to break tradition and not go to South Bend. Say Beh, Georgetown!

MOTHERLY TYPES WHO ARE ardent workers for Amnesty International and the prisoners of conscience it speaks up for at last have got respect in their own homes. All it took was U-2 and The Sting, with an assist from **Joan Baez**, in that recent cross-country, fund-raising concert tour.

Mika Koutsoyannis of Palo Alto says her son, **Alexander**, 16, fed back details of AI's work he heard in a radio lecture about the time of the San Francisco concert that were what Mika had been saying for years at the dinner table. And when U-2 and The Sting reached New Jersey on a Sunday for their Meadowland concert, Alexander got up early to record a radiocast. Mika, who is an administrator for the Stanford University sociology department, even caught some excitement in **Rene MacClean**, her 23-year-old secretary.

Palo Alto council seizes pooper scooper issue

APOLOGIES, PALO ALTO DOG OWNERS. Wish I'd never written "pooper scooper" in an earlier column. Now the City Council has gone and lawed it (the vote split along unusual lines). And that was only the beginning.

What more can be anticipated? Well, there'll be great uncertainty as to where city property begins and ends. Is school district land included? Is the Mitchell Park dog run exempt? The baylands? Can those plastic bags **Ellen Fletcher** thinks are so neat be deposited in public trash cans? Will Sanitation Service workers — the garbage picker-uppers — demand extra pay, or perhaps masks?

Let's not forget the intercity issues, either. Most of the dogs in my neighborhood are walked over to a piece of Mountain View land whose main function seems to be to provide bushes and trees. Some pooches will visit Stanford, Los Altos, Menlo Park, East Palo Alto. Will the public entities on this list adopt defensive ordinances?

When Palo Alto starts something like this, the mills of government grind exceedingly fine. The council might better have let sleeping dog doo lie.

POLICE LIKE NARROW ROADS. OK, so that's oversimplifying it by a country acre. The point is that in the estate towns where residents are likely to have large private parties, officers often earn overtime pay monitoring parking along the narrow roads.

In Atherton, for example, a willing policeman can generally log some weekend overtime to fatten the family budget. Under town ordinance, when an event at a park is expected to draw an assemblage of more than 100, at least one officer must be on duty to keep order. Although the regulation does not apply to events at private homes, Police Chief **Richard Moore** said, homeowners expecting sizable crowds usually do call the police station and hire an officer on O.T. The town pays the officer and bills the homeowner. It doesn't cost much.

Moore says his force gets about three such requests per weekend, and in June four or five. The events may be weddings, cocktail parties, reunions or whatnot. If they congest the parking on Atherton's narrow roadways, with no sidewalks and sometimes of single-lane width, help is needed.

WHEN WALDO ASHBY MARKED his 80th birthday recently at a large lawn party at the Atherton home of his daughter, **Dorothy Chapple,** the birthday boy kicked up his heels for several minutes in a lively solo dance. It would have winded most people half his age, yet the guests weren't surprised — most of them had seen Waldo dance before. When he's around, vaudeville is not dead.

Ashby, who is retired, operated a hardware store in Los Altos' downtown triangle for years. He and his wife **Helen,** Carmel residents now, made it a doubleheader by observing their 48th wedding anniversary, too. Most of the guests were from the senior set, many coming from retirement residences spread from Marin to Monterey.

Atherton Police Officer **Tim Lynch** was out front, greeting guests cordially and waving to potential parking a block or so away. Lynch said he really appreciates being able to pick up some overtime and not have to moonlight at a second job.

WOODSIDE DOES IT A BIT differently. Anyone who's having a race, a parade, a wine-tasting or some other gig that'll draw a crowd must file a public event application with the Sheriff's Department, Town Clerk **Dolores Babich** said. The regulation doesn't apply to private parties, she added, but most residents having large gatherings find it wise to let the sheriff know, and perhaps to hire some deputies or private patrolmen.

In Portola Valley, it's a little less formal, but the same advance planning is recommended if narrow streets will be clogged. The town has the power to require that special police be hired, but so far hasn't used it, Deputy Clerk **Leila Harbin** said.

ATHERTON'S CHIEF MOORE NOTED that football games keep his men busy in the fall if they want extra work. Last weekend, for instance, two officers were assigned to Menlo School, where the resident Knights were entertaining the Menlo-Atherton High School Bears. Two or three more were required when the Menlo College Oaks hosted Occidental on Saturday.

Moore said he believes almost every department on the Peninsula provides policing for special events, although desk people in the larger cities may tell you they know nothing about it. Only one town, Hillsborough, lets residents pay police directly for special service, according to Moore. He thinks that's risky from the liability standpoint.

How liquor tainted drive for women's right to vote

WHAT IS THE LEAST STUDIED major California social, economic and political event in the past century? Women's suffrage, says Dr. **James C. Williams**, director of the California History Center at De Anza College, Cupertino.

" ... In fact, historians until very recently have paid little attention to the campaign for suffrage and its larger societal significance," Williams writes in the September issue of *The Californian*, the CHC's magazine. "Only now are we beginning to understand the complexities of the issues and the campaign which joined numerous community equal rights associations and women's clubs in successfully achieving the right to vote in 1911."

While Williams sets the theme, writing women from the mid-Peninsula take over to tell the story in the magazine issue, which serves as a lead-up to a suffrage exhibit set to open Oct. 11 at the CHC headquarters in De Anza's Little Trianon building.

IN THE FEATURED ARTICLE, author-historian **Yvonne Jacobson** of Los Altos Hills tells about the suffrage campaign with special attention to events in Santa Clara County, a leading center of suffragist action. Reviewing the political sophistication the women leaders were forced to attain, Jacobson brings out something I didn't know: that the first California woman's suffrage election bid failed in 1896 by 13,000 votes. Why did it fail? Because leaders had mixed suffrage and temperance, spurring active efforts by the Liquor Dealers Association to defeat passage. In 1911 they asked the Women's Christian Temperance Union to withdraw from the forefront of the battle.

Like national leaders Elizabeth Cady Stanton and Susan B. Anthony, several prominent California leaders — Sarah Wallis of Mayfield, Sarah Knox-Goodrich of San Jose and Jane Lathrop Stanford of Stanford University — did not live until suffrage was granted. But others did, and foremost among them were Elizabeth Lowe Watson of Cupertino, Sarah M. Severance of Gilroy, Jenny Arnott of Palo Alto, Sophia Durst of Sunnyvale and Sarah Massey Overton of San Jose, the black campaign leader.

Besides downplaying anti-liquor sentiment, Jacobson observes, women campaigners catered to anti-Asian feelings rampant in 1911. Their rhetoric stressed that giving women the vote would change the world, bringing peace, uplifting purity and ending prostitution. Although the resulting change was not so sweeping, women in political action did partly bear out the prediction of the *Palo Alto Times* that they "would liberate in the political life of the state a preponderantly moral element."

IN ANOTHER ARTICLE, Kathryn Larson Aka- tiff of Palo Alto and **Judy Porter Adams** of Menlo Park profile Alice Locke Parke, the bicycle-riding letter, pamphlet and banner writer who moved with her family to Palo Alto in 1906. Locke became secretary of the California Equal Suffrage Association and supported not only suffrage and pacifism but a broad variety of causes, including vegetarianism, ending animal abuse at rodeos and granting equal parental custody of minor children.

Porter is the exhibit's research coordinator.

THE WOMEN'S HERITAGE MUSEUM, which is co-sponsoring the exhibit, is explained in another article by its director, **Jeanne McDonnell** of Palo Alto. It will seek to collect and display "multicultural materials specifically our women's history," materials which, in McDonnell's view, have been greatly neglected. As an example, she points out that we all have heard a lot about Indian arrowheads and spear points, but baskets, which played a critical role in the health and survival of Native Americans and which were a point of Indian women's pride, are not as widely understood.

THE CALIFORNIAN MISSED a chance to carry another prominent local byline, that of California Chief Justice **Rose Elizabeth Bird** of Palo Alto. Last spring, Bird devoted a substantial part of a women's history celebration speech in San Jose to the story of Clara Shortridge Foltz of San Jose, who in 1878 won her struggle to be admitted to the practice of law. Subsequently, Foltz applied for admission to Hastings College of Law in San Francisco, only to be denied by Serranus Clinton Hastings, its founder and California's first chief justice. However, Foltz took her case to the California Supreme Court and won it, along with praise for her oral argument by one justice who said, "You are not only a good mother; you are a good lawyer." Bird added: "A most generous comment for that day."

The magazine devotes a paragraph to Clara Foltz's drafting of the "Woman's Lawyer Bill" and prints her picture, but Bird's account is fuller.

Stanford library associates and the moving building

TRIVIA QUESTION: What famous architect designed a building that has stood in both Menlo Park and Palo Alto, and that remains a popular gathering place today?

Here's a clue: Eaten any baby back ribs lately?

Give up? OK, the answer is Julia Morgan, and the place is today's MacArthur Park near the Palo Alto SP (or is it Caltrans?) depot. Originally the building was part of Camp Fremont, the World War I base in the westerly reaches of Menlo Park. After migrating to Palo Alto, it was the community center for some years, then a meeting place for veterans' groups. When roof repair needs threatened to bankrupt the city, MacA PK came to the rescue.

Julia Morgan, best known for her designs of San Simeon and Asilomar, was the subject Sunday of the 1986-87 kickoff meeting of the Associates of the Stanford University Libraries. **Sara Holmes Boutelle** of Santa Cruz, whose biography and catalog titled "Julia Morgan, Architect" is due out in fall 1987, was the speaker. Trust she's including the Saratoga Foothill Club, a wooden gem of Morgan's that I grew up next door to.

CARL McDOWELL OF PALO ALTO, new chairman of the Associates, a fund-raising outfit that showers cash and treasures on the university's extensive libraries system, says the second meeting could be more controversial. On Oct. 12, former U.S. Ambassador to Mexico **John Golenar Gavin** will lecture on "Latin America: Perspectives." Gavin, a movie actor before President **Ronald Reagan** sent him south, and a Stanford graduate, had a rough time during his tour in Mexico City. He's now with Arco as VP for federal and international relations, but I'd bet people still call him "Ambassador." Gavin will talk at 3 p.m. in Cubberley Auditorium on campus; it's free and open to the public. Afterward, a reception in the Louis R. Lurie Rotunda of Green Library will open an exhibit entitled "The Rediscovery of Latin America: Europe in the Americas in the 18th and 19th Centuries."

In November, the Library Associates have two sessions slated. Photographer-author **Carolyn Caddes** of Palo Alto will talk about the making of her newly published book, "Portraits of Success: Impressions of Silicon Valley Pioneers" on Nov. 9. Then on Nov. 20, there'll be a gala reception at Lou Henry Hoover House, coupled with a showing of one of famed movie director Delmar L. Daves' films.

A HIGH-RANKING SCIENTIST at NASA-Ames, who begged anonymity, recently told a Los Altos area group the space shuttle had such a large probability of failure that it was amazing 24 flights were completed safely before the Jan. 28 Challenger accident. He blamed the press (naturally) and politicians for forcing NASA to assume a role it wasn't prepared for. Some other little tidbits: Dr. **Hans Mark**, former boss at Ames, later secretary of the Air Force, then NASA deputy administrator, and now chancellor of the University of Texas System, personally stopped seven scheduled launches earlier but wasn't there at the end of the Challenger countdown. As for giving astronauts more involvement, our mystery scientist said, that's like having stewardesses handle jetliner takeoffs.

THERE IS AN INFANT PROGRAM for developmentally delayed tots in northern Santa Clara County, contrary to what this column implied some weeks ago, and there has been for a long time — it began 14 years ago when a group of parents of babies with Down's syndrome got together. It is based at C.A.R., 3864 Middlefield Road, Palo Alto, and it serves much of San Mateo County, too.

Janina Nadaner is the director of the early intervention program, which provides specialized services for infants from birth to 3 years of age, whether delayed or at risk of being delayed.

Needless to say, C.A.R. does a lot of educating of parents of these babies, and parental participation is a large element of the program. There is a bilingual counselor/teacher to help Spanish-speaking families. A dozen volunteers assist the staff, and 43 families are enrolled.

"We are now providing significantly more home intervention to better meet the needs of medically fragile babies," Nadaner says.

IF YOU SERVED IN 2d Battalion, 410th Infantry, during World War II, **Richard M. Stannard** is looking for you. Dick, once a Palo Alto Times reporter, is retired from federal civilian service. He delights to hear from fellow riflemen. His address: 2424 Hobart Ave. S.W., Apt. C, Seattle, WA 98116.

Sarah Wallis has her day Saturday in Barron Park

HISTORY IS THE NAME of the game in Barron Park and Cupertino Saturday, or is it politics? With the 75th anniversary of women winning the vote in California as the peg, there will be a morning plaque unveiling and an afternoon exhibit opening, both with plenty of trimmings.

The state historic plaque honors Sarah Wallis, who in 1870 was the first president of the California Woman Suffrage Association. Unfortunately, her showplace house in Barron Park (acquired in 1878 by Edward Barron, whose name this sans-sidewalks part of today's Palo Alto bears) burned down in November 1936, but the plaque will be placed at La Selva Drive and Military Way, near where the ornate house stood. Ceremonies will start there at 11 a.m. There'll be refreshments, live music, people in period costumes and, inevitably, speeches.

Assemblyman **Byron Sher**, Palo Alto City Council Member **Gail Woolley**, executive director **Jeanne McDonnell** of the sponsoring Women's Heritage Museum of Palo Alto, historian **Doug Graham** of the sponsoring Barron Park Association and probably president **John Bracken** of the sponsoring Palo Alto Historical Association will join in explaining the significance of the occasion.

TWO SPECIAL SPECTATORS will be **Dan Baker** and **Chatham Forbes**. Baker has a double claim to special attention: the plaque is being put on the boundary line of his property, and he photographed the landmark burning in '36. As a boy Forbes lived at the estate, then a military school. He has helped Graham learn where various buildings were, a task eased by the survival of many trees, some tropicals, planted 100 years ago.

THE AFTERNOON PROGRAM will begin at 2 p.m. at the Little Trianon Building on the De Anza College campus, site of the California History Center, where an anniversary exhibit titled "California Woman Suffrage" will open for an extensive run. State Sen. **Becky Morgan** will speak at 2:20.

One feature of the day will be voting in a couple of antique polling booths on the suffrage measure that men faced on California's 1911 fall ballot, plus an equal pay for equal work proposition, and a law limiting women's work days to eight hours. It will be interesting to see if the polling at the exhibit exceeds the actual winning margin in 1911, which was a slim 3,587 votes.

The exhibit, sponsored jointly by the History Center and the Women's Heritage Museum, will continue for many weeks, and may later go on tour.

Kathi Peregrin of Menlo Park, CHC instructional/media associate, says an eyecatching part of the exhibit will be suffrage campaign buttons on loan from the Smithsonian Institution.

Right after the opening, **Judith Porter Adams** of Menlo Park, the research coordinator, will begin teaching a De Anza series titled "Women in the Public Eye" and featuring oral history interviews. In November, **Jane Boyd** of Cupertino, head of women's studies at San Jose State University, will teach "Western Women and Suffrage," exploring why California and five other Western states were nine to 51 years ahead of U.S. enfranchisement.

McGRUFF, CRIME PREVENTION dog of the Palo Alto Police, and **Sparky the Fire Dog**, a Dalmatian out of the P.A. Fire Department, made their first dual appearance Sunday at a Police and Fire Show at Stanford Shopping Center. I wanted to ask these canine authorities their views on the pooper-scooper ordinance, but they were busy posing in their $1,000 fur suits. **Patches**, Pacific Bell's cat, was there too, dispensing child safety tips.

Sgt. **Greg Munks** of Palo Alto's finest says that in a few months these upright characters will be joined by a newcomer, **Buckle Bear**, who'll ask preschoolers and business and community groups to obey seat belt and child safety seat laws.

McGruff, Munks, Capt. **Lynne Johnson** and Officer **Dennis Burns** recently were photographed with a group of San Francisco 49er players. However, only McGruff and the 49ers will be on posters to be distributed by Southland Corp., 7-Eleven's owner, along with child safety tips, Munks said.

ZOOFEST TURNED UP George and Greta MacLeod, former Los Altos Hills residents and now two of the Sonoma Valley's happiest vineyardists. George, who used to sell silicon and kibbitz crystal growing in the early days of Silicon Valley, and who served on the Santa Clara County Board of Education, currently is head of the Sonoma Valley Grape Growers. The MacLeods' glee had to do with a Kenwood wine made from grapes from their Indian Springs Ranch having just won the sweepstakes award at the Sonoma County Harvest Fair.

Chinese Club to celebrate 37 'profiles in excellence'

THE STANFORD AREA CHINESE CLUB is staging a reception Sunday from 2 p.m. to 5 p.m. at the Syntex Corporation Gallery/Conference Center in Palo Alto to celebrate completion of its 20th anniversary project — publication of "Profiles in Excellence: Peninsula Chinese Americans."

The book, written by **Connie Young Yu** of Los Altos Hills, portrays 37 individuals living and working in San Mateo and Santa Clara counties. Yu and many of those whose careers are traced in the book will be at the reception. The book resembles **Carolyn Caddes'** book on Silicon Valley pioneers in form, but that's coincidence, Yu said.

Those profiled are: San Francisco State College President **Chia-Wei Woo**, Hillsborough; television reporter **David Louie**, San Mateo; surgeon and fire buff **Donald Cheu**, San Mateo; heart surgeon **Eugene Dong**, Palo Alto; Kaiser Santa Clara chief physician **Chris Chow**, Los Altos Hills; dentist **Roger Eng**, a Los Altos councilman; neurophysiologist **Kao Liang Chow**, Palo Alto; engineer/entrepreneur **David Lee**, Los Altos Hills.

Also, engineering Professor **Francis Huang** of San Jose State University; chemist **Ernest K. Hung**, Palo Alto; artist/communicator **Florence Wong**, Sunnyvale; jazz producer/educator **Herb Wong**, Menlo Park; research chemist **Frank Y. Chuck**, Los Altos; Foothill College Dean **Bernadine Chuck Fong**, Los Altos; SJSU social work Professor **Peter C.Y. Lee**, San Jose; novelist **Laurence Yep**, Sunnyvale; engineer/entrepreneur **Allan Chin**, Palo Alto; developer **Stephen C.H. Lin**, Woodside; **James Dao**, engineer/entrepreneur, Hillsborough; psychiatrist **Allan Seid**, Palo Alto.

Attorney **Stephen Wing**, San Jose; Professor **Chao Mei-Pa**, voice teacher/conductor, Sunnyvale; photojournalist **Lui Kit Wong**, San Jose; businessman/community leader **Samuel Leong**, Mountain View; artist/teacher **Paul Pei-jen Hau** of Los Altos; musician-singer-teacher **Lily Chin**, Sunnyvale; educator/writer **Lily Sung** of Palo Alto; senior citizens advocate **John Chin**, San Jose; architect **Roger Chinn**, Foster City's mayor; Realtor/people helper **Henry Gee**, Mountain View; administrative coordinator **Helen Tao**, Palo Alto; entrepreneur **David Sin**, Santa Clara; inventor-cogeneration pioneer **Dah Yu Cheng**, Los Altos Hills; Municipal Court Judge **James Chang**, San Jose; director/choreographer **Bubba Gong**, Palo Alto.

In addition, two young people who live in Los Altos Hills are portrayed as scholar/athletes: **Jennifer Yu** and **Ted Huang**.

LEONARD ELY, a Palo Altan who for many years operated car dealerships in Menlo Park and before that Redwood City, got a richly deserved honor from the Stanford Associates last Saturday night: the Golden Spike Award. Ely ranks as one of the all-time fund-raisers hereabouts, and in fact is devoting all his office hours to it these days. Some of the beneficiaries of his vigorous tree-shaking have been the Santa Clara County Foundation, Community Association for the Retarded, the Gamble Garden Foundation and the university, which he has served in other roles too. Len was all but born into the Stanford "family" — he is one of Chancellor Ray Lyman Wilbur's grandsons.

WHETHER IT REFLECTS a slowing of business or increased charitable ardor, the number of corporate executives on loan to the Santa Clara County United Fund is at an all-time high this year. I have it on the authority of **Crystal Gamage** of Palo Alto that 40 execs are toiling at a long table at UF headquarters in Santa Clara, eight more than ever before. They represent the elite of the county's corporate structures, and you have to think they'll be glad to get back to their comfortable offices.

HAPPY DAYS ARE here again in Woodside. **George Sellman** is doing a reprise.

Sellman, who retired last spring after 30 years as superintendent of schools, is putting on another communitywide musical, and it all gets started tonight at 8 at a meeting at Woodside School. In the 1960s and '70s he was the motive force behind annual shows called the Follies, not only doing a lot of writing and directing but also performing himself. After the 1980 production, he decided working all day and almost all night was too much.

The revival has a special purpose: to break in the school's refurbished multipurpose room, which has been named in Sellman's honor. Through a foundation, school supporters raised nearly $50,000 for new floors, walls, curtains and lights.

How's retirement? Sellman has surprised himself by being too busy to notice. The question now is whether, after the reprise, he'll feel more like taking it easy, or find himself stagestruck again.

Veterans hospital crew can shrink-wrap your presents

COULD YOU USE SHRINK-WRAPPING? No, Sigmund, this isn't a psychiatrist joke. It's about an enterprise that's good for patients of the Palo Alto Veterans Administration hospital and good for the customers they serve, too.

Vets' Task-Force, a non-profit corporation with offices at Building 22, VA Medical Center, arranges the sheltered workshop program, its director, **Marlene Kerrins** of Palo Alto, explained. Recuperating inpatients and outpatients who join VTF start by getting a work prescription from a vocational service team. If a job is open, the newcomer joins the workshop right away; if not, onto a waiting list.

VTF's program is divided into two parts, Kerrins said. Those in the compensated program earn money by doing jobs like collating, packaging and custom cabinet carpentry. Those on a grounds crew work on big maintenance, like keeping up the U.S. Geological Survey grounds in Menlo Park.

However, it's the shrink-wrap machine that seems to capture people's fancy. It can be used to encase books or kits in plastic; Stanford University contracts to have admissions packages shrink-wrapped. Corporations order technical manuals or employee handbooks collated and swathed in clear film. And, Kerrins said, creators of art works, photographs and games love this packaging. University Games at Stanford and **Sally** and **Jack Stout** of Los Altos Hills, inventors of Opera Game, are users.

Contracts Kerrins makes with the customers pay the patient-workers. Capacity is available, so if you want your holiday packaging done early, call her at (415) 493-1413. Her husband, **Robert**, a VA employee, interfaces with the Vets' Task-Force.

IN AN ITEM ABOUT "Profiles in Excellence" last week, listing the 37 individual Chinese-Americans who were subjects of Los Altos Hills author **Connie Young Yu** took all the space. In reading this Stanford Area Chinese Club-sponsored book since then, I've been struck by the sociological power of Yu's profiles. Equally striking are the recent and pervasive feelings of discrimination she reveals, particularly among older subjects. How blind we can be to things that, in ethnic groups other than our own, are life's major concerns!

"We're hardly new here," Yu writes. "Our story is deeply rooted in California history. Chinese who came into San Mateo and Santa Clara counties worked in developing a multitude of industries.

They were workers on the San Jose railroad, miners in the Almaden Quicksilver Mine, horticulturists and field workers in the Ferry Seed Co.,gardeners and domestics at Stanford University."

But they were denied naturalization and had no civil rights. Then in 1882 the Exclusion Law prohibited further immigration of Chinese laborers.

"Only after the repeal of the Exclusion Law in 1943 and liberalization of immigration laws in the following two decades did the Chinese community begin its integration into American life," Yu says.

Despite varied backgrounds, her profilees share ultimate success at overcoming the odds. She wryly notes one other commonality — those who had to attend Chinese school in America all hated it.

LINDA HOLLISTER OF PALO ALTO writes expressing "extreme disappointment" at this column's Oct. 8 item about the Palo Alto Police and Fire Show at Stanford Shopping Center, featuring **McGruff**, the crime prevention dog, and **Sparky**, the fire prevention dog. Hey, I'm for the finest in policing and fire prevention, and think it's neat that these forces' community service people, helped by volunteers, do this education. But let Mrs. H tell about this "excellent, organized public service."

"After visiting the many exhibits," she says, "... I only wished that I had organized my 10-year-old's Webelos (Cub Scout) Den to visit it with us. My 9- and 10-year-olds were thoroughly engrossed in the entire exhibit, from the individual instruction from a Fire Department official on how to STOP, DROP & ROLL in the event of having clothing on fire to being fingerprinted by the Police Department for parents to keep in case of tragic disappearance.

" ... questions regarding safety, Halloween precautions, and reasons a family cat should be tagged for identification as well as pet dogs ... were encouraged and fully answered by caring officers.

"McGruff, touted by Winslow as wearing a $1,000 fur suit, was in fact a Troop 50 Scout, volunteering his day under a heavy mask and trench coat. His red striped socks gave him away as a youth giving a precious Sunday for a good cause.

" ... My children had such a positive day that they shared it with their classes on Monday. Their rooms sport 'SAY NO TO DRUGS' bumper stickers next to 'NEIGHBORHOOD WATCH WORKS' signs. ... I think the Palo Alto Fire and Police Departments deserve community thanks!"

Business-art partnership noted at Dunes celebration

PAJARO DUNES near Watsonville marked its 20th anniversary Sunday afternoon with an unusual program titled "Partners in Excellence: Business and the Arts." The seaside retreat, which for two decades has provided businesses and arts organizations with conference facilities, got leaders from the two communities together at a workshop designed to enhance the increasing cooperation between them.

Ryland Kelley of Ladera, president of the Palo Alto firm that developed Pajaro Dunes, Hare, Brewer & Kelley, introduced the program, and **Tom Peters**, business columnist and co-author of "In Search of Excellence," provided a commentary. Kelley noted that while shrinking government support for the arts has raised concern for the survival of our cultural institutions, businesses are becoming aware of marketing opportunities offered by the arts community.

Architect **M. Arthur Gensler**, president of the San Francisco Chamber of Commerce 2% Club, acted as moderator. Among the panelists were Dr. **Richard E. LeBlond Jr.**, president and CEO of the San Francisco Ballet, **Bonnie Earls-Solari**, the Bank of America's art program director, and **Willis J. Price**, senior VP, Chevron USA, Inc.

ANOTHER ANNIVERSARY celebration coming up is the Downtown Palo Alto Food Closet's 10th, which will be marked with a party Friday afternoon, Nov. 7. **Gretchen Emmons** says the local people who run the operation think it's pretty remarkable that an all-volunteer outfit has lasted a decade. Three volunteers, **Elinor Beaulieu**, **Mildred Reicks** and **Mary Imbernone**, have persevered through all 10 years.

The Food Closet, located at 555 Waverley St. in All Saints Church, serves between 600 and 1,200 people a month — single men, the elderly, families whose breadwinner has been laid off, and other needy folks. They are supplied with a grocery bag of what is available and appropriate, such as powdered or dry milk, honey, beans, rice or butter from government surplus stocks, and canned fruit and vegetables, tuna, bread, pasta and donated fresh fruit and vegetables. Several Palo Alto churches donate money to buy some of the food.

THE MENLO PARK CITY COUNCIL agenda for last night was so heavy that City Clerk **Jaye Carr** rated it "a three-thermos evening." Carr totes her own coffee because she dislikes the instant variety available at the council chambers. Once in a while she shakes her thermos to stir up the sugar therein. Well, she says it's sugar, but council wits sometimes speculate that olives may surface, in the great tradition begun by **Jackie Gleason**, who often showed exceptional relish for his coffee mug's contents.

WHEN THE SARAH WALLIS state historical landmark was dedicated in Barron Park Oct. 11, Palo Alto Mayor **Mike Cobb** made an unscheduled appearance. If I heard him right, Mike, an old Barron Park boy, was unexpectedly able to attend because of a change in the schedule of the girls soccer team he coaches, a team on which one of his daughters plays. So he came and introduced **Gail Woolley**, the council member standing in for him.

At the occasion, **John Bracken**, pres. of the Palo Alto Historical Association, walked off with honors for the most outrageous pun. He said it was a splendid "Sarah-mony." Even the Brownies who presented the colors must have groaned at that one.

Another chap who merits some special recognition is **Jerry Tinney**, now a masonry contractor. He donated construction of the rather special plaque that is now the pride of Barron Park.

WHEN THE OBITUARY OF Julia "Mother" Green of East Palo Alto ran last week, it identified her as the oldest known Peninsula resident. Prodded by an inquisitive subscriber, I called the Palo Alto Social Security office to see if they could verify that. **Laura Withrow**, who is in charge of the office, laughed at the question. Social Security goes by the numbers, and a local office has no information about the ages of beneficiaries, she explained.

Remembering greetings from President and Mrs. Reagan that reached a 101-year-old godmother (in San Francisco), I asked how those came about. Ms. Withrow answered that one, but out of personal experience — she'd done it for a relative who turned 88. Someone has to write the White House explaining the occasion and requesting the greeting.

As for centenarian citizens, we'd be delighted to know how many more of you there are out there.

Palo Alto High School likely to survive, in name at least

Ward
Winslow

IF AND WHEN PALO ALTO'S two high schools are merged into one, one question the Board of Education will face is what to name the surviving school. Probably this issue won't equal the angst of the site choice, for that figures to involve a game of "musical chairs" in which Palo Alto High School, Henry M. Gunn High School or Jane Lathrop Stanford Middle School (formerly Wilbur) compete for the two remaining spots — one high school and one junior high. One site may have to lose.

Still, the name is significant. Right now I'd bet on Palo Alto High School — the name, that is. It has the weight of tradition behind it, and most communities with one high school use the place name. In the Mountain View-Los Altos Union High School District, the school board closed the old high school plant in downtown Mountain View but transplanted its name to what used to be Chester Awalt High.

One cannot be too confident, however. When it came to combining David Starr Jordan and Ray Lyman Wilbur middle schools, the Palo Alto district opted for a new name: Jane Lathrop Stanford. The choice may have been low in the merit department, for Dr. Wilbur apparently did much more for Palo Alto schools than either of the other Stanford University figures, but it did honor a woman and it seemed to meet the needs of the middle school merging. Perhaps it will turn out to have been transitional.

In other cases, Palo Alto trustees have used a new name in combining schools. Sometimes they have moved a well-established name to another campus when merging two student populations.

SINCE AUGUST, THE TRUSTEES have been cogitating a letter from **Dorothy Nichols** suggesting that the district somehow commemorate her father, Walter H. Nichols, "who for 20 years shaped Palo Alto education." He came to Palo Alto in 1915 as superintendent of schools and principal of the high school, which then was on Channing Avenue. Rather quickly he put through the formation of a union high school district extending beyond Palo Alto proper, and that district erected Palo Alto High School at Embarcadero Road and El Camino Real on a site provided to the district by Stanford University.

Dorothy related that her father then saw that an architect of distinction and imagination was re-

tained, resulting in a departure from the tradition of red brick and white pillars and the construction of a Mediterranean-style school. Nichols saw to it that a full stage was built in the auditorium rather than the customary speaker's platform, helping in the growth of a strong local dramatics tradition. She noted too that the school's landmark campanile, or tower, became a rallying point for Paly loyalists decades later when a total reconstruction of the school was proposed and then was scaled back considerably amid a squall of protests.

"HE PUSHED THROUGH the Embarcadero subway to make the railroad crossing safe for students," she continued. " ... He refused a raise in salary which he felt the district could not afford.

"When the office of superintendent and principal were divided and he was offered his choice, he chose the high school. The spirit of the school was as important as any outside achievement, and one teacher told me he had never taught in a place of such good feeling. He gave the students as much freedom as they can use, encouraging individuals and not lax on discipline."

Well said, though it must have been embarrassing for Dorothy to have to say it herself. It was necessary, for not many people are still around who have the eyewitness knowledge and appreciation of that era which she possesses.

WALTER NICHOLS SHOULD HAVE been honored during the district's great postwar construction boom, perhaps at the time the second high school plant was named for Ellwood Patterson Cubberley, who had been dean of education at Stanford but whose role in enhancing Palo Alto's educational system hardly compared with Nichols'. For a long time the district resisted naming schools for its standouts, giving in during their lifetimes only for such superlative leaders as **Dr. Gunn**, the superintendent during the postwar mushrooming, and Elizabeth Van Auken, a beloved principal.

Let's hope the leadership will find a way as the trustees and Superintendent **Julian Crocker** struggle through the many tough choices that lie ahead.

In connection with all this, we can note that while schools may close, the name sticks to the site unless the school is plowed under.

A lively newspaper survives with Palo Alto High

ONE OFFSHOOT OF the Palo Alto Board of Education's decision to keep Palo Alto High School open presumably will be to keep alive the great tradition of *The Campanile*, the student newspaper.

In November 1988, the Camp will turn 70. It has been a lively journal from the start, and adviser **Esther Wojcicki** says the 1986-87 volume may top those of the last four years, all first-place winners in the Columbia Scholastic Press Association contest. **Jennifer Linden** and **Karen Rabin** are this year's editors-in-chief, succeeding **David Van** and **Craig Vaughan**. **Robert Neff**, the adviser before Wojcicki, is credited with starting the current glory train.

No put-down of Gunn High's *The Oracle* is intended. Some fine writer-editors cut their journalistic teeth there; I worked with some of them later. But I confess my loyalties are with *The Campanile*.

DOROTHY E. NICHOLS founded the paper in November 1918. Yes, the same Dorothy Nichols who for most of the years from then until last autumn was a music and drama reviewer for the *Palo Alto Times* and then the *Times Tribune*.

The Camp got started late in that school year because of the big flu epidemic. Paly High was not then at its present site but down on Channing Avenue — the student body marched to the new campus on Christmas Eve. Dorothy was the principal's daughter. She also was the commissioner of literary activities (an elected office) and editor of the yearbook, too. From 1900 on, the high school had had a paper, first named *The Red and Green* (Paly's colors in the good old days), then *The Madrono* (now the yearbook). But they were monthlies. Nichols had grander plans.

The Camp was printed biweekly at the P.A. Times, and Dorothy remembers the late Cy Henry, one of the trio who bought the Times in 1919, telling her, "You'd make a lot more money if you worked in the back room," meaning the shop. Cy was right, but Dorothy had wanted to write ever since seeing her first piece in print — an essay that won her the $5 first prize in a WCTU contest in Pasadena.

ACCORDING TO VOL. 1, the name was voted in by the student body. Dorothy admits some "finagling" about that, however. Her father, who put across the new union high school district that built Paly, wanted a Mediterranean-style building, with the tower its dominant feature.

The fledgling paper had a remarkable world view — its debut came as World War I was ending. Theodore Roosevelt's death received bulletin treatment, but there also were lots of peppery squibs urging students to subscribe, at 40 cents a year. Maybe those were written by the late Norris James, then business manager but later the second editor. **Blake Wilbur** was another of the original staff.

Dorothy isn't sure who chose the original old English nameplate, or flag. It lasted a long time, but now it has been modernized, to good effect.

LOTS OF CAREERS HAVE BEEN launched at the Camp, this columnist's included. Dorothy remembers the delight of **Mary Thygeson Shepardson**, now a distinguished anthropologist, at being named freshman reporter. James had a literary career; **Gareth Saddler**, whose circa 1940 volume won prizes, went into politics. **Bernice "Bunny" Smith McDowell** worked with editor **Dorothy Vaughn Manor**, now of Carmel, in 1927-28; they like to joke about the time Bunny's husband, **Carl** , then business manager, was listed on the masthead as "Carlotta."

Robert W. Taylor of Menlo Park, one of famed magazine writer Frank J. Taylor's sons, bequeathed the paper to me in mid '42-43 when he began speeded-up World War II studies at Stanford; Bob has has a standout career in public relations. **Ryland Kelley**, the real estate mogul, was our commissioner of publications.

THE BEST TALE OUT OF the '42-'44 era had to do with a "circus" edition that was banned because of **Dick Jennings'** fanciful cartoon of the faculty at a beer bust. Staffers-of-yore will be interested to hear that the Camp is still plowing new journalistic ground. Its two-page spread on "TEEN SEX" (that heading is in bold caps in an inch-high box) includes a survey and stories on pregnant teens, homosexuality, condom ads, AIDS, subliminal messages and sex education. If any no-no's are left, it's hard to imagine what they are.

Mushrooming town houses create a new way of life

WHAT DO SPECIAL MASTER John R. Griffiths of Palo Alto, Lighting Conversions president **Clark Williams** of Menlo Park, Asphalt Maintenance Systems owner **Barry Ericson** of Sunnyvale, attorney **Tom Fier** of Foster City and high-tech marketing executive **Hank Skawinski** of Mountain View have in common?

The answer is a keen interest in town houses and condominiums and the associations that run them. Such tracts (many are planned-unit developments) are termed "common-interest subdivisions" because residents jointly own some outer features.

These units have mushroomed of late, particularly on the Peninsula. Besides being home to many thousands, they generate new businesses, bodies of law, management styles and political forms.

WHILE SOME FOLKS NAMED at the outset have professional or commercial stakes in owner associations, a majority of the nearly 600 people attending ECHO's recent annual seminar at the commodious new Santa Clara Convention Center were homeowners who serve as a labor of love on the boards. Close to 600 associations, representing perhaps 250,000 residential units, are members of San Jose-based ECHO, the Executive Council of Home Owners, a non-profit outfit. Its executive director is **George E. Howarth** of San Carlos. **Oliver Burford** of Mountain View is president.

Some associations use professional managers, on-site or off, while others, like Skawinski's 43-unit Rock Creek Home Owners Association, near Fairchild Semiconductor, are run by their own board members. All need certain services: landscaping, banking, billing, legal advice, insurance, painting, roofing, and maintenance of paving, swimming pools, recreation centers, artificial lakes, lighting and whatnot. So the seminar attracted an array of vendors, with literature, giveaways, pitches, displays and prize drawings. Along with programs, evaluation forms, background sheets and summaries, these contributed to a paper glut. I'll never live to see a paperless convention.

THE ALL-DAY SATURDAY PROGRAM dealt mostly with the tougher problems, reflected in session titles: "Pets, People and Parking," "Preventive Maintenance Programs That Work," "Getting and Keeping Good Board Members," "Amending the Documents and Enforcing the Rules," "Delinquencies and Foreclosures" and "Avoiding Rip-Offs By Board Members, Managers and Contractors."

Skawinski told how a resident living by Rock Creek's lake couldn't stand the frogs croaking. She urged ducks as a control, but others objected. A timely chlorination of the lake solved the problem.

The documents referred to are the CC&Rs — covenants, conditions and restrictions — and bylaws governing each association. New state laws keep compelling changes in these documents.

Soon after becoming a Palo Alto town house resident, I learned association politics can be extremely intense. Now, as a new board member (it is regarded as civic duty in our neighborhood to serve one's turn), I'm getting more eyeopeners.

For instance, the Ralph Brown Act, California's open meetings law, applies to our proceedings. We are potential targets of suits for negligence, though attorney **John Garvic** of San Mateo assured us we probably are safe if we use common sense and seek expert advice when a safety issue arises.

CONSTRUCTION AND RELATED disputes keep a corps of attorneys busy. Some cases become very complex, and John Griffiths, managing partner of a large Palo Alto law firm, spends much of his time nowadays serving as special master for the Superior Courts of Santa Clara, San Mateo and other counties, trying to settle these cases before they enter the even costlier trial phases.

Griffiths and retired judges doing kindred work are making legal history. Federal courts long have used special masters for complex cases, and U.S. District Court Judges **Robert F. Peckham** and **William A. Ingram** broke in Griffiths.

When you're in Australia, say 'G'day' to Bill Lane

VISITORS FROM THE STATES are keeping U.S. Ambassador to Australia **L.W. "Bill" Lane Jr.** of Portola Valley plenty busy, according to his brother, **Mel Lane** of Atherton and Sunset Publications. The flow of people going Down Under is occasioned by the preliminaries of the America's Cup yachting competition. A flock of Yanks would like to say "G'bye" to the host Aussies and return home with the trophy.

FRIENDS OF HIDDEN VILLA is coming up against the sobering realities of operating the Los Altos ranch the late Frank and Josephine Duveneck began opening to the community long, long ago.

Frank, who was approaching his 99th birthday when he died Sept. 2, 1985, left the entire farm to The Trust for Hidden Villa, with partial funding ($7,000 a month) for its operation. The Trust holds 1,650 acres of farm and wilderness land. The operating cost will be more than $100,000 a year, once the contributions from the founder's estate expire in 1987.

"It will be up to the community to keep the green gate open as it has been for a half a century," says **Judie Wolken** of Los Altos, president of the Friends. The group is appealing for increased support and pointing out the tax advantages to most donors of advancing gifts into 1986 rather than awaiting 1987.

Earlier this year, a Hidden Villa Master Plan was completed. It states the mission of the Trust as, "To preserve and enhance Hidden Villa as a natural, historic, educational, and recreational resource using the natural setting, the farm, facilities and traditions of Hidden Villa to teach social, humanitarian, and environmental values." That's an excellent brief statement of the Duvenecks' intentions.

WHAT DOES HIDDEN VILLA OFFER? Well, young school children can go there to see what a farm is. Second- through sixth-graders can spend a day there learning about the interrelationships of living things on the farm and in the adjoining wilderness. Teen-agers and older persons will find a 24-bed hostel that has been in operation since 1937.

In the summer, there are five camping programs, one dating back to 1945, all emphasizing multicultural diversity. The goal is to offer scholarships to one-third of the campers. This year there was a new program — community leadership training for 15- to 18-year-olds.

THERE ARE WEEKEND HIKES, too, starting at the Hidden Villa parking lot at 10 a.m. This Sunday, for example, there will be a 2½-mile High Circle Trip up the Hostel Trail over Elephant Mountain and along the ridge to Ewing Hill, then down steeply to the old Boy Scout Camp location and back along Adobe Creek. **Lalu Kiesling** of Menlo Park will lead it.

Folks who'd like a more casual look-see can meet Hidden Villa's animals and vegetables during a personalized tour on the first Sunday of each month from 1:30 to 3:30 p.m. It costs $2 a person. For reservations, call (415) 948-4680.

There is more, too, and of course the value of this magnificent gift to the community will grow in the future as we seek more such oases in the foothills. Donors who like the idea of being a part of it can send checks to The Trust for Hidden Villa, 26870 Moody Road, Los Altos Hills, CA 94022.

IN NAMING THE GYM at Woodside High School for recently retired athletics director **William M. Guttormsen** of Atherton, the Sequoia Union High School District trustees may succeed in jazzing up the language: Guttormsen became known far and wide as "Mr. G" in his 28 years as coach, mentor, example and friend to thousands of Woodside students and fellow teachers. How can it help but become known as the "G-Gym" for short? There's enough jive in that name to make it catch on in places where the kids have never heard of Bill Guttormsen.

DO THE GOOD TOWNSPEOPLE of Atherton, where the registered Republicans outnumber the Democrats about 3 to 1, realize they've elected one of the Loyal Opposition to their Town Council? At least **Chris Cobey** was a Democrat (and the son of a former state senator) in 1980 when he lost a primary squeaker for the right to oppose **Bob Naylor** of Menlo Park, the splendid assemblyperson who could be heading for Congress but unfortunately is emerging a lame duck from the '86 political wars.

Stanford, Palo Alto tidbits in two historical booklets

CREDIT FOR THE FACT THAT the San Francisco-Oakland Bay Bridge was completed 50 years ago belongs to an engineer I hadn't associated with it until now: President Herbert C. Hoover. **Robert Hessen** of Palo Alto, business historian and a senior research fellow at the Hoover Institution at Stanford University, tells about it in a delightful booklet titled "Herbert Hoover and the Bay Bridge — A Commemorative Essay."

In his introduction, Hessen remarks: "It is no exaggeration to say that if Herbert Hoover had not exerted his power as president on behalf of the bridge, it would not have been built until many years later." After reading his brief, lively account, you have to believe it.

Hoover wasn't the first to propose the project; Leland Stanford raised the idea twice, Hessen says, and "Emperor" Norton commanded it in 1869 to no avail. F.E. Fowler, a San Francisco engineer, designed a span in 1914, but found both the Army and the Navy strongly opposed. Once Hoover revived the idea in 1922, while he was secretary of commerce, he pursued it doggedly, making a campaign promise in 1928 to support the project. But even as president he had to pull quite a few strings to get the bridge approved and funded through his version of a relief agency, the Reconstruction Finance Corp.

ALONG WITH STANFORD AND Hoover, several other Stanford men were very much involved. One was Professor Charles D. "Daddy" Marx, Hoover's former teacher, retired head of engineering at the university and a longtime mainstay of the Palo Alto City Council. Marx served on a commission Hoover created jointly with California Gov. C.C. Young, and later lobbied the project in Washington, D.C., as head of the board of engineers of the California Toll Bridge Authority. Ray Lyman Wilbur, on leave as Stanford president to serve as Hoover's secretary of the interior, helped out in one pinch by carrying word of a crisis to his friend Hoover from Leland Cutler of San Francisco, who had become a principal proponent. Cutler later served for many years on the Stanford board of trustees.

There are many interesting tidbits in Hessen's story, along with a marvelous picture of Hoover, looking stiffer than he did in later years, at the dedication in 1936 with Gov. Frank Merriam. Hoover is holding a golden chain as a blow torch a foot or so away cuts through it; Merriam's policy is hands off.

Hessen's booklet is available on request. Dial the Hoover Institution Public Affairs Office at (415) 723-0603 and ask for it.

ANOTHER WORTHWHILE BOOKLET, " ... Gone Tomorrow? — 'Neat Cottages' & 'Handsome Residences'," an account of historic Palo Alto houses first published as a directory in 1971 by the Palo Alto Branch of the American Association of University Women, has resurfaced. Although the original 1971 text has been retained, six of the 72 houses described have a "GONE" label plastered on their pages, like a "Sold" patch in the classified real estate advertising listings.

The proceeds of this second printing are earmarked for the AAUW's Educational Foundation Program, which provides fellowships and grants to women completing doctoral programs or master's degrees in business administration, as well as financing local research.

Six leaders of the Palo Alto branch are credited in the preface: **Carroll Harrington**, community area chairwoman; **Mary W. Lewis; Patricia McEwen; Mary Morrison**, immediate past president; **Jackie Thomas** and **Carolyn M. Ybarra. Debbie Mytels** is publicizing the project for the branch.

It's worth noting that Pat McEwen was one of the 15 women who worked on the original edition. So was Palo Alto City Councilwoman **Gail Woolley**, who is credited in the preface with inspiring the republication "on behalf of all Palo Alto residents." Indeed the reissue is a community resource, in the same league with the streets and trees of Palo Alto booklets put out some years ago by the Palo Alto Historical Association. (Although the association has not been active in publishing in the last few years, **Boyd Haight** tells me new efforts are afoot, or is it ahand?)

MOST OF THE HOUSES PORTRAYED in photographs or sketches and charted on locator maps are big old shingle or clapboard places. Daddy Marx's house at 1136 Waverley is there, by the way.

Assemblymen may change, but Alice remains constant

EVEN IF MANY RESIDENTS of the 20th Assembly District have never heard of **Alice Fresquez** of Redwood City, she is the district's great constant — here yesterday, here today, here tomorrow.

Fresquez will continue as office manager for new Assemblyman **Bill Duplissea**, just as she served **Bob Naylor** from 1978 on and **Dixon Arnett** before that. The last hurrah of Naylor's term found the other San Carlos office staff survivors, administrative assistant **Gordon Bloyer** and field representative **Dawn Clifford**, lunching at Fresquez's home Thanksgiving Eve.

Naylor himself wasn't there — he and his family were off for Lake Tahoe for the holiday weekend. His term ended Dec. 1, but don't count him out of politics. He has just formally announced his candidacy for the Republican state chairmanship, which he is favored to win in a mid-February showdown.

CHUCK QUACKENBUSH, the new assemblyman from Los Altos, was mistakenly introduced as Naylor's successor at the California Engineering Foundation's conference in Sacramento Nov. 13. Wrong. Quackenbush does, however, expect to take over Naylor's place on the Joint Committee on Science and Technology, as befits a legislator from Silicon Valley.

One more note before leaving the Assembly districts: A recent item about new Atherton Councilman **Chris Cobey** illustrated the hazards of depending on a long, if not acute, political memory. It was in 1978 (not 1980) when Cobey ran and he won (not lost) the Democratic nomination by three votes out of 38,000-plus. Then he went on to make the best showing by a Democrat in the district until **Ed Bacciocco's** recent run against Duplissea. Contrary to the trend of the item, Cobey's name was spelled correctly.

He makes the point, too, that local government service is non-partisan and "party affiliation is irrelevant." Even so, a second '86 winner in Atherton is a registered Democrat. "The cities need help from everyone, and Atherton is no exception," says Cobey.

AS THE MENLO PARK CITY COUNCIL launched into a three-hour hearing capping a three-year study last week, members were handed a briefing paper saying the subject was the Comprehensive Plan, "Preparing for the 12st Century." Calling Alley Oop's time machine!

A FEW DAYS BEFORE Gov. **George Deukmejian** promoted his old law partner, Associate Justice **Malcolm Lucas**, to the top spot on the California Supreme Court, outgoing Chief Justice **Rose Bird** received the Sally Siegel "Friend of Education" Award from the Palo Alto Educators Association. Many of the unified school district's establishment figures were on hand.

Bird got a big laugh when she said that, although she has always considered educators her friends, she felt it best to keep that quiet during her doomed campaign for reconfirmation.

A bit later **Sally Siegel**, first recipient of the award nine years ago for her educational activism, and a local leader of this year's campaign for Bird, got the floor and was waxing poetic. Quoting a line of verse, Sally turned to the honoree and said, "Rose Elizabeth Bird, I'm filled with the noise of you." Quick as a flash, the unmarried chief justice shot back: "If only you were a man!" It brought down the house again.

Although many of those present were political sophisticates, Bird's charisma was evident. Some were awed to meet the highest-ranking woman in California political history. Her height and sparkle and grace in defeat helped.

AT STANFORD, THE CENTER for Research on Women has changed its name to the Institute for Research on Women and Gender. Among other advantages, the new name does not form an acronym like "C.R.O.W." **Deborah L. Rhode**, professor of law and new head of the institute, says, "Despite substantial improvements in the status of women over the last quarter-century, American society still confronts significant obstacles to full equality between the sexes. Institutes such as Stanford's can play a critical role in identifying the roots of that inequality and the most promising strategies for change." Perhaps they'll want to talk with Rose Bird.

Not today, however. This afternoon, in the windup of the Jing Lyman Lectures, the institute will present **Bram Dijkstra**, professor of comparative literature, UC-San Diego, talking on "Ideologies of Female Illness in Fin de Siecle Culture." If you can't catch Dijkstra at 4:15 at Law School Classroom Wing Room 190, he'll be on the Bay Area book-signing circuit tonight at Printers Inc. in Palo Alto and Thursday at City Lights in SF and Cody's in Berkeley, plugging his book "Idols of Perversity." In a slide showing of the "dangerous phantasies of the beautiful people of a century ago," set for Cody's, Dijkstra says, "There are a few scenes of exemplary virtue and many more of lurid sin, but throughout, woman is shown to be dragging man through a grim trough of perversion."

AT OAK KNOLL SCHOOL IN Menlo Park, earthquake kits are being stowed in each classroom under the joint leadership of Principal **Marilyn Franklin** and PTA President **Mary Wheeler**. They contain first aid items, lights, lists of the students, name tags and the like. Superintendent **Martha Symonds** hopes that Oak Knoll's central earthquake supply center will be the first of many in Menlo Park schools.

Not every mother-to-be wants to be on television

EVERYBODY WANTS TO BE ON TV, right? Not so, **Randi Salerno** of Mountain View discovered last Thursday night at the Mid-Peninsula YWCA. Randi's prenatal and postnatal fitness class was featured in the first segment of a projected series on working women being made by **Sandra Kurtzig** for ABC's "Good Morning America." Randi reports that one expectant woman arrived for class, saw the camera crew, and promptly went home. Some other regulars apparently stayed away. But most were good sports.

Kurtzig is one of Silicon Valley's best-known working woman, as chairman of the board and founder of Ask Computer Systems Inc., Los Altos. At present she is acting as a guest correspondent, a tryout that might eventually put her to work in New York as the morning hostess. Other parts of the working women series will deal with matters like child care and how women get raises, and also figure to be filmed locally. The exercise class segment is tentatively scheduled to air in January, along with an introduction videotaped at ASK.

Rhonda Rosner of Palo Alto, who works as a market analyst at Hewlett-Packard corporate headquarters, is Kurtzig's featured subject. She's expecting her second child in April.

Salerno teaches several daytime, evening and Saturday classes that focus on stretching, strengthening and relaxing, with about 60 women enrolled. She took the class herself while carrying her daughter, **Natalie**, now 4. Then she began teaching it 3½ years ago and went on through her pregnancy with **Michael**, now 16 months.

Teaching the class is fun, Randi says, because pregnant women are "excited, friendly and warm, and there's a lot of class camaraderie."

Dianne Dryer of Palo Alto, the YW's public communications coordinator, says the classes — a 25-year tradition at the YW — will begin their winter session Jan. 5. For information, dial (415) 494-0972.

IT WAS SURPRISE DOUBLEHEADER 60th birthday time a few nights ago for a pair of prominent attorneys, **Robert R. Wood** of Menlo Park and **Gordon L. Poole** of Woodside. Their wives, **Barbara Wood** and **Lois Poole**, engineered the dinner party for more than 50 family members and old friends at Ristorante Orsi in San Francisco and got their spouses there without the secret leaking. There was an anxious moment after **Arthur B. Poole** of Palo Alto, who'll soon turn 92, said the day before he'd be seeing his son, but Lois beat back a disclosure with some fast talking.

Actually, it was Bob's birthday, but Gordon, a Christmas Day baby whose own birthday tends to get lost in other festivities, was happy to piggyback.

Wood and Poole first got acquainted as students at Palo Alto High School. Later they were classmates at Harvard Law School. Then they roomed together as young SF attorneys. More recently, each has served on the San Mateo County Republican Central Committee, but never at the same time.

Poole won the toss and spoke first, quipping that **Ronald Reagan** should have had Lois and Barbara in charge of his secret operations.

SOME REAL TRIVIA BUFF should organize a contest to see who receives the most catalogs in the mail during the late fall. And then award that family's suffering mail carrier a free course of chiropractic aid.

My wife keeps writing to what must be tremendously powerful agencies that say they'll wipe us off the lists. But somewhere there's an even more powerful outfit that generates and broadcasts new sucker lists.

Actually there are a couple of catalogs issued in late December that I consider good reading. No, pal, not the ones from Victoria's Secret and the other purveyors of flimsy next-to-nothings next to lissome lasses bent in poses that could get a sheriff in trouble.

My favorite catalogs come from Foothill Community College. The main one — a schedule, they call it — is crammed not only with a fantastic variety of courses for the next quarter, but also with upfront information that should turn the telephone directory's A pages blush-colored. Its companion piece, the Community Services brochure, is the stuff that dreams are made of, a listing of for-fees courses artfully contrived to make me want to give up a weekend and $65 and register. The only rub is I couldn't afford the time or the cash to take everything that appeals to me.

Foothill has perfected these publications as a fine art. De Anza does about as well, but the thought of getting stuck on 85 or I-280 in a rush hour going to or from makes Foothill seem totally cozy and adequate.

THE PEOPLE BEHIND this excellent work turned out to be **Linda Nanfria** of Menlo Park and **Darren Thorneycroft** of Palo Alto on the schedule (they also do the official catalog which comes out in May and costs $5.50) and **Darlene Culbertson** of Cupertino on the Community Services brochure. Darlene said some other community colleges have similar brochures, but she knows of none other with a four-color cover. Not a penny of taxpayer money goes into the brochure, by the way. Both publications are pushing opportunities for winter quarter, beginning Jan. 5.

Up 280 at Canada College in Redwood City, courses run on a semester system and are given notice in an annual catalog and a schedule each semester. While Foothill does four schedules a year, Canada needs only three. Canada's second semester starts Feb. 2.

Family traditions are strong during the holiday season

WHAT WILL YOU BE DOING on the holidays — Christmas, say, or perhaps Hanukkah — that's a tradition in your family, but perhaps a bit different from the usual traditions: family reunions and meals, gift openings, religious services and the like?

Opaline Mitchell and her grown children, **Bill**, who lives in Mountain View, and **Marcy**, a law student at Berkeley, will be going to midnight Mass at St. Mark's Church — the kids, though they're not very regular churchgoers these days, insist on it, says Opaline, a Palo Alto teacher.

Afterward they'll return to the family home to sip cider or eggnog and reminisce about Christmases past. Here's one story sure to be retold:

It was about 10 years ago. The Mitchells had lost, in three successive years, near the holiday season, Opaline's husband, Bill, then her mother, then her father. She was feeling low, and planned no Yule trimmings.

Across the street lived good friends, **Dick** and **Joan Whaley** and their five children, **Justine, Alexis, Cara** (now Cara Cole of Mountain View), **Marianna** (who has just gone to Guatemala with the Peace Corps) and **Daryl.**

Daryl went to church with the Mitchells. While they were gone, the rest of the Whaleys found a tree, decorated it with cutouts from their old Christmas cards and set it up in the Mitchells' living room. The surprise really lifted spirits, Opaline says.

MIKE BEDWELL, MENLO PARK's city manager, observed a tradition weeks ago that brought back fond memories of an earlier one. His son **Allan**, a ranger at Yosemite, organized Mike and his other son, **Patrick**, who's thinking of becoming a naval aviator, to go out about Dec. 1 and cut a tree.

It reminded Mike of when he was a kid in Escondido and his grandmother, Jessie Miller, who was the assessor and tax collector in Inyo County, would ship a spruce or a silvertip from the mountains to the beachside Bedwells. He was about 15, Mike said, before he learned you could buy a tree from a lot. And with this year's tree-cutting, he realized that it takes a week and a half of aging to bring out that good pine or fir smell.

BILL LAWSON, WHO SPENT a bunch of years as a Menlo Park councilman and mayor, may go out for a drive this holiday. He's 86, and recently got his driver's license renewed — a testimonial to his good health. Bill celebrated by buying himself a new car. He looked at Bedwell's sporty stick-shift model, but chose one with an automatic transmission.

RAY MENDIOLA, CODE ENFORCEMENT officer for Menlo Park, will be doing what a lot of families do — making the traditional trip back home for a family reunion. Ray, his wife, **Brenda**, and their daughter **Daphne**, 8, will fly to Wichita lugging presents for everyone, including Daphne. Brenda's brother, **Brian Bonous** of Portland, and his family will be there too.

A BROTHER AND SISTER who both live in Palo Alto, Ruth Spangenberg and John Beahrs, will be devoting some holiday conversation to another brother, **Dr. Oliver "Bud" Beahrs** of the Mayo Clinic, who has a rather special assignment coming up. A few days ago Dr. Beahrs was named President **Ronald Reagan's** chief medical adviser, and will coordinate the chief executive's prostate surgery on Jan. 5 at Bethesda Naval Hospital. The surgeon will be Bud Beahrs' son, Dr. Randy Beahrs of Minneapolis, a urologist.

How did this change in the president's medical care come about? A family tie! It seems that the senior Dr. Beahrs is a protege of the late Dr. Loyal Davis, who was First Lady **Nancy Reagan's** stepfather.

THE IRREPRESSIBLE JIMMIE GRUBER of Palo Alto tells about a Palo Alto Bnai Brith pre-Hanukkah luncheon last week where he faced the task of making *latkes*, a potato pancake that's a special part of the Jewish Festival of Lights. Gruber, who used to be in the hotel and restaurant business in New York, says it's getting harder to find help for this task, though his loyal wife **Alice** and a friend, **Lorraine Apfelberg**, always pitch in, because you have to peel and shred potatoes, mix in eggs and flour and salt, then fry them. For a crowd of 50 or 60, that's work.

This year Jimmie found the quick way in a supermarket, "a fantastic replica" put out as "Golden Patties" by Ore-Ida with all the right ingredients. He coupled the *latkes* with jelly doughnuts, which are favored in Israel.

FOR ALLIED ARTS GUILD volunteers, the holiday may be a relief after their 50 percent off sale yesterday. Mary Lyn Moseley of Palo Alto, one of the vols, thinks a visit to the Rodin Garden or some of the exceptional contemporary sculpture at Stanford University is a good way to spend part of a holiday.

ROBERTA YEE, FOR MANY YEARS the guiding spirit of the Palo Alto-based Chinese Community Center, reports that the center dispatched 75 baskets of Christmas goodies last week to the On Lok senior center in San Francisco. The baskets contained knitted hats, Chinese groceries, sesame candy and a Chinese calendar.

Liberated from geography

TODAY BEGINS A NEW CHAPTER in the 20-month history of this column. It is released from an obligatory focus on events and residents in the areas covered by the Menlo Park and Palo Alto editions. By the same token it is freed to harp upon a persistent theme: the myriad harmonics struck by the mid-Peninsula's places and people.

There'll be new opportunities to take longer, deeper looks at institutions and people known from Cupertino to San Carlos, and at some of our subregion's common denominators.

Regular reporters henceforth will occupy Column 1 of the Neighbors section front, which is as it should be. They are on the beat full-time and need a spot for developing ideas and items that don't quite fit into standard news and feature categories.

What's more, their mugs can take a turn on the bird-cage floor — I figure an inside-the-section spot is better protected. Of course, some friends whose once-over-lightly of the paper means just flipping through the sections will ask whatever happened to me.

This minus will be plussed out by more consistent runs in the Mountain View, Sunnyvale, Redwood City and San Mateo editions.

SOME GOOD STUFF MAY BE going to the Palo Alto City Dump, **Gloria Brown** fears. As acquisitions chairperson of the Palo Alto Historical Association, she is asking people who decide to "clean all that old junk out" to screen their throwaways to be sure nothing PAHA could use is scrapped.

Dorothy Nichols just set a great example by donating the clippings and programs she compiled in 50 years as a music and drama reviewer for the Times Tribune and the Palo Alto Times. The collection now is housed at the History Corner of the Main Library on Newell Road, where **Steve Staiger** turns from librarian to official historian a couple of times a week.

Gloria is aiming especially for documents, photographs and other memorabilia relating to life or events in Palo Alto, from the 1940s through the 1960s — especially the '40s.

Have I got a scrapbook for her! It's full of odds and ends from the '40s so ephemeral I thought no one would ever want to look at it except my kids. (It turned out the kids weren't interested.)

VIRGINIA SATIR, WHO PIONEERED family therapy hereabouts and projected the idea internationally through her teaching and writing, is about to put on a local workshop with a fresh basis. Well, fresh in the sense of relating world peace to her trademark emphasis on the need for good communication, whether in families or professional relationships.

The conference, titled "World Peace Begins At Home," will take place Jan. 30 and 31 and Feb. 1 at the First United Methodist Church, 625 Hamilton Ave., Palo Alto. It is being sponsored by that church and two others, St. Mark's Episcopal and Grace Lutheran, and by the Midpeninsula Peace Center. The cost for all sessions is $35 per person, or $60 a pair. For more information, call (415) 328-8940.

Judging by the creativeness and impact Satir has shown in similar workshops earlier, this one should be of great interest, for she'll be talking about how to create the necessary conditions for a more peaceful, loving, healthy world. Presumably local leaders of Palo Alto-based Beyond War will tune in, too.

A few months ago, the brochure says, Satir agreed to sit on the Council of Elders for the International Congress of Nobel Laureates for World Peace. The result of that therapy is yet to be reported.

INSTITUTIONS COME AND GO. On Christmas Eve, we made our customary trip to Ming's on Embarcadero Road. It's Ming's Villa now; the interior has been remodeled (with the front door repositioned in a spot that seemed a lot windier) and the menu has been overhauled.

Bill Wang, my favorite waiter, was nowhere to be seen; indeed, the entire serving crew appeared to be new, and did a great deal of conferring over orders. The food was different, and it was very good. Somehow the place looked smaller; the various rooms are more decisively separated.

Speaking of badly located doors, the front door of the main Palo Alto Post Office on East Bayshore Road is situated so as to send icy January blasts right at the postal clerks on counter duty (and the Postal Patrons usually standing in line).

Don't architects pay heed any more to orientation? Clerks there also must look directly into the setting sun for a number of fall and winter weeks. Save our postal clerks!

IN THE NEW ORDER OF THINGS (with the old, our area's heritage, kept much in mind) I'll try to touch base with some places and institutions whose renown is general in half a dozen communities or so.

For instance, the Allied Arts Guild in Menlo Park; Kaiser Hospital in Redwood City; Skyline Boulevard where it snakes through Woodside, Portola Valley and Palo Alto; Alta Mesa Cemetery; Stevens Creek; El Camino Hospital in Mountain View; the Downtown Triangle in Los Altos; NASA/Ames and many others.

Suggestions about themes and common-denominator places, people and institutions are always welcome. Let's honor our interties!

A master of peace advocacy

VIRGINIA SATIR WAS TEACHING in Germany last year when a shadow passed over her. Not so far to the east, the Chernobyl disaster occurred, and the winds blew radiation to her location. She was advised to wash her hair and her clothing daily and to take other precautions.

That was when her concern for peace began to come into sharper focus. "I thought, There's more that can happen in the world," Satir told about 450 rapt listeners Friday night in Palo Alto. "I realized that every time I was part of a transaction that got someone healed, I was making peace." She saw her whole career as having been devoted to creating conditions so people can have health and peace.

So, at 70, the renowned therapist and teacher of therapists is turning her insights about communication and people's behavior to the service of peace. She says the planet is opening up, and conditions are ripe for an evolutionary leap. All over the world, as she views it, people are seeing a new alternative to the old choices of attacking or defending, dominating or submitting. It's to be real, to be equal to each other.

PEACE, BY SATIR'S DEFINITION, is not the absence of war but "the harmony of the self in action, ... the harmony of all human beings." As a mandala, or slogan, she suggested saying to yourself: "Peace is the harmony of my parts."

A lot of Satir fans were in the audience and, as she noted, some of them had seen elements of her presentation before, but not in the peace context. She used a rope trick — a group of people representing parts of the self connected along a clothesline — to show that when each acts with no heed for others, all get tied up, but that by paying attention to one another and moving in harmony, the parts can work together.

For years I'd heard about Virginia Satir — she lives in Menlo Park and with Jules Riskin and the late Don Jackson was one of the family therapy pioneers at Palo Alto's Mental Research Institute — but I'd never seen her in action before. It didn't take long to grasp why people swear by her. She's a master teacher, entertaining, enlightening, at once simple and profound.

"WORLD PEACE BEGINS AT HOME" was the program title, and it developed that my one-time stablemate in the editorial stall, Jay Thorwaldson, had suggested it. Jay, the Palo Alto Medical Clinic's communicator, has lined up Virginia Satir to speak May 2 on family communication at a Life Skills Conference for local teens at Palo Alto High School.

Another discovery was that Marion Booth, another former associate (in a church activity), had put the whole program together, enlisting three churches and the Midpeninsula Peace Center as sponsors. Virginia paid tribute to Marion's drive and follow-through, remarking, "If anything is going to be done in this world, human energy is going to do it." Satir's own energy is formidable.

"I give everybody a push any way I can," she said. "I say go do it. ... We don't have to wait for somebody to tell us it's OK."

A special feature of the evening was Debbie Koshelnek's singing in signing of "I Want to Live." This Canadian-born young woman had deaf parents, and did most of the outside talking for her family. Her first public "singing" brought down the house.

Jim Snodgrass, an old friend who was blinded in an automobile accident years ago, was there, wearing a "Hiroshima Never Again" button with a bit of green ribbon. It replaces a ribbon he used to wear that said: "Nuclear Hostage." Jim got the idea from the Iranian hostage crisis, reasoning that the stocks of nuclear weapons capable of killing every human in the world umpteen times over make prisoners of us all.

CALLING FOR THREE MEN and three women to come on stage, Satir paired them up to demonstrate the "small universe" of combinations possible: man-man, man-woman, woman-woman. The man and woman, for example, might represent husband and wife, father and daughter, or mother and son. Or two countries. She asked one in each pair to kneel in a posture of supplication, and later had the non-kneelers hang on the partner's back. The point was to demonstrate that people are uncomfortable with un-level or clinging relationships. "We'll never come to real peace until we know how to stand on our own feet," she said. Among people or nations. Each person or country has the power to change — and to look at power in a new way: as the whole integrated self.

As evidence of new possibilities for Earth's humans, Satir said she has been invited to Moscow to teach family therapy there for a month. "As long as you don't call it politics, you can go anywhere," she remarked.

Scout makes baylands accessible to handicapped

THERE'VE BEEN SOME CHANGES MADE at the Lucy Evans Baylands Nature Interpretive Center in Palo Alto. Thanks to **Hugh Fox's** Eagle Scout community service project, a new self-guided nature trail designed for the visually handicapped and hearing impaired leads out from the center. The center itself and its boardwalk also have been modified to be wheelchair-accessible.

Fox designed and carried out construction of the trail, and prepared a narrative tape and an illustrated booklet describing the different aspects of salt marsh ecology at each of 11 stations. Tape players can be checked out from Junior Museum naturalists at the Interpretive Center. The neat little booklet has sketches and vivid accounts of the habits and lifestyles not only of such plants as fennel, salt grass, fat hen and pickleweed but also of such shy creatures as the salt marsh harvest mouse and secretive types including the pintail duck and the California clapper rail.

Hugh Fox

The trail was opened Sunday afternoon with fitting civic hoopla. Besides giving persons with disabilities a chance to get to know the baylands, the project should lure additional able Peninsulans to one of the area's distinctive attractions.

ALONG WITH TROOP 627's FOX, leading enablers of the project have been Supervisor **Mearl F. Carson** and naturalist **Ted Chandik** of the Junior Museum and **Arthur de Genova**, a member of the city's Task Force for Disability Awareness. Carson took a special interest because he incurred extensive hearing loss during World War II Air Force duty and has worn hearing aids for 40 years. More recently, his wife suffered a partial paralysis and has had to struggle to regain the ability to walk short distances. De Genova, who has taught citizenship classes for many years, also is toiling to overcome a disability.

No one knows how many Palo Altans are disabled in one way or another — perhaps one in five, de Genova guesses. He says he was surprised to learn there are more folks who hear poorly than who see poorly. De Genova is considering launching a magazine to be called *Challenges* about matters of interest to the disabled. He presently publishes a biography journal.

Chandik's wish list is topped by a video camera-recorder for recording seasonal baylands changes, de Genova says. Also wanted is a tactile map to help unsighted visitors get the lay of the marsh, so to speak.

One last tidbit for long-time baylands fans: **Harriet Mundy**, who along with the late Lucy Evans did a lot to save the baylands, was here on a visit during the recent high tides. She lives in Pennsylvania now and is over 80. Part of the marsh is named for her.

IS IT HARDER NOWADAYS to lead or play an active role in any sort of organization? **Pat Cawood** of Menlo Park, a trainer who has worked with many Peninsula groups over the last 18 years, says yes. It used to be easier, she says, when an agency had three publics: its board of directors, its clients and its fund donors. Now there may be as many as 10 to 15 publics to be responsible to, with a diverse board, a more variegated public, advocates among people served, monitoring organizations and the works, not to mention balancing the budget. There are whole new layers of interaction, Cawood says.

Cawood is about to launch a course titled "Facilitative Management," which she describes as the first of its kind in the Bay Area. "Facilitation" has been in trainer lingo for about 10 years, but it doesn't wear well, Cawood says — I'd guess thoughts about bathrooms get in the way. "Management" sounds serious.

The thrust of her course came through clearest to me when she said people trained under management theorists like Peter Drucker knew all about plans and organization and deadlines, but tended to come a cropper because the work had to be done by human beings. Humans have been known to block progress, or render minimum output, for their own reasons.

So Cawood aims to help leaders develop multiple perspectives for dealing with the complex, multidimensional situations of the '80s. Part of the emphasis is on integrating logical, analytical thinking with subjective, intuitive thinking.

The course, offered under the aegis of the Volunteer Center of San Mateo County, will begin Feb. 3 at the Burlingame Library Community Room, 480 Primrose Road, and run in day-long sessions once a week for six weeks. **Trish Ronald** of San Mateo is Cawood's primary backup. Others on the presenting team are **Virginia Levick** of Atherton, a therapist who works with families and children and group process; **Nancy Yeend** of Palo Alto, arbitrator and negotiator; and **Jean Litts Burkhardt** of Redwood City.

Hewlett-Packard, Foothill team up to build sports fields

YOU SAY YOUR COMPANY SOFTBALL teams can't find a place to play? How about trying what Hewlett-Packard is doing? HP is chipping in $112,000 for development of two new softball diamonds and a soccer field at Foothill College in Los Altos Hills. The string is that HP will get to use the fields for its interdivision employee sports leagues from 5 to 9 p.m. weekday evenings from mid-April through mid-September for the next 15 years.

The community college, which now has just one softball field, will gain new venues for day use by P.E. classes and sports competition. The fields, in the college's plans for 10 years, according to Foothill President Tom Clements, are under construction next to parking lot T. "Play ball!" will be heard this summer.

At HP, Betty Gerard in corporate PR says employees are keen about the idea, which may be the first deal of its kind between a business and a community college. It was negotiated by Barbara Hensley, coordinator of Foothill's business and industry interchange program, and Steve Chell, HP's manager of Bay Area employee and community programs.

IN CASE YOU WONDER WHY HP NEEDS so much softball time, consider that last year — limited by a shortage of playing fields — the company held its softball leagues to only 48 teams (24 men's and 24 coed), with about 800 employees playing.

"We welcome the chance to consolidate our interdivision sports leagues in one location and know we have the security of a long-term agreement," Chell said. He pointed out that HP already contracts to use Foothill's gyms for interdivision basketball and volleyball leagues. Until now, various city recreation departments and school districts have accommodated HP softball. In fact, the season probably will start in May at Cooper Park in Mountain View. Meanwhile, with the new turf in prospect, HP is looking at organizing an interdivision soccer league.

If you're an HP stockholder, take comfort in Chell's assurance that profits from an "HP Way to Play!" sports apparel program will help finance the deal.

Watch for an agreement like this one in Japan before long. Meanwhile, school districts with spare sites might consider plowing under extra classrooms and using the land for softball. Corporate capitalism is coming to bat.

COMPANIES SHELTER SPORTS GROUPS in other ways, too. For instance, last Saturday night Ampex Corporation's glass-walled cafeteria building in Redwood City was the scene of a meeting of the National Air-racing Group Inc. Improbable as it may seem, this professional air racing unit is Peninsula-based. Frank Ronco of Sunnyvale is president, Bar-

bara Snow of Cupertino secretary, John Clark of Santa Clara treasurer, and Pierre Wildman of Mountain View and John Crocker of San Mateo directors.

The racing doesn't take place locally — Minot, N.D., and Reno are the '87 race meet sites. And the membership, consisting of raceplane owners and pilots and related retinues and enthusiasts, spills all across America.

In a recent NAG newsletter, Chuck Aro tells of going to a recent motor sports show at the Santa Clara Convention Center and finding some of the world's most exotic racing hardware there — but no air racing stuff. That'll be remedied next year.

What do air racing buffs do at a monthly meeting? Besides a little business, last Saturday they saw slides of the '86 Reno Air Races and aviation movies.

SOME WOMEN WATCH MICHAEL SWAN on television because he is "not only debonair, but deliciously dangerous," as Suzy Mallery, president of Man Watchers Inc., said when she put him on her outfit's latest list of "Most Watchable Men in the World." However, other fans, including Lucy Smith of Palo Alto watch him because he's a local boy who's making good.

Swan's Scottish brogue is heard on "As the World Turns," the long-running soap opera. Earlier, he appeared in series called "Cliff Hangers" and "Hot Pursuit," and "Wheels," a miniseries. He has had other TV parts in "Murder, She Wrote," "M.A.S.H.," "CHiPs" and "The Incredible Hulk."

Before he "went Hollywood," Swan lived in Palo Alto, attended Paly High, Menlo School and Foothill College, acting in several Foothill productions.

MY FAVORITE WAITER, BILL WANG — actually he's more a maitre d' or restaurant owner type — is alive and well in Sunnyvale. About the time an item ran here last month lamenting his absence when we dined at the new Ming's Villa Christmas Eve, Bill, his wife, Pat, and their two teen-age daughters, Christine, 14, and Karen, 12, turned up at the table next to ours at Rudolfo's of Palo Alto. It was old home week and before we were through, Bill — a sort of Chinese Yul Brynner type — had brought around owner Art Alfinito and head chef Dionisiu Lee. Rudolfo's (which has a palpable ambiance of friendliness) still feels threatened with eviction by the city in 1993, so Alfinito remains eager to meet potential new allies. As for Lee, his ancestry and nations of past residence are a story you have to hear yourself.

It has always puzzled me how all these restaurant guys know each other. Maybe they meet at some secret place for Saturday lunch or Monday dinner.

Woman scientists at USGS create a day care center

THE "GEO KIDS" ARE COMING! The first on-site day care center in the U.S. Geological Survey will open at Western Region Headquarters in Menlo Park this spring, and the parents setting it up — mostly woman scientists — are thrilled and proud and still a trifle awed that Uncle Sam would help them.

Debbie Trimble of Redwood City, a geologist who manages the radiocarbon laboratory, began a campaign for a child care center 3½ years ago. Since then, she has delivered two babies of her own (**Jamie** and **Greg**), and with colleagues has sold "the Survey" on the idea of making space available, incorporated the non-profit Menlo Survey Day Care Center Inc., raised $7,000, secured a loan, and begun the process of hiring a director and teachers.

Easier recited than done. When Trimble learned she was pregnant and decided to try to get a child care center, she discovered the effort had been made before, to no avail. "They kept telling me no," she recalls. Then she got an ally: **Carol Ann Hodges** of Woodside, assistant chief geologist of the Geological Division. Trimble convinced Hodges a current child care need existed, and would grow in the future.

IN MENLO PARK, THE USGS has 120 professional women, out of a personnel total of about 1,500. They are trained in the sciences, and perhaps that accounts for their success. Trimble and her team spent a year and a half working up their proposal to the Survey Committee. They investigated regulations and requirements, and surveyed day care need.

"The way we approached it is the reason it sold," Trimble said. "We didn't plead from an emotional base. We laid it out like a scientific project. We had facts and figures — we got our ducks in a row. When questions were asked we were prepared to answer them. The fact that we'd really researched it impressed management."

The proponents made the point, too, that the child care center will benefit employees. Government salaries are not very competitive, Trimble said, but the on-site day care will give the USGS a recruitment tool and a way to offer something to support its staff.

PART OF THE BREAKTHROUGH occurred when **George Hargrove** of Mountain View became administrative officer and championed day care. Then Trimble & Co. found that the General Accounting Office had put out a memo stating that federal agencies could offer space for child care. Next the memo was enacted as Public Law 99-190, providing that government agencies could offer space when available to employee groups, unions or outside (for-profit) groups, provided 50 percent of the space is allocated to children of federal employees. The agency may provide rent, utilities including telephone, office supplies and furniture, security and janitorial service. But no federal funds may be spent to run the center.

At Menlo Park, there is no surplus building space, but USGS offered a site, plus utilities. So the non-profit corporation is leasing a modular building with an option to buy. It'll be placed on what once was a parking lot. **Pete Seeger** should add a stanza about that.

THE $100,000 BUILDING is being ordered this week, Trimble said. Fund-raising has been going on for the past six months and $7,000 has been collected. Landscaping of the playgrounds is about to proceed — geologists **Kathy Harms** of Santa Clara and **Jennifer Hardin** of Half Moon Bay are designing it. Equipment has been donated. Foundation grants are being sought, because the board wants to enlarge the building soon and go beyond the startup capacity of 52 kids, from infants to kindergarteners.

Peggy Bruggman of Redwood City, a part-time USGS physical science technician and an accomplished oboeist, organized a woodwind octet for a benefit concert in November. The musicians had never played together before, but they liked the group, now named Sirocco, and may do a second concert. Other fund-raisers past or forthcoming are a cookbook, Bay cruise, De Anza College flea market rummage sale, and an art auction April 25 at the USGS.

Just about then the day care center will open weekdays from 7 a.m. to 6 p.m. It is a cooperative; the parents will take part in running it and commit time to help care for the tots, and also pay a fee. Learning through play will be the philosophy.

OTHER LEADERS IN THE DRIVE have been **Katherine Pringle** of Menlo Park, a hydrologist, and her husband, **Malcolm**, a geologist; **Lore Winterman-Sturm** of Newark, on the National Cartographic Information Center staff, and her husband, **Tom Sturm**, also with USGS; geologist **Jane Nielson** of Mountain View; engineer **Pat Showalter** of Mountain View; hydrologist **Pat Cascos** of Boulder Creek; secretary **Robin Rebello** of Newark; geologist **Sean Stone**; and geologist **Michael Clynne**, Debbie's spouse.

While planning, the Geo Kids' sponsors got technical assistance from the San Mateo County Child Care Coordinating Council. **Bill Fisher** of Sunnyvale, who is just starting a new outreach program for victims of Alzheimer's disease, but who ran a child care center in Chicago for 12 years, spoke to the leaders. They took a look at Syntex Corporation's near-site day care center at the former Cubberley High School in Palo Alto, and adopted the idea of a co-op from the Stanford Cooperative Day Care Center on campus.

A vision of more funds for photos

Photography at Foothill College is a creative art, and that includes presenting and supporting it, as well as learning and doing it.

Marion Patterson of Menlo Park became the full-time department head in September, buoyed by the administration's decision to spend $50,000 to renovate the photo lab last summer. The center of the lab was gutted and rebuilt, with full wheelchair access, and the building was ready to support the new AA degree in photography (with an expressive emphasis).

The equipment, however, was something else. The studio lights were archaic, some of the enlargers were more than 25 years old, and color equipment was next to non-existent. And the budget was all but exhausted.

PATTERSON IS A resourceful person. The late Ansel Adams was her photographic mentor. "He was like a father to me," she says. As a former staffer at Sunset magazine, a free-lancer known for her nature and travel work and a part-time teacher at De Anza College in Cupertino and then Foothill in Los Altos Hills since 1968, she has built a reputation and taught many people to "see" — the crucial knack in photo work, to her mind. So she called in some markers. In December she mailed a "Dear Friend of Photography at Foothill College" letter, asking for donations to buy equipment and slating an open house to show off the remodeled lab.

Although fewer than 100, mostly former students, responded with checks, they responded handsomely. Donations ranged from $10 to $500, and 23 of the donors gave $100 or more. Gifts to the Foothill College Photography Trust Fund totaled more than $4,100. Initial use of the money has been to set up new color processors for negatives and prints.

Marion had set up recognition levels for donors — nameplates on equipment for those who gave $500 or more, names on a special plaque for the $100-$500 class. There were two $99 donations, and while one might think them shy about being listed on a plaque, it might just be that they wanted the "less than $100" prize: Patterson's signed photo of Mount Everest by Moonlight, a fabulous 3½-hour time exposure.

SOME BIG NAMES IN CAMERA WORK are on the donor list. **Carolyn Caddes** of Palo Alto, whose book of portraits of Silicon Valley pioneers is a smash, spoke at the open house. **Liz Duveneck Dana** of Los Altos Hills, whose sensitive shots of kids and farm animals appear on Hidden Villa brochures, helped out. So did **Virginia Adams** of Carmel, Ansel's widow, and professionals who studied with Marion, such as **Steve Mangold** of Mountain View, **Mark Tuschman** of Menlo Park, **Bill Powell** of Los Altos and **Helen Golden** of Palo Alto. **Charles W. Halleck** of Los Altos, a retired judge and a student in the beginning photo class, did a photostory on the department's expansion for the Los Altos Town Crier.

Patterson hopes donations have only begun. The department could use equipment as well as cash, particularly 35mm, 2¼ by 2¼ and 4 by 5 cameras and lenses, and strobe lighting with various studio doodads. She's hoping for some corporate grants to help with bigger ticket items and notes that it wouldn't hurt companies to send executives up to study picture-making as a stress-relief activity.

DE ANZA HAD THE JUMP ON Foothill in photography and has been awarding AA degrees for some time. Its emphasis, however, has been vocational, while that at Foothill has tended toward fine art. **George Craven** at De Anza, who only recently turned the department head duties over to **Shirley Fisher**, originally hired Marion.

Foothill's enlarged program has four tracks leading to an AA: fine arts photography, photojournalism, professional/technical (for jobs in laboratories and studios, or free-lancing) and interdisciplinary. The latter track delves into film, television, commercial art, advertising and computers.

"The whole field is changing so fast," Patterson said. "Basically we teach seeing — if you can see well you can move between fields, such as video, motion picture, still, computer graphics. And photography is becoming increasingly digital."

To serve interdisciplinary interests and rapid developments, the faculty — all part-timers save the chairperson — bring a variety of talents to bear. Current instructors are **Mike Ivanitsky** and **Deva Hymen-Breisch** of San Jose, Steve Kizer of Palo Alto, **Lescher Dowling** of Sunnyvale, **Dale Boyer** of Mountain View and **Bob Dawson** of San Francisco.

The lab is a busy place. Between 250 and 300 students a quarter are enrolled in photo courses, daytimes, evenings and even weekends (under the full-pay community services program). In the film developing room, about 20 students can process at once. They come in all ages from 18 up; numerous women in midlife have found photography a pleasing avocation.

"**I WANT IT TO BE THE BEST** in the state at this level," Marion says. "We've got a great faculty, a nice facility, good administrative support and we're in an ideal location — Silicon Valley." A course titled "Photography and the New Technologies" is coming up, by the way. But fundamentals won't be neglected. Patterson likes to work with beginners, and says, "We try to teach all the basics in the first class."

Ward Winslow

Many lessons to be learned in traffic survival workshop

IN AN EXERCISE OF investigative journalism for your benefit, dear readers, your columnist spent two long evenings last week in a National Traffic Safety Institute "traffic survival workshop" at Palo Alto High School. Well, there was one other reason (the same reason 29 others went to "traffic school"): to wipe a citation off my driving record.

Joe Falkowski of Belmont, our instructor and a man well aware of the flaws of bureaucracy, warned us it might not happen. He advocates waiting four to six weeks after the warrant date (mine's in June), then going to a DMV office, paying $3 and filling out a form to get an abstract of your driving record and make sure the system worked and purged your ticket.

Falkowski managed to get all 30 of us to say where and why we were cited — about one-third on Embarcadero Road for speeds like 37 in a 25 mph zone. Some were irate to be ticketed at 5:30 a.m. when no one else was on the road, except the cop they didn't see. Falkowski defended tight enforcement on Embarcadero, noting all its residential and schools traffic, but the two 5:30 a.m. stories surprised him.

Alma Street and Stanford Avenue are other speeder pitfalls oft-mentioned in the classes at Paly, he said. Some of our number met the CHP on a freeway, including one girl who wanted recourse against the guys who sold her a radar detector that didn't work while she was doing 70.

NO COMMON SPEEDER, your columnist was the only one there for being in a collision. It happened on a December night when I was driving my wife's new car. Luckily she was along and didn't deem it my

NO COMMON SPEEDER, your columnist was the only one there for being in a collision. It happened on a December night when I was driving my wife's new car. Luckily she was along and didn't deem it my fault. After making a full stop where Seale intersects Newell (and the stop sign is 30 feet back from Newell if you count the bike path), I pulled out to turn left. The 16-year-old girl seemed to come from out of nowhere, doing 45 or 50. We were stopped when she hit us; there was no time to back up. After we all checked out OK, she realized she had the right of way. The investigating officer agreed, yet suspected her of speeding.

It was my first plastic car crash. What would have been a modest fender bender in the days of heavy metal cars did $3,000 damage to our car and probably $2,000 or more to the other. Heck, until a few years ago I'd never owned a car worth $3,000 after it left the sales lot.

THE TWO NIGHTS SEEMED grueling — 6:30 to 10 p.m. are awful hours. The first date was St. Patrick's Day, and our class had three Mikes. We started out doing workbook exercises, and in a section on values I found myself sounding angelic. But soon we all were freely admitting we speed often, and violate other laws, too.

The group struck me as rather academic, with some highly articulate people who took part eagerly in small-group discussions of such topics as raising the 55 mph limit, Santa Clara County's most congested areas — "all major intersections" — and how you rate the traffic justice system. The conclusions about the system were that it serves its purpose by catching you now and then, but is impersonal and unresponsive if you truly feel you are innocent. Joe said our group was not untypical. He also teaches, by the way, at Serra High in San Mateo and San Jose City College, where 20 such classes may run all day Saturday.

THERE WAS NO REAL GROUSING that I heard. As a 40+-year driver, I learned useful things from the four films and the discussions. For one thing, the old "allow a car length between you and the car ahead for every 10 mph" rule is out. The new rule says, allow the distance you go in two seconds, at whatever speed. You are taught how to gauge the distance.

Also, it was a survival course in a practical sense, for Falkowski threw in some tips on not getting arrested and what to do in common emergencies. Facts were applied on how little time speeding saves you, and the insane follies of driving after more than one drink.

Safe driving is in my forebrain now, though that may wear off. Meanwhile, I'm contemplating the CSAA's observation that "accident" is a misnomer; driver error is found in 92 percent of all collisions. By the way, Falkowski smoked out the (to me) startling fact that every person in the class had been in at least one crash.

A classic story of the first day in first grade in Mayfield town, 1922

IN THE MARCH ISSUE OF *The Tall Tree*, the Palo Alto Historical Association's bulletin, **Lillian Ledoyen Kirkbride** of Palo Alto does full justice to the story of her first day of school back in 1922, a little over three months after her French-speaking family moved from San Francisco to the Town of Mayfield. She, almost 7, and her brother **Maurice** (now of Los Altos), 5½, were to enter first grade together because the old Sherman School had no kindergarten. The North County Courthouse now occupies the site of the school, a tall two-story wooden building with a much embellished tower.

Young Lillian had worried whether her teacher would understand her if she asked to go to the bathroom.

"To our surprise," she writes, "we weren't the only foreign children; Mayfield was a melange of Italian, Spanish, Oriental and French inhabitants." Which reminds one that many fine local families' breadwinners came humbly to help build parts of Stanford University — and stayed to thrive.

Maurice must have suffered more than his big sister. "Maman" had sent him to school in the cosmopolitan garb of SF — short pants buttoned to a matching top, white shoes and handknitted knee-length socks. Besides that, he had long, naturally curly hair. Needless to say, he was jeered by the older Mayfield boys. "They tugged at his pants, asking, 'Are you a boy or a girl?' " Lillian tells what happened next:

"The first day came to an end at last and we started for home. I was so anxious to tell maman everything that had happened I ran ahead, leaving Maurice behind. ... She cut me short when I started to rattle on and asked, 'Ou est Maurice?' She was still scolding me when we found him in the middle of Lincoln Street crying his eyes out. (Lincoln was renamed California Avenue when Palo Alto annexed Mayfield in 1925.)

"When he finally stopped crying, he told maman how the boys had teased him, so instead of going home we went to the barber shop where he got his first real-boy haircut. From there we went down the street to Shield's drygoods store where he was outfitted in the knickers and shirts the other boys wore."

Mrs. Kirkbride pays a marvelous tribute to her two primary grade teachers, Mrs. Doherty and Miss Janet Thain, both sensitive women who eased their "foreign" students' speedy Americanization.

A MEMBER OF STANFORD's Class of '35 is still shaking her head at a metropolitan paper's account of the death earlier this month of screenwriter Waldo Salt, '34.

Along with his two Academy Awards for screenwriting ("Midnight Cowboy" in 1969 and "Coming Home" in 1978), there were two standout facts about Waldo Salt. One was that he entered Stanford at age 14 (and did fine). Secondly, his career suffered because he was called to testify before the House Un-American Activities Committee, clouding him in McCarthy-era suspicion; then the hearing was canceled at the last minute and the committee was abolished before he appeared.

The Associated Press story in the met left both those facts out. How's that for stripping a man of his distinctions? And how did the lady know? Well, I think she lived it. But she also had an obituary from *The New York Times* to prove her point.

A special retreat, hidden in Woodside, for 'artist in residence'

IT WAS A GIFT from my son and his bride that I dined the other night with the Djerassi Foundation's Resident Artists in Woodside. **Edward Winslow** and his dance partner, **Mary Ann Willoughby,** have been there a month and hope a cancellation will let them stay on longer.

Being invited to be "in residence" is a rich opportunity for an artist in whatever medium and of whatever age, especially the young. Their meals and housing are provided, and they are free to create, without distractions such as telephones. Better yet, they mix with other creative persons — composers, sculptors, writers, poets, filmmakers, dramatists — and exchange ideas in a setting where time seems to stretch to allow ample reflection.

MANY WOODSIDERS would not identify this retreat as being in their town. It is over the Skyline and a few miles (which seem like 20) down narrow, curvy roads, in one of those woods-fringed bald spots with a view — often through fog and wind — to the ocean. Edward and Mary Ann had a studio in a 12-sided roundhouse with a dance floor fit for a ballroom. By chance I arrived the night they were showing their work-in-progress modern dance choreography to the other residents. The excerpt from a program meant for 1988 sparked animated discussion, so much so that the pair performed it again, a bit modified, touching off more discussion.

LATE LAST YEAR, writer **Jane Ayres** and photographer **Bob Andres** did an excellent spread on this retreat, relating how the program took shape after Pamela Djerassi, a working artist, died in 1978 and left her 600-acre ranch to the foundation started by her father, **Dr. Carl Djerassi,** the noted chemist and an aspiring writer. Initially, talented women were invited to live at the ranch for a year, but it proved too lonely, and in 1982 the foundation trustees broadened the program to include a dozen or more artists at a time.

The trustees pick the invitees on executive director **Sally Stilman's** recommendation. Some stay three months, some shorter periods. Most of those present were on their first tour, but one, author **Millicent Dillon** of San Francisco, a former Palo Altan, was on her third retreat. Each has been quite different, she said.

A young writer, **Dart Lindsley** of La Jolla, was invited on Millicent's recommendation. The celebrated poet, **Vikram Seth,** who studied economics at Stanford University but now is writing full time and living in his native India, no doubt was sought out by Stilman. Another poet, **Alicia Ostriker,** is on leave from Rutgers University. **Vernie Gusack,** a playwright whose home is in West Los Angeles, had applied after hearing about the foundation in a roundabout way; years ago, she enjoyed a similar retreat at Yaddo in the East.

JAMIE EDMONDS, who is on staff but really should be printing poems born of his years in Turkey, said America has about 40 such retreats now, some only for, say, painters. Jamie is helping the Djerassi Foundation raise half of its $300,000 annual budget from outside sources. He noted that besides freeing up the artists for a while, a secondary goal is to foster collaboration among them, a dream not often realized.

Mary Watkins of Berkeley, composer and jazz pianist, has a sector of the roundhouse. Another studio there is occupied by **David Nash** of Wales, who does striking wood sculpture with a chain saw, using only down timber. His exhibition at the Museum of Modern Art in San Francisco opens today. Yet another sculptor present is **Hartmut Bohm** of Lunen, West Germany. So is his fellow countryman, Berlin filmmaker **Michael Krause.**

Palo Alto has lost a number of fine longtime teachers

PALO ALTO'S TEACHING ESTABLISHMENT will be shy a few hundred years of experience when classes resume in the fall. Forty-eight retirees who were honored at a recent party had, among them, 1,017 collective years with the district.

Not all of them were in teaching jobs, of course. Some were administrators, some classified personnel. But a lot of teachers sang swan songs, and many were in the 20- to 40-year bracket.

The party is an annual event sponsored jointly by the Palo Alto Educators Association, the classified employees' outfit, the Board of Education and the Palo Alto Unified School District. **Pat Einfalt** served as mistress of ceremonies and presented the retirees. Superintendent **Julian Crocker** and trustee **Carolyn Tucher** dispensed the handshakes, hugs, certificates and plaques.

For dramatic effect, Einfalt worked up the experience ladder, but that's not journalism. Let's just say that the dean of the group was **Florence Turner**, with 44 years, mostly at Palo Alto High School. And Turner wasn't present — she'd gone to Los Angeles with a delegation to claim Paly's distinguished high school award.

TWO LONG-TIMERS, Paul Ford and **Dewey Johnson**, were accorded special honors by the PAEA, which is the teachers' own organization, sometimes called a union. **Dorothy Hargrove**, new PAEA president, bestowed the laurels. Ford, who finished his career at El Carmelo School as a classroom teacher, served an earlier hitch as a principal. He told the crowd that when he joined up it was called the Palo Alto Teachers Association and dues were $1 a year. Johnson, whose formal handle is **DeWayne**, taught social studies at Paly High; Hargrove said PAEA especially valued him for practicing participatory democracy and sometimes disagreeing.

PERHAPS THE BIGGEST HAND of the day went to **John Martin**, assistant superintendent for educational services and a pivotal figure in the administration for a number of years. Another high-ranking retiree is **Robert E. McLean**, assistant supe for personnel and payroll; also, two principals, **Gene Tankersley** at El Carmelo and **Lon Andrews** at Addison.

Others in the 30-years-plus class were **Dick Finch**, language teacher at Cubberley and Gunn high schools, and **Joyce Bryson**, who finished at Ohlone.

ALLAN F. BROWN of Menlo Park, head of a Palo Alto contracting firm, had two meals Friday at Waverley Place. The first was lunch with an old acquaintance, **Leonard Ely**, the second dinner with his CPA and, as a surprise added attraction, a roomful of friends and relatives there to celebrate Brown's 60th birthday. The coup was the work of his wife, **Marilyn**.

Allan's three younger brothers — **Lawrence, Donal** and **John** — were there, but his older brother, **Robert**, widely known in recent years as Mr. Portola Valley, was off on another trip to Germany. Likewise, two of Allan's three sons — **Davin** and **Stephen** — were on hand, but the third, **Bowen**, was in New York pursuing his musical career. He drums.

Ely ate at the restaurant twice, too.

TWO SISTERS, Katharine Bailey of Palo Alto and **Mimi Howarth** of Atherton, are due to head for Maine soon to visit their father, **Dr. Henry Lewis**, a clergyman who held temporary charge of St. Mark's Episcopal Church in Palo Alto about 15 years ago. Lewis will be 94 in September; more remarkable is that he has just finished another book, having published his autobiography a few years ago.

Few clubs have endured
as long as Booktasters has

BOOKTASTERS recently passed its 25-year mark. The anniversary means little, although it elicited reminiscences at a festive potluck. What's remarkable is that this group of Peninsula women has stayed so close and constant for so long a time.

Lots of clubs form (or used to) around a common interest — reading, bridge, poker, sewing, etc. Few prove so lasting.

When Booktasters got started, most of its members were sending their youngest children off to kindergarten, or perhaps were still nursing one. **Sharlie Hutchinson** (now **Grispini**), then the wife of a scientist at

Ward Winslow

Stanford Research Institute (now SRI International), was the prime mover, abetted by **Sally Holland, Jean Coblentz** and the late Carol Miller. "Let's start a group," Carol said, and they did.

IN FORM, IT IS a simple organization. No officers, no dues, virtually no rules except to stick to the subject of the day. Just signup lists for hostesses and book reviewers at the monthly meetings. The hostess can tell everyone to bring-brown bag lunches if she wants, but usually there's a tasty meal. The current membership runs to 14, with five others on the inactive list (three moved away but stay in touch).

"We had similar backgrounds, tastes and points of view," Sally explained. All treasure the printed word; most are accomplished writers, and artists in other media as well. When you hear one say she is "just a housewife," you'd better be on guard. **Nancy McLaughlin** of Portola Valley, for example, has strong scholarly credentials.

Their husbands run the gamut: surgeons, airline pilots, business and industrial executives, clergymen, attorneys, inventors, the head of a high-tech Silicon Valley firm. As an editor, I was lucky to marry into this well-jelled and lively company.

LOUISE SPANGLER of Los Altos reviewed **Betty Freidan's** "The Feminine Mystique" at one of the first meetings. The women — and it's really a women's group, although husbands attended and even reviewed once at the outset — discovered they were not highly assertive feminists; their interests range far and wide.

Jean Coblentz, at whose Sunnyvale home the club's birthday party took place, went "outside" with her special talent and has been reviewing books at Channing House for 15 years; she also is on the Stanford development office staff. **Marnie Furbush** of Los Altos Hills edits *Imprint*, the Stanford Library Associates' journal.

One early member, **Pat Cairns**, who ran a Los Altos nursery school, later moved to the Sea Ranch and has written an animal book somewhat akin to "Bambi." Sally Holland, of Menlo Park, writes travel commentaries. **Susie Smith** of Los Altos Hills is renowned for her charming paintings of bandana-wearing ducks and pigs. **Elaine Tanner** of Palo Alto is a whiz with tropicals and other flowering plants. Lou Spangler edits for Houghton Mifflin Co. **Martha Jeffs** of Mountain View and **Holly Winslow** of Palo Alto are teachers.

Poems by the late Janice Brumbaum of Los Altos, published after her death, revealed a significant talent.

The "book club" is seen variously as "a therapy group in time of trouble" (Holland), "an oasis" (McLaughlin), and "an escape from career and children" (Cairns). One member, **Lois Bennett** of Stanford, an SRI systems analyst, confessed not having been able to read a book in years. "I am an audience," she said.

Battle against 'taxation without representation'

THE BIGGEST THREAT to passage of the 5 percent utility tax measure on Palo Alto's Nov. 3 city ballot may well be **Richard J. Herzing**, a retired Sequoia Union High School District teacher.

Herzing is one of about 175 residents of Monroe Park, a district roughly bounded by El Camino Real, Adobe Creek, the railroad tracks and San Antonio Road. His part of Monroe Park is in Palo Alto, but remains in the Los Altos Elementary School District.

The utility tax would raise roughly $3 million a year for the Palo Alto Unified School District, a pass-through from the city, which is sort of loaning its claimed ability as a charter city to bypass the law requiring a two-thirds majority for a tax measure and do it with a simple majority. Los Altos Hills and Stanford campus residents, although in the PAUSD, would escape the tax, while their children would benefit if the measure passes.

Herzing, outraged at the injustice to himself and his neighbors (and to a pocket of Whisman School District residents along San Antonio Road), is staging a one-man campaign. He's out to stir up every neighborhood group and anyone else who'll listen to him denounce the proposed tax as deceitful, vicious, and, in his case, "taxation without representation," as he can't vote on Palo Alto school trustees or issues. He argues, too, that a utility tax is unfair to seniors, who like the heat turned up a bit.

THE MEMORIAL SERVICE for Dr. Harry Rathbun, which filled Stanford Memorial Church on a Saturday evening, was remarkable, which is no surprise considering his long and remarkable life. It consisted mainly of readings from "Jesus As Teacher," a book by Henry Burton Sharman on which Rathbun and his wife, **Emilia**, based much of their religious teaching, and classical music selections that were his favorites.

Beyond War, the movement to which he was spiritual godfather, has received "a most generous response" of contributions in his memory, according to **Bev Sorensen** of Menlo Park. The money is being used in the organization's general fund rather than for a special purpose, such as a scholarship, she said.

IN RESEARCHING the above item I wound up talking to **Jim Burch**, one of Beyond War's leaders, who currently is stationed in Des Moines, Iowa. Why Iowa? Elementary, Watson, those early presidential caucuses. Burch says Beyond War, 50 to 75 strong in Iowa, has easy access to the candidates there — he already has met eight of the dozen hopefuls. The caucus process requires them to persuade voters to turn out on a cold February night, so they look for any potential support. Beyond War also is maintaining a presence in New Hampshire, Jim said.

THERE'S ANOTHER PENINSULA OUTPOST in Cincinnati, according to **Ruth Spangenberg** of Palo Alto, who writes from there reporting on the Frank Duveneck Show at the Cincinnati Art Museum. "The genius and diversity of his art is amazing!" she says. One Peninsula connection is that Frank Duveneck the artist was the father of the late Francis (Frank) Duveneck of Los Altos; another is that a second Duveneck exhibit is on right now at the Triton Museum of Art in Santa Clara. And there's a third: The curator for prints, drawing and photography at the Cincinnati Museum is **Kristin L. Spangenberg**, Ruth's daughter. Kristin will be lecturing next month on "Prints and Drawings by Duveneck and His Circle."

Lest I bend the local angle too sharply, be it noted that the senior Duveneck was born in Covington, Ky., just across the river from Cincinnati, and after living and working in Munich and elsewhere in Europe, ultimately returned to teach at the Art Academy of Cincinnati. His life is chronicled in a new book, "Unsuspected Genius," by **Robert Neuhaus**, who, Mrs. Spangenberg reports, was at the Cincy show.

FELICITY TSE, president of Ming's Villa in Palo Alto, tends to wince when customers tell her they dined at the rebuilt restaurant shortly after it opened late last fall. The reason is that construction delays disrupted her staffing plans, and the service was not at peak efficiency for a while. All is running much more smoothly now, she says, and **Bill T. Wang** of Sunnyvale, former head waiter at Ming's, is back on a part-time basis to advise the staff on the fine points of Peninsulans' tastes.

Also playing a more visible role is **Vicky Ching** of Palo Alto, representing the other partner family. Tse's husband, **Francis**, is a prominent anesthesiologist in Berkeley; Ching's husband, **Robert**, is what Wang describes as "a business doctor."

As for the cuisine, it's an extraordinary departure from standard U.S. presentations of Cantonese fare.

Area's federal laboratories getting new assignment

HOW MANY FEDERAL LABORATORIES are located between, say, Sunnyvale and Redwood City? The biggies should be easy: NASA's Ames Research Center at Moffett Field, with about 5,000 employees; the U.S. Geological Survey, Western Region, in Menlo Park, 3,676 employees; and Stanford Linear Accelerator Center, west of Menlo Park, with 1,500. That's three. There are four more, one each in Moffett Field, Palo Alto, Stanford and Menlo Park. Keep guessing.

The seven, together with California's biggest, Lawrence Livermore National Laboratory (8,000 employees), and Lawrence Berkeley Lab (3,688), stamp the Bay Area as a federal research and development citadel, Uncle Sam's part of Greater Silicon Valley.

AN ENLARGED DUTY ASSIGNMENT lends added luster to the federal labs from the standpoint of civilian industry. Congress enacted the Federal Technology Transfer Act of 1986, and President Reagan followed up with a plug in his 1987 State of the Union address and then a strongly worded Executive Order in April, telling all federal agency heads to get with the task of commercializing federal technology to make the nation more competitive.

The new law shored up weaknesses in the Stevenson-Wydler Act of 1980, making clear the authority of federal labs to transfer technology and pushing down the authority to the laboratory director level — on paper, at least. It offers federal scientists and engineers incentive, too — royalty payments of up to $100,000 a year to inventors of super widgets.

FOR ALL THE LAWS AND ORDERS, federal technology transfer isn't yet moving at warp speed — far from it. So more than 70 industrial research executives and federal laboratory directors and technology utilization officers got together recently at Ames Lab to brainstorm how to make it work better.

They found themselves in inspirational surroundings. They met in the Numerical Aerodynamics Simulator Building, apple of Ames Director **William F. Ballhaus Jr.**'s eye, and Ballhaus himself welcomed them. Quoting **Larry Milov**, Ames's technology utilization guy, Ballhaus said the center has the biggest R&D budget of any organization in Silicon Valley, and is SV's sixth-largest high tech firm.

Ballhaus not only is a shooting star (he recently received the presidential rank of meritorious executive for his outstanding accomplishments); he also is known within NASA as one of its most entrepreneurial lab directors. He is strongly for technology transfer, which has been part of NASA's mission since the law founding it was enacted in 1958.

DESPERATION IS A GREAT motivator of technology transfer, Ballhaus told the visitors. In 1975, when he was doing computational research, some people from Rockwell sought to use an Ames wind tunnel to crack a tough aerodynamic problem. Ames scientists concluded Rockwell's problem couldn't be solved with wind tunnels in the time available, and suggested trying a computational approach. So Rockwell sent a person up to work with Ballhaus for about a month, learning how the Ames computer code worked and modifying it in order to take it home and teach Rockwell designers how to use it.

It all worked, and the benefits weren't Rockwell's alone, Ballhaus noted. By saving a program, Ames got recognition and evidence of the first payoff of a massive six-year NASA investment in computational fluid dynamics. Rockwell had a new technology and a company expert who then could train others.

Among the sequels, from the Ames standpoint, is its supercomputer complex, with two powerful units, a Cyber 205 and a Cray XMP. Two more are being negotiated, Ballhaus said, and "a year from now we will have a machine that's about four times more powerful than the Cray 2." More than that, the complex puts researchers right into the fluid flows, in a "virtual environment," so they can study the physics of it as if they were swimming around.

WHY SHOULD INDUSTRY want the transfers? R&D is darned expensive, explained **Michael L. Bandler**, president of the California Engineering Foundation and Pacific Bell's network engineering boss. Besides, Bandler added, at last report the $55 billion a year federal investment in R&D was only bringing back a return of about 3/1000ths of 1 percent to the Treasury. Bandler cited Stanford University and Stanford Research Park as a model of university-industry cooperation. Later on, **Gordon Longerbeam** of Lawrence Livermore said Stanford has the best formula he knows of for sharing patent royalties: a third to the inventor, a third to the university and a third to the department or other sub-unit.

Workshop sessions brought out a lot of ideas for making transfers fly, along with a curious factor reported by Chevron Research Company's Dr. **Robert Moore**. Both federal lab/industrial research people are dogged by worries about giveaways — in one case giving away public property, in the other company property. Now that the improved laws have provided a way, there's still a problem of will, it seems. In fact, although authority to negotiate deals has been handed to them legally, some federal lab directors say they still feel the heavy drag of headquarters bureaucracy. As for industry, the consensus at the Ames forum was that it will have to be more active in seeking out what federal gems it could use, usually after costly development work. So, it'll all take time.

OH YES, THE OTHER four labs. There's the Aviation Research and Technology Lab at Moffett, with 278 people; Sondrestrom Radar Facility, a National Science Foundation outfit at SRI International in Menlo Park (141); the Veterans Administration's Rehabilitation R&D Center in Palo Alto (60); and the Artificial Intelligence in Medicine lab at Stanford (20), a Department of Health and Human Services unit.

Selling a house isn't what it used to be ...

THE WIFE AND I SOLD A HOUSE and bought another this year, and believe me, it ain't what it used to be. It's more — close to unbelievably much more.

It would only grieve younger people who've recently borne the awful travail of modern first-time buying to read how easy it once was. Instead, I'll address those who haven't been in the market for a decade or three about how complicated it has become.

Lest anyone who bought a few years back think he knows it all, let me add that recent court rulings and disclosure laws have made paperwork sprout like foothills grass after our fall rains. The situation also has left real estate people and related professionals scared to death of being sued, and with reason.

BUYING UP ISN'T quite the struggle that making a first purchase is, not if you're on the escalator. Indeed, it seemed deceptively easy. Just as we discovered our new dream house, its price happened to tumble by an amount that would have bought the same house back when it was built 20-some years ago. The owners already had moved to Sacramento and were getting desperate. A relocation service was entering the act, the import of which we didn't immediately grasp. It turned out mostly to be a headache for our marvelous agent, **Imogene Chancellor**, requiring her to dispatch bales of copied paper via couriers again and again.

Buying a house will teach you instantly how fast you can (or can't) get funds you fancied were liquid. Everyone seems to be operating on the float.

Hiring an inspector is one modern custom I applaud. **Alan Huntzinger**, a former city official, insisted on a new roof. He also found armies of termites the termite man had missed in a courtyard wall, and we began to feel sorry for the sellers, who had to pay for that plus a survey and new fencing where a fence had strayed onto neighbor **Kay Muranaka's** land.

The title company made appalling mistakes — names spelled wrong, items omitted. And a bank involved in a loan delivered its check to the wrong place. Despite our pleas and escrow officers' promises, we had to go to Campbell to complete a transaction that should have been done in Palo Alto. Buyer or seller, you need to check and recheck all details.

SELLING WAS GOING TO BE a snap. Didn't we have the most desirable town house in town? Heck, it was better than a town house — it was a Planned Unit Development unit. Turned out we were lucky if folks called it a town house and not a condominium, which comes lower in the pecking order or higher on the hard-to-sell scale, as you will.

Nowadays you don't just sign up with a realtor, set an asking price, put it on multiple and prepare for lookers. Oh no, under new disclosure rules you're supposed to reveal every flaw, down to how many times the washing machine overflowed. Or the cat. You fret about whether there's asbestos around. If you can't qualify to execute an affidavit of nonforeign status, the tax boogeyman 'll gitcha, I guess.

For about 30 bucks a consulting geologist will attest that your place is in "an area of moderate potential for liquefaction, lurching and lateral movement." Imagine how that plays with a buyer from Peoria!

THE MULTIPLE TOUR is a marker date. Suited, booted sales aces (mostly women) come in droves, piling out of BMWs, Mercedes and Cadillacs like the dozen circus clowns used to emerge from a Model A. They go through the dwelling in a trice, sizing up instantly whether it will suit any client of theirs. They leave behind enough business cards to paper a hall. Later, our agent will resort to baking goodies to lure them back.

Even before the ugly truth dawned that the place wasn't going to sell right away, we prepared to take a bridge loan, a third mortgage designed to liberate (at ruinous cost) the equity to apply on our purchase. This required a loan broker to get us a gross sum from a bank we'd never heard of. His demands for a financial soul-baring were worse than the IRS or even FAF (college financial aid) ever imposed.

AS THE HOUSE SHOWED, lookers found faults we'd never noticed. They eyed the quiet church nearby suspiciously. They saw an upkeep nuisance in the tiny back lawn — our pride.

We disdained a low offer with bizarre terms, presented ceremoniously by an agent given to derogation. When panic set in, we were persuaded to replace our jolly burnt orange carpet with a characterless beige. At last, it worked. Then the buyer's inspector found hairline cracks to fix that never bothered us.

One last round with another title company brought more glaring errors. But at last we were free to spend our spare time culling the glut of bucks-seeking mail the purchase brought on — and worrying whether there could be cause for a latent lawsuit.

This politician can't be kept
off the phone, surgery or not

YOU CAN KEEP A GOOD POLITICIAN DOWN, but probably not off the phone.

Sally Siegel, a Palo Alto educational activist if ever there was one, is mending nicely, thank you, from recent major surgery. She was barely out of the recovery room, it seemed, when she resumed quarterbacking arrangements for a meet-the-candidate party she'd arranged earlier to have at a neighbor's home. Sally couldn't attend, but she called every shot that one could call *in absentia* via Pacific Bell.

One admiring fellow townswoman, former Chief Justice **Rose Elizabeth Bird,** commemorated Sally's pluck by giving Siegel a trophy that Bird herself had received as an integrity award.

That wasn't all. Still abed almost on the eve of the election, Siegel issued a handbill challenging an endorsement editorial and some ad copy she didn't like.

In a way, the late Lou Fein, another ardent educational activist and one with whom Sally rarely agreed, outdid her. I notice that Lou got in his last licks posthumously in the Palo Alto school ballot measure arguments. They'd been written, of course, before a massive brain aneurysm stilled his voice.

CHUCK KUBOKAWA, who was a Palo Alto City Council candidate some time back, is a new board member of the California History Center Foundation at De Anza College, Cupertino. So is **Mardi Gualtieri Bennett,** a former Los Gatos councilwoman and state Assembly candidate who now is a historic preservation consultant. Both are serving under the presidency of **Yvonne Jacobson** of Los Altos Hills, the historian and author. The vice president is **C.A. "Sy" Sivertson** of Saratoga, who was Kubokawa's big boss for a time while Sivertson directed NASA Ames Research Center, where Chuck still toils.

The History Center, by the way, is looking for artifacts that illuminate the lives of Chinese immigrants in California earlier this century. They'll be displayed with a Central Coast photo exhibit in February. Clothing, household items, tools and the like are sought; some members of former missionary families that were stationed in China probably have just the thing. Potential lenders may call (408) 996-4712.

MAIL CALL: A RECENT COLUMN titled "Selling a house isn't what it used to be" drew more than the ordinary amount of reaction, most of it amiable. Perhaps the reason for the exceptional interest is that, as branch manager **Nancy Russell** of First American Title Guaranty Company in Palo Alto writes, "Buying or selling a house is usually one of the more stressful experiences of a person's life."

Russell was moved to write by my mention of some flagrant escrow errors. "I felt it a duty to my fellow escrow and title employees," she says, "to attempt to shatter some of the myths or at least shed some light on the mystery of our profession, one that seems to be an easy target for abuse."

After the "stressful" remark, she adds: "You (the buyer) just want to get it done. But once you have entered the world of escrow, it seems like these nameless entities called lenders, agents, appraisers, termite companies and title/escrow companies are planted along every step of the way to prevent you from closing.

"Actually," Russell continues, "it is our function to expedite real estate transactions. Time and human nature have proven that a simple exchange of dirt and a handshake don't cut it. So services such as what we offer have evolved out of necessity and in this consumer-oriented society today, we are looked upon as protection for 'the little guy.' "

"CONTEMPLATE YOUR OWN TRANSACTION and multiply it by 20 or 25 and imagine your escrow officer dealing with your situation an average of that many times a month," Nancy suggests. "Each 'file' has its own quirks and dilemmas, with agents, principals, lenders, insurance agents *et al.* using the escrow officer as the ultimate coordinator of the 'deal.' With deadlines set by all of the above, life at an escrow branch is geared to a level of high intensity. And believe it or not, we try to emanate an air of calmness for our clients ... "

"You see," she explains, "most of us love what we do, though we do consider ourselves masochists. ... Most stumbled into the career as an accident and ... learned the trade by on-the-job training and a lot of self-initiative. ...

"I know of escrow officers who meet clients at their homes, stay till 9 o'clock at night to finish a set of papers and perform other daily 'miracles' to get each client's escrow closed on time. ...

"In 1986, a booming year for anyone in the real estate industry, we worked until 9 and 10 o'clock at night over the holiday season (traditionally a busy time for the title industry), much to the distress of our families. ... It was awful ... but we had a job to do and did it, and this year we can say we survived 'Escrow '86' and hope it never happens again.

"Nothing in any profession could be much better than the exhilaration of completing a tough escrow. ... And the buyer and seller walk away, thinking that I just did my regular old, nothing-spectacular job. They got their house or their money and they won't have to think about escrow for a while. But I did it, and that is a great feeling. I wonder how many others can say that about their jobs?"

Hothouse wizardry is alive and well

IF YOU ARE ENJOYING the usual flowering plants this Yuletide season, apart from poinsettias, credit your nursery with having clever suppliers who work some hothouse wizardry.

In home gardens, things have been crazy for many weeks. Christmas cactus at our house bloomed luxuriantly, but finished by Thanksgiving. Likewise a sasanqua camellia, deciduous magnolias, rhododendrons and azaleas. And ours is by no means the only place with unseasonal flowerings to report. Agapanthus are ahead of themselves all over the Peninsula, and roses are blooming so late they're liable to miss their winter naps.

Dieter Lach, owner of Podesta Nursery in East Palo Alto, a wholesale grower, says very warm nights in October and November affected azaleas. Because cool nights didn't harden them at the usual time, they couldn't be forced into early bloom for Christmas sale, he explains.

Other nursery people don't identify any specific reason, but most are aware of some freak plant behavior. **Chris Best**, a salesman at Roger Reynolds Nursery in Menlo Park, points out that sasanquas at the Palo Alto Cultural Center, which usually bloom in January, did their thing in October.

MARGE FARWELL, the title character of Mrs. Farwell's Rhododendron Nursery in Woodside, says she just advises gardeners to enjoy it when they report their "rhodos" blooming early. Some are two or three months ahead of schedule, she adds, and that is producing some "very peculiar color schemes" in her Skyline plant beds. As for azaleas, she notes that they're just a form of rhododendron — a form with minds of their own.

Juan Navarro, owner-manager of the Ladera Garden Center, reports that his suppliers have been able to meet his demands. **Leo Goria**, manager of Woolworth's Garden Center in Palo Alto, suggests that it's not all bad — English primroses in 4-inch pots have been available since mid-October, months early. Goria believes a cold fall can cause more problems than a balmy one. Mid-December's chill is doing its bit, of course. And right now we're more likely to have trouble with high water than with high temperatures.

THE HIGHEST DAYTIME TIDE of the year was supposed to occur by this evening, and if it's raining, you might want to head for high ground. On the other hand, if you want to watch what happens when the baylands flood thoroughly, head out Palo Alto Yacht Harbor (which might give the false signal of looking like it could still support boats of any significant draft). Dec. 22, some oldtimers will recall, was date in 1955 when San Francisquito Creek (and others) flooded. So if there's a prolonged warm rain, as there was in '55, make for the hills.

HERE'S A TIP FOR ANYONE who still needs Christmas decorations and ornaments. The Allied Arts Guild in Menlo Park will have them on sale Wednesday from 9:30 a.m. until 5 p.m. at half-price, according to **Marion Deane**, manager of the traditional sales room. You may have to fight off volunteers who've grown attached to certain splendid items.

A MEMBER OF THE FOUNDING staff at the Palo Alto Medical Clinic, probably the last, died in San Francisco last week. Ida R. Steller, the original office manager, was 103½. She had survived for decades after having extensive cancer surgery.

IF YOU'VE DONE ALL YOUR SHOPPING and have anything left in your Christmas budget, there are lots of places where a modest check will do a world of good. One is the American Red Cross, Palo Alto Area Chapter, 400 Mitchell Lane, Palo Alto 94301. Or the Senior Coordinating Council of the Palo Alto Area, 450 Bryant St., Palo Alto 94301. In activities like these, a contribution is heavily leveraged by the efforts of many volunteers; in the case of the Senior Coordinating Council, the leveraging is increased by support from the city of Palo Alto, United Way, and county and school contract funding.

Another deserving activity is the Sensory Aids Foundation, 399 Sherman Ave., Suite 12, Palo Alto 94306. This foundation uses technology to help capable, motivated blind and deaf people get jobs nobody thought were possible.

The tale of Grandfather and the garbage wagon

NOWADAYS CITY CREWS repave a street while hardly bothering the neighborhood, and sanitation crews man gleaming trucks that gulp down garbage with nary an errant smell or scrap. But it wasn't always like that, not even in Palo Alto.

That point is witnessed by the following story, appropriate for a time of deluge — the midwinter jicker, Dr. Seuss called it. For the tale, we're indebted to the storyteller, **Henry Bolton Post** of Bakersfield, Palo Alto High School Class of '34, and to **Lillian Kirkbride** of the P.A. Historical Association.

THE TIME IS a rainy winter day in the 1920s. The place is 1229 Webster St., Palo Alto. The event is "Grandfather and the Garbage Wagon."

Young Henry, age about 8, is in the bay window seat, watching the outside world pass by. His grandfather, Capt. Arthur John Hutchinson, and two cronies, retired Stanford Profs. Frank Angell (for whom Angell Field is named) and C.D. "Daddy" Marx, have interrupted their chess-playing for tea and Lorna Doone cookies. (Many deemed Marx the father of the city utilities.)

. Post says even today he cannot call our modern conveyances with their pulverizing machinery garbage trucks. "To me they are and always will be garbage wagons — four-wheeled, high-sided wagons with the large diameter wheels to the rear, drawn by a team of draft horses with burly men who came to your back door with burlap sheets, which were spread out to receive one's castoffs." The bearer climbed up a ladder and swung his bundle over the wagon side, spreading its contents to mix with an already nauseating collection.

"IN THOSE DAYS WEBSTER STREET, being on the perimeter of the city, was only paved in the middle and by midafternoon it was a quagmire." The garbage wagon was well loaded by the time it arrived at 1229, with the sodden mess weighing several times what it should. "Our collection and those of the immediate neighbors must have been just enough to do the trick, because when the driver said 'Ho' to move on, the horses pulled and strained and slipped in their traces, but the wagon stuck fast. The driver's lashing of the horses with the reins and the crew's curses in Portuguese and Italian did no good. The rear wheels just went deeper into the ooze." Then, with a snap, the rear axle broke.

"I thought by this time to acquaint Grandfather as to what was transpiring, as I knew he (who once raised race horses) would be incensed at the belaboring the poor horses were taking," Post writes. Just as the old gentlemen reached the living room and could see the drama, a crewman laid a hard whip cut across the back of one poor steed, which, stumbling from the blow, sat haunches down in the mud.

"GRANDFATHER IN HIS TRUE authoritarian military tone acquired as an officer in the Royal Welch Fusiliers of the British Army said, 'Angell, you're a younger man than I, go outside and stop that infernal ass from beating that poor helpless animal.' By the time Dr. Angell had gingerly plowed across the gooey mess, the crew had decided to lighten the load, and one pulled the handle which caused the wagon bed to tilt backwards, and the whole stinking, wet mess was deposited across the street from Grandfather's house.

"This was too much for Grandfather and to the telephone he stormed. Before he was through all officialdom in the City Hall had heard his rage, from the city engineer to the city clerk to the police chief and on down through the Health Department, Board of Public Works and any other unlucky official he could reach. From army experience he had not much use for civilian officialdom and no words of regret from them would placate them. He was the maddest Englishman I have ever seen ... "

It was Saturday evening, so the garbage load spent that night and the next in the street, while downpours continued. All the crew from Public Works could do Monday morning was to spread the pile around as they now couldn't separate mud from garbage.

"WITH THE EVENTUAL DRYING OUT come spring, and the passing of other vehicles over the pile, the garbage load was further spread and ground beneath the dirt," Henry Post relates. "In a few years Webster Street was paved as one can see it now, but if one had occasion to jackhammer away four inches of concrete in front of the old Darsie home driveway, he might find a rusting, moldering memorial to the early 1920s buried beneath the subbase, and I could tell him how it got there, and all about Grandfather and the Garbage Wagon."

Children's Health Council capitalizing on church connections

IN RESEARCHING ITS "VIVA ITALIA" theme for the Summer Symphony at Stanford's Frost Amphitheater July 17, the Children's Health Council is finding some interesting connections. For one, there's quite a local legacy from the mosaics at Stanford Memorial Church.

Judy Donnelly of the Stanford development office, who is on the symphony committee and a former CHC board member, is in touch with descendants of Antonio Salviati, at whose studios in Venice the mosaics were designed just after the turn of the century. The company is still in business, and the university orders tie tacks and lapel pins from Salviati as gifts for volunteer fund-raisers.

Someone else who shares the legacy is **Jo Guttadauro** of Palo Alto, whose step-grandfather, John Pelligrini, worked on the church as an apprentice and later ran a tile business. Jo   is known for prodding the City Council on "Project Mobility" to provide taxi service for the elderly and disabled.

Carolyn Reller, CHC symphony chairman for the third year running, and **Jack Alexander**, veteran physical arrangements chief, decided that the Palo Alto Jaycees deserve a reward for having set up seats at the amphitheater for a number of years. So guess what they and their spouses or significant others are getting? A spaghetti feed, at the Palo Alto Medical Foundation Auditorium.

LOS ALTOS HILLS IS ABOUT TO corner the market in professional engineers' officials. **Norman Bergrun** will be installed June 18 at an annual meeting in Santa Clara for a one-year term as president of the California Society of Professional Engineers, 3,000 members strong.

Charles Wright, also of "The Hills Hills" (as early council critic Fred Gutt used to delight in saying), will be dubbed CSPE vice president for the northern region. From farther up the Peninsula, **George Zinckgrah** of San Mateo will become treasurer.

Bergrun says that, unlike the technical societies under which the various kinds of engineering majors organize, the professional engineers have a primary objective of service to the public. That means professionalism, ethics, and higher quality products. If an urgent safety issue arose, the PEs might well lend their lung power to a whistle-blower, Bergrun avows. In such a situation, he says, you need "a big flywheel."

You may have heard Bergrun on a radio talk show. He also heads the public policy section of the American Institute of Aeronautics and Astronautics, whose regional chairman is **Lew Peach** of NASA Ames. In that role, Bergrun sometimes undertakes to explain why America should strongly support space exploration.

MORE THAN 300 ASSOCIATES, relatives and friends gathered two weeks ago at Ridge Vineyards on Montebello Road overlooking Cupertino (and, on a clear day, a great deal more) at a memorial for beloved winemaker David R. Bennion, who died March 28 of injuries suffered in an automobile accident. A number of speakers, beginning with his wife, **Fran**, recalled episodes of his life or qualities of his character, and his musically talented offspring and their mates wafted plaintive string selections on the breeze.

Among those reminiscing were two of Bennion's partners in launching the renowned winery, **Hew Crane** and **Charles Rosen**, both SRI colleagues. Crane recalled that some of his and Bennion's work on all-magnetic logic was still helping run the New York subway, but added, "Dave's life was much richer than that little bit of technology." He was a "complexifier" whose passion for detail could sometimes try one's patience, Crane said, and he also was "absolutely honest" — a point several later speakers echoed.

Rosen noted that after they bought the 80-acre property for "$50,000 or so," it was Bennion, a born farmer, who left SRI to become the winemaker and vineyardist.

Wine historian **Charles Sullivan** said he thinks of Dave Bennion as "the burly, gentle Paul Bunyan of the wine revolution." Many members of the Santa Cruz Mountain Vintners, which Bennion founded, were present.

The program had a surprise ending. **Warren Douglas**, who still lives next door to Ridge, arrived to describe how in October 1963 he bought a case of the first zinfandel (blended with cabernet) released by the winery. He then unwrapped the very first bottle, which the winemaking partners had signed, and presented it to Fran, saying: "After 25 years it's coming home again."

District loses 31 employees
(706 years) to 'graduation'

ALONG WITH THE MANY OTHER JUNE GRADUATIONS, the Palo Alto Unified School District has a special one to send off its retiring certificated and classified staff members. This year, 31 employees with a combined 706 years and 11 months of service were feted on a warm afternoon at the Cultural Center.

The Board of Education, California State Employees Association, Palo Alto Educators Association and the district's management team sponsor the party. Can you believe that after all the plaques and certificates are handed out they pop some champagne?

Pat Einfalt, assistant to the superintendent, acts as mistress of ceremonies at these gigs (her voice carries), and it was she who termed it a graduation. Superintendent **Julian Crocker,** citing a scene of an Italian family at table in the movie "Moonstruck," said he thinks of it more as a family gathering with all its complex emotions. One thing you can count on in a family, he told the retirees, is that you'll always get a welcome home.

Liz Kniss, school board president, pointed out that the individual experience the district is losing will never really be replaced.

LEADING THE LIST OF retiring teachers was **Robert P. Anderson,** who taught for 35 years, most recently at Gunn High School, followed by **James R. Johnson,** Jane Lathrop Stanford Middle School, 32 years; **Frank Ratliff,** Gunn High, 31 years; **Ken Sanner,** central office, guidance and psychology, 31 years; and **Sally Herriot,** Palo Alto High School, 30½ years.

Those in the two-decades-and-up category were: **Barbara Peterson,** special education at Palo Alto High, JLS and the district's continuation school, 28 years; **Evelyn Louthian,** Walter Hays School, 27 years; **Rosemarie Moore,** special services psychologist, 26 years; **Fran Olexo,** Hoover School, 26 years; **Shirley Worthen,** Addison School, 25 years; **Janet Helin,** elementary music team, 22 years; and **Holly Winslow,** elementary music, 20 years.

Others were **Melva Lenox,** Palo Verde/Duveneck resource specialist, 17 years, and **Miyeko Tanaba,** Palo Alto High, 16 years.

THE MOST VETERAN of the classified staff retirees were **Theresa Regan,** Instructional Materials Center, 24 years; **Joan Walker,** Jackson Hearing Center secretary, almost 23 years; **Emmett Portales,** senior plumber, 22 years; and **Helen Kelly,** Business Services secretary, 21 years.

Right behind them were **Larry Queen,** Jordan site custodial supervisor, 19½ years; **Norah Chrupalo,** Briones School children's attendant, 18 years; **Agapito "Pete" Rin,** Palo Alto High custodian, 18 years; **Lavelle "Lovey" Seebauer,** maintenance clerical specialist, 16 years; and **Betty Dehn,** word processing, 6 years.

INCOMING P.A.E.A. President **Maggie Benz** announced the teachers' association's WHO ("We Honor Ours") awards to **Ev Louthian** and **Holly Winslow.** About then a cork popped.

ALTHOUGH HE WON'T BE PRESENT, the spirit of **Craig P. Calkins** will be strongly felt at the Palo Alto Concours d'Elegance at the Stanford Intramural Field on Sunday. Calkins, a New York Life of Palo Alto insurance agent who lived in Sunnyvale, died last fall after the 20th Concours. He was a founder and co-director of the classic car show and, in the estimation of the sponsoring Palo Alto Lions Club, its "chief architect, sparkplug and guiding spirit." So the Lions have dedicated the 21st annual Concours in his honor.

In addition, a Craig P. Calkins Award has been created by the University National Bank and Trust Company, where a trophy will remain on display. The double award will honor the person selected by the Lions as contributing most to the success of the current Concours with a silver bowl, and — with a trophy — the most interesting car in the show, as chosen by the bank (read Carl Schmitt, its chairman and a longtime Concours supporter). The bank also is sponsoring a new award at the show called the "Gallery of the Greats" — 10 cars of special distinction or interest.

George Paddleford and **Erv Austin,** co-directors of the 1988 Concours, had a big hand in setting up the awards. The Lions Club has also established a Craig P. Calkins Memorial Fund.

WHEN THE SENIOR CENTER of Palo Alto celebrates its 10th anniversary on June 29, there'll be a clever theme: "Our Second Wind for a Second Decade." Directors of the Senior Coordinating Council of the Palo Alto Area have whipped up quite a set of events at the center at 450 Bryant St., beginning with open house from 10 a.m. to 3 p.m. From 3 to 3:45 p.m. there will be a "Thank you, Palo Alto!" program featuring Mayor **Jack Sutorius,** Supervisor **Dianne McKenna,** and Palo Alto Chamber of Commerce President **Gary Cavalli,** with a roll call of honored guests and presentation of awards.

Looking at a 'false spring' and its effects

EVEN WITH AN EXTRA DAY in it, February 1988 didn't deliver enough rain to float a tadpole. The many warm days before the recent fogs set in added up to a "false spring." Which is not so bad, of course — day after day was gorgeous, helped along by flowering trees that blossomed early. But early is the operative word; nature's cycle is a bit out of kilter.

Up in the Midpeninsula Regional Open Space District's Skyline preserve, ranger **Dennis Danielson** reports, three of the first-blooming wildflowers, hound's tongue, milkmaid and Indian warrior, were out at the 1,000-foot level by mid-February, about one month ahead of par. Trails are in good condition, not overly dry and not muddy, and people have been using them so heavily that parking lots are full weekends. Danielson puts weekend usage at twice normal.

Permanent streams are flowing, some of them fed by springs. Yearling deer are surviving better than normal (though last year was good, too) and Danielson says he's seen none of the "blue tongue" disease reported up north.

Open-space technician **Frank Olson** adds that lizards and snakes are out ahead of schedule, and an abundance of raptors such as hawks and owls can be seen aloft as you drive along Skyline Boulevard.

DOWN PAGE MILL ROAD A BIT, in Palo Alto's Foothills Park, trees and shrubs are greening up real quick, ranger **Lester Hodgins** says. Families have been out in force, flying kites, watching the lake refill (the rangers expect to have it open in two or three months), and admiring the dazzling, mustard-splashed vistas. Buckeye hasn't bloomed yet, Hodgins reports, but its swelling buds are under close scrutiny.

Down lower still, in Menlo Park's playgrounds and parks, the dry spell has had its benefits. Little League season will open with the baseball diamonds in prime condition, according to **Jerry Hornibrook**, public works supervisor. That's because park crews had ample time to work through the backlog, instead of staying indoors on rainy days fixing sprinkler heads.

WARD WINSLOW

BY THE BAY, THE SALT MARSHES aren't affected because they're governed by the tides, says **John Walton**, the big, genial ranger at Palo Alto's Baylands Interpretive Center. Walton goes on to say, however, that he has noticed the birds are singing their courtship songs ahead of season, or at least they were before the fog set in.

Warm, dry February's effect on the birds, beasts and botany is not without parallel among the human populace, Walton adds. Teachers have been calling in sooner than they typically do to set up field trips, so humans are responding, too. The sap is rising.

BACK WHEN AGRICULTURE, not technology, was king in Santa Clara County, the county subsidized rainmaking. March 15 was considered the end of the rainy season insofar as the cloudseeding contracts were concerned. So unless this year takes another crazy turn, climatewise, only two weeks remain for fattening up the old rainfall average.

If dry weather persists, fire danger in the hills may be high, for the heavier fuels are dry already. Grass, on the other hand, may be somewhat stunted. The wildflower season could close early and ingloriously

What's more, my car, parked under a pine tree, showed up with a heavy pollen dusting a few days ago. The allergy season could be starting early, too.

How Sally Siegel used her eyes and the bridge table

SALLY SIEGEL'S OBITUARY last week could only begin to suggest why she was an effective force in regional education politics and Palo Alto city affairs. For one thing, it said nothing about her eyes.

Those eyes were the outstanding feature of her visage, and she knew how to use them to express a thousand unvoiced statements, approving, cajoling, showing mock horror or astonishment or disdain and the rest of a vast repertoire. Her musical speaking voice helped drive home her points.

Sally was an ultimate insider, too. She made it a point to know who was who and who thought what, and she wasn't in the least reluctant to feed in information where she thought it would do the most good. Even when she disagreed with someone she usually listened carefully and sought common ground. After all, her aim was to support public education in the broadest way, and that was a purpose anyone might be persuaded to share, sooner or later.

IT HAPPENS THAT the Siegels were our neighbors in recent years, and now and then we went to their house for a bridge game. This was a time of trial for Dr. **Elmar Siegel**, who is a serious duplicate bridge competitor, for Sally was a careless player and the guests weren't much better. It all tested Elmar's vibrant wit, and a stupid play could trigger a scolding.

Sally's attention was not on cards but rather on gleaning scraps of useful information from a music teacher active in the Educators Association and a journalist who'd been through a lot of election campaigns. She launched a lot of trial balloons at that bridge table, and it was great fun to witness her in her political action mode.

SALLY LIKED TO HAVE ACCESS to the movers and shakers, but she put loyalty ahead of that. Her continued support of Dr. **Wilson Riles** for state superintendent of public instruction after it became evident that **Bill Honig** would upset Riles is a good example. She also went down, without a whimper, with former state chief justice **Rose Bird's** ship. And not every action by a local superintendent deserved the backing she gave it, or so her bridge cronies thought.

One of Elmar's gag comments went like this: "I've always believed that one should perform social services for the community, and I've given my wife." Sally would do a good imitation of cringing while he said that. He also had a line about how his wife was married to a rich man whom he had never met. Come to think of it, their timing could have played in vaudeville, honed as it was in 49½ years of marriage.

Unfortunately, Sally was almost comatose at the end, so there are no parting bon mots to report. She'd be pleased, I believe, if people would remember her as a lifelong crusader for a good public education as every American's birthright.

THE COMMITTEE FOR GREEN FOOTHILLS is beginning its second 25 years this month with a $25-a-head celebration. The event is set for Sunday, May 22, from 2 to 5 p.m. at the Woodside home of **Louise M. Davies.**

Guest of honor at the party will be **Mary C. Davey** of Los Altos Hills, who has compiled a long and enviable record as a conservationist. While serving on the Hills council, she persuaded the town to buy the 50-acre Byrne Preserve, a park open to all. Mary also was one of the seven founders of the Midpeninsula Regional Open Space District, has been active in CGF and did long stints with the Forum on Community and the Environment and the Peninsula Conservation Foundation.

Davey has been a leader in groups dedicated to the environment, fair housing, education, women, minorities and senior citizens. Possibly she absorbed political smarts at her mother's knee — her mother was the first women to enter the U.S. Foreign Service.

Lois Crozier-Hogle of Palo Alto will introduce the honoree, and there'll be a mariachi band and south-of-the-border taste treats. Those who want to attend may contact CGF at 1019 Forest Court, Palo Alto, 94301, or call (415) 949-5393, for further information. A donation of more than $25 for the CGF's work is, by the way, acceptable.

AN ADDENDUM TO a recent item about the history celebration and reunion Saturday, May 14, at the Westinghouse Iron Man Museum in Sunnyvale: The sponsors believe there are former Joshua Hendy Iron Works employees in the community whose names they do not have, and they want them to know their attendance would be welcome. Just call John Mallory at Westinghouse, (408) 735-2627, to make arrangements.

Not everyone is enamored with cable TV installation

OUR NEIGHBORHOOD MAY BE one of the last in Palo Alto to get cable television, because it has underground utilities and a small planned unit development residents association to boot. Yet, we were told the other night we're involved in a precedent nevertheless — an unpleasant one.

Before relating that story, though, let me set the scene. First, cryptic communications in the cheapest photocopy form began to arrive at the door. Then a few simple markings appeared on the street. Those markings were almost worn off the pavement when a vivid new set in Day-Glo colors appeared. Applying them would be an ex-graffiti vandal's dream job.

Next the heavy equipment moved in: monstrous rigs to haul in smaller pieces on giant flatbeds, pavement rippers, jackhammers, cable dispensers and whatall, plus panel trucks and command cars. They treated the local crossroads, a three-way arterial stop, as if it wasn't even there, and came close to squashing a few residents' small cars in overshooting their turns and backing up.

THE PRECEDENT BEGAN to shape up in mid-afternoon. A McCourt Cable Systems crew, the installers, drove some javelin-like stakes to mark the site of the TV line extender box to be put between Kay Muranaka's lot next door and ours. Evidently they "skinned" the main electrical supply line. Kay phoned us to ask if our power was cutting in and out like hers. It wasn't, but we'd had a few flickers; had it gone out entirely, I'd have lost a couple of hours' work on the computer.

Kay's video cassette recorder was knocked out of action (are VCRs and cable TV mortal enemies?), her electricity was behaving weirdly and she was worried that refrigerated food might spoil. She called the city.

In due course, some Palo Alto city electricians responded. After study and testing, they decided it wasn't a city problem, and advised us to summon a private electrician in the morning, saying McCourt would pay for it. We made neighborly plans to do that.

Before the evening was over, however, a new rally formed around the big electrical box in the sidewalk. City, McCourt and maybe even Pacific Bell guys surrounded it and shined spotlights — it was reminiscent of a surgical team at work in an operating room. Once we were totally blacked out. At length, McCourt's on-the-scene boss told us his company would have an electrician there in the morning. He said it was the first time such an incident had happened.

MORNING CAME AND SUDDENLY word was passed that getting repairs was our responsibility. The Muranakas were furious, not least because the presumably "hot" probe had been left in all night where some kid might touch it. Finally, my wife reached a responsible official at City Hall and won the day with the argument that it was the city's responsibility because we hadn't asked to have the work done and it was occurring on a public easement. The city electrical men swiftly completed repairs once the responsibility was declared to be theirs.

At this writing, drilling continues. Furrows crease the pavement. Our line extender pedestal box has uprooted a juniper, and the woman of the garden has promised an exotic vine will soon conceal it. Elsewhere in the area pale green toadstools have sprouted, little domed cylinders of varied heights, all faintly phallic. Some of them stand where the gardeners who mow the tiny lawns will surely curse and kick them; one was put in an ivy patch and already is half covered.

Cable TV is not wildly popular in our precinct right now, and some are vowing eternal opposition. But Paul Gullixson, the expert reporter on this matter, says about 40 percent of the potential subscribers in Palo Alto are signing up, enough to make the system viable. I suspect there'll be more than half ultimately.

WHEN THE PENINSULA CONSERVATION Center Foundation gave its Conservationists of the Year Awards to Florence and Phillip La Riviere and Assemblyman Byron Sher on May 5, there was a fair amount of levity. Sher rendered that inevitable when he took up the cause of the banana slug, but that wasn't all.

In presenting the honors to the couple, Palo Alto Councilperson Emily Renzel quoted liberally from letters from their Palo Alto neighbors, attesting to seeing them come and go at all hours and often finding them in the midst of long-distance phone calls to legislators, all in the cause of preserving wetlands and expanding the national wildlife refuge. Phil, a retired Varian Associates staffer, was cited too as a "swamp physicist" for his measurements of the impact of wetlands management plans — documents that impressed federal authorities.

Writer Paul Steinhard made the presentation to Sher as one long dedicated to environmental issues, a leader in protecting forests and resources, a campaigner for proper controls of hazardous materials and waste management, and, of course, the champion of the banana slug.

DR. ALLAN SEID OF PALO ALTO has been elected to a second four-year term on the board of the National Institute Against Prejudice and Violence. Seid, a psychiatrist, is national president of the Asian Pacific American Coalition U.S.A., and an outspoken foe of anti-Asian violence in the nation.

The institute is the only national center of its kind — a clearinghouse for materials about prejudice and violence and policies for coping with such issues, a research organization into causes and effects, and a helper of various groups which confront issues of bigotry.

Fog a big factor in local weather

Even in a year like this one, Sausal Creek in Portola Valley is flowing, as always. **Herb Dengler,** the town's resident naturalist, says it never dries up.

Why doesn't it go dry like nearby Corte Madera Creek? Fog, Dengler explains. The same fog that came to our rescue after a day of 106-degree weather.

JULY AND AUGUST normally are the Bay Area's foggiest months. The pattern is well known. A high-pressure ridge camps out over the Pacific, sending fresh winds blowing onshore, bearing moisture. As they pass over cold water near the shoreline, the moisture condenses. Now the winds send the fog billowing up the western slopes. Finally checked by warm updrafts on the easterly side, the fog clouds cling like a skullcap to the Skyline. Although warm air from the inland valleys stops the fog intrusion during midday, in the evening and in the cool of the night it filters in, only to be burned off again by the sun the next morning.

Sooner or later the ocean winds ease off, our days get hotter, the rising inland air creates a vacuum that pulls in more marine air, and we're off on a new cycle.

HOW DOES ALL THIS keep Sausal Creek flowing? Well, says Herb, in some places there is considerable precipitation associated with these climatic effects. It's called fog drip.

Dengler cites a study on Cahill Ridge done by an ecologist named Oberlander in 1951. He collected data over a three-mile stretch from July 20 through Aug. 28.

In that 39-day period, a 200-foot-tall redwood in a protected part of the forest dripped 1.8 inches, as measured by the scientist's rain gauges. A 125-foot redwood that stood open to the incoming fog banks dripped 8.9 inches — almost a quarter-inch a day. A Douglas fir, also about 125 feet tall, registered 17.1 inches. And a 20-foot tan oak, with large leaves like a chestnut's, designed by nature to capture a lot of water, recorded 58.8 inches!

"This is why the creek runs year-around — it's fog-fed," Dengler explains. Corte Madera and San Francis-quito creeks may look dry, but there's some under-gravel flow there, too, similarly fog-fed.

THE FOG DRIP is spotty. Just 200 feet from those water-precipitating trees you could find a very dry chaparral patch, Dengler notes. The drip also creates some interesting effects. On the Morshead estate in Portola Valley there's a grove of redwoods underlain by a carpet of yellow violets, formally named *Viola sempervirens.* Driving to La Honda, you find wet spots where the road passes under redwoods.

THE BURNED FOLIAGE left on some lowland trees by that all-time scorcher July 17 is not so evident in the native trees of the foothills, Dengler says. But they seem to have been dropping their leaves earlier this season. As the water table gets lower, they automatically shed leaves — madrones in May, buckeyes now, bay laurels soon. Poison oak seems ahead of its usual withering schedule, he adds.

SEPTEMBER USUALLY brings our hottest days during its first two or 2 1/2 weeks, though not quite a match for that 106. The fog machine begins to run down because the prevailing winds slack off. There are still some breezes, created by the interplay of inland and coastal air and thermals, but as the high-pressure ridge loses its poof, the fog thins. At the beaches, days in autumn and fall often are the most glorious of the year.

BAYLANDS LEVEES and boardwalks near the Palo Alto Nature Interpretive Center see a good deal of foot traffic in August. There's a nature walk at 2 p.m. every Saturday and Sunday, and on Thursday, Aug. 11, at 7 p.m., there'll be an evening jaunt to view creatures not often seen by daytime visitors. This Sunday, starting at 9:30 a.m., there'll be the summer marsh walk — a two-hour traipse to observe summer plant production and nesting birds.

For those who'd rather ride, a bike tour of the baylands is set for this Saturday, Aug. 6, at 9:30 a.m. Bring binoculars and a windbreaker, the naturalists advise.

All these look-sees start from the center at the end of Embarcadero Road.

WARD WINSLOW

The advantages of staying put

What does it take to qualify as an oldtimer around here? Fifteen years? Thirty? Fifty? And is it worth it, or is life ultimately more interesting if you keep moving?

Sure, it depends on a lot of variables: personality, the community's stage in its own life cycle, fortune, fate and dozens of others. Still, I think the advantages usually tend to favor the stay-putter, if the locale affords opportunities, or he or she can make them happen there.

If that's true, it's good, for societal forces around here tend to prompt young adults who've once dug in to hold their ground. With the monumental cost of home ownership, buying up is inhibited and improving where you are may be easier than jumping to and fro.

THESE ARE THE MUSINGS, dear reader, of someone who has lived in or around Palo Alto for nearly 45 years since high school days. People like me have seen classmates become captains of industry and commerce, based on personal capabilities, but also on being in the right place at the right time.

Some had to be patient, like the orchardists who ate dandelions during the Depression but, decades later, sold their crop land for millions. Some rode the growth waves that ran strong here even before "Silicon Valley." Some had qualities that catapulted them to the top while the area scribed by a 20-mile radius from, say, Homer and Alma became one of the most influential on earth.

NOW AND THEN I WORRY whether **David Packard** is writing his autobiography, or at least memoirs. It's none of my business, of course. Still, my worry has a basis. Dave (and his partner, **Bill Hewlett,** too) clearly prefers acting in the here and now to re-chewing the past. Both men come across as touchy about references to their fabulous earnings (despite all the great things they've done with their money), and neither has ever sought the kind of personal glory garnered by **Lee Iacocca** or **Chuck Yeager** with the help of their ghostwriters.

Packard probably was amused, if he saw it, by a recent headline describing him as "a Hewlett-Packard official." Zounds! He cofounded a world leader among technology companies. He was a principal architect of the Palo Alto school system in its salad days, and had a lot to do with Stanford University's present eminence. He was the No. 2 man in the Defense Department in the '70s, and in the '80s headed up two of our nation's key presidential commissions.

When Dave Packard speaks out, thoughtful Americans from coast to coast listen, and find wisdom in his words, whether they agree or not.

What's more, Packard does a good job of writing. His observations on a tour of the Soviet Union decades ago, printed in an HP house newsletter called "Watts Current," stand out in memory as exceptionally trenchant reportage. His reflections on his experiences in innovation, management, academia and government would command a broad, attentive audience. So let's hope he reaches the same value judgment his friend Mr. Hoover did and takes time to illuminate his eventful life for posterity's benefit.

PEOPLE VALUE LONG associations and dedicated service. The funeral last month for veterinarian Aldo Cascinai, who was drowned on a fly-fishing trip, reportedly was standing room only. Dr. Cascinai, 63, had a big family and lots of friends in the South Palo Alto Lions, but many who paid their respects were dog and cat owners who loved the man for his dedication. **Mildred Nelson** of Palo Alto attests that he'd turn out at any hour at the 24-hour vet service he set up to care for a sick pet — and worried owners. The animals were calmed by his mere touch, Millie says, and his kindness impressed everyone.

DURING A HAIR-DO appointment a few days ago hairdresser **Paul Spiteri** and my wife recalled it had been 25 years since their first collaboration. They calculated he must have cut 12 1/2 feet of her locks, all told. But someone's always more of an oldtimer. A customer of 33 years' standing is about to treat Paul to a trip to India.

Billion-dollar fun at Raychem

It may have been the biggest party ever thrown in Menlo Park, though it wasn't the only show around that day. Stanford versus Southern California drew a larger crowd, but Raychem Corp.'s billion dollar bash was one for the books.

The company's employees (about 4,500) and their families made up the turnout of 15,000 on Saturday, Sept. 10, at the Raychem campus on Bayfront Expressway off Bayshore Freeway near Marsh Road. The party didn't cost a billion — it was a celebration of Raychem's passing $1 billion in annual sales in 1987-88. The theme, of course, was "Thanks a billion!"

Paul M. Cook, chairman and CEO, and **Robert M. Halperin**, president and chief operating officer, were portrayed on the cover of the invitation in a staid annual report pose. "What's a proper way to celebrate a billion-dollar year?" the legend asked. Inside, Cook and Halperin were shown in party hats giving the answer: "Have serious fun."

SERIOUS FUN, RAYCHEM STYLE, differs somewhat from the usual Silicon Valley gala. For one thing, employees were deeply involved in planning the party and staging many of its entertainments. For another, it was nonalcoholic, in keeping with the family spirit and to the relief of the provisioners, since it ran from 1 to 9 p.m.

The event took place in the company parking lot, which was closed the day before to enable employee teams to decorate with multicolored banners and balloons. Workers were bused into the plant from outlying points that day. And while there was no Mickey Mouse theme, an oft-heard comment was that "It's like Disneyland."

An opener event was a centipede parade, with departments competing like Bay to Breakers teams. Snacks and beverages were served all day, and carnival rides and a kiddieland were in operation. Five stages were occupied by the likes of **Pride and Joy**, a motown review type;

Johnny Baron and the Bel-Aires, a rock group; the country western **California Cowboys**; **Raychem Review,** an employee talent show; and assorted other circus and samba acts and roving performers. Another stage was a big dance floor.

CHICKEN AND RIBS, the latter cooked by MacArthur Park, Palo Alto, were on the dinner menu from 4 to 6:30. Then at 7 came the main event: Some speeches followed by rock 'n' roll star **Kenny Loggins**. A huge fireworks show topped it off.

Taste Catering of San Francisco, headed by **Timothy Maxson**, stepped out of its usual gourmet specialty to feed the multitude, and reportedly enjoyed hotdogging it. The task took 500 servers, and the provisions list went like this:

18,000 hot dogs

70,000 beverage servings — soda, juice, milk and coffee

3,000 hens

30,000 ribs (counted by the bone)

25,000 frozen juice and ice cream bars

15,000 pounds of ice

Plus quantities of nachos, carton candies, sno-cones, peanuts, popcorn and salad

My peek at the victuals list came through my daughter, **Lynne Winslow,** who coordinated the food and beverages. She reported the party-goers really had a good time. As for Raychem, she pronounced the company "about the nicest client I've ever worked."

THERE WAS ANOTHER big party in Menlo Park six years ago. The count for that one was about 12,000. Raychem gave it, too. It was the company's 25th anniversary party. At that time Raychem described itself as a radiation chemistry company, as its name implies. Now it is called a materials science company, indicating its broadening into new technologies: fiber optics, liquid crystals and gels, and others.

Greenmeadow's venerable history

Know what's the second-oldest community association in the nation? It's south Palo Alto's Greenmeadow Community Association Inc., says its president, **Doug Mecham.** One in Boston may be older, but look out — Greenmeadow has passed the 33-year mark and is going strong.

Our house is just beyond Greenmeadow's pale, but owing to a special rule they have, we were able to become users of its swimming pool and thereby association members. The pool, surrounded by a park, meeting rooms and a nursery school setup, is the heart of this sector of mostly Eichler homes near the Cubberley High campus.

Although the facilities facilitate it, the activism and community spirit of the residents are what make the association tick. There are quarterly membership meetings, meetings to hear political candidates, meetings to discuss issues, band practices, a good newsletter and lots of other trimmings. Plus a championship youth swim team.

GREENMEADOW HONORED one of the leaders behind all this recently by giving **George Ebey** the first Greenmeadow Association Service Award (his wife, **Leonor,** was cited as the power behind the power). Ebey, now 81, was assistant superintendent of schools in Portland before he moved to Palo Alto and became a consultant. He served as third president of the association; then founded its Scholarship Fund (and, in a stroke of organizational genius, roped all past association presidents, or prex as they say in GM, into doing its work). Ebey also edited Meadowlark, the newsletter, for 5½ years, and has been confidante and friend to other prex since his term.

By the count of **Ralph Whitaker,** another early president, 30 prex have served 34 terms, and 15 still live in Greenmeadow. A couple became city councilmen, **John Berwald,** (prex No. 1) and the late Dr. Christian Zweng.

ACCEPTING THE HONOR, EBEY noted among other things that **Pete McCloskey,** before he went to Congress, had negotiated purchase of GM's land from the late Joe Eichler for a bargain $10,000. (McCloskey was among the 130 persons present.) Typically, Ebey gave something back to the association: a cherished myrtlewood gavel, now inscribed in part, "GM Prex Power, A Community Leadership Commitment" and a Fourth of July handbell, entrusted to **Jack Hamilton,** president of the Scholarship Foundation.

The outsize cake for the occasion (it took three bakers and three icers) said: "Let George do it ... He already has."

THE SPACIOUS PATIO at Sacred Heart School in Menlo Park was the setting recently for a party celebrating the 40th anniversary of the Universal Declaration of Human Rights. It was an Amnesty International gig, engineered by AI's local guiding spirit, **Ginetta Sagan** of Atherton. The party was short on speeches and long on food and music, and the crowd reflected the success of rock group U2 and colleagues in rallying youngsters to AI, as well as a faithful corps of older Peninsula devotees.

"BY THE SWEAT OF Thy Brow: The Story of Labor in Santa Clara Valley" is on as the fall and winter exhibit at the California History Center in the Trianon Building at De Anza College in Cupertino. Except during noon hour, it's open from 8 a.m. to 4:30 p.m. Monday-Friday and 10 a.m. to 2 p.m. Saturday.

With photos, placards, tools and text, the exhibit traces organized labor's rise from the grim New Almaden quicksilver mines in the 1860s. It details founding of the forerunner of the present Central Labor Council a century ago, a surge during the Depression when cannery workers finally organized, then troubles in the 1960s as the economy changed.

I have just one complaint with this fine exhibit, co-sponsored by the Santa Clara County Central Labor Council, AFL-CIO. It forgot to mention Emerson Street (his name, not his address) of Palo Alto, who won labor many friends in 17½ years through 1977 as the council's business representative.

"PASSING FARMS, ENDURING Values," the exhibit related to the book by **Yvonne Jacobson** of Los Altos Hills, has just moved into a permanent home at the San Jose Historical Museum in Kelley Park. It's in a plain brown barn hauled in from the Stevens Ranch in Coyote, but inside features photos, text, a big prune grader and a wagonload of fruit lug boxes from once famous ranches throughout the valley. The photos, especially, tell the story of the family farms that existed before "Silicon Valley" with their lush crops, human dignity and ethnic diversity.

A gift from the David and Lucile Packard Foundation helped mount the permanent exhibit.

Not too late to experience Filoli

Filoli has six wells and some reservoir storage "up the canyon," but they're all dry. So the magnificent estate in Woodside is limping into November on bought water — 75,000 gallons a day, at least in summer's heat.

Even so, Filoli has survived this second drought year running with only one major loss: a terrace lawn between the mansion and the canyon that's been allowed to die. Presuming the rains come this winter, Filoli's crew of 13 gardeners doubtless will have a new swath of greensward sprouting by spring. And don't think the browning lawn is Filoli's only one.

Come Saturday at the end of this week and Filoli's 1988 tour season will end. When it reopens in '89, quite different flowers will be in bloom, rain or no.

IN CASE YOU HAVEN'T experienced Filoli, it's a grand place which from nearby I-280, or even Canada Road, shows a low profile. In fact, from the roads it is hard to believe a 450-acre estate with a very large country house could be so unobtrusive. It lies a little south of the Spring Valley Lakes, and for good reason: William B. Bourn II, who built it in 1916, owned the Spring Valley Water Co. (and the Empire Mine near Grass Valley, a big gold producer that likely did more than the water service to build the estate).

Bourn had the mansion designed by noted architect Willis Polk. He liked the site because of its resemblance to the Lakes of Killarney area in Ireland, and he used the house and grounds to entertain on a massive scale.

After the deaths of Mr. and Mrs. Bourn in 1936, the estate was acquired by Mr. and Mrs. William P. Roth. Lurline Roth, the daughter of Capt. William Matson of the shipping lines, lived there until she was 85, when the 40 steps to her upstairs suite evidently became too taxing. In 1975 she deeded it to the National Trust for Historic Preservation — house, garden, and 654 acres, along with an endowment of $2.5 million to help pay the upkeep, now in $1 million or so a year.

Mrs. Roth continued to take an active interest in Filoli, and remained a frequent visitor, until her death the day after her 95th birthday.

THE PROPERTY NOW IS administered by Filoli Center, a nonprofit corporation run by a local board of trustees including leaders in the horticultural, academic, cultural and business sectors. They are backed up by Friends of Filoli, a volunteer support group with numerous social and cultural activities. It must be fun, for there are 700 volunteers and 200 docents who lead tours of the house and gardens.

It's a good bet that all the docents are accomplished and entertaining tour leaders, but I thought we were especially lucky to be guided one recent afternoon by Victor K. Thompson of Portola Valley. Vic is a Stanford professor emeritus of architecture and has been active in the Filoli leadership, and the information nuggets he dropped were fascinating. For all his love of structures and their lore, he considers Filoli's gardens even more outstanding than the house.

Vic's wife, Marianne, was along too and told us on the QT she'd never seen the place in less bloom — news to us, as the sasanqua camellias, the rose garden, the colorful "Chartres garden" (so called because it emulates the stained glass of the famed French cathedral) and lots more flowers were spectacular. Marianne is a concert pianist who recently played in a pair of two-piano recitals in Ladera and Palo Alto, and she has played in the Filoli grand ballroom during past musical entertainments.

OTHER FASCINATING DOCENTS you might draw include the Roths' twin daughters, Lurline Coonan of Woodside and Berenice Spalding of Hillsborough. Or David Patterson of San Mateo, who is 85 now. Patterson began his service at Filoli at age 14, and was with both the owner families as well as doing a stint with the Crockers in Hillsborough. He was Mrs. Roth's last butler.

Tours can be arranged by phoning (415) 364-2880, but, as noted above, they are off from Nov. 5 until some time in February.

Fond memories of elections past

Elections used to be a lot more exciting back when precinct officials delivered ballot bags to the Palo Alto Times and people hung around the Times to see the returns posted.

That was a long time ago, before computers revolutionized the vote counting and television reshaped campaigning. Excitement is hard to maintain when you can learn most of the results before the polls close here.

CERTAINLY THE TOP all-time thrill at Stanford came in 1928, when Herbert Hoover's election was proclaimed. The Hoovers were at their campus home, now called Lou Henry Hoover House, and students, faculty, townspeople and John Philip Sousa's band all rushed up the hill to offer congratulations. The band had been playing a campus concert.

Probably no one remembers that event more vividly than Carl E. McDowell of Palo Alto. He was on the concert staff, put the request to Sousa and procured two buses to carry the band up near the Hoover home. Then it fell to McDowell to introduce the maestro to the president-elect. "It was the biggest moment of my life," Carl says.

In 1932, McDowell was at the Hoover house again, this time for a low point. He recalls that the defeated president, dead tired, stood at the foot of the stairs and shook his hand.

IN THE POSTWAR YEARS, Palo Alto had one of the finest Republican precinct organizations in the state. Dorothy Custer remembers that its leaders were all personal friends, yet reflected all shades of GOP opinion. "If we could take old Palo Alto, we could deliver the city for our candidate," she says. "Even though we disagreed on many things, we worked well together."

Mrs. Custer worked hard in 1960 for Vice President Richard Nixon, and he did edge out John F. Kennedy in California and in Palo Alto.

Hugh March and his wife, Carol, also were active in the '60s. Hugh remembers it as "hands-on" precinct work, going door to door in the days when doing that felt comfortable. "There was a captain for virtually every precinct in town," he says. "It was really a neighborhood concept, ... and it was social as well as political."

A "foot soldier" who grew into larger responsibilities, Gloria Brown cites 1968 when Nixon barely won over Hubert Humphrey as "the most exciting night of my life, waiting for those votes to come in." So dedicated a party supporter was Gloria that, the week before her daughter was to be married, she recruited her son, David, then a Paly High student, to go with her to Turlock and canvass for a special election. Her candidate, Claire Berryhill, won by 12 votes — and she and David had gotten out 20!

ED SCOYEN, now retired as a Municipal Court judge, has a different perspective. While a law student at Stanford, he grew angered over *Time* magazine's reporting of the Truman-Dewey race in 1948. "I went down to University Avenue where the Democratic headquarters was in two rooms over an old store," Ed relates. "When I volunteered, they hugged me and kissed me and gave me 19 precincts to cover." When Truman won, he adds, the campus group whooped it up — "it was like beating USC."

In '50 and '52, Scoyen adds, a frequent response when he rang a bell and identified himself as a Democratic worker was (in hushed tones), "Who told you?" It wasn't respectable to be a Democrat in Palo Alto then. But in 1954 that began to change, he says, and in 1958 the party, led by Edmund G. "Pat" Brown, swept the state offices. Since then, the Democrats have done well in Palo Alto.

NIXON CARRIED Palo Alto in 1960, and won in both Santa Clara and San Mateo counties. Since then, Democratic candidates have prevailed in Palo Alto, as Paul Gullixson details in his history column today, including Jimmy Carter in the Ronald Reagan victory of 1980.

Menlo Park has gone with the winner more often in recent decades. Atherton and Woodside are solidly Republican, even to backing Barry Goldwater in 1964.

'Sixty-four was a costly loss for the GOP. Hugh March points out that in that election, Goldwater supporters who mostly weren't party regulars won in the primary but could not broaden their candidate's base enough in the general election. March says he sees a lot of parallels with Michael Dukakis' campaign this year.

You may know a closet celebrity

Have you ever discovered that someone you know and like casually is actually a celebrity, or a noteworthy personage?

Peter Neumann and I met through our dogs, at the Cubberley High track, or thereabouts. We like each other — at least I think we do, though doubt can creep in when that old "Love me, love my dog" saying gets to caroming around in my head. Our dogs are not friends — no way. What they form is a moving indignation rally at the ends of two strained leashes.

Now and then there's an intimation that these pooches, Peter's Baron, a Doberman, and my Dustin, a mix of Rhodesian ridgeback, German shepherd and maybe a tad of wolf, could become pals. If only Dustin would relax his unrelenting hostility. A couple of times one or the other has broken away from the leash restraint, and the dustup all the barking leads one to expect hasn't occurred.

ONE DAY PETER'S MUG appeared on the front page of a morning newspaper. He was being quoted as the reigning Peninsula authority on hacker-induced computer disorders. He's employed at SRI International, and he's a blooming expert on what the press invariably used to call computer viruses. That's changing. In the crisis affecting UNIX operating systems coast to coast the culprit was a worm. And Peter, who lectures to the National Science Foundation and testifies before congressional committees on this matter, has pointed out that the threat in certain cases is far more a time bomb than a virus.

OLD ACQUAINTANCES, met in a new setting, take a while to recognize, sometimes. This year my wife took up a new hobby: pottery glazing. She kept mentioning a marvelous character she'd met in a Midtown shop where she went to buy greenware and paint, or whatever the stuff that produces the color and shine is called, and to have pieces fired. So one day I went along.

The character was rather tiny, very forthcoming and utterly charming. She had that folksy, slightly schoolmarm quality that it seems to take to deal with a steady flow of hobbyists who often need instruction. And there was something familiar about her.

Off I went on a banking errand, and then headed back past the shop, BAM Ceramics, toward the car. Then it struck me, and I stuck my head in the door to confirm it. She was the woman who used to give bridge classes at the Lucie Stern Community Center, Ethel Chedekel.

Ethel and her husband, Art, run their little business with a style all their own. For instance, they're giving out their own set of Ten Commandments, revised for 1989. Number III says, "Thou shalt clean up your work area. Your mother doesn't work here." Then there's VII: "Don't tell me you put on two heavy coats. I know I told you to put on three."

HOW ABOUT A LOW-cholesterol, fat-free, smoke-free, alcohol-free dinner for the holidays? A couple of dozen people tried it at the Palo Alto Medical Clinic's nutrition department a few days ago, and they came away raving about the eggplant and white bean casserole, among other dishes.

The diners, said dietitian Jennifer Ingco, were alumni of four of the department's classes: cholesterol control, "Keep It Off" (weight management), smoking cessation and stress management. Other popular dishes they brought for the potluck included chicken and tomato with fetta cheese, salad with imitation crab (made from fish), bean salads and potato spinach casserole.

A FORMER COLLEAGUE, Jay Thorwaldson, the clinic's designated communicator, is making a related announcement this week. The clinic is offering what he calls "a priceless gift certificate" printed on parchment. It entitles the recipient to take a smoking cessation class, "a $150 value investment in life," Jay says.

Al Werry to celebrate 100 years

Neither Thanksgiving nor Christmas is the big event this year at one Palo Alto home. **Alfred E. Werry** is turning 100 on Dec. 15, and his family is celebrating with a bash on Sunday, Dec. 11.

Werry ranked as Palo Alto's oldest living merchant when, at 95, he retired from his business, Werry Electric, on University Avenue. The store closed three years ago, and he still misses it. His daughter, **Ellen Bergren,** says he'd really like to be back in business.

AL WERRY WAS BORN in Mayfield, known now as the California Avenue district, in 1888, the youngest in a Stanford brick mason's family of seven. He was 3 when they moved into the sixth house in the burgeoning hamlet of Palo Alto, on High Street where Zack Electronics is.

After attending Palo Alto High School — the *old* Palo Alto High on Channing, that is — Werry became a commuter, taking the train to San Francisco to attend Cogswell Polytechnic College (now in Cupertino). He graduated from Cogswell in 1909, worked briefly for a company building Diesel engines, then started working for Palo Alto contractor Fred Roller. Soon Werry bought out his boss, but by 1916 they were partners again, running an electric business, including sale and repair of electrical appliances. Werry wired Peninsula homes as far out as Woodside and Sunnyvale.

When the business moved for the third and last time in 1922 to University and Waverley, Werry was criticized by other merchants for locating so far out in the sticks. Time was on his side, however, and the shop became a favorite of generations of townspeople. From 1945 on he owned it outright until the last few years when his son, **Al Werry Jr.,** served as proprietor.

THE CENTENARIAN-TO-BE lives now with his daughter Ellen and her husband, **Al Bergren,** in a house at Hamilton Avenue and Fulton Street that Werry bought in 1935 for $5,500. His other daughter, **Kathryn** and her husband, **John Childress,** also live in Palo Alto now, and so do Al Jr. and his wife, **Ann.** The tribe includes four grandsons, **David Werry** of Denver, **Scott Werry** of Palo Alto, **Kevin Childress** of Chicago and **Mark Childress** of Palo Alto, and one great grandson, **Mark Childress** the younger, also of Palo Alto.

They'll all be joined by relatives from New Zealand and Australia and lots of merchant friends at the Sunday afternoon party at the Garden Court Hotel. More than 100 are expected, and they should find the honoree in fine fettle, troubled only by a hearing difficulty.

Again on the 15th the venerable gentleman will greet friends from 2 to 4 p.m. at an open house at his home.

Even that won't end the milestone marking. Werry is looking forward to receiving his 75-year pin from the Masons in March. He still turns out now and then for Palo Alto Rotary Club meetings and events at the First United Methodist Church, which his parents played a large role in founding.

JULIE JEROME, who received the 1988 Sally Siegel Friend of Education Award recently from the Palo Alto Educators Association, is the first honoree in a long time to make it by the inside volunteer route.

PAEA President **Maggie Benz** explained in presenting it that the idea of the award is to honor a strong supporter of public education and one who has "the undying belief that public education is a basic foundation of a democratic nation and worth the struggle that insures its continued existence."

Sally Siegel, who died earlier this year, was the first recipient a decade ago and personified those qualities.

A little more than a decade ago was when Julie Jerome began volunteering in the math lab at Green Gables School. She became the lab's coordinator, then entered a PTA whirl that propelled her into officer posts and ultimately to the Palo Alto High School unit presidency.

Meanwhile, Jerome found time in 1982 to become a teacher's aide, and still is. In recent years, she has also made her mark in Leadership Palo Alto, Committee 2000 Facilities and Enrollment, the Palo Alto Foundation for Education, Palo Alto Adolescent Services and other advisory posts.

Quite a tour de force. Bravo!

Late in 1993 Al Werry turned 105. He was named the honorary chairman of Palo Alto Centennial 1994.

We got our money's worth in Gunn's 'golden age'

A lot of people who worked with Henry M. Gunn regard him as the best superintendent of schools Palo Alto ever had, and speak fondly of the 1950s and two years of the '60s as "the golden age of Gunn."

Dr. Gunn died Dec. 22 at his Mount Madonna home of a stroke. He was 90.

Tully C. Knoles Jr., who joined PAUSD in 1937 and served under six superintendents before retiring in 1972, ranks Gunn "way up" among them. Knoles, who now lives in Healdsburg, recalled that Robert Littler and **David Packard** were the trustees on the search team that plucked Henry Gunn from his presidency of the Oregon College of Education. Earlier he'd been superintendent of the Eugene schools.

"He took the district at a time when it was just getting ready to expand explosively," Knoles pointed out. Palo Alto had good schools and a strong Board of Education, but it wasn't then nationally recognized as a "lighthouse district," as it later came to be. "Henry was a real leader," Knoles said. "He had a totally supportive board, and he encouraged us to try new things."

WHAT RESULTED WAS not only a school management team that handled rapid physical expansion without mortgaging the future for state loans, but also one that encouraged the testing of new educational theories.

In the scramble to build and staff schools "Henry Gunn always kept a little bit ahead," said **Ben Page**, Stanford professor emeritus of geology and a school board member in that era.

How Gunn contrived to stay ahead is a bit of a puzzle, for while the number of schools doubled and the enrollment almost tripled, he maintained an open-door policy. District employees revered him because he was never too busy to talk to any of them about educational issues or personal problems. Teachers recall, too, that he was a frequent visitor in their classrooms, and one whose pop-ins were welcome, not unsettling.

A FREE FLOW OF IDEAS among administrators, classroom teachers and board members became a trademark of the district, Knoles said, and was continued later when **Harold Santee** was superintendent. "You had an opportunity to speak your piece," Knoles said.

It was "an atmosphere of great warmth," he added. **Betty Rogaway**, who has recorded oral histories with Dr. Gunn and many of his cohort, made the same point. "Almost everybody involved then says those were the days ... the golden age of Gunn."

What made the open-door policy so valuable was that Dr. Gunn was "a damn good listener," and able to draw people out, Knoles said. He almost never dealt in a "we and they" context. "And he had a great big smile — with dimples."

At a community appreciation dinner in April 1961, **Jack B. Power**, then board president, announced that the district's third high school would be named Henry M. Gunn Senior High School. At the same event Tully Knoles, a recent past president of the Palo Alto Chamber of Commerce, bestowed upon Dr. Gunn the Distinguished Citizen Award — the sixth the chamber had given in 50 years.

FOR A WHILE IN the mid-'50s it was my privilege to cover the board for the *Palo Alto Times*, so I can say a personal amen to all of the above. Henry Gunn seemed to project authority effortlessly, probably because he'd done it all in his pre-Palo Alto career. I'm told, too, that he could be fearsome in disciplining an incompetent or misbehaving employee.

The times favored him. That became evident later in the '60s when student and teacher unrest welled up, collective bargaining battles took shape and voters began to resist bond measures.

Nobody's perfect. After Dr. Gunn left to teach at San Jose State, the district spent some time shoring up a system so decentralized that kids transferring between Palo Alto schools might find their new class using a different textbook.

In the light of today's bloated executive salaries, it's noteworthy that Dr. Gunn took the Palo Alto post for $11,500 per annum. If he ever topped $20,000, our clip file doesn't show it. We sure got our money's worth, and then some.

WARD WINSLOW

Palo Altan's link to the emperor

The death of Japan's Emperor Hirohito closed a significant chapter in the life of one Palo Altan, Tomoe Tana. Mrs. Tana, now 75, a writer of poetry since she was a girl of 10 in Japan, has been a perennial entrant in the emperor's annual poetry contest.

The contest dates back more than 1,000 years, but only since 1884 have commoners been allowed to enter. Fifteen poems from many thousands submitted from poetry-crazy Japan and, indeed, all over the world, are chosen to be chanted at the occasion each January. This year, of course, the ceremony was canceled.

Tomoe Tana herself won a coveted invitation to the emperor's poetry party in 1949 while she was living in Richmond. However, she did not learn of her honor until after the event had taken place, and hence missed attending. Two years later she moved to Palo Alto.

In 1956, Lucille M. Nixon, who had been tutored by Mrs. Tana in both *waka* and calligraphy, became the first person not of Japanese descent to win an invitation. Mrs. Tana was perhaps more thrilled than Miss Nixon, then an elementary education consultant in the Palo Alto school system.

LUCHI NIXON THOUGHT at first she could not afford to attend the ceremony. At that point, the *Palo Alto Times* called editorially on President Eisenhower and the State Department to make funds available to send her as a cultural exchange gesture. With Sen. Thomas Kuchel's prompting, the government did help, but arrangements were made only after Miss Nixon insisted — characteristically — that Mrs. Fumiko Ogawa of Los Angeles, a naturalized U.S. citizen who also was a winner, receive the same aid.

Lucille Nixon was killed 25 years ago, on Dec. 22, 1963, in an auto-train crash at King City. Subsequently Palo Alto named an elementary school in her memory. There mementoes of her 1957 trip to Japan are displayed.

AKIHITO, THE NEW emperor, is said not to write *waka*, the stylized, 31-syllable, five-line poems sought for the contest. Perhaps there is a convention to get around that, because the high point of the ceremony in Hirohito's day was for the emperor's poem to be chanted five times while all others present stood.

There is a link from Akihito to Tomoe Tana. It was Elizabeth Gray Vining, a friend of Miss Nixon's and former English tutor to the then crown prince, who commended Mrs. Tana to Miss Nixon.

True to her beloved friend's memory, Mrs. Tana asked to have the 25th anniversary of Miss Nixon's death called to public attention. She may have been the only one to note that Dr. Henry Gunn, Palo Alto superintendent in most of Miss Nixon's time, died last month on the same day of the year as she had.

MRS. TANA IS A highly acclaimed poet in Japan. For the past three years, she has been the second-place winner in the Yasukuni Shrine Poetry Contest. The widow of a Buddhist priest, she went to Foothill College after her children were grown to study English in order to translate her husband's voluminous diaries from the time of their World War II internment — separately, by an added, cruel stroke of fate. One of the three diaries is finished now.

When Miss Nixon was invited to the party, Mrs. Tana wrote five poems of congratulations and offered them to the paper. However, she would not permit their being used in English only, saying the Japanese must be given too, for the Japanese subscribers. Here is one:

Nippon-wo
Sono-na-kumoi-ni
Toitaki-kokoro
Uta-ni-yose
Nikoe-agetari.
Translated, it says:

She knew the Emperor would be pleased with the poem and now the honor says that that is true.

Miss Nixon also brush-stroked one *waka* that could be an epitaph for Hirohito. The English version reads:

Dutifully transmitting
To a nurturing nation
Noble cultural riches,
Cherished from ages past,
His Majesty fulfills his trust.

Rubber pedestals for quake safety

Remember Jack Benny's gags about Anaheim, Azusa and Cucamonga? Well, I've just been to Cucamonga to see the first U.S. structure built with "base isolation." It's the Foothills Law and Justice Center, serving half a million residents of western San Bernardino County. Its basement and four floors rest on about 100 rubber pedestals, one under each column.

When an earthquake strikes — and Rancho Cucamonga is a seismic hotspot — these big shock absorbers will dampen most of its energy rather than transmit it, amplified, to the structure above, or so the designers say. To calm skeptics (and insurers, no doubt), there are stub ends of the frame's huge steel beams just a few inches above the foundation — a fallback feature, so to speak.

THE IDEA OF THE TWO-DAY meeting arranged by the California Engineering Foundation was to raise consciousness about this means of not merely keeping large low- and mid-rise buildings standing in a moderate to major earthquake, but stopping them from being bent out of shape and incurring ruinous damage to the contents, which may be worth far more than the structure. Thus hospitals, command centers and other emergency facilities can ride out a shake and remain in service when they're needed most.

The wisdom of this notion has hit home in other temblor-ridden places. Japan, for one, has 20 very large public buildings built with base isolators. If all this seems somewhat remote from the Palo Alto area beat, believe me, there are connections. Please read on.

The Law and Justice Center houses 16 courts with extensive computer and teleconferencing systems. County officials are keen on base isolation, though it has been tested by only a minor quake so far — a test its instrumentation showed it passed with flying colors.

ALL DURING THE SESSIONS I kept wondering if base isolation had been considered for the new $20.9 million courthouse under construction in San Jose, a six-story and basement layout in the Hedding Street complex, not so far from where the Santa Clara County Courthouse dome collapsed in 1906.

Inquiries finally led me to the project architect, Richard B. Campbell of Hoover Associates of — guess where? — Palo Alto. Campbell, it turned out, had formerly been a partner in Reid & Tarics of San Francisco, the firm that designed the Palo Alto High School reconstruction. More importantly, one of its principals, Dr. Alexander Tarics of Belvedere, is the leading apostle of base isolation. An offshoot of his firm had designed the system for Rancho Cucamonga. So from his past, Campbell knew all about base isolation.

IT WAS CONSIDERED for the new Santa Clara County courthouse, Campbell said, but was not deemed necessary. He sees the isolators as indicated for hospitals, structures housing very sophisticated electronics systems, or laboratories with racks of chemicals sure to be sloshed by intense ground motion. The courthouse, he said, won't contain much in the way of computers.

Far be it from me to challenge an architect's professional judgment, but I keep wondering when we'll make a start on our own fault-riddled turf.

Actually, there've been minor starts. A Berkeley firm that designs rubber isolators with lead cores has installed a pair at the target end of the Stanford Linear Accelerator Center O-ring building. A Bayshore Freeway overpass in San Mateo County also sports some.

One conference speaker, Professor James Kelly of the UC Berkeley civil engineering faculty, who runs the big shake table over in Richmond, said the principle isn't so new. He found a 1909 British patent for a crude form in the Stanford Engineering Library, with a reference indicating that the notion dates back more than a century.

Kelly couldn't resist spicing up his rather technical talk by showing the famous photo of the statue of zoologist Louis Agassiz impaled head down in the Stanford Quad pavement after the '06 quake. He got a laugh with the old wheeze: "It was said that he went from the abstract to the concrete."

Another speaker was Charles Thiel of the Stanford faculty, a consulting research engineer. He chose to note that base isolation may not fit some situations, and to advise the engineers-heavy audience how to appeal to corporate decision makers and building owners to spend somewhat more for high quality construction. They're likely to act, Thiel said, if they perceive a potential loss as business-ending or ruinous in terms of market share. Talking by engineers in terms of first costs and damage is less effective, studies show.

Lastly, one of the listed attendees was Bob Lanning of Hewlett-Packard Company, whose title is earthquake program manager. I take that as a good sign.

Council switches from Sousa to 'Viva Italia'

SORRY, JOHN PHILIP SOUSA FANS, but there won't be a replay at this year's Children's Health Council Summer Symphony XXIX on July 17. However, conductor **Keith Brion,** who impersonated Sousa at Stanford in 1986 and 1987, will be back, doing his Italian number.

(For those of you who don't read Roman numerals any better than I do, that's No. 29, the Summer Symphony having a seven-year jump on the Super Bowl.)

The Sunday afternoon benefit performance at Frost Amphitheater on campus this year will hew to the theme "Viva Italia," a health council source reveals.

Works of Rossini, Verdi, Mantovani, Ponchielli, Puccini and others will be on the program, with the San Jose Symphony Orchestra performing under Brion's baton.

Vocal soloists will be **Kathryn Wright,** soprano, who has performed extensively with the Texas Opera Theatre and appeared with other opera companies and symphony orchestras, and **Noel Espiritu Velasco,** tenor, who has been hailed as "one of the Philippines' national treasures." At the end of the concert there'll be a Neapolitan sing-along.

IN DEPARTING FROM THE Sousa tradition after two successful years, the health council is on the lookout for embellishments that might fit the "Viva Italia" theme without making it seem like a pizza party. So historical nuggets that tie Stanford's earlier days to people of Italian descent — for example, the artisans who inlaid the mosaics on the facade of Stanford Memorial Church,— or that relate to famous Italian artists who performed locally, are in demand, according to health council volunteer **Phyllis Johnson.**

Anyone with a stirring suggestion is invited to call **Ruth Kaplan** at the health council, (415) 326-5530. Hold the bologna for now — save it for your picnic on the green that afternoon. Even pizza might get in. I have the impression that provender inspections at Frost aren't as stringent as at Stanford Stadium.

HUNDREDS OF PERSONS VISITED the Varian Associates Research Center in Stanford Research Park on a recent Sunday to see an exhibition of photographs, Portfolio IV by the late Ansel Adams, titled "What Majestic World." Adams originally printed the portfolio in 1963 in memory of Russell Varian. This time the exhibition honored Varian's founders, Russell and his brother, Sigurd, and the 50th anniversary of their invention of the klystron, the traveling wave tube that was instrumental in the development of radar, that powers electrons on their mad course at the Stanford Linear Accelerator, and that still helps get your airline flight home safe as well as working medical wonders.

Hosts and hostesses were members of Varian Associates' first families, present and, mostly, retired: **Dorothy Varian, Ed** and **Artemas Ginzton, Norm** and **Natalie Pond, Tom** and **Dorothea Sege,** and **Myrl** and **Ruth Stearns.**

Photographs of the Varian brothers were included, and Adams' magnificent scenics were captioned with philosophical musings from Russell Varian's journals and lines by his poet father, John, lovingly selected in both cases by Dorothy Varian.

SPEAKING OF POETS, C. Shan Solomon of the Palo Alto Unified School District's Transportation Department is due to become a published poet in April with three poems appearing in the American Poetry Association's Anthology.

Sharon Heyler, a Palo Alto advanced programs resource teacher, has been honored by a unit of the California Association for the Gifted and the Association for Education of the Gifted for her outstanding contributions to educational programs, and particularly for her work with students, teachers and programs for "more able" students, the latter evidently being dubbed with the current euphemism for "gifted."

Tony Mazzaferro, Gunn High School music teacher, has been selected to direct the San Francisco Bay Area Music Educators High School Conference Band at its 1988 annual conference at Chabot College. Part of Mazzaferro's doctoral dissertation on the life and musical works of Roger Nixon will be appearing in an international band music publication, the Journal of Band Research.

Dinah's keepsakes about to become more valuable

Among my souvenirs of Paly High days in the early '40s are a menu, charred around the edges, and a napkin monogrammed "DS" and also charred, relics of the May 1942 fire that put Dinah's Shack out of business.

Memory does not yield up just why I acquired these keepsakes; probably because a staffer of *The Campanile*, Paly's student newspaper, considered a good local fire fair game.

Dinah's had to close because of the late-night fire, but not for long. As **Paul Gullixson** already has detailed in his column, the restaurant — then exceedingly popular, especially among Stanford students — first moved into an abandoned eatery next door, then rebuilt. Judging by the look of it today, with exposed piping still showing, they may have hewed to the original 1926 construction scheme.

MODERN BUSINESS competition is about to do what the fire failed to do. After one false start, Dinah's now is due to close April 2, and manager **Paul Partti** says this date is firm. Its trade has been brisk, as generations of Stanford students who carved their initials in the bar or danced and frolicked there have flocked back in for farewell visits.

Ralph Whitaker called my attention to the fact that he and his wife, **Meredith**, went there on their first date in 1947. That reminded me that my wife and I had dined there on our first date,

some years later. Ralph also recalled that his pledge class in a Stanford fraternity, after hell week and initiation, had gone to eat at Dinah's with the rest of the chapter, all equals at last.

WHAT MAKES DINAH'S incipient demise especially sad for oldtimers hereabouts is that it is the last of the famous down-the-road places one went to from dry Palo Alto in order to be able to buy a drink as well as a meal. Others, such as Longbarn, L'Omelette and Chez Yvonne, expired earlier. They ranked between roadhouses and watering holes, and each had character and charm, along with generally good food.

Other good places to eat locally also have folded over the years. Bertrand's in Menlo Park, near Willow and Middlefield, was one. Another was "Sticky" Wilson's on University Avenue in Palo Alto. Mountain View had a great all-the-chicken-you-can-eat place; as a kid I was impressed by stories of Stanford roughs who had starved themselves for a couple of days and then assaulted this establishment, setting trencherman records.

PART OF THE BILL of fare at Dinah's is burned away on my 1942 menu, but the prices remain intact. They ranged from $1 for ham steak to a top of $1.45 for sirloin steak or Dinah's Special Combination. Chicken was $1.25 or $1.35. If you wanted only hors d'oeuvres (over 42 varieties), the charge

was 65 cents; evidently the term smorgasbord had not penetrated our menus yet. Pie was 15 cents, ice cream a quarter, coffee a dime. "Dinah's makes a delicious mint julep — takes ten minutes," a line in small type at the bottom says.

Our sentimental journey a few nights ago revealed that only chicken and the catch of the day are marked under $10 now, so prices are up tenfold or better.

PALO ALTO HISTORIAN Steve **Staiger** says the fire loss was reported as $60,000, the equivalent of a fair number of meals. His records show Dinah's was back in business, at the temporary location within 48 hours.

No one currently on the staff of more than 50 can relate these experiences first-hand. Waitress **Winnie Goughlin**, who has been at Dinah's 37 years, is the dean, followed by **Barbara Pierce**. Chef **Gerhardt Steiner** is a 25-year veteran.

A RECENT MEMORIAL SERVICE for Ken Peters, who spent his whole career as a music teacher in Palo Alto schools, was notable not only for a large turnout but also for the musical program. **William Whitson**, a student of Peters when he was a first-year teacher, brought his Palo Alto Chamber Orchestra. **Teresa Merchant** directed the Gunn High School Chorale, and another teacher, **Mary Driscoll**, sang. Pianist **Robert Bowman** and harpist **Celeste Misfeldt** also rendered tributes.

Little 'Eeerma' was a handful

WARD WINSLOW

Irma must be home now with her family in Concordia, near Mazatlan. Her mother, even after a month's respite, is probably at wit's end trying to make this 27-month-old wear a hips-and-knees brace for the week it supposedly will take her to forget she doesn't like it. Her mama must also wonder what sort of *norteamericanos* hosted her child.

In the four weeks Irma lived with us, she grew a month older, gained a bit of weight, learned new tricks, and once came home utterly drunk on a tranquilizer she was given so she wouldn't wiggle while being scanned in a magnetic resonance imager.

In the same four weeks Holly and I aged about five years, discovered how far from childproof our house is, practiced the imperative as never before in Spanish and English, and learned why grandparents like to have small grandchildren around for only so long.

IRMA CAME NORTH from Mexico with a van load of kids destined for treatment at Shriner's Hospital, arranged through the Hesperian Foundation. The foundation's home base is **Trude Bach's** house on Hamilton Avenue near downtown Palo Alto. Irma was by far the youngest in the group, and Trude, busy with older children with serious disabilities, needed some help.

Holly's daughter, **Carol Thuman**, a sometime worker at Hesperian, nominated her mother. I was in Southern California at a conference, and though I had a telephonic veto opportunity, failed to grasp the consequences of saying *"si."*

Soon after I got home Holly came down with the flu, and it was Irma and me, *mano a mano,* for the next week. Outside work all but stopped, except during her naps. I relearned why the mothers of 2-year-olds look so harried.

IRMA WAS INITIALLY accompanied by an 11-year old polio victim, **Maria Isobel.** Maria was good with the tot, but desperately missed the older kids and adults who understood her rapid-fire chatter. She soon went back to Trude's, and with my wife ill, Irma bonded to me. After recovering, Holly had to fight to regain status as household boss.

I don't know if Irma is mechanically gifted or if every 2-year-old who falls into command of easily tired sixty-somethings would have exploited the opportunity to squeeze every tube, open every container and unscrew every knob, but this one did. She showed a bent for plumbing, too, and an irrepressible fondness for keyboards — piano or computer — or any electronic gadget with buttons or knobs. The *tele* was to watch at times, but also to play with if other activities paled.

LA SENORITA PEQUENITA proved plenty inventive despite her handicap. Indeed, she left for home just before mastering self-leveraging techniques and a method of using a plastic laundry basket to get to things we thought were stashed beyond her reach.

A charmer at the grocery, wowing checkers with curls, sweet smiles and roguish eyes, she could turn monster at home with a more familiar audience. She'd stand us one at a time or *todos,* including the family dog, and her willpower was as amazing as her refusal to accept being crossed. "No" is the same in both tongues, and all of us voiced it often and forcefully.

WE RENTED A CAR SEAT, borrowed a stroller, and bought enough supplies to discover how much toddler-care items have changed. The car seat and a ride in *el caro* became the best invitations to *siesta.*

Irma nicknamed us, of course. Mine was *"el goppo,"* which Trude and Holly tried to tell me was flattering. Holly had to fight a masculine appellation.

Until the last few days, Irma's prime link with her home seemed to be her *"patos,"* babytalk for *zapatos,* or shoes. When she woke up each day, locating the shoes was desire numero uno.

IRMA LEFT US RELIEVED and a trifle lonesome, and probably in hock to the water cops — she loved to flush toilets. We'll wonder for years how she's doing. There's no guarantee it'll work the same in reverse, for, although she showed evidence of a firm parental hand, she never seemed to pine for or talk of her mother.

The letter "i" in Spanish is pronounced as Americans say "e," and using the American words she learned ("hey!" "bubbles," "why," and "hello" among them), I signed off with "Bye bye, Eeerma."

DAVID PACKARD
IN HIS OWN WORDS

The lure of one professor

David Packard has proved a major figure in the modern history of Palo Alto. The company he and William Hewlett founded made the city the launching pad of the electronics industry and remains Palo Alto's largest employer. He also helped shape events as a Board of Education member and Stanford University trustee. This is the first of a three-part interview he granted to Ward Winslow, a former managing editor of the Times Tribune.

Q. The other day a friend of yours, Mary Kennedy, mentioned

MONDAY

Packard recalls the building of city schools, HP's moves outside Palo Alto and the development of Stanford Industrial Park.

TUESDAY

A look at the development of the Hoover Institution, Stanford Shopping Center and Japanese competition.

that when she was a student at Stanford, she

HEWLETT-PACKARD

Electronics industry pioneer David Packard was first attracted to Stanford during a family visit to California in 1929.

hadn't paid much attention to the town; she didn't really become conscious of it until later. Was that your experience, too?

DP: I didn't pay much attention to the town while I was at Stanford — I was doing everything I

Please see LURE

LURE/

could to learn to be a good engineer and didn't get involved in any social problems. Others on campus were all worried about the war over in Spain. The only thing I did get involved in to some extent' was a movement called Technocracy, which was to solve all the problems in the world with better technology. It turned out to be a false premise. The idea was that if you used the best technology, you could build more reliable products, including a razor that would last your lifetime.

Q. When did you become conscious of the town?

DP: I guess it was really when I got involved in that school board election in the late '40s.

Q. But that was long after you had started your company.

DP: Yes, we started our company in 1939. At first we spent all our time trying to get the company going. Bill Hewlett was an Army Signal Corps reserve officer. He got called to active duty, and I was left here to run the company, so I spent all that time during the war on that, and didn't have any reason to get involved in the local situation.

Q. But you might have gone to Pueblo, Colorado, or stayed in the East, or picked some other place. Why did you start it in Palo Alto?

DP: Because of Fred Terman. Fred Terman was the first professor who had a course in radio engineering, which has since become electronics. His textbook on radio engineering was the most widely used text in the world through World War II. Now, I'd started in ham radio when I was a youngster. As a matter of fact, I was the secretary of the local radio club in Pueblo in 1924 when I was 12 years old. My father was a lawyer, and he wanted me to be a lawyer. But I had decided that I wanted to be an electrical engineer; I didn't necessarily want to get involved in radio, because it wasn't all that big a deal in those days.

During the summer vacation in 1929, I drove my mother and sister out to California. We visited some old friends, and a few relatives in the southern part of the state. One of my mother's friends lived in Palo Alto, and she had three daughters, the oldest of whom had just started at Stanford. So we visited the Neff family in 1929. I'd heard a little about Stanford before I came, so I went over and learned a bit about the engineering program.

I had planned to apply to the University of Colorado, which had a good engineering school, but I thought, I'll come out and apply to Stanford. They probably won't admit me, but I'll just come out anyway. They admitted me, so that's how I ended up here.

We had a ham radio station at the Engineering Corner. Fred Terman had a laboratory in the same building. I used to go over there to work in the amateur radio station, and I didn't really know very much about Fred Terman. But he stopped by one day when I was a junior, and said he'd checked up on my grades and everything, and thought he might be able to let me take his graduate course in my senior year. So, I thought, that's a very good idea, and I did that.

That's when I got acquainted with a lot of former Stanford people who had established businesses around here, because part of this course was to visit places like Heintz and Kaufman, John Kaar, who had an operation here in Palo Alto, and Philo Farnsworth in San Francisco, and Charlie Litton in Redwood City. This was in the middle of the Depression.

Bill and I had been talking, and said, if we can't get a job ourselves we'll just start our own company and make a job for ourselves. Fred encouraged us to do that. He said, "You fellows have had better education than any of these fellows that have businesses, and you ought to be successful at it."

During the war I stayed here and operated the company. Fred Terman had been asked to head up what was called the Radio Research Laboratory at Harvard. The background of this was that President Roosevelt, by 1940, had decided that the Allies would probably not be able to prevail against Germany without the help of the United States.

Roosevelt thought that the best thing he could do at that time would be to help with some of the scientific work, because the British had been doing work on radar, which made a big difference in the aerial battle of Britain.

So FDR asked Vannevar Bush to invite scientists and engineers and doctors to undertake a project to use science and technology to develop weapons. When we got in the war this program was expanded. At its peak of activity, 35,000 scientists and engineers and doctors from universities all over the country were working on this project. Some of them were working on the atom bomb — that was a very specific program.

But a very large number were working on conventional technology, and this is something that isn't widely known: They had worked on improvements for radar and countermeasures for radar. They had also worked on the proximity fuze, which was the fuze that would explode a shell before it hit the target. This made a big difference in the anti-aircraft business, because you didn't have to hit the airplane, you just had to get close to it.

Q. Did HP do any work on weapons in this program?

DP: The company had developed a number of instruments for work at audio frequencies by 1940 and some of them were used in the development of these weapons. For example, a number of our audio oscillators were used in the production of proximity fuzes. I had a close personal relationship with the scientists at the Naval Research Laboratory.

With their help we developed microwave signal generators and other instruments needed for radar and radar countermeasures. We also undertook the development with NRL of a complete radar countermeasure system for shipboard use. It could make the ship appear in the wrong position in the enemy radar. We had delivered the first unit, which was being tested by NRL when the war ended.

Q. I see.

DP: Those weapons were what enabled us to win the war in Eu-

LURE/ CONTINUED

rope. The Battle of the Bulge was a big tank battle. Our forces had proximity fuzes in the shells in their tanks; the Germans didn't. That made it possible for us to have our shells go over at precisely deadly height above the German tanks and decimate their tank force. That was the deciding factor in the battle.

All these weapons are also what enabled us to retake the islands all the way across the Pacific and Japan. We would have won the war against Japan without the atom bomb because of this other technological development; the atom bomb brought the war to a conclusion without a larger loss of life because it would have been a very expensive matter to try and make landings in Japan — it would have cost them and us probably a million more casualties. So it was a good outcome.

Anyway, Fred Terman came back to Stanford, and set up a research laboratory supported by the Office of Naval Research. This was at Vannevar Bush's recommendation, because he came out of the war feeling very strongly that the use of science and technology to win the war was an indicator of what could be done in the following years.

He put it this way: The extent to which we use science to win the war against disease, to develop new industries, and to maintain the strength of our military forces, to a very large extent will determine the future of this nation. That was the premise on which this whole research program was set up.

So I was very supportive of Fred Terman's effort, and all this fuss about research overhead at universities went clear back to that period.

Q. So it was the proximity to Stanford and Fred Terman's program that persuaded you to stay here?

DP: Well, there were some other things. Let me go back to the question of how I got involved in some things in Palo Alto. I had graduated from Stanford and then spent 3 1/2 years back in Schenectady with General Electric. All this time I was trying to learn as much as I could about how to manage a company because Bill and I were about to do that.

Also during the war I spent a lot of time looking at new management approaches and practices. I remember very clearly a meeting set up by Paul Holden — this might have been before we got into the war or very early in it.

Paul Holden was professor of industrial management at the Stanford Graduate School of Business, and he invited a group of people who had companies around the area working on defense business to a conference, and I was included although we only had a small number of employees then.

Somehow we got into a discussion of the responsibility of management. Holden made the point that management's responsibility is to the shareholders — that's the end of it. And I objected. I said, "I think you're absolutely wrong. Management has a responsibility to its employees, it has a responsibility to its customers, it has a responsibility to the community at large." And they almost laughed me out of the room.

Q. What did that come from?

DP: I'd been studying all these things, and I'd thought a lot about what management's responsibility should be. I was a little ahead of my time, but obviously that's the name of the game today. That was really the genesis of my interest, and my company's interest, in the communities where we had plant locations, and Palo Alto is just one of them.

The idea is that the environment in which our people work has a good deal to do with the success of the company, and it's to our advantage to make that environment as attractive as possible.

We were a little out in front with that philosophy. Other people had put it into practice, but we went along with the frontrunners on that whole idea.

Q. Did you have a labor supply problem in the early years?

DP: Not really. We didn't need a whole lot of people. It was difficult to get good technical people because they were in such demand with the various aspects of the war, and most of them were drafted. A few for one reason or another were not drafted, and we were able to get exemptions for a few people. But we simply hired people without any experience.

I had some manual dexterity tests that we gave to see how well they put nuts and bolts together. We just selected some people who could do things with their hands, because that was a large part of the job at the time.

Q. Right after the war, were many people looking for jobs?

DP: Yes, lots. One thing that happened then was very important to the company. Fred Terman took a great deal of interest in what Bill and I were doing because he'd encouraged us to do it. He pointed out that our success was going to be determined by attracting the best technical people we could get. By this time, before 1950, he had a good graduate program in what was essentially electronics.

He said, "Tuition pays about half the cost of a graduate student. If you're willing to put up the other half of the cost for half a dozen or so students, I'll guarantee that we'll admit anybody you hire and enable them to take graduate work at Stanford."

This was great leverage. I traveled around the country and already knew some of the deans of engineering and other key faculty people at various places, and I could get them to identify their top two or three students. Then I'd tell the students, you come to work for us and I can get you into Stanford to do your graduate work.

That enabled us to attract some of the top students from all over the country. It was a tremendously important part of our early strength. We had developed some instruments that came from the laboratories at Stanford; they weren't any great scientific advances, they were developments.

And also, as I described earlier, I got acquainted with some people at Naval Research Laboratory, and on a personal basis they helped us to develop a line of test equipment for microwave and high frequency. So by 1950 we had a fairly broad line of general-purpose test equipment.

Then, when the whole electronic business was revved up in the Korean War, all these electronic companies were our customers, and that resulted in a very rapid period of growth. For one or two years our growth was 2-to-1; we doubled every year.

And that was a challenge — to get people to move in and get them working.

DAVID PACKARD
IN HIS OWN WORDS

Post-World War II objectives: expansion for HP, Palo Alto

David Packard has proved a major figure in the modern history of Palo Alto. The company he and William Hewlett founded made the city the launching pad of the electronics industry and remains Palo Alto's largest employer. He also helped shape events as a Board of Education member and Stanford University trustee. This is the second of a three-part interview he granted to Ward Winslow, a former managing editor of the Times Tribune.

Q. Did HP's growth at that time put any strain on the town?

DP: No, I don't think so.

Q: It was going on its own track and expanding too.

DP: No strain that I know of. I ran for the school board, and we did fairly well in getting our schools set up. Again, there were two or three things that looked like they made sense to us — to me, at any rate, and I had more to do with this than anyone. First, there was obviously going to be an increase in school population.

Q. A friend of yours,

Please see **PACKARD, A-7**

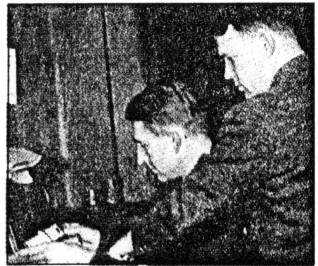
HEWLETT PACKARD

The innovative audio oscillator is tested by David Packard and William Hewlett in a Palo Alto garage in 1939.

DAVID PACKARD: IN HIS OWN WORDS

PACKARD / 'We ought to keep our growth down and not expand very much ... that's probably consistent with what the city would like'

CONTINUED

Mary Kennedy, said you went out there and counted the lots and figured out how many kids they were going to produce.

DP: Well, it wasn't quite that, but all you needed to do was find out how any babies were born each year and put some factor in to account for the influx, and you'd know how many kids you were going to have in school in any grade in the following years. A little third-grade arithmetic is all it took.

The other thing was, they were having competition for architects on different schools, and I said, "Why are we wasting money on different architects? Let's design a standard classroom and a standard elementary school. Then we can make a few modifications." So we got Birge Clark to do this and cut out all the competition in architecture. Those two things made it possible for us to meet the classroom needs, and keep the system within budget.

Then Noel Porter (Hewlett-Packard's manufacturing direc-

tor) got active in the City Council and Bill Hewlett at the hospital. At one time, three of us were involved in some of the major city projects. That was when I think the city got a little concerned that we were taking a larger part than we should, so we realized that and backed down a little bit.

Q. This resistance from around town was just kind of political chirping, wasn't it? Was it really a big obstacle?

DP: No, it wasn't any great problem. But I guess the first demonstration of it was, you

---

In giving the interview to the Times Tribune, I imposed one condition: that it not be cut without my consent. The Oakland-Berkeley hills fire broke out late Oct. 20. With a big story to handle, I thought the editors might ask to put off Part 2. They didn't, even though it ate up much of their news space that day.

know, we had a very good relationship with Elinor Cogswell when she was the editor of the Times. We'd go to Elinor — I did this many times with school problems — and tell her what we're doing, and why we're doing it, and give her a lot of background, and she would use her judgment about when to make disclosures about it. And the fellow that followed her ...

Q. Al Bodi.

DP: Bodi. I asked him if he'd be willing to work with us. No, he said, anything you tell me I'll publish whenever I want. Well, that was the end of our cozy relationship.

Q. Was there ever a time when you felt that in these political things you were shaping the future of the community?

DP: I never really thought about it in those terms.

Q. Certainly the school expansion would qualify.

DP: I've always looked at this as something that needs to be done, and my philosophy has always been that you get your satisfaction in life from doing something. Once you've done it, you ought to forget about it and do something else.

Q. The school district was able to keep financial independence at a time when all the other districts were going on double sessions with state aid. Did that come out of your own philosophy? Financial independence is sort of in Palo Alto's history, too.

DP: Actually, no, I shouldn't take all the credit for this. There was another fellow who gave very good input — Ernie Kump.

Q. The architect?

DP: Yes. I think it was Ernie who had the idea that you ought to have a standard design for all your schools. And then of course, Bob Littler was also a very strong person on the board at the time. By planning properly, and building to a plan, you could meet your

space requirement on an orderly basis and you could also plan to build up your teachers and so forth.

One other factor was very important: We needed to have a good superintendent to be the head of the school system. We had a fellow that wasn't very good and we had some legal problems with him. We got Henry Gunn to come down. I interviewed him in Portland and I interviewed several other people, one in Winnetka, Illinois, and we decided that we were going to try to find the best person we could to come to Palo Alto. I think Henry Gunn is about as good a fellow as we could have found anywhere. He did a great job for our schools in the early years. So there were a lot of things that went together, and obviously these are not all my own ideas. I tried to pick the brains of everybody I could to get good ideas.

Q. The financial independence strain ran through the way you financed your own company and the school district.

DP: Also that was largely a question of the confidence of the community, because you had to have a two-thirds vote to pass a bond issue. We had managed things well enough so the community had confidence in the way the schools were being operated, and we always used to win. We never lost a bond issue here, as I recall.

Q. Certainly not in your time on the board. A long time afterward they put a Palo Alto High School remodeling issue on the ballot with several different choices, and that was a mess.

DP: They've obviously had some troubles since then, because the enrollment has gone down and they have surplus buildings, and now it's probably going to come back up again. Anyhow, it's just an entirely different problem.

Our family foundation has been trying to help in some of these areas. In some schools the Spanish population is over 50 percent now, and a lot of the kids can't speak English, so you have a horrible problem. I'm not going to solve that one.

Q. Has Palo Alto worked well as the headquarters for your company?

DP: It's worked fine. They've gotten a little wound up in all these crazy environmental ideas in the last few years that I don't agree with. I've thought that we probably were too heavily involved in Palo Alto. But on the other hand it's an attractive place to live and it's an attractive area for engineers, so there are some compensations. We've had just as good success in attracting people at all levels at our facility at Colorado Springs, and there the cost of living is about half what it is here.

But we've got so much historical involvement here now that I don't think there's any likelihood of our moving out. I do think that we ought to keep our growth down and not expand very much, and that's probably consistent with what the city would like anyway.

Q. When did the point come when your manufacturing jumped outside of this town?

DP: In the mid-1950s we had everything centered here. We realized that a good many of our competitors that specialized in certain types of instruments needed attention, although very few competed with us all the way across the board. So we divided the company up into engineering and manufacturing and marketing groups that would deal with specific types of competition — a structure to match the particular market for our electronic products.

We were a partnership up until 1947, when we incorporated. Then, in 1957, when Bill and I still held all the stock, we put some

I had sent Al Bodi, my longtime boss, an excerpt covering Dave Packard's mention of him. At a dinner at our house soon afterward, Bodi spoke spiritedly about how it hadn't been just Dave Packard "but also his partner, his production manager, his wife, his attorney, his secretary" and maybe more who were involved in running the town. From a newspapering viewpoint, Bodi's stand was absolutely right.

stock on the market, and later we sold some more. That made it possible for us to acquire companies, and we acquired the F.L. Moseley Co. in Pasadena, which made strip-chart recorders. Later on, we acquired the Sanborn company, located in Waltham, Mass.; they made electrocardiographs. And a company just out of Wilmington, Delaware, that made instruments for chemical analysis.

So our moving some of our own operations out into other parts of the country coincided with buying these other companies within three or four years toward the end of the '50s.

Q: Why couldn't manufacturing continue to expand here?

DP: It could have for some time, but at some point we'd get to the place where it was just too expensive to manufacture products here. Colorado was a lower labor cost area, even fairly early on.

Then we got involved in Europe. We had some problems in foreign operations in that the foreign country wanted us to manufacture some products in their country. They didn't want to just spend their money buying our products, they wanted to benefit themselves. So we had pressures to establish a plant in Germany, that was the first one, then in England, and then we had a joint venture in Japan in the early '60s, a little later than the others.

Q. Did you have something to do with the creation of the Stanford Industrial Park?

DP: Yes, in this sense: We were one of the first tenants, and Lockheed was an early arrival. Varian got started first, and I was on their board, and so was Fred Terman. As his program at Stanford built up, a lot of companies wanted to do what we did with it and have a close relationship with Stanford. So I worked with Fred on this business. I'd funnel people over to him and he'd make a pitch on the great advantages of being close to Stanford. Then he'd send them over to me and I'd keep backing him up. We had a kind of

HEWLETT PACKARD

During the mid-1940s Lucile Packard (left), Flora Hewlett, Bill Hewlett and David Packard enjoyed a Hewlett-Packard Co. party. The company that Hewlett and Packard had established in 1939 still was in the early stages of its development at that time, but it already had made significant technological contributions to the Allied war effort during World War II.

a one-two game we played for a couple of years. In that sense we did have quite a bit to do with getting people started out here.

Bill Shockley decided he wanted to come out and set up his operation here. I'd known him, and offered to help him. He didn't have the slightest idea about how to do anything. So he'd call me up every day or so the first few months he was here and say, where do you buy pencils, how do you hire a secretary, and all kinds of things like that. We tried to be helpful to people coming in.

Over the years a great many Hewlett-Packard people have left and set up their own businesses. That's been sometimes our fault for not having the right kind of opportunity for them, or not seeing it; on the other hand, we found that generally they've been good friends and good customers, so we've tried to help them. I think

we were probably more of a factor in the first few years of the Industrial Park — the late '50s and early '60s.

Q. You went on the Stanford board of trustees in mid-1954. Were you still on the Palo Alto Board of Education then?

DP: Yes, I was on the school board at the same time.

Q. You must have been busy.

DP: I dropped off the school board pretty soon. It was too much to do both, but they did overlap.

Q. Did the Stanford trusteeship involve a lot of work with the city in working out the shopping center and some of the land uses?

DP: It did. Actually, my first assignment as a Stanford trustee involved medicine. Stanford had decided to move the medical school from San Francisco down to Palo Alto, and that was just starting.

Lloyd Dinkelspiel, the chairman of the Stanford board, asked me if I'd kind of take over the situation and see if I could help work it through well. So I took some time and got acquainted with the medical school people in San Francisco. I already knew a lot of the Palo Alto Clinic people — there were a lot of my old friends there. What I discovered very quickly was that none of the people in San Francisco wanted to come to Palo Alto and none of the people in Palo Alto wanted them to come. So I learned about the innate obstinacy of the medical profession early on.

Q. What'd you do about that?
DP: Well, I made a rule which is still referred to as the Packard rule. It's that they were going to come down here whether they liked it or not, and they were going to set up some rules and they were going to have to work with the Palo Alto doctors. Actually that went along all right, but there were real problems, and it turns out that those problems are still with us today. We had the same problem getting the (Lucile Salter Packard) Children's Hospital relationship with the university medical school worked out.

That was a big involvement — I spent a lot of time on that. They didn't know what to do with the hospital in San Francisco that the medical school operated. So three or four of us trustees ran the hospital for a year or so. We finally were able to give it to the Presbyterian Church, just to get rid of it.

Q. Franklin Lane Hospital?
DP: Yes, Lane Hospital. I had a lot of good friends up there. Frank Gerbode was just starting open heart operations at that time. I was there one day when he was about to do one, and he asked if I'd

like to watch. I said sure, so he put me on a stool right behind him so I was looking right over his shoulder. The first thing he did was to cut this young girl about from here around to here *(gesturing)*. I began to get a little dizzy and had to walk out in the hall. I finally went back and got interested and watched through the whole operation. And I got to know a lot of those people at the medical school in San Francisco very well.

Henry Kaplan was a very skillful, highly talented radiologist, and he was involved in the first use of the linear accelerator for radiation treatments. He took the view that none of the doctors outside the medical school knew a damn thing. I don't know how he'd developed that attitude because, after all, they'd taught these people. It's just a crazy situation.

Then I was involved in the whole Stanford land development program. You may recall that the original plan was that the university would develop an integrated community. There would be a shopping center, industrial development, and some residential property, so it'd be a complete community.

Colbert Coldwell provided invaluable advice on the land development program. Alf Brandin did a wonderful job of implementing the whole program. There were two reasons that having extensive residential development on the Stanford property was a big mistake: One is that you couldn't get anywhere near as much money for residential property as you could for commercial or industrial property, and secondly, you'd be inviting in a bunch of dissidents who were going to object to

everything the university did.

So we essentially cancelled the residential program. They've done a little bit of it, but it's still very low key, not anything near what was planned.

There was another interesting aspect of that. Herm Phleger, who had been a member of the board of trustees for a number of years, a very distinguished attorney in San Francisco, was in the State Department in the Eisenhower administration. While he was in Washington, he kept track of what we were doing out here. We decided that because leases were not common in the United States, Stanford would have to have 100-year leases — nothing else was saleable. Phleger kept writing and saying you're crazy to lease the land for 100 years; you should have a lease no longer than 50 years.

We finally succumbed to his argument, and it turned out we got just as much for 50-year leases as we could have got for 100-year leases. Both the industrial development and the commercial development have done very well.

Fred Terman had another interesting idea. In attracting industrial companies to locate in this area and encouraging them to have an informal association with Stanford, he didn't think it was desirable to have any patent or royalty license requirements at all — they could use whatever information they could get.

In the long run, people in those companies would contribute far more to the university than it would ever get from any patent licenses. And that's what has happened.

© 1991 by Ward Winslow

DAVID PACKARD
IN HIS OWN WORDS

Influence was enormous, no matter where you look

David Packard has proved a major figure in the modern history of Palo Alto. The company he and William Hewlett founded made the city the launching pad of the electronics industry and remains Palo Alto's largest employer. He also helped shape events as a Board of Education member and Stanford University trustee. This is the last of a three-part interview he granted to Ward Winslow, a former managing editor of the Times Tribune.

Q. I know that you knew Herbert Hoover quite well.

DP: Yes, I got to know him quite well.

Q. In your role as a trustee, did you ever read up on Leland Stanford's original ideas?

DP: I didn't do very much on that. Of course, I read a lot about Herbert Hoover because I knew him and was interested in him. I got acquainted with President Hoover because, while I was chairman of the Stanford board, he was very con-

Please see **PACKARD**

PACKARD / Many community roles

CONTINUED

cerned that the faculty was taking over his Hoover Institution. He was really almost paranoid about this; he didn't want those left-wingers to be involved in his institution. He had set the Hoover Institution up to do research on his work but also he somehow had a very strong bias against faculty people.

I remember there was a book that he had objected to, written by a Stanford professor named Robert North, entitled *Moscow and Chinese Communists.* Hoover thought it was terrible. I read the book and didn't see anything very

much wrong with it. But I was growing very concerned that Stanford was getting too much involved in social issues, and, as I put it, that they had converted themselves from an institution for education to one for social reform in the 1960s. I wasn't in complete agreement with this, and I'm still not. So I was very strong in saying it, and I thought the Hoover Institution would be an important counterbalance for this trend in the university.

The issue was that President Hoover wanted to have the Hoover Institution established to demonstrate the evils of communism. And some of the university professors didn't want to have an

COURTESY OF STANFORD UNIVERSITY

Among David Packard's friends was President Herbert Hoover, whom the industrialist knew while he was chairman of the the Stanford University Board of Trustees and later would visit for breakfast whenever he was in New York City. Packard regularly sided with Hoover when there were philosophy disputes with the university.

institution dedicated to research with the results predetermined. We went round and round on that; it was a difficult issue. Easton Rothwell was the head of the Hoover Institution then, and Easton and Virginia were good personal friends of mine, and this made the situation more difficult. So I tried to work out something. Every time I went to New York I used to have breakfast with President Hoover in his office in the Waldorf Tower.

We finally got it worked out on the basis that the founder of the Hoover Institution has the right to say whatever he wants to say about the institution and its studies, and that shouldn't deteriorate their ability to do objective research. Well, (Stanford President) Wally Sterling never agreed with this, and he thought that after Hoover died that he'd get it put back where he wanted it. Fortunately, enough of the trustees agreed with me so we didn't let it get put back.

So that's how I got to know Herbert Hoover. He was a very good friend. He used to invite Mrs. Packard and me down to his houseboat in Key Largo, Florida, every year in January. I was there on the week of the inauguration of Jack Kennedy. President Hoover flew up for the inauguration, but the weather was so bad he couldn't land.

So he came back to Key Largo and we watched the inauguration over TV there in his houseboat. I think that the Hoover Institution has been an excellent balance. As you know, Glenn Campbell is kind of an abrasive fellow, and he asks for trouble and doesn't do much to avoid it. But it's now pretty well established, with George Shultz and some of the people there, that it's a legitimate and an important part of Stanford.

Q. Was the shopping center created while you were on the board?

DP: Yes, the first year. The thing that I was interested in was that our real estate adviser paid very careful attention to having the right balance of shops in the center. He knew how many shoe outlets and how many clothing outlets and how many of this and that and the other thing would make sense — he gave us a lot of detailed advice. Alf Brandin was the one who administered all this, and Alf did a great job in handling that program.

Q. It sort of knocked the pins out from under the University Avenue merchants for a while. Did they complain to you?

DP: Yes. Of course, that was just a precursor of what's happening all over the country now. All over the country you see malls taking business away from the old community or city centers and downtown areas. That was a problem in Palo Alto.

Q. You mentioned the Stanford Linear Accelerator electric power line, and that reminded me of Pete McCloskey. Pete was our first home-grown federal politician, at least, to get elected from right around here.

DP: Well, Pete was ... it was actually Herman Phleger who was concerned because this power line that they were going to run from the substation up beyond 280 cut across his property, and that's what he objected to. So I met with Pete — matter of fact, I was on the board of PG&E at the time, so I was right in the middle of that one.

It would have been possible to string the line underground, but an underground line with high voltage is a very expensive proposition, and it could hardly have been justified at the time. The federal government essentially paid for all of the linear accelerator facilities that the university was to operate, so there was no university money involved. There was no way you could have got the federal government to put up enough money to put a power line underground.

Q. I also remember you standing off the State Highway Commission over I-280; you represented the university in the hearings on the route determination.

DP: I've kind of forgotten.

Q. They gave you a rough time that day, as I remember — maybe that's why you suppressed the memory.

DP: *(laughing)* Well, I've had a rough time lots of times.

Q. Of course, with your Washington service and perhaps putting younger people in charge of some of the operation of the company, you've maybe moved away from the community a bit, but have you continued to keep an eye on things?

DP: No, I don't have time. Except through our family foundation.

The foundation has supported a number of programs here in Palo Alto over the years. School music is one of the things we've supported that's been very important in this community and others around it.

My son David learned to play the trumpet in grade school, and he got to be very good; he almost ended up undertaking a career in professional music. A shortage of funds stopped all the music programs in schools here. So one of the things our foundation has done in the last few years is to provide money or equipment so that all the schools could have music programs. That's pretty well in place all over the area.

Q. John Young (HP's present CEO) made a forecast in 1978 about seeing the end of the Industrial Park, or the Research Park as they call it now, as a manufacturing entity. Of course it has pretty much turned to research now. Do you see that as ongoing perpetually?

DP: Yes, there's no way you're going to do very much manufacturing here locally.

Q. Do you think the research function will continue here?

DP: Well, it's more than the research function. I think the research function and being the headquarters for some companies.

Look at it this way: These changes started to occur in the mid-1960s. That's 20, 25 years or so from 1939. Up until that time our direct labor was about 30 percent of our sales dollar. It's down to less than 5 percent now. That's partly because in those days you assembled components, and you had lots of wires, and you had to solder the wires and resistors and capacitors together, and it took a lot of handwork and time.

Now those components are all put in large integrated circuits — almost a million times as many components as you'd get in a product before. Those are done in automated processes — it's just too small and too concise to do by hand. Our first products had five or 10 vacuum tubes in them. Vacuum tubes in those days cost, oh, maybe $1.

Now a product will have the equivalent of 20 or 30 million vacuum tubes, and the cost of the integrated circuits will be $2. So the cost involved has changed in character. That's probably not going to get very much different. But some of the automated processes can be done here and that's one way of building up supply.

We've had some problems in this country with Japan because Japanese companies are very communicative — they work closely together. They manufacture their own integrated circuits and their own ships and steel plants and automobiles and everything else, thus they've got a big base to spread the cost around. So it's difficult for us to compete in that sense.

On the other hand, our company competes very well in Japan. We have very good business in Japan, and we've sold a lot of products that were manufactured in the United States to Japan, and vice versa — both ways.

But the cost of labor in Southeast Asia, Mexico, Brazil — and probably it's going to be true in a couple of the Iron Curtain countries in Eastern Europe as well — gets down to a different order of magnitude. So that's where your handwork is going to be done. We'll still have some manufacturing because we still have to produce a number of things. You can't run a country or run the world on information only; you've got to have something to have information about.

Do you have the background going back to the beginning of the century on Palo Alto's involvement in wireless telegraphy?

Q. Federal Telegraph, yes, and all that. Did you pick up any people from that era?

DP: Well, there was one fellow who was very important. Cy Elwell was the fellow who went over to Denmark and got the patents on the Poulsen arc, which was the key mechanism for all radio through World War I. Lee de Forest invented the vacuum tube here in Palo Alto in 1906, and that didn't come into active use until

at least 10 years later. There was a reason for that: They had to learn more about vacuum technology and thermal emission and so on. That work was largely done by people at General Electric and Bell Labs.

But Cy Elwell and Lee de Forest had no love for each other.

Elwell moved back here and he didn't have very much money. So out of kindness we gave him a job. He didn't do anything useful for us, but we had a lot of fun hearing him talk about the early days of wireless and radio.

The person outside of Fred Terman who was probably most influential in helping us get the company started was Charlie Litton.

Charlie was a very unusual person, and I probably learned as much from him as I learned from anybody else. The background of those people, Ralph Heintz and Charlie Litton and Philo Farnsworth and Fritz Kolster, the fellow who invented the radio direction finder, and Peter Jensen, who invented the magnetic coil loudspeaker — those were all done here in the beginning.

Q. Outside the technical friendships and so on, were there people in the social and political community you looked to as leaders early in your career?

DP: There were a lot of people who participated in the school program and were helpful there. Bud Hubbard was a very good friend of mine, and he was more influential on the county level than he was with the city.

Q. Do you think that Palo Alto is over the hill?

DP: No. It's just a different city than it was, and it's not going to change very much from the way it's going.

I guess the story is that I'm not as enthusiastic about all these things, like the fellow who was sitting on a lot at a crossroads and great big buildings grew all around him. And a fellow stopped by and said, "There have sure been a lot of things developed around this property of yours." And the owner replied, "There sure have, and I've been against every one of them."

© Ward Winslow 1991

David Packard misspoke slightly about Lee de Forest, who actually invented his audion or three-element vacuum tube in New York in 1906. De Forest made key improvements in Palo Alto in 1912 upon discovering its amplifying and feedback properties. At the time the interview ran, I was ignorant of these details and hence made no correction then.

DAVID PACKARD, DOER EXTRAORDINARY

by Ward Winslow

In the spring of 1942, David Packard, a 29-year-old electrical engineer who headed a small manufacturing firm, was pleased to be among the San Francisco region defense industry leaders invited to meet with Stanford Professor Paul Holden, then academia's top management guru. It wasn't easy to squeeze more time from a 15- to 18-hour work day, but Packard looked forward to mental stimulus and hearing how more seasoned executives were coping with the myriad problems posed by World War II. He had no inkling that he himself would voice the evening's profoundest challenge.

At the time it took an effort not to let your spirits sag. America still reeled from Japan's hammer blows at Pearl Harbor and other United States and Allied bases in the Pacific and Far East; the Coral Sea and Midway battles that began the U.S. turnaround lay ahead.

In North Africa, British and German desert troops were locked in a seesaw campaign. On the home front, war production was gaining slowly — and its grinding demands had left everyone attending Holden's huddle weary from care and overwork.

Still, Holden was not to be missed. A key adviser to the Office of Production Management's priorities division, he had close ties to the OPM chiefs in Washington, D.C. His much-hailed textbook on management, published a year earlier, had magnified his renown.

The industrialists present were mostly from big companies: Food Machinery & Chemical, Standard Oil of California, Westinghouse Electric, Kaiser Industries. Packard's partner, William Hewlett, an Army reservist, had been ordered to Signal Corps duty again, this time for the duration. Employees of their three-year-old electronics firm were working double shifts on parts for secret defense devices along with less esoteric measuring instruments. Years later, their Palo Alto neighbors learned of their contributions to the proximity fuzes that gave the Allies a vital edge in the air war and enabled beleaguered GIs to rally and win the Battle of the Bulge. The microwave signal generators for radar and radar countermeasures came later — just too late to be used in World War II, but soon enough to count in the four decades of cold war that recently ended.

In the group, dark-haired David Packard clearly was the new kid on the block. He was hard to miss, for he stood six-feet-five and projected a commanding personality. Yet everyone present was surprised when a David-and-Goliath confrontation evolved (though the David, like his biblical namesake, was destined for greatness).

After a good deal of talk about expediting production, the topic swung around to management. Holden soon posed his pet question: What is the responsibility of management? Then, Packard remembers, the professor declared: "Management's responsibility is to the shareholders — that's the end of it."

"I objected," Packard recalls. "I said, 'I think you're absolutely wrong. Management has a responsibility to its employees, it has a responsibility to its customers, it has a responsibility to the community at large.' And they almost laughed me out of the room."

His stand had been characteristically blunt; the derisive rebuff left Packard undaunted. He'd bucked the conventional wisdom before. He was one of Stanford's football "Vow Boys," who had pledged each other never to lose to the University of Southern California Trojans — and didn't. So Packard stuck by the belief he'd formed while studying management on

To provide context for the story Dave Packard told in the interview, I researched Professor Holden and developed this article. After a couple of attempts to market it, work on the book overwhelmed me, so I put the article aside until now.

his own a few years previously while he worked for General Electric in Schenectady, N.Y.

Graduating in the midst of the Depression, he and Hewlett had agreed that if they couldn't find jobs, they'd start a company and make their own jobs. That led to the two young engineers founding Hewlett-Packard Company in 1939 at Palo Alto, in Stanford's shadow. They adapted an invention by Hewlett to fill their first big order: special sound equipment for the Walt Disney film, Fantasia.

Before the war began, HP had installed an incentive compensation plan that rewarded employees for improving productivity. It enabled the workers to earn big increments in their base pay despite wartime wage controls — 100 percent over base by the war's end.

It is worth noting where they got this idea. Their mentor, Frederick E. Terman, Stanford professor of radio engineering (electronics by an earlier name), had encouraged them to start manufacturing electronic measuring equipment, and even loaned them cash. Terman was a friend of Melville Eastham, founder of General Radio Company of Cambridge, Mass., then the largest and best company in the field. Terman suggested that Eastham meet Bill and Dave (as everyone in HP knew them), so he stopped by Palo Alto to visit.

"I thought he would be concerned about our plan to compete with GR," Packard remembers, "but instead he said he thought our competition would be a good thing because new methods of measurement and new types of equipment were more readily accepted by the market if several companies were involved instead of only one."

Eastham told them about GR's unusual incentive compensation, not precisely profit-sharing, but a plan that rewarded employees for improvements in their productivity. HP adopted it; Packard, who usually took the lead in administration, as Hewlett did in engineering, was not only decisive and strong-mind-

ed, he was a good listener, too.

So when Packard took issue with Holden, HP already had begun managing for the benefit of its employees. They, in turn, had produced more, which meant more profits could be plowed back into growing the business. The partners then were the sole owners, and their main concern was to establish a successful enterprise. So it was not unnatural — if unconventional — to look to management responsibilities beyond their own profits.

Soon after the war ended, HP's order backlog dropped sharply, and a reduction of the wartime work force occurred. With the market changes, there came a shift to more standard profit-sharing. Once past the postwar rough spot, the company prepared a full line of electronic measuring instruments and was ready early in the 1950s when demand soared. For several years, business doubled annually.

Later, in lean times, HP would furlough its whole work force rather than fire anyone. And after the partners went public and sold some stock shares, employees were offered a chance to buy in.

Packard welcomed Fred Terman's proposal that HP offer graduating engineers it wanted to hire the tuition and time off the job to do graduate study at Stanford. This magical recruiting aid bewitched one top brain after another, building an array of technical talent.

As for serving the community, many HP executives held local public offices — Packard himself sat on Palo Alto's school board, planning for a "lighthouse" district that kept pace with the baby boom. Then he became a Stanford University trustee and helped to create Stanford Industrial (now Research) Park and the Stanford Shopping Center, both big tax earners for the city of Palo Alto.

By then HP had become a major local employer. Why should such a firm offer leadership in public affairs? Packard explains: "The idea is that the environment in which our people work has a good deal to do with the success of the company, and it's to our advantage to make that environment as attractive as possible."

In relating to its customers, Hewlett-Packard stood behind its products and listened attentively. HP also stayed friendly with employees who left to start their own businesses — Apple Computer co-founder Steve Wozniak is a striking example. "We found that generally they've been good friends and good customers, so we've tried to help them," Packard says.

The industrial park — a prototype for others that now dot the nation, and often cited as the most successful of them all — was another brainchild of Fred Terman, who by then was dean of engineering and on his way to becoming Stanford's provost. Terman and Packard played a one-two game in encouraging other high technology companies to locate at the research center. One of their catches was William Shockley, co-inventor of the transistor at Bell Labs in New Jersey. Eight young scientists who worked for Shockley and then broke away in a dispute over his management practices went on to form Fairchild Semiconductor in Palo Alto. Led by Robert Noyce, they developed the integrated circuit — the computer-on-a-chip that's credited with touching off "the second industrial revolution."

Once World War II was won, HP focused its attention on producing instruments to enhance science and engineering, first the measuring instruments, then complex calculators that weaned many an intrigued engineer from the slide rule, then computer equipment. Packard is a believer in the doctrine propounded by Vannevar Bush, who headed the wartime U.S. science and technology effort. Packard quotes Bush's thinking this way:

"The extent to which we use science to win the war against disease, to develop new industries, and to maintain the strength of our military forces, to a very large extent will determine the future of this nation."

Dr. Bush's vision took shape in the form of federally supported research on campuses throughout America, with the Office of Naval Research as overseer. Therein, Packard points out, lay the genesis of the current research overhead controversy that so embarrassed Stanford in 1991 when gleeful congressional probers revealed a few glaringly misallocated costs.

Packard's role as a Stanford trustee landed him in two touchy middle-man situations.

The first arose when he was asked to smooth the way for a move by Stanford's teaching hospital and faculty from San Francisco to the campus at Palo Alto 35 miles to the south. He found the San Francisco professors at loggerheads with the Palo Alto physicians, who had a stake in the new hospital that was to serve both the medical school and the community. To deal with what he wryly called "the innate obstinacy of the medical profession," Packard made a rule saying, in effect, "YOU WILL GET ALONG." It worked, at least for a while.

Packard's friendship with former President Herbert Hoover drew him into another peacemaking task. Hoover, who lived to be 90, became very suspicious in his final decade of the aims of some social science professors. He wanted the Hoover Institution at Stanford — the vast library collection on war, peace and revolution he had had assembled beginning in the aftermath of World War I — devoted to exposing the evils of communism. Faculty members proved loathe to engage in research "with the results predetermined," as Packard put it. A compromise was finally struck recognizing Hoover's right to say what he wanted about the institution and its studies without detracting from its scholars' ability to do objective research.

After Hoover's death in 1964, there were efforts to undo this accord but Packard and other trustees stood firm. Packard foresees that the Hoover Institution will remain "a legitimate and an important part of Stanford," especially now that former Secretary of State George Shultz is ensconced there, playing a major role as a distinguished scholar and host to visiting statesmen.

David Packard also said yes over several decades to pleas from the White House to try to improve defense production for all America's benefit, as deputy secretary of Defense and most recently as chairman of a presidential commission on defense management. Arguably, if that panel's recommendations had been carried out by industry and government officials, there'd have been no recent procurement scandals.

When he took the Pentagon job, as "inside man" with Defense Secretary Melvin Laird in 1969-71, Packard put his fortune in a trust. Despite HP's emphasis on science, some of its revenues would inevitably come from federal contracts. So the $22.3 million earnings of the trust during Packard's federal service were disbursed to U.S. colleges and universities — a patriotism bonus, as it were.

Professor Holden never yielded fully to Packard's philosophy, and perhaps with good reason, for it was easier for HP as a partnership initially to pursue such uncommon notions than it would have been for a public company. Even after HP reorganized as a corporation and later put its stock on public sale, the founders held large blocks of stock; they felt free to take a long-range outlook even if it bore a cost at the quarterly bottom line. However, when Holden revised his management textbook in 1968 he did put in a section on external and employee relations recognizing the new thinking about multiple responsibilities. Even then, Packard's vision, although shared by some other companies, was ahead of general industrial trends. Its time has come only recently.

As HP grew to global scope, Packard and Hewlett became billionaires and, through philanthropy, kept acting to improve an ever-larger community. The family foundations the two established have made major donations to Stanford University, largely for new science and engineering facilities. In April 1991, the 142-bed Lucile Salter Packard Children's Hospital at Stanford, named for the late Mrs. Packard, was dedicated with the help of Barbara Bush. Of the financing for the $100 million hospital, $40 million came from the Packard family foundation, and David Packard shared the toil of raising additional funds.

The foundation also supports America's largest program of unrestricted grants to young university faculty in science and engineering — five-year fellowships of $500,000 each. That time span and that sum reflect Packard's belief in providing resources adequate for a task.

In 1994, Hewlett and Packard together gave Stanford $25 million to establish Frederick Terman Fellowships for junior faculty members in engineering and sciences, including funds to help them set up costly new laboratories.

Another Packard family project is dedicated to preserving at least one of the fruit orchards for which Los Altos was famous before the land became more valuable for homes and industrial sites. Through an endowment, an 88-acre apricot orchard surrounding the Packard home in the Santa Clara Valley foothills is destined still to be growing its juicy delights a century hence. Like the children's hospital, the apricots were one of Lu Packard's cherished concerns.

Two interests of the couple's offspring also led to investments for the public weal. When Julie Packard and her sister Nancy Burnett joined several other young marine biologists in developing the Monterey Bay Aquarium, their parents' foundation put up the whole $40 million cost. What's more, their father, reveling in a chance to do some independent engineering, designed three ingenious systems to simulate

DAVID PACKARD, DOER EXTRORDINARY

ocean water movement. A surge tank, a crashing wave machine and a gentle beach tide regulator add realistic impact to the exhibits in this largest U.S. aquarium.

The trumpet-playing talent of son David Woodley Packard lies behind the foundation's donations to buy instruments for school music programs, which had become hamstrung by fund cutbacks. Another project the son has thrown his energies into, restoration of the Stanford Theatre, a large art deco movie house in Palo Alto, as a showplace for films from Hollywood's golden years, complete with theater organ music, also received backing. Its future is iffy, however, because it has not become a self-sustaining operation, as father Packard deems proper.

A critic in the early 1990s labeled David Packard a plutocrat — a practitioner of government by the wealthy. That pejorative term blinks the fact that Packard started with almost nothing but an education and from the very beginning enhanced the well-being of his associates, his community and his country.

In the midst of a long interview, I asked Dave Packard if he ever felt that in his political activities he was shaping the future of the community. He said he'd never thought of it in those terms; instead, he thinks in terms of things that need to be done. Then this extraordinary doer added:

"My philosophy has always been that you get your satisfaction in life from doing something. Once you've done it, you ought to forget about it and do something else."

Fifty years after the night they laughed at Dave Packard's ideas on management's responsibilities, it seems fair to say he has proved his point and had the last laugh. Chances are he has already forgotten about that and set out to do something new. ∎

PALO ALTO: A Centennial History — ERRATA

When *Palo Alto: A Centennial History* was published by the Palo Alto Historical Association in October 1993, it turned out to contain a few errors. At this writing it is uncertain if there will be a second printing to supplement the 7,500 copies printed initially. Even if there were, corrections might be too costly to manage.

For those reasons, I want to use this opportunity to set the record straight. This involves correcting errors of fact and setting forth a few significant omissions.

The year when the late U.S. District Court Judge Robert F. Peckham swore in Judge William A. Ingram to the federal bench was 1976. It is given incorrectly in a caption on page 239.

Attorney Roland C. Davis picked up three statements requiring correction or further explanation. Paul Gullixson, editor of the Palo Alto Weekly, wrote a column about one of these — a statement on page 118 that the Pedro de Lemos house on Waverley Oaks had been the first in the city to sell for more than $100,000. Davis noted that a house he and his wife owned, located at 345 Coleridge Avenue, had sold in 1967 (five years earlier than the De Lemos house) for $105,000, and that the real estate agent involved had said this was the second highest price for a Palo Alto residence sale at the time.

Perhaps the most serious error in the history appears on

page 76 in the form of a statement that Ralph Emerson Welles had led the Palo Alto Community Players for more than 40 years, starting in 1934. Davis noted that after only 18 years as the Players' director, Welles embarked on a new career as a U.S. ranger in Death Valley studying and scientifically recording the habits and lifestyles of big horn sheep. Ralph Schram then became director of the Players, as a plaque near the Community Theatre's front door honoring both men informs. Schram was the director from 1951 to 1974. When Schram died in 1985, John McClintock wrote a tribute in the Peninsula Times Tribune quoting TheatreWorks artistic director Robert Kelley as saying that TheatreWorks had been virtually "invented" by Schram.

Thirdly, Roland Davis clarified a statement on page 185 regarding Palo Alto Hardware, which was founded by the grandfather of his wife, nee Harriet Allen, a native Palo Altan. The book says: "In the years before World War II other well-known downtown businesses included Ben Allen's Palo Alto Hardware on University at Bryant."

Benjamin Graves Allen opened his hardware store in Palo Alto in 1903. This landmark store, perhaps with a change of location, was operated continuously by the Allens until Benjamin Graves' son W.B. Allen (Mrs. Davis's uncle) sold it in the 1950s

and retired. The buyer, David Haight, served for a time as mayor of Palo Alto and ultimately closed the business, including a branch in the San Antonio Shopping Center in Mountain View. Haight subsequently became an apostle of the Church of Jesus Christ of the Latter-day Saints, a member of the LDS ruling body in Salt Lake City, Utah.

In 1993, Larry Hassett opened a "new" Palo Alto Hardware at Alma Street and Channing Avenue. In it is displayed a photograph of the interior of the old downtown store, including a picture of Benjamin Graves Allen that was in the old store for many years.

Another longtime downtown business worthy of mention was Stark's Bakery on University Avenue. Everett Stark won renown for many rare specialty items. After retiring, he helped his son Dick, an early retiree from Spectra-Physics, start Page Mill Winery in Los Altos Hills.

Although the first Palo Alto Children's Theatre production at the Lucie Stern Community Center was correctly reported, Michael Litfin has pointed out that the Children's Theatre's true first play, given at Community House, was "The Perfect Gift" in December 1932.

Litfin pointed out also that the Palo Alto Junior Museum's initial move to the Community Center, cited on page 77, was to the basement of the Children's

ERRATA — continued

Theatre, not the Community Theatre.

On page 214, a section on telephone service in Palo Alto says it became "a favored exchange, one that got innovations early." Virgil P. Flint, who was manager of the exchange in the 1930s, has pointed out that long before the DAvenport exchange dial installation was completed in 1948, the first step-by-step dial switching in Palo Alto was introduced in 1934.

Two persons who have served as bridges between the Stanford and Palo Alto communities did not receive appropriate attention in the book. Jing Lyman, wife of University President Robert Lyman, played a leading role in the campaign to defeat Proposition 14 and the creation of Midpeninsula Citizens for Fair Housing. Andy Doty, for many years Stanford's director of community relations, helped the city and the university to understand one another and often eased tensions between them through personal initiatives.

There ought to have been included a picture of Mayor and longtime Councilman J. Pearce Mitchell, for whom Mitchell Park is named. Here is a photo of the former Stanford registrar at the opening of the park in 1957 with his grandson, John Clifford Mitchell, who is also the grandson of Mrs. Mary Edith Jones Clifford, one-time Santa Clara County welfare director.

Another who perhaps merited more attention is Edward C. Thoits, who served on the City Council for 40 years and who was a guiding spirit in the formation of a volunteer fire department and its later conversion to a professional department.

The long school board service of Lois Hopper, a daughter of Stanford President Ray Lyman Wilbur, might well have been mentioned.

In the acknowledgements, the help given me by C. David Burgin, the editorial director who led in designing the Peninsula Times Tribune, was unfortunately omitted.

In the sports chapter, on page 275, swimmer Caren Cramer's name is misspelled, a slip Keith Peters noted.

Dr. Mitchell giving his great-grandson a ride around the new Mitchell Park at the dedication, April 1958

How one family made the big move to East P.A.

By Ward Winslow
Special to the Mercury News

'FOR sale," the classified ad read, "picket fencing, motorcycle parts, pickup truck bumpers, house to move." That last item caught the eyes of Foster Curry and his wife, Nancy Leech, urban homesteaders in East Palo Alto.

Buying the house, moving it from Mountain View, hooking it up and making it home became a central focus of their lives.

It solved their landscaping problem on a ¾-acre lot.

Also their living-space problem, their what-do-we-do-after-the-baby-comes problem, their floor-plan problem and, to a large extent, their home-financing problem.

Today the transplanted house is the heart of Patchwork Farm, as the couple call their spread on Bell Street. Curry and Leech, both 29, 2-year-old Devon and baby Lauralyn, born in December, are snug in just what they wanted: a 1920s farmhouse.

And a farm it is. Fifty new fruit trees await planting, and there are vegetable and herb gardens. In pens and a low barn out in back live two pregnant Nubian goats, ducks, a flock of chickens and two black sheep. Three bags of wool sit ready to spin. Honest.

Patchwork Farm also is the case history of one creative way to clear the high hurdle to Peninsula home ownership.

Rolling in a house — the right house — wasn't easy. But it's proving to be a neat answer to their housing need. They're committed to living in East Palo Alto, which they think has the Peninsula's best weather and is great for raising children. Curry, a recent appointee to the city planning commission, says, "We have a 50-year plan." How'd it all happen? Here's the synopsis: They bought the land and first lived in a tiny cottage on it.

While they were considering building a home, they read the ad and found the house. Moving it, and

See HOMESTEAD, Page 2

This feature got me in trouble with Mike Kidder, then Times Tribune editor. He thought I should be writing exclusively for them; I contended I was a free-lance writer. Actually, Carolyn Snyder, formerly Times Tribune assistant managing editor and now Mercury News special sections editor, had heard of the story and assigned it to me.

Settling in East Palo Alto

resuscitating the cottage, entailed many frustrations and delays. For a while they lived in a trailer on the lot while working on the other structures, including a garage the city required them to build.

Do-it-yourselfers, they've put in many hours of sweat equity.

Still, it's being repaid liberally. They have the homestead they wanted, and the house alone is worth nearly four times what it cost to install.

Another player in all this lives four doors away: Jane Leech, Nancy's mother, an apartment manager. She found the land and cottage, saw the "house to move" ad and spotted ads for two other necessaries: an Airstream house trailer and a buck stove.

A chance meeting

Leech grew up in East Palo Alto, and she and Curry both attended Ravenswood High School in its last two years. Mere acquaintances then, they went their separate ways and met again by chance in 1981 at a building materials store.

"She was buying stuff to patch her mother's roof, so I ended up going along to help," Curry said.

After marrying, the couple lived in Monterey. By then, Curry held bachelor's and master's degrees from Stanford in geophysics. Leech, a University of Michigan graduate, took a master's at the Monterey Institute of International Studies in teaching English to foreigners.

"We'd been thinking of moving overseas . . . (to) work in France or the Middle East," Curry said. "Then this place came up for sale." It cost $80,000, their biggest investment. The assessor figured the land at $60,000 and the 500-square-foot cottage at $20,000.

"We lived in the cottage for over a year, with all our stuff crammed in," Curry recounted. "We knew we wanted to build something, and if we started from scratch we figured it'd probably take us three years to build it by ourselves. And we wanted to start a family.

"House-moving companies are real good at locating houses for you for $500 or a thousand bucks," Curry said. One firm touted a three-bedroom stucco ranch house due to be moved from Atherton, but the couple soon saw it wasn't right. Then the ad came up.

"We went down there and looked, and the guy had an acre lot that was packed solid with junk," he said. It was on Joaquin Street, where an office complex now stands, opposite Shoreline Amphitheater.

A $4,000 offer

The seller wanted $20,000 but he only had two weeks to sell.

Curry and Leech sat tight. The developer who acquired the lot then offered the house for $4,000.

"We could have waited," Curry said. "We could have gone out there the day they were going to demolish it and probably have gotten it for $500, because the demolition crew was getting $3,000 for getting rid of the house." But they liked the house, and met the developer's price in October 1984. It took months to get the permits required for the move, so their find had to be parked nearby.

"We had to pay $500 a month rent for six months just to have it sitting there on an empty lot," Curry said. "Boy, that guy was making out," Leech added. "He had another house sitting empty on that space, too."

Working with East Palo Alto officials, they became aware of a bias against moving houses into the community. It stemmed from the Oregon Expressway project in Palo Alto, when, Curry said, a lot of houses were moved across Bayshore Freeway and "people would just slam them in and turn a quick buck." Thus the city of East Palo Alto requires a project to be completed within three months; the applicant must live in the house.

Curry regards the first case as impossible, because the work entails the move, pouring a foundation, plumbing, and any painting, exterior work and re-roofing needed. The second, he adds, isn't very enforceable, especially if an owner's funds run out.

"We feel lucky that we pulled this one off, because we got it fairly cheap and ecologically it makes a lot more sense," Curry said.

"Once somebody's gone to the trouble of building a whole house, to just tear it down and put it on a landfill seems like a waste." They also pulled off a house movers' no-no — moving the fireplace (after dismantling the chimney). Testing this in the move to the empty

After two moves, the house and the family are settled into East Palo Alto.

Settling in East Palo Alto

lot, Curry found the fireplace had slipped a few inches and recruited his dad, David Curry of Menlo Park, to help him jack it up.

After the final move, he jacked it up again and installed the wood-burning stove Jane Leech had located.

To clear the house site, the couple moved the cottage nearer the

---

'We feel lucky ... we got it fairly cheap and ecologically it makes a lot more sense.'

— Foster Curry

---

street, leaving it up on blocks for remodeling. Then the main move was delayed because of street work in Mountain View. So they had to live in the house trailer during Leech's pregnancy with Devon.

"It was OK in the winter, too," she recalled. "It was pretty snug."

Adventure marked the main move. Curry had left 30½ feet between the cottage and the neighbor's fence. The house was 30 feet wide and 50 feet long. So he warned the neighbor a corner fence post might have to be taken down.

They also had to clear cars from one side of the road. Signs the city provided didn't fully do it, so Curry took his mother-in-law door-to-door "because she has a better way with people.

"She'd go up to the front door and say, 'Now listen, honey, the house is going to be rolling by in the morning and here's your car parked on the street. Do you really think that they're going to take the house back, or that your car's going to get moved?' And so they'd say, 'Well, OK, maybe you're right.'"

The move was supposed to be done between 3 and 4 a.m., and Curry and Leech went to Mountain View to watch. First they found that a gravel truck owner had, as asked, moved his cab, but not two trailers. The house movers slid them to the side, then nudged them back after their load squeezed

past.

At San Antonio Road, an airplane tire, one of 18 on the three dollies under the house, blew out and had to be replaced with a spare. "By then the morning commute was starting," Leech recalled.

Sleepy people driving on East Bayshore Frontage Road did double takes when they saw the house coming, Curry said, and even school buses had to back up when drivers found they were cut off.

A close call

Finally the house movers swung their burden onto the lot, just clearing the fence post as its owner watched apprehensively. Curry had had a back hoe dig foundation trenches; they fit almost exactly.

The movers were disappointed not to be hired to dig the foundation, he said, but he wanted to do it himself so he could make the crawl space twice as deep as required and the concrete walls thicker.

He also put in a 1-inch water line, and later used framing clips rather than toe nails to attach the house to the foundation sill.

"We expect to survive the next earthquake quite handily," he said. Curry and Leech also are thinking about adding a second story, in which case the built-in extra capacity will serve well.

"It was Halloween (1986) when we finished the foundation," Leech said. "We had our first party in it while it was still up on blocks.

It looked like a perfect Halloween house — cobwebs everywhere, and dust," she said.

Lawrence Anderson, a semi-retired partner in the house-moving firm, told Curry he'd moved the house once before, about 25 years earlier. It was uprooted from the 500 block of Everett Avenue in Palo Alto to make way for an apartment house.

A modern house of 1,500 square feet probably would have three cramped bedrooms, Curry said. "This is two bedrooms so it's pretty spacious. Big rooms, big kitchen and we have a dining room. The lot faces due south, and sure enough at the south end there's a sun porch. The north end faces the street. We

were lucky in many ways." A mud room flanks the sun porch and opens onto the barnyard.

Besides the barn and new garage, there's a sizable one-story shed that sheltered family furniture during the move. The cottage in front, fully renovated, now is rented, which helps pay the mortgage.

"We just refinanced, and we got a pretty good return on our labor," Curry said. Moving and fixing up the house cost about $30,000 — $4,000 to buy it, $3,000 to park it for six months, about $6,500 for the two-step moving, plus fix-up labor and materials.

The garage cost another $5,000.

The refinanced house, deemed "essentially custom construction," was appraised at $115,000. "It cost us 30 or 35, so it's gratifying." Curry is quick to say that buying a house to move is not for every owner, every house or every lot. But he derived a special side benefit: his contractor's license.

Coupling earlier experience as a carpenter's apprentice with his work on the Bell Street buildings, he'd logged enough years to qualify just as the old licensing setup ran out. Now owner-builders have it tougher.

A software engineer for Develco, Inc., in San Jose, he says he might try full-time contracting if oil development ever goes sour.

Patchwork Farm is in the Faber tract, which was subdivided into large lots in keeping with poultry colonizer Charles Weeks' turn-of-the-century belief that a family with an acre of land and a flock of chickens could live happily.

Neighbors have goats, chickens, horses and pigs. City ordinances allow two of a kind, and stretch for new litters. So as not to become too fond of goat kids, Leech said, she simply names males "Meat" when they're born.

"After commuting on the Bayshore and having a lousy day at work, it's good to come home and milk a couple of goats," he said. "It keeps your mind off your troubles."

Free-lance writer Ward Winslow lives in Palo Alto.

An addition to the Palo Alto home of Beverly and William Grossman makes room for her parents.

RE-BUILDING BOOM

Banner year for remodeling

'Don't move; improve,' homeowners seem to agree

By Ward Winslow
Special to the Mercury News

A Menlo Park couple are almost doubling the space of their 900-square-foot bungalow. The project began in March, but change orders, delays in getting materials and difficulty in finding subcontractors (of 13 tile firms contacted, only two would bid) have pushed the hoped-for completion date from July to September.

Their experiences put them in good company as thousands of Peninsulans this summer remodel their homes and compete for goods and services.

Residential remodeling is setting records nationally this year, with the Peninsula at the leading edge. Local reports peg the current quarter as the busiest yet.

The reason is evident. In cities where single-family home prices are sky high, residents find remodeling to get the kind of home they want easier and less costly than "buying up." New city restrictions on additions and remodeling — and fear that even tighter rules will be adopted soon — are quickening activity, officials say.

What's exceptional on the Peninsula are the permit value amounts and the scope of the work. Jobs from $100,000 to $300,000 are not rare, and one showy remodeling job in Portola Valley topped $1 million. Such big jobs often change the fundamental character of a house, contractors say.

The boom is having the effect of splintering professionals into specialties ranging from utmost craftsmanship to computer-aided planning and from elaborate design services to new

See REMODEL, Page 6

Homeowners who remodel share the goal of fulfilling their housing needs without moving

Building in some elbow room

REMODEL, from Page 1

matchmaking for small contractors. (See related story on this page.)

Nationally, remodeling hit the $100 billion mark in 1988, federal census data show; 1989 is expected to go $5 billion higher.

In Palo Alto, chief planning official Carol Jansen noted in a recent proposal to tighten the city's allowable floor-area ratio that "single-

family building activity has risen from one-half to two-thirds of all permit activity." Permits for remodeling and additions outstrip the few for new homes.

Palo Alto figures for the first half of 1989 show 488 remodeling and additions permits totaling $12.4 million. Even with two slow months included, these half-year totals are well ahead of 1988, when

there were 915 permits totaling $21.68 million in valuation for the entire year. Jackie McDonnell of the city's building staff said plan checks are four to six weeks behind, indicating a busy summer. "I wouldn't be surprised if we doubled (last year's figures) this year," she said.

Olga Shalygin — Special to the Mercury News

The new peninsula in the kitchen of Palo Altan Flo Braker, author of "The Art of Perfect Baking," will be her baking center

RE-BUILDING BOOM

Booming Menlo Park

Menlo Park's chief building official, Donald E. Johnson, said his city's total valuation for 1988-89 was twice that of 1987-88, and that this year's remodeling activity seems greater. However, Johnson has been able to add staff to cut plan review time.

Mountain View also has increased its staff, Building Inspector Ray Coates said.

In Los Altos, building official Vance Phillips said the 1988-89 building totals showed substantial jumps in permits and valuations and a decline in new residences built.

Phillips said that a bid of about $100 a square foot for remodeling or additions is typical.

Lynn Comeskey, owner of Mountain View-based Mac and Lou Construction, said that just in June, he signed contracts equal to half his 1988 dollar total.

Homeowners who remodel share the goal of fulfilling their current housing needs without moving. But the factors driving their needs differ widely.

William C. and Beverly Grossman are adding all the space the city allows to their sizable south Palo Alto home to make room for her parents, George and Emily Storm. The Storms, married nearly 60 years, sold their home in El Monte, east of Los Angeles, to finance the $90,000 project.

Grossman, a radiant heating specialist, has acted as the general contractor. He subcontracted the concrete and carpentry work but installed much of the wiring, plumbing and heating himself. George Storm, 80, a retired roofer, is talking about putting on the composition shingles.

Initially, Grossman chose a plan from a mail-order book. After modifying the design a couple of times, he hired an engineer to draw more precise plans.

Working along with city

"The city building department was very helpful," he said. It shot down his plan at one point, but for

Ceramic tiles, under plastic, were spared for Flo Braker's new kitchen

what he considered good reasons: safety and how the addition would blend with the neighborhood. (Two-story homes flank his lot, and no one has voiced objections.)

The two-story, 1,655-square-foot addition has a living room, master bedroom, family room, bathroom and utility room-sewing room downstairs, and a bathroom, bedroom and sitting room upstairs. All are spacious. The doorways are wide, in case a wheelchair must ever go through them, and the stairs are wired for an elevator chair.

Construction began June 1 and moved along rapidly. Work had to be halted in August until funds were released from escrow.

The one amenity the addition lacks is a kitchen, because a single-family home is allowed only one.

Though two kitchens could have been useful to Flo Braker, that rule meant she and husband David had to remodel the existing kitchen in their Palo Alto home.

Flo Braker, a baking consultant and cookbook author, needs a more commodious and fully equipped kitchen than most folks.

But because she was busy bringing out a new cookbook and heading the San Francisco Professional Food Society, the Brakers hired

Nancy Cowall Cutler of Palo Alto to design and oversee the project.

They settled on a plan to remove a wall, open up the room, put in custom cabinets, marble and new kitchen appliances.

Getting professional help

"Even though the kitchen was going to have professional equipment, Flo still needed a warm kitchen, welcoming for guests and family," Cutler said.

Cutler is an interior designer who has specialized in kitchens and bathrooms since she remodeled her own kitchen nine years ago.

Her projects typically involve removing an interior wall and have run from $36,000 into six figures, she said.

She writes the specifications, usually gets two bids and arranges a contract with one of several contractors she likes to work with — Thompson Sako in the Brakers' case. Then she orders the materials and oversees the project.

Organization's the key

Cutler's formula for avoiding hang-ups is: "Get really organized in the beginning and order well in advance." Decisions about windows, doors, fixtures, faucets, tile and the like should be made before work starts, or close to it, she said.

As for choosing a design professional or a contractor, Cutler advises getting several recommendations from acquaintances, checking referrals, visiting a job or two, making sure to see professional qualifications and double-checking that all materials are ordered.

But even when homeowners take precautions, there still can be problems.

One Palo Alto couple, who added a wing onto their house and remodeled the old part last year, spent six months deciding on a contractor. They talked to six or seven companies whose bids ranged from the high $50,000s to the mid-$80,000s. The low bidder was inexperienced, they decided; they liked the second-highest bidder's can-do attitude, willingness to explain how he'd do things and kudos from neighbors.

A wrench in the plans

All went fairly smoothly until only part of the window order arrived, including some wrong items. A corrected delivery was promised in six weeks but took 10. The contractor, who'd been ahead of schedule, finished 2½ months late and indicated he lost money.

Tiling was another problem. The owners noticed the tile spacing getting wider and wider — the subcontractor was trying to stretch a short supply of material. When the contractor returned from vacation and saw the inferior work, he ordered it torn out and hired another tile contractor to finish — six weeks late. The job, due to be done by Labor Day, ran on until Thanksgiving.

In good times, everyone's a specialist

By Ward Winslow
Special to the Mercury News

AS HOMEOWNERS feather their nests in this boom year, remodeling pros seize the chance to make their own work more comfortable.

Yellow Pages ads saying "no job too small" may be outdated. Certain highly reputed artisans rely only on word-of-mouth, not the Yellow Pages, and are choosy about jobs.

"Every job is different, every home is different, every customer is different," says general contractor Alfred S. Braun of Palo Alto.

In remodeling, he might have added, every contractor's operation tends to be different.

His company, Braun Builders, is known for its focus on one job at a time. He uses a small crew — eight currently, but usually four — of generalists who can do everything: partitions, Sheetrock, wiring, plumbing, painting, though at times he hires subcontractors to speed progress. His son Randall, who has a degree in design, can do plans.

"That way, we can schedule the work efficiently," he said.

Lynn Comeskey, owner of Mountain View-based Mac and Lou Construction, works with a crew of about 20 divided into small-job and big-job teams because he believes different personality types are required. Although his crews often do specialized work, he may use up to 12 or 14 subcontractors on a big job.

"You want to bring a cooperative group together," he said. "A low bid (by a subcontractor) is not as important as whether he's reliable and does good work."

A typical big job used to be a two-room addition; today, it's two or three additions to different parts of the house, plus kitchen and bathroom remodeling.

As an example, Comeskey cited a Menlo Park job: two bedroom additions, a dining room extension, a new entry with an adjoining powder room, the creation of two bedrooms from one and a changed traffic pattern.

Plemons Construction Co. is known as a premier Palo Alto remodeling firm. Scott Plemons said he has had to turn a lot of people away this year — or ask them to wait six months to a year.

Custom craftsmanship is his hallmark. He works with a crew of six, often teaming up with architects, and subcontracts painting, plumbing, electrical and tile work.

He turns down designs he dislikes, saying "I don't want word going around that I built that ugly thing."

What his clients want, he said, is the old house in the old neighborhood, updated, its architectural integrity intact. He scorns people who thinks remodeling is too much work, who "bulldoze perfectly good houses to build speculative houses to make money."

Going from high craftsmanship to high technology, George Morgan, owner of Morgan Construction of Mountain View, advertises computer-aided design as part of his service.

Morgan uses a digitizer to estimate the materials needed and applies the computer to design, price estimation and scheduling.

"A time-and-materials contract stands some chance of saving people money," Morgan says, by removing the padding — or "fudge factor" — in a standard remodeling contractor's bid.

For about two years, Hinton & Associates of Mountain View has been playing matchmaker between homeowners and "good, small contractors who personally perform all work."

John Hinton and his partner, Colton Carmine, both with contracting backgrounds, maintain a list of about 100 contractors and specialty people whom they refer, depending on the job requirements. They charge the contractors "a nominal fee," but the service is free to the homeowners.

The business tries to screen those it lists, but cannot stand behind their work, Carmine said.

GENE TUPPER — PALO ALTO TIMES

As it crosses the San Francisquito Creek bridge in 1951, a steam locomotive passes El Palo Alto.

New role for El Palo Alto

Abstraction with roots in city symbol dominates Centennial logo

BY WARD WINSLOW
Special to the Mercury News

El Palo Alto

BY WARD WINSLOW
Special to the Mercury News

SINCE the days of the dons, a tall redwood tree has been the south Peninsula's central landmark. Now El Palo Alto has a new role as the city named for it approaches its 100th birthday. Long the symbol of both the city of Palo Alto and Stanford University, the tree — in a form reminiscent of a Chinese brush painting — dominates the logo of Palo Alto Centennial 1994.

The logo created by Mark Ryan, a Salinas graphic designer, beat out 104 other entries in a statewide contest. Ryan drew 400 versions of his image before picking the best.

"I knew it had to be an abstraction yet have its roots in the fa-

Could today's landmark not be the tree the Spaniards saw? Historian Dorothy Regnery said Palou's 'tower' might have stood near Middlefield Road.

miliar symbol we all know," he said. " . . . My tree is frozen in time, yet it could still be evolving."

More lifelike drawings of the tree appear on the seals of the city and the university. On football-season Saturdays, a costumed mascot — at times looking as much like a palm tree as a redwood — dances with cheerleaders, Dollies and the incomparable Leland Stanford Junior University Marching Band.

The real redwood behind the images still stands just east of the CalTrain tracks on the south bank of San Francisquito Creek — the Palo Alto-Menlo Park and Santa Clara County-San Mateo County border.

Time's ravages have battered it and roused fears for its continued existence as "the first official liv-

ing California landmark," as a plaque set in 1926 by the Native Sons of the Golden West calls it.

Yet with the help of misting pipes and guy wires installed by city tree crews, it may live to witness more anniversaries. During Palo Alto's 75th anniversary in 1969 a tree dubbed El Palo Nuevo was planted in Mitchell Park, just in case. It remains an understudy for the starring role held by a tough old sequoia sempervirens.

In 1769, Don Gaspar de Portola's expedition camped near the tall tree after the first sighting by Europeans of San Francisco Bay.

Five years later Father Francisco Palou told in his diary entry for Nov. 28, 1774, of reaching San Francisquito Creek. "Near the ford it has a grove of very high redwoods," he wrote, "and at about a hundred paces farther downstream another very large tree of the same redwood. . . . from a distance it looks like a tower."

Palou erected a cross nearby to mark a possible mission site. But the next party, arriving in March 1776, realized the creek dried up in summer and opted for a site by the Guadalupe River in Santa Clara, where Mission Santa Clara was founded in 1777. The grove Palou noted is gone — possibly undermined in the flood of 1862.

Juan Bautista de Anza, leader of the 1775-'76 expedition, and Father Pedro Font mapped the area. Font sketched a redwood with one trunk, estimating it as more than 135 feet high and 15½ feet around.

One of the mysteries of El Palo Alto is why Font did not show the

twin trunks documented by a sketch in 1867 and a photograph in 1875. Did the second trunk grow later, as some scholars have guessed?

Photographs of 1886, 1888 and 1891 show a single trunk. Possibly the other fell in the stormy winter of 1885-'86, but that has yet to be dated precisely.

The tree marked one corner of the estate Gov. Leland Stanford bought in 1876 and built up as his Palo Alto Stock Farm. There he bred and developed trotting horses famed across America.

Emory E. Smith, a Stanford professor and a pioneer Palo Alto trustee, wrote in a newspaper years later that after the twin fell Gov. Stanford "bulkheaded the remaining tree, but its crown is broken, its glory of feathery branches has departed, it is now but a gnarled relic upon the top of which the Stanford class flag is annually planted."

A count of the rings requested by Gov. Stanford pegged the fallen trunk as at least 960 years old.

As the university was being built, Stanford helped Timothy Hopkins get a loan to buy a town site across the railroad line — today's downtown Palo Alto.

By then Stanford had been elected to the U.S. Senate. Returning from Washington, D.C., in 1889, he was surprised to learn Hopkins had named the subdivision University Park, thinking Stanford wanted "Palo Alto" reserved for his horse farm.

Worse, to Stanford, the only land west of today's El Camino Real he had been unable to buy had been subdivided and marketed as "Palo Alto." Stanford filed a lawsuit contesting the name use. Later his agents negotiated an out-of-court settlement. With the lot-buyers consenting, University Park became Palo Alto and the other tract College Terrace.

Could today's landmark not be the tree the Spaniards saw? Historian Dorothy Regnery said Palou's "tower" might have stood near Middlefield Road, where fording the creek was easier.

Oblivious to its lore, the ancient tree clings to its place as trains and years go passing by.

An imprint on American medicine

Dr. Russel V.A. Lee's pioneering health-care attitudes have been carried on through his sons

PROFILE

Sixth in a series of notable families whose Palo Alto roots go back 100 years

BY WARD WINSLOW
Special to the Mercury News

PROFILE

BY WARD WINSLOW
Special to the Mercury News

SAVE for its vineyard, Boronda Farm's old center — the beautiful hilltop adobe with a splendid view into Palo Alto's Foothills Park — is gone.

Also gone are its denizens, Dr. Russel Van Arsdale Lee and his wife of 54 years, Dorothy Womack Lee. She died in 1972, he in 1982.

The Lees' imprint remains indelible, however, throughout American medicine and especially in Palo Alto. It also lingers at the family compound they built in a remote corner of town — a place bypassers often take for Los Trancos Woods or Portola Valley.

In 50 years as a physician and 42 years on the Stanford Medical School faculty, Russ Lee preached and practiced preventive medicine, group practice and prepaid health care. He led colleagues in starting the Palo Alto Medical Clinic in 1930, and later its research arm, the Palo Alto Medical Foundation. He dreamed up Channing House, the retirees' residence with lifetime health care through the clinic.

Dorothy Lee, for her part, helped create Foothills Park.

Together, the Lees produced their proudest accomplishment: a family of four sons and a daughter. All five graduated from Palo Alto High School, Stanford University and Stanford Medical School.

Three of the brothers practiced at the clinic, two of them for most of their careers. All four have echoed in one form or another their dad's ahead-of-the-times health care thinking and his penchant for bold initiatives.

Peas in a pod? The family resemblance is evident in tousled hair, lanky builds and merry blue eyes, and the brothers remain close. But don't be fooled. Each has widely divergent interests and a distinctive personality.

In 50 years as a physician and 42 years on the Stanford Medical School faculty, Russ Lee preached preventive medicine, group practice and prepaid health care.

Dr. Richard Stanford Lee, the eldest, is an obstetrician. Retired from the clinic, he also has given up driving in sports car races. But he devotes 29 or 30 weekends every year to serving as chairman of the physicians for the Sports Car Club of America, going to race meets at Laguna Seca, Sears Point, Atlanta and other venues.

"Uncle Dick is the only person I know who built his house with an auto mechanic's pit in the garage," said a niece, Barbara Paulsen, a clan archivist of sorts.

Dick Lee's best-known activism involved women's reproductive rights. He helped get California's abortion and sterilization laws changed.

The second brother, Dr. Peter V.A. Lee, first taught at Stanford Medical School while it was in San Francisco and then switched to the University of Southern California. An internist and family practitioner, he chairs the USC medical school's department of community medicine. An amateur cellist and opera buff, he often flies north for Bay Area opera performances.

Dr. Philip R. Lee, a rheumatologist, currently is a leading Clinton administration apostle for health care reform. In the Department of Health and Human Services, he is assistant secretary for health and U.S. Public Health Service administrator. It's his second tour in Washington, D.C., though he's more

See LEE, Page 4

Russel Lee, center, with sons Hewey, Dick, Peter and Phil, from left

PROFILE

■ **LEE**
from Page 3

often flying around the country than perched there. His first hitch was when Lyndon Johnson was pushing through Medicaid and Medicare.

Is Phil Lee trying to complete his dad's agenda? "He'd certainly be very much in favor of the Clinton proposal," he said.

At 69, Phil Lee, former chancellor of the University of California, San Francisco, was first reluctant to serve in the Clinton administration. But he seized the opportunity after seeing how committed to reform Bill and Hillary Rodham Clinton were. "It's something I've cared about for the last 40 years," he said. "I seem to have a lot of energy left to take it on and it's a chance to participate in a very substantial way."

Despite holding firm opinions, Phil Lee is renowned as a skilled negotiator, a talent likely to be needed in the coming showdown on universal health insurance.

Dr. R. Hewlett Lee, a general surgeon, stayed closer to home. In 33 years at the clinic, he had a hand in administration most of the time. From 1982 to 1989 he was executive director. He remains on the medical foundation board and is an administrative consultant.

Being locally based did not stop Hewey Lee from making waves. He was instrumental in getting California to ban the insecticide DDT. He and Palo Alto colleagues fathered minimal breast cancer surgery, posting better results than mastectomies, he said. In a term as president of the Santa Clara County Medical Society, he engineered a controversial stand against the Vietnam War.

His retirement is a busy one. In addition to handcrafting furniture and taking and printing color wildlife photographs of birds and flora, he serves on the boards of Stanford Hospital, Mid-Peninsula Bank, Age Center Alliance and Peninsula Blood Bank.

Dr. Margo Lee Paulsen did not practice medicine, instead raising children with her husband, Dr. James A. Paulsen, a clinic psychiatrist. She died in 1973 of an intestinal ailment for which her father had tried to find a cure.

No parental pressure

Russ Lee didn't insist on his kids becoming physicians.

"When most of us made our decision to go on in medicine, he was not here," Hewey Lee said. "He left the day after war was declared by the United States in 1941. . . . He was gone almost until 1946."

The senior Dr. Lee entered what was then the Army Air Corps, rising to become Air Force chief of preventive medicine, personal physician to Secretary of War Henry Stimson and Air Force Chief of Staff Gen. Hap Arnold, and a colonel. (He was also personal physician to a long string of Stanford University presidents.)

All his sons also did tours in the service. Dick Lee, an Air Force Reserve flight surgeon, was recalled three times to active duty in the Philippines, Korea and the Cuban missile crisis.

Until 1950 the family home was on Gerona Road at Stanford. Russ Lee, who'd grown up a poor minister-turned-beekeeper's son in Utah, was proud that its swimming pool and open space helped his vigorous youngsters develop. The Lee boys were known for swimming and water polo prowess.

Dr. Russel Lee was a leading figure in medicine at Stanford.

Together with Drs. George Barnett and Anna Barnett, the senior Lees co-adopted two orphaned daughters of a medical school professor friend, Jane Langnecker Stratte (now deceased) and Leslie Langnecker Luttgens. Both married physicians. Luttgens, who was the first woman Stanford student body president, currently sits on several major Bay Area corporation boards.

The family compound takes root

In 1950 the senior Lees bought land in the foothills and built their adobe dream house. There Russ could indulge in a favorite activity, horseback riding, while Dorothy tried raising karakul sheep.

After some years, the couple invited their offspring to buy parcels of the brushy, hilly land for $10 an acre. And they helped them build homes along the road down from the adobe. First Dick and his wife, Louise, built. Then Hewey and his wife, Betty. Then Phil and Kitty, then Margo and Jim.

When the clan assembled for a feast, there might be anywhere from five to 10 doctors at the table. "Medicine was almost never discussed," Hewey Lee said. What then? "Everything else."

Twenty grandchildren remember life at the Boronda Farm compound as very special. Between the oldest and youngest cousins the span was 11 years. Peter's L.A. tribe often stayed much of the summer.

"We grew up as siblings. That was the most special thing about it," Barbie Paulsen recalled. "We'd wander in and out of any house and share each other's parents. Sometimes it was easier to talk to an aunt or uncle about something than to your own parents.

"Mom (Margo) was a focal point for the cousins. Ours was the first house, at the base of the steep hill.

"Out in the open terrain we let the rattlesnakes be, but if we saw one near the houses, we'd find a grown-up to kill it, cut off the head and bury it deep, then throw the body over the hillside. Once we noticed that one headless snake's heart was still beating. So Mom hooked up a gen-

PROFILE

■ LEE

erator and gave us a biology lesson."

Barbie remembers being cut in several accidents while an avid tree climber. "Hewey put stitches in my head three times before high school — I was never in an emergency room. We had doctors on call."

What the grandchildren do

Only one of the 20 grandchildren has become a physician. Dr. Richard David Lee of La Honda is in family practice with the Stanford Midpeninsula Health Center. True to family form, when Barbie was having her first baby five years ago, Ritchie, then doing an OB residency, showed up to assist.

Hewey and Betty joke that their children steered clear of medicine after living with a surgeon father's awful hours.

For some of the 20, it was no joke. Paul Lee, Phil's son, recalls his grandfather's telling him that no other profession was as gratifying, and how the lives he'd saved made him feel good.

Paul had been premed as an undergraduate. When he announced plans to become an architect, his father pressed him to stick with medicine. Paul said bluntly that he'd made his decision.

Yet not all bonds to health care were sundered. As an Oakland architect, Paul Lee works primarily on long-term health care facilities. He and four others originated the International Healthy Cities Conference, and drew his father as co-chairman and keynoter to its San Francisco-Oakland sessions earlier this month.

Others among the grandchildren work in health care.

Louise Lee, Dick's wife, is a nurse. So is their daughter, Patty Piantanida of Woodside. Patty and her husband, Tom, a biology researcher, both race sports cars. Dick and Louise's oldest son, Rusty, is an auto mechanic and lives in Marin County. Their youngest, Peter Michael Lee, is in film work in the Los Angeles area.

Peter V.A. Lee's oldest daughter, Martha, does archaeological services at Yosemite National Park, and recently brought out a book on California Indian basketry. A second daughter, Susan, formerly a geologist, is working in real estate. She and her husband, Gordon Reetz, a geologist, live in Oxnard. Cathy Lee of San Francisco is studying for her Ph.D. in clinical psychology; her special interest is gerontology, a field her grandfather pioneered. Attorney Peter V.A. Lee Jr. recently joined a Los Angeles area law firm.

Their mother, Sharon Gardner, who originally trained as a nurse, is now a caterer. Their stepmother, Belinda Fischer, is an attorney in the L.A. area.

Phil Lee's daughter Dorothy lives on the Greek island of Mykonos. Paul and his wife, Karen Marker, a school psychologist, live in Oakland. Amy Lee lives in Phil's house at the compound; since deciding not to make a commitment to medicine, she's become known for creating handwoven interior decor fabrics using intricate computer-controlled designs. Margie Lee, a horseshoer, lives in Palo Alto, as does Theodore, who manages a video store and the computer network in the Palo Alto law office of his mother, Catherine L. "Kitty" Lee.

Phil Lee's wife, Carroll L. Estes, directed the Institute

for Health and Aging at the UCSF School of Nursing before the couple left for Washington.

When Hewey Lee retired, the first thing he did was to build a house near his own under the direction of his son Stan, a general contractor based in Marysville. Daughter Virginia, a nurse at the Stanford Chest Clinic, lives there with her two children. Another daughter, Phyllis, took a doctorate in animal behavior at Cambridge University in England, and now teaches there. Eric Lee, Hewey and Betty's other son, raises catfish near the Salton Sea south of Palm Springs. A nationally ranked water skier, he opens his three lakes to water skiers to help aerate the fish.

Geoff Paulsen, Jim and Margo's son, lives in Cupertino with his wife, Janine, a former nurse. He is a senior analyst in Santa Clara County's risk management department, and remains on call as an emergency coordinator — a job he did during the 1989 earthquake. Barbie Paulsen and her husband, Bart Smaalders, live in San Jose. Bart is a software engineer for Sun Microsystems; Barbie was on the board of Peninsula School in Menlo Park, where some — but not all — of the Lee families sent children. Now that her children are 5 and 3, she is thinking of resuming a Lee clan newsletter. Sally Paulsen of Burlingame is pursuing college studies.

At present the great-grandchild count exceeds two dozen. Most of them were on hand, along with the rest of the clan and former wives, last August when the descendants of Dorothy and Russel Lee met at Boronda Farm to celebrate the 75th anniversary of their marriage.

There was no winemaking, a highlight of August reunions up to the mid-1980s. The patriarch's house and vineyard had been sold to Vinod Khosla, a founder of Sun Microsystems, who tore down the adobe and built a huge residence. Scott McNealy, Sun's CEO, bought the Paulsen house. William Hewlett, co-founder of Hewlett-Packard Co., had bought 100 hilltop acres decades earlier.

Russ Lee used to tell of earning $5 million in real estate deals within three years after retiring from the clinic. Hewlett, the son who handled his business affairs during his last decade of life, said his father firmly believed in the value of land — but not of stocks or insurance.

Hewey Lee also revealed that his mother really was behind the Foothills Park land gift.

When a plan to build hundreds of houses there was proposed, she declared: "Not on my half, and my half is every other yard!"

Thus the Lees' values live on in the park, their hometown and their burgeoning tribe. Traces of the patriarch's provocative style, wit, creativity and non-conformity can readily be found in the Lee progeny near and far.

PAUL SAKUMA — JEW FAMILY COLLECTION

Thirty-six members of the family of the late Rose Tong Jew gathered at Lucie Stern Community Center when she was honored in January at a Palo Alto Centennial tribute to the "Creators of the Legacy."

Letting language do its work
P.A. clan still speaks with prominence

WHEN the Palo Alto Centennial paid tribute in January to 54 "Creators of the Legacy," Rose Tong Jew's contingent was the largest present.

"She opened her heart to everyone," her citation said. Dozens of descendants represented one family's flowering in many fields: commerce, entertainment and the arts, industry, education and volunteer service. While clearly of Chinese ancestry, they all were speaking in English — and therein lay one family's formula for success.

Rose and her husband, Ngum You Jew, settled in Palo Alto in 1912. Their laundry, store and residence were on Emerson Street between Hamilton and Forest avenues. They probably were the first Chinese-Americans to own Palo Alto property.

In the town's first years, and again a decade later, vociferous opposition to Chinese laundries, restaurants and residents had surfaced, but the Jew family's charm transcended it.

Ngum You's death certificate says he was born in Mayfield on July 27, 1878. How his parents came to be in the hamlet centered at today's El Camino Real and

See FAMILY

Rose Tong Jew stands near the arches of the Stanford quad in the early 1920s. The couple settled in Palo Alto in 1912.

■ FAMILY

California Avenue is unclear. In that era, Chinese were involved in farming, railroad-building and work on Peninsula estates, but very few had wives with them.

Before long, one family story goes, they sailed for China and resettled in Canton province's Chungshan district. There Ngum You's siblings were born and he grew up, accorded special respect as "the

highest in his generation."

Between his late teens and late 20s, he bought passage in steerage on a ship bound for San Francisco. Even for a U.S. citizen by birth, readmission to America was fraught with difficulty, so he may have had to await a propitious time.

Another explanation, supplied by his son Thomas, is that he was born in China, not

Mayfield, and in order to enter the United States procured a "paper name" — a common practice then.

Where Ngum You was born hardly matters, for once he reached San Francisco's Chinatown he prospered as a merchant and entered a "matched marriage," arranged by the parents and a middleman. Photographs show San Francisco-born Rose, his bride-to-be, as beautiful, slim and elegant.

Her unusually progressive father, Tong Tom Sing, was a respected translator in Pacific Coast courts and immigration offices. He owned a San Francisco cigar factory and stores. Believing in the value of education, he insisted that his seven daughters and one son learn to speak English and stay in school. That bucked contemporary custom, which was to give girls less schooling than boys.

After the Jews settled in Palo Alto with their son Paul, eight more children were born, beginning with Lillian in 1913. After her came Vivian, Doris, Thomas, Albert, Louis, Mary Jane and Barbara.

Chop suey PR

In 1914, Rose's father staged a public relations coup. Together with the young couple, he put on a chop suey dinner for more than 30 American guests at the laundry building. The Palo Alto Times wrote up the Chinese New Year event, relating the menu and how Rose's three younger sisters and brother "sang several sweet songs in the American style" and

CENTENNIAL FAMILIES ■

■ FAMILY

led everyone in singing "America." Toastmaster Tong said his people desired to "obey all the laws of the town and to have the protection of their friends."

The Jews' store-front home at 647 Emerson, next to the laundry at 651 Emerson, had about 10 rooms, a courtyard and a stairway up to a building in the back.

Part of the house served as a general store carrying cloth, thread, corsets, high-button shoes and the like.

"The house was always full, and no one had a key," said Lili Wong, now an artist in Scottsdale, Ariz. "How could we make that many keys? It was open all the time, like a revolving door, in and out."

"My father was really kind-hearted," said Doris Yep of Palo Alto. "When immigrants came over and didn't have a place, he let them stay there until they could get on their feet. Many times he helped the Stanford students who came from the Orient to start. That's how we got our Chinese education — some of them taught us."

Prime volunteer

Rose Jew liked volunteering. She became the liaison between the town and the Chinese in and around it, translating for immigrant wives who saw physicians and learned they were pregnant, assisting at births, making arrangements. She never took any pay. Her family nicknamed her "the employment agency" — she often filled requests from local residents to find a maid or a cook.

Ngum You's laundry prospered, and he acquired three restaurants — the Canton Cafe in Redwood City and two in Palo Alto: the Shanghai Cafe on Emerson and the Varsity Grill on University Avenue.

All the Jew children graduated from Palo Alto High School except Vivian, who died in her teens of spinal meningitis. Paul, class of 1932, won renown both as a track

and basketball star and a self-taught dancer who earned three encores at the Boys Stunt Show.

A college scholarship awaited Paul, but instead he incurred his father's ire by setting out with a buddy to see the country, then going to Hollywood. Performing as Paul Wing with Dorothy Toy, his partner for more than 30 years, he worked the U.S. theater circuit and ultimately reached the Roxy on New York's Broadway and the London Palladium. Toy and Wing often were lauded as "the Chinese Ginger Rogers and Fred Astaire." They did tap, ballroom and acrobatic dancing, ballet and impressions.

The family comedian

Paul entertained at the 50th reunion of his Paly High class, and danced into his late 70s, adding comedy routines. The film "Forbidden City USA" featured him.

His brothers and sisters attended college and followed their parents' examples in more traditional ways.

Doris, who became Mrs. George Yep, managed The Bamboo, a Palo Alto take-out food business, then worked as an administrative assistant. Tom carved out a career locally as owner of Jay Realty. During World War II, both Paul and Tom fought in Europe.

Albert, who as a youth tinkered with radio, worked for Stanford Research Institute (now SRI International). Then he teamed up with a friend, Fred Kruse, in electronics experiments in the Jews' garage.

In 1949 the two combined their first names and set up Alfred Electronics, moving into a specialty in microwave instrumentation. Their company went full-time in 1956, locating on Commercial Street, and in 1961 became one of the first small firms to move into Stanford Industrial Park (now Stanford Research Park). In 1969, after reaching a sales volume of about $6 million a year and employment of 150 per-

JEW FAMILY COLLECTION

Ngum You Jew, above, arrived in San Francisco from China in the early 1900s.

Vociferous opposition to Chinese residents had surfaced, but the Jew family's charm transcended it.

sons, Alfred was sold to the Singer Co. and became part of Singer's Instrumentation Division. Albert Jew died in 1976.

Love for cars

Cars fascinated Louis. He lined up early to become one of the first drivers through the new University Avenue underpass at the railroad tracks in 1940. During the war, he served with the Flying Tigers in the China-Burma-India theater. En route home, he brought as a stowaway an orphaned Chinese lad who had been his squadron's mascot. The case of Chin Ta Bin, now called Steve

CENTENNIAL FAMILIES ■

■ FAMILY

Chin Jew, drew widespread notice, yet eight years went by before Congress passed special legislation enabling Rose Jew to adopt the engaging boy.

Louie went on to become owner of a large automobile dealership, Richmond Mazda. Steve, who has been a preacher, is an executive of KM Products, a mineral supplement firm in El Cajon.

Mary Jane married a Stanford classmate, David Toy, who became a dentist. Barbara, a student of art and costume design, married Robert Lee, a San Francisco businessman. Mary Jane, now divorced, lives in the East Bay and works in public relations. Barbara lives in San Francisco. Both have been volunteers with the Salvation Army and On Lok, a Chinatown agency serving senior citizens.

Homeward bound, almost

In 1925, Ngum You prepared to take three of his sons to China for a few years of schooling. He called off the trip after receiving word that his mother had died. After that, a fire at the laundry, Depression business losses, long years of war in China and finally several strokes blunted any ambition he may have had to retire to China as a millionaire. He died in June 1945 at age 66, shortly before his sons returned from war service overseas.

Rose Jew devoted many more years to her family and community before her death at age 88. Her survivors included 22 grandchildren and three great-grandchildren (there are now 15).

In the second generation, Lili's son, Jeffrey Wong, is a partner in a San Francisco law firm. Her daughter, Judy Wong Haren, is an entrepreneur. She has three children.

Doris Yep's daughter Robin Kwong co-owns Maximart Pharmacy in Palo Alto. Son Richard Yep is assistant executive director of the American Counseling Association in Alexandria, Va. Each has one child.

Tom Jew has two sons and two grandchildren. Jon Jew is a sales manager in Iowa. Gerald Jew is a

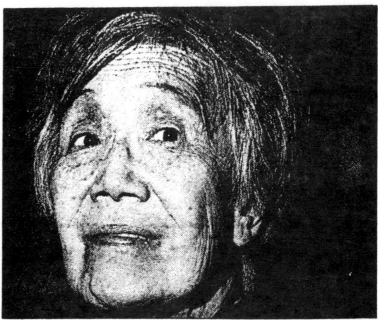
DAVID TOY JR.

Rose Tong Jew in a portrait circa 1973, when she was about 86.

roof and floor contractor in Palo Alto.

The late Albert Jew's children are Broderick Jew, a certified public accountant in Palo Alto, and Becky Tennanes of Palo Alto, formerly a personnel manager in San Francisco. Each has two children.

Louis Jew's son Ted, a photographer, heads Chic Clique, a firm with studios in San Mateo and San Leandro. His daughter Dyanne is an artist in Newport Beach.

One of Mary Jane's four children, Leland Toy, a renowned kite designer, died in 1992. David Toy Jr. is a graphic designer and account manager with Visicom Design Group, Palo Alto; he has one son. Sunny Lynn Toy Birkette of San Mateo is an administrative assistant with the Stanford University School of Education; she has two sons. Philip Toy is an operations agent with USAir Group.

Barbara Ann Lee has four children. Two are executives of their father's Hawaii & San Francisco Development Co. in Emeryville, Janet Lee, vice president-treasurer, and Brian Lee, vice president. Terry Lee is an entertainer-actor based in Beverly Hills, and Carol Chung, of Orinda, a receptionist, has two children.

Steve Chin Jew's children are Phillip Chin Jew, who is working toward a master's degree in electronics; Sharon Haberman, a homemaker in Oceanside; and David Chin Jew, a salesman in the San Diego area.

Evidence of anti-Chinese discrimination is readily found in the files of the local press and other sources, but Ngum You and Rose Jew's children say they experienced none in Palo Alto.

"I never felt it," said Lili. "People were very nice to us, I guess because my mother was so nice to everyone."

"We all spoke English all the time," said Doris Yep, who can understand but not really speak Cantonese. "I know there are many families that did feel prejudice, and I think that's probably because they spoke Chinese in front of Caucasian children."

On tour as a dancer Paul did encounter bias in various places. Only then, he said, did he realize that "Palo Alto is so different," with people who are kind and say hello and act down-to-earth.

Rodney Jew, Albert's son, was left out — a slip corrected in the Mercury News March 11 in a report on pro bono service by his multimedia firm, Corporate Design Strategies, to Palo Alto Centennial 1994.

A struggle for a better way of life

The trolley stopped right in front of Seaman "Pop" Harris' shoe-shining shop on the Stanford campus.

BY WARD WINSLOW
Special to the Mercury News

NOW, more than a century later, it can be told. One of Palo Alto's earliest settlers was a black man, Seaman Harris, who broke away from sharecropper life in North Carolina by stealing a bale of cotton, selling it and buying a train ticket west. A fugitive. A person driven to a single crime to save his family from grinding poverty. A Jean Valjean of the American South, like Victor Hugo's character in "Les Miserables," whose theft of a loaf of bread haunted him cruelly.

This vignette will be featured April 16 when the city celebrates the 100th anniversary of its incorporation. It is Ruth Anne Gray's account of how, four generations back, her great-great-grandfather reached Palo Alto, put down roots and headed a family that has produced several of the Palo Alto-Stanford community's best-loved individuals — Pop Harris himself, Mac Hinson and Fran Hinson.

Anne Gray is one measure of how far the family has come. She describes herself as the first Palo Alto-born black woman to have earned a bachelor's degree at Stanford University.

Toddler Ruth Hinson in 1920.

Seaman Harris' place in Palo Alto's early years is well documented. But the story of how he got there is new. Harris was born into slavery in 1852. In 1863 he was freed by President Abraham Lincoln's Emancipation Proclamation, although the Civil War did not end until 1865. Evidently, he lived on a plantation as a boy, and was allowed to learn to read.

See FAMILY

Special Correspondent – 199

Spinning a bale of cotton into a new life

■ FAMILY As he grew, he engaged in tenant farming. Harris was married young to an even younger bride, Amanda, and they had 13 children. Some of them died young in the harsh conditions.

Anne Gray describes herself

as the first Palo Alto-born

black woman to earn a

bachelor's degree at Stanford.

At 35, Seaman Harris decided to try to break away from sharecropper misery and start a new life. So with his purloined grubstake, he bought a one-way railroad ticket, leaving his family behind. Why he chose California, and then Palo Alto, which was only a subdivider's plat at the time, will probably remain a mystery.

Ninth in a series of notable families whose Palo Alto roots go back 100 years.

He arrived in 1887, the year ground was broken for construction of the university. One news account in 1924 stated that Harris, then 71, "is known to every Stanford man for ages back." It said he worked for some time as an expressman, then as a porter at the railroad station, "and for the past seven years has been on the campus as its chief shoe-polisher."

A photograph shows him outside his bootblack and shoe repair shop at Stanford University's trolley stop. By then he was widely known as "Pop" and used his nickname on the sign.

Voter rolls as early as 1896 attest to his presence, and in 1897 "S. Harris" was listed in the weekly Palo Alto Times as one of 100 signers of a petition asking for the resignation of the town-

ship constable, who had shot down a black man on the streets at midday.

After working hard for seven years, Harris was able to buy land, have a house built in 1896 and send for his wife and surviving children. He owned property in Block 49, bounded by Lytton and University avenues, Middlefield Road and Guinda Street. Fulton Street divided the original block, and Harris built at 422 Fulton.

One daughter who came west, Etta, is pictured in an 1897 photograph of Channing School students. The picture appeared on the cover of "History of Palo Alto, The Early Years" by Pamela Gullard and Nancy Lund, published in 1989.

Different account

Arthur Smith Gray Jr., Anne's younger brother, understands the story differently. As he heard it, Seaman Harris had done livery work and was good with figures. He became a compiler for other sharecroppers near Charlotte, N.C., and handled the cotton sales and money changing — until he absconded.

Whichever version is accurate, the purloining of the cotton bale symbolizes the essence of the story.

"He believed in God and had a

strong religious bent," Anne Gray said. "I think he felt very hopeless. It was the only way he saw he could escape and leave the South."

"Probably the worst thing he ever did was to steal that bale of cotton. To come here, he had to be separated from his family — he paid for it in many ways. He was an upright person and tried to be an outstanding citizen," she said.

Seaman Harris was almost 80 when he died in 1931. He had outlived his son, Andrew, who worked as a Palo Alto bootblack for decades.

It was neither Andy nor Etta Harris who extended the family line in Palo Alto. Martha Jane (Seaman and Amanda's second born) was 13 when she married Mark Dennis in North Carolina. One of their three children, Pearl Blanche, born in 1895, came to Palo Alto in 1903.

Pearl's father died while she was still an infant, and her widowed mother later married T.J. Honeycutt. Martha Honeycutt died in 1952.

In 1914, Pearl, then 19, entered what Anne Gray termed "sort of an arranged marriage" to Isaac MacDuffey Hinson in North Carolina. The next year they moved to Palo Alto, where Pearl had worked earlier as a mother's helper.

CENTENNIAL FAMILIES ■

■ POP HARRIS

Shoeshine shop

"Mac" Hinson became a community favorite like Pop Harris. Most Palo Altans knew him for his shoeshine and repair shop, which had several University Avenue locations over the years. In about the last decade before he retired in 1972, the business operated as the Old Reliable Shoe Shine Parlor; Nathaniel Flowers was Mac's partner.

A news feature story in 1948 related how Mac had shined the shoes of Herbert Hoover and family in Hoover's pre-presidential years.

Another customer was Stanford President Ray Lyman Wilbur. Mac said he shined Wilbur's shoes for 16 years before he ever saw his customer's face. Wilbur, a busy man, sent his shoes to town with members of the family. And when Wilbur went to Washington, D.C., in 1929 to become Hoover's secretary of the interior, he still sent his shoes home for Hinson to polish.

What the story missed was Hinson's other roles. He played baseball for the Palo Alto Stars in a blacks' league. He was a founder of Palo Alto's University African Methodist Episcopal Zion Church in 1918 (and in 1976 the last of the founders to die).

During the Depression, the church had a crisis — its members could not pay the mortgage. Palo Alto's white community helped out in what historian Guy Miller called one of the town's finest hours, and over five years

Mac Hinson at the family's new home at 425 Middlefield Road, Palo Alto.

Early settler Pop Harris escaped poverty with stolen bale of cotton

Mac Hinson and son Fran change a tire on the car Mac loved; Hinson and wife, Pearl Harris Hinson.

▪ POP HARRIS

the mortgage was paid off. What no one reported then, however, is that Mac Hinson's aggressive fund raising in both the business district and the small black community underpinned the success.

Hinson helped persuade a North Carolina friend, Jerry Harrison, to settle in Palo Alto after his World War I Army service. Harrison became a porter at the train depot and when he retired 22 years later could boast that he never lost a bag.

Mac and Pearl Hinson had three children, Francis Lawrence, Hildegarde Jane and Ruth Dennis, born in 1915, 1916 and 1918. They later divorced, but both lived in town into their 80s. Francis Hinson became better known as Fran.

'Everyone was his friend'

Businessman Eddie Hoffacker, who attended grammar school and high school with him, once said: "He was one of the most popular guys at Palo Alto High. Everyone was his friend; no one was his enemy."

Fran and Eddie played football together. "He was quick and he was tough," Hoffacker said. Fran wrestled, too. He was also musical, playing the violin and piano, and he had art talent, though his

sisters outdid him there. Up until 1943, he worked as a bellman at hotels in Palo Alto and San Mateo.

When he entered the Army during World War II, Fran Hinson ran into far more discrimination than he had known on the Peninsula. He was sent to an all-black ammunition supply outfit, and saw duty in the European theater, gaining the rank of sergeant.

He told the family that once he and most of his unit were pulling away in a truck when they looked back and saw an ammo dump explode from shellfire, killing three buddies left behind to guard it.

In 1948, he established Fran's on Lytton Avenue at Cowper Street. He sold newspapers, magazines, books, tobacco, candy and other items. For a time the shop offered shoe shines, too.

His sister Ruth clerked there. She had attended San Mateo Junior College and then San Jose State College, majoring in art.

"She was not able to get a teaching job in California," Anne Gray said. "Her professor recommended she go to the South, but she found the black colleges didn't have art programs — they were too poor."

Over the years, Fran's popularity grew. Customers liked his

Born in 1895, Pearl Blanche came to Palo Alto in 1903. In 1914, she entered "sort of an arranged marriage" to Isaac MacDuffey Hinson. This photo is circa 1910.

Ward Winslow is the principal author of "Palo Alto: A Centennial History," published by the Palo Alto Historical Association. Information: (415) 322-2205.

Art Gray wears Palo Alto High's school colors to his 20th class reunion in 1993. Classmates are, from left, Bob Rice, Jeff Williams and Vince Sturla.

CENTENNIAL FAMILIES ·

■ POP HARRIS

friendly style, and he often introduced them to each other. Before handing out copies of the Sunday New York Times, he'd inventory the sections out loud. For all his chatter, he seemed a loner, reluctant to talk about himself. Yet when heart trouble befell him in 1983, some of his regular customers formed Friends of Fran and sold prints of a painting of his shop to help pay his hospital bills.

He died in 1984. The present proprietors of his landmark shop have kept the name Fran's Market.

Fran Hinson never married. Hildegarde, an outstanding artist, died in her early 20s. Ruth was married in 1945 to Arthur Smith Gray, who had served in the Army ammo unit with Fran. Their children are Ruth Anne, who goes by Anne, and Art Jr. Both attended Lytton School (as two generations of the family before them had), Jordan Junior High, Palo Alto High School and Stanford University.

At Stanford, Anne studied art and the humanities. She sculpts in her favorite medium of ceramics, lives in Sunnyvale and works as a project administrator for a Silicon Valley high technology firm.

This old house

Art Gray Jr. conducts a Peninsula home renovation business, and helps a friend part time with a start-up electronics components firm. He resides in a house on Middlefield Road that his grandfather, Mac Hinson, first built — back to back with the house Seaman Harris had built at 422 Fulton in 1895. That house has been rebuilt and is no longer in the family.

"I'm glad he chose Palo Alto to settle in," Art Gray said. Ruth Gray, a lifelong Palo Altan now lives at Lytton Gardens, just across the road from the family home.

Before handing out copies of the Sunday New York Times, Fran Hinson would inventory the sections out loud.

In 1948, Francis Hinson established Fran's on Lytton Avenue at Cowper Street, which sold newspapers, tobacco, candy and other items. The present owners have kept the name Fran's Market.

Index

About the Author

My parents had lived in a bungalow on Kingsley Avenue in Palo Alto for a while before I was born in San Francisco in May 1927, but their doctor and a set of grandparents were in The City.

As one of a class of only 13, I attended Saratoga Grammar School and then, for one year, Los Gatos High School. Our family moved to Palo Alto in mid-1941 and I entered Palo Alto High School, then a three-year school, as a sophomore. Because Bob Taylor, editor of *The Campanile* in 1942-43, left early to attend Stanford University on an accelerated wartime schedule, I became editor of the student newspaper and kept the post until my graduation with the Class of 1944.

Entering the World War II Navy V-12 program, I was sent to the University of Colorado, and later was transferred to the Naval Reserve Officers Training Corps program. The pay remained the same — an apprentice seaman's — but the program covered college tuition and books, plus room and meals and uniforms. What's more, we could buy sea stores cigarets, lifting our popularity with girls who smoked.

In June 1946, the Naval Reserve mustered us out. I was processed at Camp Shoemaker in Alameda County — now a jail, isn't it? The Navy invited us back into the revamped NROTC program, and I returned to finish at Boulder with a dual major, Naval Science and Journalism. As sports editor of the Silver and Gold I earned a few bucks closing pages at night down at the *Boulder Daily Camera* office.

Finishing at CU in March 1948, I headed home by bus via Ely, Nevada, where I found a smarter classmate had nabbed the sports editor's job by telephoning. Back in Palo Alto, I resisted the enticements of papers in Williston, North Dakota, and Gallup, New Mexico, and worked as a *Times* stringer until a full-time job opened up. The rest is indicated in the clips.

After retiring as managing editor of the *Times Tribune* in July 1984, I started a home-based writing service in 1985. Locally, I've always lived either in Palo Alto or north Los Altos. Holly and I have seven children between us, and late in 1993 the youngest of them put us in the grandparents league — at last. Welcome, Melinda Marie!